UNDERSTANDING THE POLITICAL ECONOMY OF THE ARAB UPRISINGS

UNDERSTANDING THE POLITICAL ECONOMY OF THE ARAB UPRISINGS

Edited by

Ishac Diwan

Harvard Kennedy School of Government, USA
and Economic Research Forum, Egypt

World Scientific

NEW JERSEY · LONDON · SINGAPORE · BEIJING · SHANGHAI · HONG KONG · TAIPEI · CHENNAI

Published by

World Scientific Publishing Co. Pte. Ltd.
5 Toh Tuck Link, Singapore 596224
USA office: 27 Warren Street, Suite 401-402, Hackensack, NJ 07601
UK office: 57 Shelton Street, Covent Garden, London WC2H 9HE

Library of Congress Cataloging-in-Publication Data
Diwan, Ishac.
Understanding the political economy of the Arab uprisings / edited by Ishac Diwan.
pages cm
ISBN 978-9814596008 (hardback : alk. paper)
1. Arab Spring, 2010---Economic aspects. 2. Arab countries--Economic conditions--21st century.
3. Arab countries--Politics and government--21st century. I. Title.
JQ1850.A91D59 2014
909'.097492708312--dc23
2014000053

British Library Cataloguing-in-Publication Data
A catalogue record for this book is available from the British Library.

Cover image © Abdulrahman Jaber, www.ajaber.com

In-house Editor: Chye Shu Wen

Typeset by Stallion Press
Email: enquiries@stallionpress.com

Printed in Singapore by B & Jo Enterprise Pte Ltd

Preface

Most of the Arab Uprisings must be considered revolutionary events, involving a violent stirring of society with profound consequences for each national political economy, that have yet to run their course. Attempts to create legitimate new political orders have so far been unsuccessful, while the process of unruly change continues, making prediction difficult. This is more so as the uprisings also took place at a time of economic recession among their European neighbors, cutting off, or very much reducing, valuable flows of investment capital, tourism, and official aid. Naturally, efforts to understand why the uprisings took place, and what effects they have had so far, are of the greatest importance. Even though we must also know that everything we say and write will be subject to future qualification and amendment.

My own contribution to this volume sees the 'genesis' of the uprisings in a build up of popular pressure against powerful Presidents who not only aspired to control every aspect of economic and social life but also, with the encouragement of a small number of crony-capitalists, to pass this system of control and personal enrichment on to their sons. Hence the young people in Egypt, Tunisia, and parts of the Arab East were faced with the depressing prospect of being ruled by members of the Mubarak or Ben Ali families for life.

What actually caused them then to mass together in Maidan Tahrir in Cairo or the Avenue Bourguiba in Tunis was first seen through the optic of some kind of a 'tipping point' leading to a giant outburst of popular enthusiasm. But, over time, observers like Ishac Diwan and Fadhel Kaboub have examined some of the deeper political economy structures involved. In Ishac Diwan's case, his research into public opinion polls led him to assign great importance to shifts in middle class opinion about its own place in a Mubarak-dominated Egypt where power and influence were skewed towards a club of cronies whose economic interests were of an inward-looking variety base as they were on their control of the major national monopolies such as electricity, gas, and steel. While in Fadhel Kaboub's analysis, it is the breakdown of the major instruments of political control that had previously bound both the Tunisian middle class and organized labor to the regime.

Given the fact that the main aim of all the uprisings in the Arab republics was the replacement of a system dominated by presidential dictatorships by one loosely described as 'democratic', it was perhaps inevitable that most followed a roughly similar path in which elections to a constituent assembly were won by religious parties or movements, the only organization with real grass-roots support and led by men whose long years either in jail or exiles spared them from any possible allegation of corruption.

The problems that followed can then be examined in two mutually reinforcing ways. One, taken by Caroline Freund and Melise Jaud, is to focus on the general difficulties faced by almost all the world's polities that have attempted to create 'democracies' *de novo* in the last 50 years. That nearly half failed is obviously no surprise. But there is still much to learn from the attempt to identify the main variables involved, and then to apply such lessons to similar processes which began in the Arab world in 2011. The second, is to look more closely at the problems involved when, after a period of mass mobilizations with the streets and squares filled by millions of people, Arab revolutions try to institutionalize themselves and come face to face with a mismatch between what Jillian Schwedler calls the logic of 'inclusion-moderation' principle and the fact that electorally-successful Islamist movements can be drawn away from the center by pressures to demonstrate their core commitment to a conservative set of religious beliefs. The result, as we have seen, has led, to military intervention in Egypt, and to a complex period of political bargaining and coalition-building made more difficult by deteriorating economic circumstances in Tunisia.

As for the central subject of corruption itself, Jeffery Nugent provides a rich and comprehensive analysis that allows us to evaluate the degree of its seriousness in the Middle East in terms of both states and sectors of national economy, followed by some useful suggestions as to possible policies for its future control. Also welcome is the comparative aspect of his study in which he finds that, while Middle East corruption was not as serious as elsewhere in the developing world to begin with, it then began to increase, being 'positively associated' with such related factors as the systems of taxation, political instability, and competition from the informal sector.

Later chapters look at Turkey, Iran, and Indonesia for help in providing lessons that might be helpful in understanding the political economy of the Arab uprisings. Izak Atiyas lauds the Turkish example of ways to enhance competition by introducing a regulatory framework that limits arbitrariness and discrimination by state authorities *vis-à-vis* the private sector while also using state power to make the market work more efficiently by preventing anti-competitive behavior. Hasan Ersel examines the transformation of political Islam as a result of the widening of multi-party regimes to allow mass participation in the political process and so the promotion of particular sectional demands, as well as encouraging revisions in certain basic republican concepts such as secularism. The result is a trenchant reminder that where you have religion, you must also have its opposite. Athough, given the present travails of constitution-making in Egypt and Tunisia, it is not clear whether 'secularism' is quite the right word to cover that bundle of notions that attempts to define both national identity and the relationship between 'din' and 'dawla' (religion and state power). It is a chastening reminder too, as Ersel concludes, that in global terms the establishment of 'sound institutional basis for multi-party democracy and a market economy is a long and difficult process'.

As with Turkey, the evolution of what Hadi Esfahani and Esra Gürakar call 'social orders' in Iran has been in place long enough to be able to observe the impact on it of major regime changes, some of them produced by military coups, others by popular movements of a revolutionary type. Where the contemporary Arab situation would seem to differ is in the absence of the type of foreign interventions and military alliances that marked the Iranian as well as the Turkish story. Nevertheless, the fact that both countries have offered themselves to the Arab world since 2011 as competing models of institutional and policy frameworks, makes them a very interesting source of comparison, both in terms of what seems to promote economic development and what does not.

Lastly, for those looking for a perhaps more optimistic conclusion, we have Akhmad Rizal Shidiq's and Philips Jusario Vermonte's upbeat account of Indonesia's successful consolidation of democracy since its major 1998 political and economic crisis, notably the response of political Islam to the holding of modern democratic elections, a process marked by its own movement towards greater moderation and accommodation as it adjusted to the 'new institutional settings' produced by the crisis.

'Men make their own history' as Marx famously states in his *Eighteenth Brumaire of Louis Bonaparte*, 'but they do not make it as they please, but under circumstances existing already, given and transmitted from the past'. Among many other things, this provides powerful support for the notion that, in revolutionary situations like those of the Arab Spring, the fight is against existing structures within the political economy which, whether in the shape of concentrations of economic power or the persons who control the security services within the 'deep state', limit what basic changes can be achieved, including the redistribution of income or the introduction of a representative democracy. The contributors to this volume are to be congratulated for the many skillful ways they use a Political Economy approach to provide trenchant evidence for this significant point.

Roger Owen
A.J. Meyer Professor of Middle East History Emeritus
Harvard University

Contents

About the Editor

Ishac DIWAN is currently a lecturer on public policy at the Harvard Kennedy School of Government. He is also the director for Africa and the Middle East at the Center for International Development at Harvard University, directs the research program on the "Economic and Political Transformation of the Arab World" for the Economic Research Forum for the Arab Countries, Iran, and Turkey, and is a member of the Global Economic Council of the World Economic Forum on the "Arab World". Dr Diwan got his Ph.D. in Economics from the University of California, Berkeley. He has published extensively on issues related to international finance, development, and political economy, with a focus on Africa and the Middle East. He is also a practitioner he recently served as the World Bank Country Director for East Africa (2000–2005), and West Africa (2005–2010).

About the Contributors

Izak ATIYAS received his BA from Boğaziçi University Department of Economics in 1982, and Ph.D. in Economics from New York University in 1988. He has worked as a senior economist at the World Bank in the Private Sector Development Department in 1988–1995 and at Bilkent University as visiting Assistant Professor of Economics between 1995–1998. He has been with Sabanci University since 1998. Currently he is the coordinator of the Master's Program in Public Policy. Since January 2011, he has been Director of TUSİAD-Sabanci University Competitiveness Forum, which undertakes research on Turkey's international competitiveness. His research areas include productivity, industrial policy, competition policy, regulation of network industries, and privatization.

Hasan ERSEL received his Ph.D. in Economics from Ankara University in 1971, where he worked as a faculty member until 1983. He served as Chief Research Officer at the Capital Market Board of Turkey (1984–1987), General Director of the Research, Planning and Training Department of the Central Bank of the Republic of Turkey (1987–1991), before becoming its Vice Governor (1991–1993). He worked for the Yapı Kredi Bank as Senior Executive Vice President (1993–2003) and as a Member of the Board of Directors (2003–2004). His published works are in the areas of monetary economics, welfare economics, and political economy. His latest book is *Linear Algebra for Economists* (with F. Aleskerov and D. Piantkovski) (Berlin: Springer, 2011). He is a research fellow at the Economic Research Forum (Cairo).

Hadi Salehi ESFAHANI is a Professor of Economics and Business Administration at the University of Illinois at Urbana-Champaign. In addition, he currently serves as the Editor-in-Chief of the *Quarterly Review of Economics and Finance.* He is a member of the Board of Trustees of the Economic Research Forum for the Arab Countries, Iran and Turkey, and a founder and member of Board of Directors of the International Iranian Economic Association. In the past, he has served as the Executive Secretary and the President of Middle East Economic Association and as the Director of the Global Studies Program and the Center for South Asian and Middle Eastern Studies at the University of Illinois. He has also worked for the World Bank as a policy research economist and consultant. He has received BSc in engineering from the University of Tehran and Ph.D. in economics from the University of California, Berkeley. His research focuses on the role of politics and governance in economic policy formation.

Caroline FREUND is a senior fellow at the Peterson Institute for International Economics. She was chief economist, Middle East and North Africa, World Bank (2011–2013). Prior to that she worked in the Research Department of the World Bank. She was also senior economist at the International Monetary Fund (2006–2007) and economist at the Federal Reserve Board (1997–2003). Freund works primarily on economic growth and international trade and also writes on economic issues in the Middle East and North Africa. She has published numerous articles in economics journals and has contributed to many edited volumes. Her work has also been cited in leading magazines and newspapers, including *BusinessWeek, Economist, Financial Times, Wall Street Journal,* and *Washington Post.* She is on the editorial board of *World Bank Economic Review* and is a member of the Center for Economic Policy Research. She received a Ph.D. in economics from Columbia University.

Esra Çeviker GÜRAKAR is an Assistant Professor at the Faculty of Economics and Administrative Sciences at Okan University, Istanbul. Dr Gürakar's research interests are institutional transformation and political economy of institutions in Turkey and Iran. Her main focus is on formalization of rent-creation and rent-distribution mechanisms; judicialization of politics versus politicization of judiciary; and the limits of third party enforcement from an open access order based organization in the process of institutional transformation. Dr Gürakar's current research is on the political economy of public procurement in Turkey, where she studies the political economy implications of legal amendments to the Public Procurement Law and the limits to straightforward EU-required reform in public procurement system.

Melise JAUD is an economist in the Chief Economist Office of the World Bank's Middle East and North Africa region. Her research primarily covers international trade in particular the determinants and impacts of firms' export dynamics and growth, food safety issues in trade, and policy reforms in developing and transition countries. She also works on political economy issues in the Middle East and North Africa. Prior to joining the World Bank she has worked as an economic advisor to the Ministry of Agriculture in Mozambique. She received her Ph.D. from the Paris School of Economics.

Fadhel KABOUB is an Associate Professor of Economics at Denison University and a Research Associate at the Harvard Kennedy School of Government and the Levy Economics Institute. His research focuses on the political economy of the Middle East and on job creation programs in developing countries. He has been an elected member of the editorial board of the *Review of Radical Political Economics* since 2006. Dr Kaboub's research has been widely published in academia and in the international media. He is currently working on a book project about the political economy of the Arab Uprisings.

Jeffrey B. NUGENT received his Ph.D. in Economics from the New School University and is professor of Economics at the University of Southern California. He is also affiliated with the Institute for the Study of Labor and the Economic Research Forum. As a Development Economist, he has worked on a wide variety of issues, problems and analytical techniques and in and on a variety of countries from Latin America, Africa, South and East Asia, and especially the Middle East and North Africa. In recent years, much of his research has made use of new institutional economics and political economy perspectives. He has published in both leading and applied journals and serves on the editorial boards of several journals.

Roger OWEN is A. J. Meyer Professor (Emeritus) of Middle East History at Harvard University and a former Director of Harvard's Center for Middle Eastern Studies. He previously taught Middle East political and economic history at Oxford University where he was also many times the Director of the St Antony's College Middle East Centre. His books include *Cotton and the Egyptian Economy* (Oxford University Press, 1969), *The Middle East in the World Economy, 1800–1914* (I.B. Tauris, 1993), *State, Power and Politics in the Making of the Modern Middle East, 3rd Edition* (Routledge, 2004) and *Lord Cromer: Victorian Imperialist, Edwardian Proconsul* (Oxford University Press, 2004). He is also the co-author (with Sevket Pamuk) of *A History of the Middle East Economies in the Twentieth Century* (I. B. Tauris, 1999). His most recent publication is *The Rise and Fall of Arab Presidents for Life* (Harvard University Press, 2012) — a political history of an era when most presidents were becoming more and more monarchical in their style of rule, which effectively came to an end with the revolutions of the 'Arab Spring'. He has written a regular column for the Arabic newspaper, *Al-Hayat*, since the late 1980s.

Jillian SCHWEDLER is Professor of Political Science at Hunter College and the Graduate Center, City University of New York. She is member of the Editorial Committee of *Middle East Report*, published by MERIP, and member of the Steering Committee of the Project on Middle East Political Science (POMEPS). Dr Schwedler is author of numerous books and articles, including *Faith in Moderation: Islamist Parties in Jordan and Yemen* (Cambridge University Press, 2006) and *Policing and Prisons in the Middle East: Formations of Coercion*, with Laleh Khalili (Columbia University Press, 2010). Her articles have appeared in *World Politics, Comparative Politics, Journal of Democracy, Middle East Critique,* and *Middle East Policy*, among others.

Akhmad Rizal SHIDIQ is a lecturer and research associate at the Institute for Economic and Social Research, University of Indonesia (LPEM-FEUI). He has extensive research experience especially in development economics in Indonesia. At the time of writing his chapter for this book in 2011–2013, he was a former Research Fellow at Ash Center, Harvard Kennedy School.

Philips Jusario VERMONTE is the Head of Department of Politics and International Relations at Centre for Strategic and International Studies (CSIS) Jakarta, Indonesia. His research interests are electoral and political party politics in Indonesia and Southeast Asia.

Acknowledgments

Earlier versions of Chapters 1–5, 8 and 10 were previously published in a March 2013 'special issue' of *Middle East Development Journal* (Vol. 5, No. 1). Earlier versions of Chapters 6, 7 and 9 were previously published in the Economic Research Forum (ERF) Preceedings Volume, "Corruption and Economic Development: Selected Papers from the Economic Research Forum 18th Annual Conference."

Introduction

UNDERSTANDING THE POLITICAL ECONOMY OF THE ARAB UPRISINGS

Ishac Diwan

The popular uprisings witnessed by the Arab world in 2010–2011 have been a revolution of the mind and joyful democratic moments when citizens came together to discover their common yearning for dignity and liberty. The real revolutions, however, have started happening post-uprisings, in the hard work to build new rules, organizations, parties, and institutions that are the tangible substance of democratic progress. Each country has been projected onto its own trajectory of change. Elections are bringing to the fore new political players and new constitutions are being written. New regimes are not yet consolidated, power is still contested everywhere, and experiments with change from within are ongoing in some countries in an attempt to avoid costly social explosions. Yemen, Libya, and Iraq face daunting challenges of reconstruction of their polity, institutions, and infrastructure. Syria is burning with little hope for a quick resolution.

The economic situation has deteriorated everywhere, at a time when popular demands for jobs and better services are higher than ever. Reality has made a comeback — it is now clear that not everything before the uprisings was bad, or that everything that emerges will be good. It is not an exaggeration to say that the Arab world is at a crossroads, facing enormous challenges as well as opportunities that can lead to different countries gradually improving their democratic path, experiencing an authoritarian retrenchment, or falling in outright chaos. In effect, and in various degrees across the countries of the region, the uprisings have revealed the existence of three crises of state, capitalism, and society, all of which require a better understanding of their evolution and interactions to support favorable future outcomes.

On the political side, the quick rise of political Islam post-uprisings, the remobilization of the liberal camp after a short period of disarray, and the ensuing polarization of politics have constituted a successions of big surprises, which have each led to a reassessment of our understanding of these societies. Islamic parties, empowered by years of organized opposition, have become central political actors, but their early first experience with governing, in Tunisia and Egypt in particular, have produced public discontent, driven in part by the fear that their possible takeover of institutions will reduce the space for pluralism in politics, and in part by their inability to turn around the economic situation quickly enough. The coming of age of society needs to be understood better, including a dynamic of social polarization that is currently in full swing. But it is also clear that it will be much more difficult to monopolize power in the future than it had been in the past.

In retrospect, there were large underlying changes that have occurred over the past several decades, which were obscured by the seeming immutable reality of authoritarianism. The middle class has become more active over time and now aspires to become more influential politically. The modernizing aspirations of more educated youth have becoming increasingly more frustrated over time, and they have now learned how to resort to the street in strategically smart ways. Labor unions, long dominated by the state, have been increasingly pushed by workers with accumulated grievances to become more assertive and they are now better organized and are increasingly playing central roles in militating for change. All these transformations must have been gradually picking steam over the past decade, but they were unleashed into the open by the uprisings in the manner of a dam exploding. The social tensions that are now expressed openly are starting to generate all sort of new conversations, sometimes in a chaotic way. New actors, empowered by new constituencies, are attempting to fill a yawning political vacuum created by the fall of the longstanding autocrats. More than any time since the 1940s, the future is now pregnant with possibilities. Several models of social organization have been tried in the past — from socialism to state and crony capitalisms. Governance, state, markets, and even identities are in various measures in a state of crises and re-invention. What type of approaches will work now, given the changing political landscapes? Where would old policy solutions work, and where will new solutions need to be imagined?

This is an opportune time to develop new research areas that focus on the essential changes that have occurred in the region over the recent two decades and that bring the region's central concerns about state, the economy, and society into a closer dialogue with the international political economy literature. Methodologically, the Middle East as an area study has in the past focused more on an essentialist approach that exaggerates the specificities of the region. The recent developments dispel any remaining notion of exceptionalism and have opened up the range of possible socio-political outcomes, thus bringing into the field less deterministic theoretical considerations. They also call for a more analytic and detailed account of the economic and social forces unleashed post structural adjustment — an area of study that is still relatively thin, and for a close examination of the post-uprising developments.

The complex transitions that are unfolding open up a host of issues for debate. The economies of the region remain confronted with old problems of economic instability, increased inequality, lack of jobs, poor quality public services, and poor insertion into the global economy. The big questions on the table are both positive and normative. A better understanding of political economy drivers is necessary positively, in order to imagine better policies and institutions *given* the new political conditions; and normatively, to come up with suggestions for the next phase that can improve political and developmental outcomes.

More specifically, from the vantage point of *after* the uprisings, how do we, the economists and social scientists working on this region, create a factual narrative about the past, its rising inequalities, cronyism and petty corruption, and indignities, in ways that enlighten the current conversations and help in the process of the constructing a better future? How do we reassess the interests of the various socio-political players and of their potential, constraints, and stakes, in ways that make the analysis of economic reforms and institution-building more useful and constructive?

The Chapters in this edited volume start tackling some of these big issues and by so doing, advance our knowledge about the drivers of current affairs. At the same time, they open up a new range of questions for future research. The importance of studying the political, social, and economic transformations in more unified ways is now apparent. The emerging research agenda, which we use as a framework in this book, can be organized around three main axes:

(1) Exploring the contours of a rational and coherent framework to understand the drivers of change that led to the ongoing revolutions, but that can also explain the past and the survival of authoritarianism for nearly three decades after the roll-back of the state that started in the 1980s.
(2) Exploring the dynamics of the ongoing transitions, how the live political forces are likely to evolve, and what are the determinants of whether a democratic path will be consolidated. This includes a better understanding of the social forces at play, and imagining the welfare-improving policies that would be desirable, feasible, and politically supportable in the near term in order to generate virtuous cycles and avoid getting stuck in a low equilibrium transition trap.
(3) Discussing in more depth some of the main tensions that have led to the uprisings — the two main themes explored in this book concern the rise of crony capitalism in the past and the connected questions about how to shape the future evolution of capitalism, and how to reform the state in ways to improve social services and enhance social justice.

A cross-cutting theme is the necessity to learn from experiences of change in other countries with similar characteristics — social polarization, rising inequality, or cronyism are not Arab specificities. In addition, in spite of many similarities among the countries of the region, there are also long recognized country specificities that need to be considered such as their degree of dependence on oil revenues, their degree of ethnic fragmentation, or the difference between republican and monarchic systems.

**

On the issue of the genesis of the revolts, there is a broad convergence of views among the authors in this volume. The main theme that comes across relates to how the roll-back of the state that started in the 1980s and the incomplete move to markets that accelerated in the 1990s interacted with a broader socio-political context to ignite the uprisings.

While the approaches are different, what emerges are the contours of a coherent framework that explain the persistence of autocracy until 2011 and its eventual collapse in some countries. Moreover, in trying to explain the genesis of the uprisings, the Chapters start unearthing rich narratives about the evolution of social and economic structures over time, which help in thinking in more disciplined ways about possible future outcomes as well.

What are the key elements of such a framework? The emerging account in this volume begins with the roll-back of the state and the decline of public services in the Arab republics that had the lowest access to oil rents, which palpably increased insecurity among non-elite populations. With the narrowing of the fiscal space of the state and the adoption of market-oriented reforms, the social constituencies of authoritarian rulers gradually shrunk, and a class of privileged, well-connected elites emerged, which profited from special access to economic opportunities. The rise of crony capitalism across the region reflected shifts in economic structure, with the growing *de facto* exclusion of the middle classes from opportunities for socio-economic advancement. Perhaps most important, cronyism and rising economic insecurity fueled perceptions of inequality and violations of norms of social justice. In the richer oil countries, increased transfers reduced, at least for now, the emerging tensions. Where tensions related to ethnicity were high, such as in Syria or Iraq, the removal of autocracy opened up the issue of the renewal of political settlements. In all cases, the inter-linkages between economic and political grievances point to the value of a political economy perspective in understanding the Arab uprisings and their aftermaths.

Several Chapter in this volume contribute to this emerging account and discuss the consequences of the youth bulge, the rising education and aspirations, a more autonomous middle class increasingly frustrated by a perceived rise in the inequality of opportunities, in the midst of an environment with rising repression and cronyism under-delivering on the jobs front.

Roger Owen recounts the broad historical and economic path leading to the uprisings. He argues that the system of personalized Arab presidential power based on a strong security state had its origins in the assertion of national sovereignty in the dangerous post-independence world of the 1950s and 1960s which became more monarchical in character over time. He discusses how the attempt to perpetuate itself by passing power on to the ruler's son was related to the appearance around each ruler of a small group of crony-capitalists who used their privileged access to secure state monopolies which they then schemed to protect after the ruler's death. In his account, both developments, that of family dictatorships, as well as their associated corruption and cronyism, account in large measure for the emergence of the uprisings.

Fadhel Kaboub, by developing the Tunisian story, brings out the roles of socio-economic inequality, youth unemployment, corruption, and government oppression in the making of the uprisings. He argues that given the extent of repression under Ben Ali, the overthrow of his regime could not have taken place had it not been a leaderless revolt. In the process of exploring the factors that maintained stability until the forces of the Tunisian revolution were unleashed, Kaboub's analysis reveals the radical social transformation that took place since the early 1990s which led to the breakdown of the social contract, and the gradual drift of the middle class away from its implicit support of the Ben Ali regime.

In my Chapter, I start by arguing that the old models used to understand the region are not helpful in understanding the genesis of the uprisings, because they were focused on explaining the persistence of autocracy, and that as such, this literature has not looked sufficiently into the underlying social and economic transformations, since regimes seem immutable. My analysis focuses on two key aspects of the past that are relatively under-studied: the development of crony capitalism, and the parallel shift in social attitudes towards democracy, inequality and redistributive policies, and political Islam. My analysis is largely quantitative. I document social changes in Egypt using opinion surveys, and I assess the magnitude of cronyism using stock market and corporate data. The arguments that I sketch connect economic development (especially fiscal policies and the rise of crony capitalism), social change (rise in both aspirations and grievances), and political change (a more autonomous middle class splitting away from the autocratic coalition). The overall picture that emerges includes:

- The roll-back of the state in the mid-1980s, but without democratic opening, led to the rise of an elite capitalistic class allied with security circles, enforcing its dominance with the use of security tools to repress its opposition and economic tools to co-opt the middle class.
- The closer state-business relations did not develop into a successful industrial policy, but rather, into an economic system of gift exchange with moderate performance, which taxed growth and thus did not create sufficient good jobs; but that also generated additional grievances by unbalancing politics, and leading to a rise in income inequality.
- Increased fiscal pressures, driven in large parts by rising subsidies and lower tax revenues led to deteriorating social services and lower public investment, further eroding social mobility, hurting the poor and the marginalized regions, and leading to a rise in class identification.

**

The second theme that is discussed in several of the Chapters relates to the enormous difficulties being encountered during the ongoing transitions, and the question of the consolidation of democracy.

Caroline Freund and **Melise Jaud** look at the historical regularities around the world and find that not all transitions succeed: of the 90 countries that have changed regimes in the last half century, only 46% experienced a successful transition to democracy, 39% failed, and 15% moved gradually to democracy. Their Chapter explores the initial conditions associated with transition and with its success. Based on a statistical analysis of the past, they find that gender equality, the lack of natural resources, the lack of conflict, and urbanization significantly affect the likelihood of regime change and the durability of democracy. Contagion effects from experiences in neighboring countries are also important determinants of success. The results cast doubt on the possibility of quick wins in many countries of the region, except possibly in Tunisia, which satisfies most of the conditions for a successful transition (low natural resources, high female literacy, and a tradition of a parliamentary system). If democracy stabilizes in Tunisia, their results on the existence of regional contagion suggest that it will have positive implications that extend well outside its borders.

A set of questions closely associated with transitions and investigated in this volume relates to the need for a better understanding of past social developments. One of the main mysteries of the uprisings is that it started in countries that were doing better economically, and they were driven by youth from the middle class. These are not the losers from liberalization, but rather, the would-be-winners, and they could have been driven both by modernization forces as well as by frustrated aspirations. At the same time, there were poorer social groups that joined the movement after it was sparked. In my Chapter, I try to test empirically, using country level variations in public opinion in Egypt, which of the two most common explanations of 'revolution' elsewhere in the world applies best to the Egyptian case: the emancipative effects of rising education on the one hand or the rising levels of grievances related to inequality on the other. The main questions I ask are: have the opinions of the main socio-economic groups about the desirability of democracy changed over time? Are the youth of the middle class leading opinion change? Can the change in opinions be correlated with either a rise in aspirations, or grievances, or both? My results suggest that the middle class increased dramatically its support for democracy between 2000 and 2008, and that this was accompanied by a large increase in the perception of inequality. While the youth may have mobilized more than other age groups in protests, the analysis does not support the view that their views differ from those of their parents on the desirability of democracy at the present juncture. To the extent that the underlying forces driving public opinion are connected to skilled youth unemployment, it seems that the parents of Egyptian middle class youth became as unhappy as their children about the lack of job opportunities, compelling them to favor regime change and democracy. Instead, the data indicates that support for democratization came from two simultaneous drivers. On the one hand, support for democracy increased among those most concerned by the rising inequalities and they expected democratization to lead to a more redistributive state, with this drive particularly prevalent among lower income individuals. On the other hand, there was also a large increase of support for democracy among those driven by modernization and emancipation motives. This drive was more prevalent among the more educated individuals, and it was correlated with high levels of support for other modernization values such as support for gender equality. Overall, the middle class emerged as the strongest supporter of democracy, because it is at the intersection of these two forces.

A related line of investigation concerns the role of political Islam — did it contribute to the demise of the old order? The result in my Chapter, again based on the World Value Survey data for Egypt, confirm the results obtained by the Arab Barometer project (Tessler 2012), which is that the demand for democracy is positively correlated with support for political Islam: people favor more democracy and more Islamism at the same time. Some more detailed results also emerge. Adherents of Islamism did not support democracy as much as secularists in 2000. By 2008 however, middle class supporters of Islamism become, like secularists, a force for democratization. This finding suggests that Islamism acted as a conservative veil for the poor only, trumping their class interests. Islamists were not central actors in the uprisings that toppled authoritarian rulers, but their role in society and politics may have contributed to the defection of the middle classes from authoritarian coalitions, a key step in the breakdown of authoritarian rule.

Jillian Schwedler looks deeper into the evolution of political Islamist parties by exploring how the moderation hypothesis applies after the uprisings — this hypothesis states that political parties moderate their view once they start to participate in the political process in order to appeal to larger constituencies. Political inclusion is a major concern for democratizing states. Among the many groups excluded and repressed by the former regime, which should now be included and which excluded? And who decides? After the uprisings, a wider range of political actors have become directly engaged in debates and processes of political transition. Her Chapter explores the inclusion/moderation hypothesis with special attention to Islamist groups and asks whether the central tenets of the argument that inclusion leads to moderation, which was made in the past in the context of rules of participation set by autocratic regimes, still holds in the more open and dynamic environments of the post-revolutionary contexts, particularly in Tunisia and Egypt, where Islamists have done well in free and fair elections. She argues that in unstable and changing institutional contexts, the logic of the inclusion-moderation hypothesis is less likely to be present, particularly when more extreme opposition groups challenge Islamists to prove their core commitment to a conservative religious political vision. In particular, the main Salafist groups aim mainly at pressuring moderate Islamists to reduce the extent of their moderation. Indeed, the success of Salafi groups at the polls and in the streets has resulted in a shift of the political center to the right. In such contexts, the pressure becomes on the leftist and secular groups to move toward a more religious center by moderating their secular views. Short of doing that, a process of polarization gets under way, with the attraction to a 'center' being replaced by a logic of polarizing constituencies around two different preference peaks.

Hasan Ersel, and **Akhmad Rizal Shidiq** and **Philips Jusanio Vernmonte** bring evidence from Turkey and Indonesia to bear on several of these questions, and by doing so, offer important lessons for the Arab region. Ersel shows how the consolidation of a multi-party system and of a private sector dominated economy in Turkey emerged as interplay between politics and economics, and took half a century to get Turkey to where it is now — a still imperfect democracy. In the process, both mechanisms described by Schwedler took place: Islamic parties moderated, and secularists moved towards the new center. The Turkish political system was transformed into a multi-party regime that allowed participation in the political process. These developments led to a change in the political demands of the different segments of the society (including the Islamic political community) and to revisions in fundamental political concepts (such as secularism). Although Turkey has not been able to reach its long term goal of becoming a developed liberal democracy, the steps taken during this period enabled the smooth transfer of power to the Islamic-based AKP in 2003 elections. Turkey's experience reveals that establishing a sound institutional base for multi-party democracy and market economy is a long and difficult process. It requires the resolution of a series of conflicts among different interest groups and securing wide public support in an uncertain environment.

In looking at Indonesia, Shidiq and Vermonte argue that moderation forces can also arise from the exigencies of the electoral process itself. They argue that over time, the Islamic parties largely 'dissolved' into the polity in Indonesia after their positions became more moderate and less distinct from other parties across the political spectrum, and how decentralization was used to regenerate the political class. The total votes obtained by the Islamic parties consistently dropped over time, from 35% in 2004 election 26% in 2009 elections. They offer three explanations for this phenomena. First, voters with Islamic preferences have over time seen that the Islamic parties were too fragmented to win elections, and they have found alternative channels outside the electoral arena to pursue their interests — non-party Islamic organizations have mushroomed since the fall of Suharto in 1998, advocating the implementation of Islamic laws in more articulate ways than Islamic parties. Second, political parties have tended to shift to the center, trying to project the image as parties that are not too secular or too Islamic, in order to accommodate the aspiration of the conservative electorate. For example, the nationalist Golkar have become in favor of the implementation of *sharia.* At the same time, the Islamic parties have pursued moderate agendas by portraying themselves as pluralistic and inclusive parties in order to seek support from the largely moderate and secular Indonesian society. Third, the nationalist secular parties, such as Golkar and PDI-P, have started to compete with Islamic parties in developing a network of social services that helps them in maintaining their support base. As a result of competition, some of the Islamic parties have even distanced themselves from the Islamist agenda, particularly that of turning Indonesia into an Islamic state. Moderation is increasingly believed to get votes and political campaigns have increasingly projected strategies that emphasize a clean and caring party, anti-corruption, wealth redistribution, and social welfare, as opposed to explicitly religious agenda such as the establishment of an Islamic state.

**

A third class of issues that receive a lot of attention in this volume concerns the performance of capitalism in the past. The specificity of the region in this respect resides in the fact that economic liberalization operated in an environment where political competition remained limited. Why did this 'regime', despite what looks on paper like extensive economic liberalization, not deliver the type of private sector growth needed to absorb productively the youth bulge? Is there evidence that political connections played an important role in the rise of large economic concerns? How did the politically connected firms benefit from privileges, especially in countries where banking was liberalized? Can the low firm dynamism that is observed in most countries, including the problems of the 'missing middle' and the low levels of innovation, be attributed to the regime of political connections?

This is a large research agenda, which is now active globally, and needs to be opened up in the Middle East in order to understand better what type of capitalism is taking root in the region, and how the ongoing political transformations could influence its development, and thus, future economic performance. The ubiquitous nature of grand corruption in the Arab world, and the underlying exclusion mechanisms are discussed in several of the Chapters and are seen as a major stumbling block to progress on the job creation front.

Jeffrey B. Nugent sheds light on the extent of corruption in the region, and how this has changed over time. He shows that while earlier corruption in the region had not been as serious compared to other developing countries, more recently it has been on a sharp rise in most countries. He shows that from firm surveys in MENA countries, ordinary (or micro-level) corruption seems to be positively associated with certain other obstacles to doing business, such as tax administration, crime, political instability and competition from the informal sector. Nugent identifies several determinants of corruption and corresponding anti-corruption measures. After discussing relevant findings from around the world with anti-corruption policies, he describes evaluation methods that can serve as a guide for future anti-corruption efforts in the region.

However, while the design of anti-corruption programs is an important concern, it begs the *political* question: under what political conditions would such regulations be supported by governments and be allowed to work? The Chapters in this volume tend to view corruption and cronyism not as a sickness that can be cured on its own, but rather, as the outcome of a system by which authoritarianism extends its influence to the 'private' market sphere, and whose correction therefore require the type of political changes that have been ushered by the uprisings. A competitive economy tends to foster a competitive polity, since competing parties can finance themselves from diverse economic players by promising to represent their interests. Thus, autocratic rulers were reluctant to open up the economy and when they liberalized markets, they did so by concentrating economic power with their 'cronies', entrepreneurs that were selected for their loyalty rather than their skills, and which received privileges under condition that they do not support the opposition.

The Chapters in this volume explore two facets of the type of state-business relations that have grown post-economic liberalization: the impact of authoritarianism on business performance, and the impact of cronyism on governance. For example, Owen and Kaboub describe how autocrats restricted the heights of the economy to capitalist elites that they could trust, both to support their political needs financially, and to prevent opposition forces from developing support in society. Esfahani and Gürakar show how the Shah actively managed the Iranian business elite in ways to support his political goals. As discussed above, Owen also argues that cronies were a major driving force to bring sons of presidents to succeed presidents for life. Ersel shows how such systems can unfold: in Turkey, the economic liberalization of the 1980s facilitated the rise of the so-called Anatolians tigers, and these new players became more active politically and in turn, facilitated the rise of the AKP in the 2000s.

Hadi S. Esfahani and **Esra Ç. Gürakar** delve deep in the historical and structural factors that sustained authoritariasm in Iran in order to understand the factors leading to change. Their Chapter examines the evolution of social orders in Iran since the early 20th Century and relates the country's economic performance to that process. The study is enriched by comparisons with Turkey. They base their analysis on the limited social orders framework developed by North, Wallis and Weingast (2009), and argue that the core political settlement among the elite has been dominated by individuals and groups that have been more effective in organizing and controlling the means of violence. While many aspects of the system and the dominant groups have changed in significant ways over time, the transitions have not supported the development of impersonal rules and independent private organizations. This has been in contrast with the situation in Turkey where the army's collective rule and the role played by the European Union (EU) have allowed impersonal rules and long-lived private organizations to grow and gain strength. While Turkey's gains could in their view be reversible, they were nevertheless necessary in preparing the country to transit to a more open access order. The implications of the analysis offer insights for the Arab countries that are going through political transformation by pointing out that while institutions are central to development, they are not politically neutral because they affect income distribution. Often, institutional progress will occur when it benefits the elites, and the new rules will gradually be extended and opened to benefit broader constituencies.

In my Chapter, I attempt to develop a sense of magnitude on the size and impact of cronyism. I use an event study methodology to shed some light on Egyptian cronyism. First, I identify a set of politically connected large firms, which allows for a assessment of the impact of cronyism, including comparisons between connected and non connected large firms. Using an event study of stock market reaction to the revolution, I estimate the value of political connections at about 23% of the connected firms' value (the same magnitude estimated by Ray Fisman for Suharto's Indonesia). I then compare the past corporate performance of connected and unconnected firms and show that connected firms grew immensely during 2004–2010 (seven folds, compared to no growth among non-connected firms), increased their market share relative to their non-connected competitors, and borrowed much more than their competitors. However, while they were in profitable sectors, they were less profitable than non-connected firms in the sectors in which they operate. This indicates that to a large extent, industrial policy was captured by private interests and was not effective.

With the political winds shifting, it may become possible to push back the political constraint which has restricted the growth of the private sector in the past. New regulations to improve competition should become possible should regimes become more representative of the interests of the population. This requires a policy and regulatory framework in which political authority is constrained in its ability to discriminate among firms on the basis of political connections.

Izak Atiyas describes the global best practices on the type of rules and institutions needed to control corruption and enhance competition, drawing on the experience of Turkey. He argues that establishing a non-discriminatory policy and regulatory framework entails institutional remedies whereby substantial amount of decision and rule making authority is delegated to agencies that are relatively independent from the government and individual ministries. He discusses the objectives and characteristics of this delegation, the nature of the independence, and other dimensions such as accountability and transparency. Turkey's experience shows that such delegation can happen, albeit imperfectly and in ways that are not uniform across sectors. But even in its imperfect form, where the *de facto* independence of the new agencies is questionable, he shows examples where the new rules of the game did have some bite in limiting the extent of capture. The role of Independent Regulatory Agencies in particular, in his assessment, was associated with better performance in reducing corruption. The Turkish experience seems to suggest that institutions that enhance competition play a role in creating an environment that is more conducive to investment and growth. But his Chapter also shows that Turkey benefited from particular circumstances that may not be present in the Middle East, such as the occurrence of the macro-financial crisis of 2001, the influence of international organizations, and the perspective of accession to the EU. Moreover, it is noteworthy that in the case of Turkey, enhanced transparency and accountability in some sectors occurred simultaneously with increased political discretion in others. The jury is still out, then, on whether the new institutions will survive political dynamics if the EU anchor becomes weaker.

**

A last theme that was developed in several Chapters in this book, albeit in less detail that the themes discussed above, is that of state budgets and macroeconomic policies. Several authors see a deterioration of the macroeconomic situation during transition as an inevitable phenomenon, especially that the international community had no ready-made mechanism to support the countries in transition. The revolutions themselves have weakened the macroeconomic environment, with capital flight accelerating, and foreign direct investment (FDI) and tourism collapsing. It is well know that the macroeconomy and growth always deteriorate during transitions — the challenge is to recover quickly. There is a broad recognition that improving politics will be essential for recovery. But it is also likely, unfortunately, that economics will have to deteriorate further before politics improve, with the risk of countries getting stuck in a low equilibrium transition path, whereby a deteriorating economy slows the transition, and *vice versa*. In Turkey, Ersel reminds us that it took a major financial crisis (in 2001) for the emergence of more discipline macro policy (by the AKP). In Indonesia, the political crisis of 1998 was caused by the Asian Financial Crisis that had engulfed the country. In the uprising countries, no clear constituency for macroeconomic stability has emerged yet, and new regimes are pushed by high aspirations towards populist and short-sighted policies, rather than in-depth reforms. At the end, the relevant political economy questions in several of the countries that will not be able to avoid a financial crisis may well be how to exploit the coming financial crises in order to establish a constituency for more stable economic order in the future.

The related issues of fiscal policy and the health of state services received little attention in the volume, a reflection of the poor state of the current literature, which is to a large extent a reflection of the lack of access to data and information in the past. The Chapters by Kaboub and myself on Tunisia and Egypt respectively suggest that the patterns of public expenditures and taxation changed gradually over the past two decades to reflect the increased dominance of elite capital in the governing coalitions and the roll-back of the state. Besides outlining the issues of petty corruption in the provision of social services, and the deterioration in the quality of services which has led to their quasi privatization, several of the Chapters highlight the underlying political reasons for the rise in subsidies for goods that go predominantly to the richer parts of society. Clearly, more work is needed to understand the current incidence of public finance in order to suggest reforms that can accommodate in the short term the change in preference of the new governments which will likely represent the interests of the middle classes and the poor more than in the past, and which can increase the effectiveness of the state over time.

The walls of intellectual fears have been broken, and the unfolding events have lifted the veil from a complex social, political, and economic inheritance. Much of what is in this volume could not have been written in the Arab world just three years ago. Since then, a new regional space has been opened for more honest and enlightened discussions, dialogue, and learning. In many ways, the future will be shaped by the ongoing conversations and by their effect on collective action.

THE GENESIS OF THE UPRISINGS

Chapter 1

THE POLITICAL ECONOMY OF ARAB PRESIDENTS FOR LIFE — AND AFTER

Roger Owen

1. Introduction

The overthrow of a series of long-term dictatorships was clearly the major aim of the revolutionaries of the so-called 'Arab Spring'. And remarkably successful they were. In a relatively short period of time, three republican presidents for life (Zine El Abidine Ben Ali, Hosni Mubarak, and Muammar Qaddafi) have been deposed, two others (Bashar Hafez al-Assad and Ali Abdullah Saleh) have been forced into the fight of their lives to defend themselves, and two others again (Abdelaziz Bouteflika and Omar al-Bashir) much weakened, although by a variety of forces not all directly connected with an active youth rebellion. If we add the Anglo-American overthrow of President Saddam Hussein of Iraq in 2003, the only republic that did not experience some major upheaval was that of Lebanon where its tradition of a weak Christian presidency has long been constrained by institutions and popular forces from all of the sectarian communities.

In what follows, I will examine the trajectory of the post-independence Arab presidencies as they mutated from presidencies for life into something more monarchical, given the increasing desire of rulers and regimes to perpetuate themselves, usually by selecting a son or other relative to act as the president's successor. I will then look at the reasons for the widespread opposition these presidential regimes aroused, the attempts to replace them with a new political order by means of new constitutions and newly elected parliaments, and finally, the problems encountered in dealing with the members of the old dictatorial regimes along with their legacy of pervasive security apparatuses and crony-capitalist monopolies, not strictly limited to the Egyptian case, of a well-entrenched military establishment. In doing so I will deal with examples from all the Arab republican presidencies, from Iraq and Yemen in the east, to Algeria in the west, noting that not only did the Arab

Spring bring the Arab states together in a way they had rarely been before, but that it also provided examples and warnings which were rapidly passed from one state to another across North Africa and the rest of the Middle East.

2. The Establishment of Authoritarian Presidencies for Life

Following independence sometime after the Second World War, many of the Arab states established strong, centralized republican presidencies, either by getting rid of an existing monarchical structure (Egypt, Libya, Iraq, Tunisia, Yemen) or by a series of military coups (Algeria, Sudan, Syria).[1]

Given the fact that similar processes took place elsewhere in the post-colonial world, it is reasonable to suppose — with Mohamed Ayoob — that this was the result of more general global processes concerning the protection of newly-gained sovereignty and the desire to promote unity (of language, education, culture, etc.), modernization, and development via popular mobilization, as well as by measures to redistribute income such as land reform and state-lead industrialization (Ayoob 1995). But there were also significant Arab features of this process as well, notably the demonstration effect of the type of state-building efforts pursued by President Nasser in Egypt followed by the policy of partial economic liberalization begun by his successor, President Sadat.

Central to such a system of control was an emphasis on regime security based on some combination of the army, the police, and often competing internal security organizations. Important too was the creation of a large state bureaucracy consisting of separate bureaucratic fiefdoms run by men close to the President but not necessarily under his direct control, like Nasser's friend and Minister of War, Abdel-Hakim Amer.

Nevertheless, there were also some significant differences in the actual conduct of affairs between the various regime, best understood under three general headings:

(i) The presidents of states with a long tradition of centralized power (Algeria, Tunisia, Egypt, Iraq, and Syria) were able to rule more or less by decree, while those with more extensive and unruly domains (Libya, Sudan, and Yemen) were forced to continue the more traditional methods of negotiating with local power-brokers while practicing a loose policy of divide and rule.

(ii) Over time, reliance on the army as the main prop of the regime gave way in Egypt in particular to that of the police and the intelligence services which turned them into more obviously police states.

(iii) There was also a tendency for regimes which had originally sought a multi-class base to rely on a more middle class one as statist development policies could not longer be afforded. This base also began to be replaced by those of a mixed

[1]Note that Qaddafi never actually called himself 'President' preferring titles like that of 'Brother Leader'.

public/private type, making the main sources of tension exist between the middle class and regime cronies on one hand, and the middle class and the police, on the other.

Over time, such dictatorial regimes attracted the label of 'authoritarian' — a form of government first identified by scholars working on Latin America, which assumed the creation of a single center of power that controlled every aspect of political, economic, social, and cultural life, including state-ownership of the country's major means of production. In many cases this definition was supported by a second assumption, that of the crushing of anything that might be called 'civil society', a notion much in vogue after Poland and the other eastern states began to free themselves from Soviet rule at the end of the 1980s. But note too, that with respect to both definitions, recent research has begun to question the comprehensiveness of state control over every aspect of political, economic and social life, preferring to stress the existence of pockets of opposition within groups such as organized labor, as well as in geographical regions where the exercise of state power was limited by the existence of quasi-independent communities such as rural villages and loosely-organized tribes. In Egypt, Libya, and Tunisia, it was such entities which were often in the forefront of opposition to the dictatorial regimes and which formed important political constituencies to be competed over by the various parties that stepped into the electoral arena after the Arab Spring.

3. Republican Presidents Become More Monarchical

Once established in power, and no longer subject to the threat either of foreign intervention or military coup, presidents like Gamal Abdel Nasser of Egypt, Habib Bourguiba in Tunisia and Houari Boumediene in Algeria, seem to have assumed that they would remain as 'presidents for life' without this ever being recognized as part of actual constitutional practice. To start with, they were content to live and work in quite humble circumstances. But, beginning at least as early as the 1970s in the case of President Sadat of Egypt, there was an observed tendency to flaunt their power, to live in palaces, and again in the case of Sadat, to promote his wife to a kind of equivalent of America's 'First Lady'.

Other pressures were at work in the case of Syria where President Hafiz al-Assad's grave illness in 1983/4 appears to have prompted senior members of the minority Alawi community to place the protection of their communal interests in the Assad family's hands. And others again in those countries which undertook the internationally-promoted process of building up the private sector in the early 1990s via policies of privatization and the encouragement of foreign capital with often the further effect of placing vast wealth in the hands of crony-capitalists of an oligarchic, monopolistic type, some of them either related to the president's family or able to marry into it.

The result, in all cases, was a situation in which presidents, their families, their cronies, and many of the oligarchs shared a vested interest in ensuring the permanence of the regime as the best way to preserve their own privileged positions. They had to protect their positions not only against possible future change but also against other would-be monopolists within their own society who might press to share some of the spoils. This was of particular importance to those who had either obtained former state-monopolies — steel, the manufacture of cars or chemicals, etc. — or the monopoly right to import certain scare commodities, not to speak of access to cheap credit from state banks, privileges which they needed the state to protect. Indeed, so tight was the connection between private monopoly and state power that it is possible to imagine a direct correlation between the number of major inner-circle crony capitalists and the size of the economy at large, perhaps 25 or so in Egypt, and perhaps 15 in Syria.

For most rulers and most regimes, the most obvious way to secure its permanence was to ensure that dictator fathers were succeeded by their sons, a practice begun in Syria in the 1990s and then putatively extended to Egypt with the grooming of Gamal Mubarak beginning in the late 1990s; Libya, with the return of Saif al-Qaddafi from London in 2008 and Yemen. More problematic was the situation in states like Tunisia, where the President had only a very young son born in 2006, and in Algeria and Sudan where the President had no son at all.

Just as problematic, as it soon turned out, was the situation in Libya and Yemen, where the presidents' several sons were often at odds with each other over control of state resources. But, whatever the case, the whole question was rendered moot by the overthrow of some of the dictatorial families in 2011 after which, as the Secretary General of the United Nations, Ban Ki-Moon noted, it seemed most unlikely that even those who manage to survive will attempt to adopt this particular, and now almost wholly discredited, solution to the problem of succession (Karam 2012).

4. Pressures Within the Dictatorial Regimes that Account for Their Overthrow

For a period in the 1990s and early part of the 21st Century it seemed to most observers, whether inside or outside the Middle East, that the Arab authoritarian presidencies had found a winning formula for survival based on making themselves coup-proof and then relying on a combination of surveillance, control and fear, tempered by occasional elections. This formula was tested and further sustained in states like Algeria, Tunisia, Egypt, and Syria where there were constant reminders that the ruler alone stood between society and either chaos or government by religious extremists. Indeed, in the case of many, the monarchical presidents seemed to become even stronger over time thanks to the obvious support they received from the United States and its allies as a result of their role in the 'war on terror', announced by President Bush shortly after the 9/11 attacks. Though notionally committed to the idea of their transition towards popular democracy, successive visitors to Cairo and elsewhere like Bush's Secretary of State, Condoleezza Rice, were content to give the presidents only the slightest tap on the wrist concerning their anti-democratic practices.

True, there were signs of some small signs of middle class opposition, for example, Egypt's Kifaya ('Enough') movement launched in what seemed like a vain hope to prevent the succession of Gamal Mubarak. But such was the confidence that each president seemed to display, and such was the secrecy that enveloped actual regime practice, that most of the warning signs were missed. These included significant splits with the elite itself, for example, military opposition to Gamal Mubarak based on his perceived weakness in dealing with the Muslim Brotherhood. They also included the increasing influence of more basic social trends such as the progressive impoverishment of the middle class relative to the top one or two percent of the population, and the growing impact of what demographers call the 'youth bulge' by which the numbers of young persons in the Arab world between 15 and 35 more or less doubled from 1980 to 2010 (Fargues 2012).

In any case, it was a tiny spark that led first to the rapid overthrow of the Ben Ali regime in Tunisia in January 2011, and then to the huge demonstrations in Cairo's Maidan Tahrir later the same month which revealed just how weak and unprepared most regimes were for the popular uprisings that either overthrew them or, when they encountered armed resistance, catapulted their countries into a species of civil war. Although many millions are so aggrieved, it is impossible to isolate just one or two of the factors which led to the pan-Arab uprisings. They would seem to have had most to do with each kleptocratic regime's desire to perpetuate itself; the sense of hopelessness that this engendered, combined with the regimes' inabilities to satisfy the economic needs of a rapidly-growing population left each regime almost completely bereft of mobilizable popular support once the uprisings began. The once formidable military proved unwilling or unable to put them down by sheer brute force.

5. Major Political and Administrative Problems Involved in the Development of New Structures and a New Arab Order

As world history is witness, major revolutionary events take years, sometimes decades to unfold before a stable new political structure has been built. In the Arab Middle East, as with everywhere else, the building blocks were supposed to be a combination of popular elections and a constitution to be legitimated by its general acceptance as an emanation of the people's will. But if the practice of electoral democracy and constitution-building was not difficult enough, there were other problems which were to prove in some ways almost as complex and divisive, notably the proper punishment of members of the deposed regimes, the transfer of their wealth and of the structures that sustained it back into state hands. Another problem was the wholesale reform of regime institutions such as the police, the judiciary, and the system of education including the eradication of what Middle Easterners, following Turkish practice implementing a 'deep state'.

Writing as of early March 2014, three years after the revolutionary processes began, progress towards a new constitutional order had proceeded furthest in the three North African states of Tunisia, Libya, and Egypt. Given the many problems involved, a commendable attempt by the new governments to associate the 'people' at large in the drafting process via elections, which were almost inevitably won by the better organized religious parties and movements, is a notable achievement owing much to a general wish to adhere to the timetable drawn up immediately after the revolutions. But it has also had the effect of producing deep nation-wide divisions concerning some of the basic articles in the new constitutions which are complicating the attempt to address the major economic and educational problems each country faces after so many years of dictatorial mis-management and neglect.

Note too, that elsewhere in North Africa, little institutional change has taken place in republican Algeria apart from a general weakening of President Bouteflika's position due to persistent illness. Nevertheless, he remains sufficiently part of the system of power to seek an unprecedented fourth term in office sure in the knowledge that his opponents will face unmanageable bureaucratic obstacles if they try to stand against him.

Turning now to the Arab East, the Syrian regime instinctively dug in its heels in the face of unarmed demonstrations that, in its complete isolation from the ordinary people, it chose to regard as the work of deranged agents of foreign powers. If there was any rationale to this heavy-handed military response it can be derived from a habit of mind that believed it was necessary to re-establish the usual state of fear before contemplating the offer of any meaningful concessions from a position of strength. The result, as is well known, is that what used to be regarded as a relatively cohesive society has begun to come apart in ever more destructive and violent ways, making many parts of the country virtually ungovernable with neither the regime not a fractious set of opposition groups able to gain the upper hand.

As for Yemen, the stalemate between the regime and various types of armed and unarmed (mostly student) opposition created in the summer of 2011 has been managed by outside forces, notably the United States and Saudi Arabia. Central to this process was a special election in February 2012 that led to the replacement of President Ali Abdullah Saleh by the country's vice-president who was then charged with the task of writing a new constitution followed by overseeing new elections for both president and parliament in 2014.

Nevertheless, considerable tensions persist including a military standoff between those parts of the army controlled by Saleh's sons and those by an opposition. This has been further exacerbated by the fact that, as a result of a deal brokered by the Gulf Cooperation Council (GCC), the ex-president was able to obtain an amnesty for himself after returning from hospital in Saudi Arabia, leaving the new government unable to question him about the size and the whereabouts of his private assets tentatively valued at some US$25 billion, the ill-gotten fruits of his nearly 40 years in power.[2]

---

[2]An estimation of Ali Abdullah Saleh's Salary. See "Yemeni government grants President Ali Abdullah Saleh, his kids and staff total immunity." *Now Morocco Blog*, January 9 2012.

6. Economic and Legal Problems: Tunisia, Egypt, and Libya

Three years into the Arab Spring, the only countries where reforms have gone far enough to confront the major problems involved in both disposing of the old structures and trying to establish new ones, are the adjoining states of Tunisia, Libya, and Egypt. I will deal with these problems under three headings: trial and punishment of the leaders of the old regime and members of their families, the restructuring of the crony-capitalist economic order, and the longer-term reform of the such basic institutions as the police, the educational and legal systems and, in Egypt, the anomalous role of the military.

6.1. *The trial and punishment of the leaders of the old regime*

In only one of the three revolutions under consideration did the former president for life, Hosni Mubarak, stay in his palace until he was arrested with his two sons. Of the others, one, Ben Ali, fled to Saudi Arabia with his wife, while the second, Qaddafi, was killed by his own people along with several of his sons, leaving one son, Saif, to be captured by the angry people of the town of Zintan and a second son, Saadi, extradited from Niger in March 2014.

Then came what proved to be the very difficult question of for what exactly those who remained should be put on tried. One possibility, advocated by the International Court of Justice at The Hague, was for 'crimes against humanity', an interesting notion from an international perspective but one that found little favor in Libya as it would have meant surrendering Saif al-Qaddafi to what was regarded as a foreign judicial process. As of early March 2014, the question remained on hold subject to prior reform of what passes as the Libyan legal system.

A second, chosen in Egypt, was to legitimize the whole process, not by some concept of revolutionary justice but by trying Mubarak for two crimes already on the statute book: murder and corruption; in one case, for giving orders to the police to shoot demonstrators, and in the other, for conniving with a crony-businessmen to sell Egypt's natural gas to Israel at lower than world market prices. Neither charge could be made to stick, leaving the former president under arrest but in a kind of legal limbo.

There is an important lesson here, just as there is in Tunisia where the new regime also decided to try Ben Ali in a military court, albeit in absentia, on charges of both the theft of state assets, and of ordering the deaths of protestors. While it possible to understand the logic of trying former presidents for crimes already on the statute book like murder, there is a strong case for Mohamed Hassanein Heikal's argument in the Egyptian newspaper, *Al-Ahram* to the effect that, as Mubarak's crimes were essentially political (rather than legal), the matter should be left to the elected representatives of the people to decide (Ezzat 2011).

Whether members of a popular assembly would actually want to take responsibility for so serious a task is another matter. But it would certainly have the advantage of encouraging a debate as to what, precisely, the former dictator should be held accountable for in terms of the harm he committed against, not just the lives of several generations of his people but also their legitimate expectations, including all the things they might have done if they had not been prevented from doing so.

6.2. *The restructuring of the old crony-capitalist economic order*

Though there can be no doubt that the crony-capitalist economic order established in Egypt, Libya, and Tunisia was bad for the economy in general, as well as for the health of state and private enterprise at all levels of activity, there is a great deal about its history and operations which still remains unknown for many obvious reasons. For one thing, the vast sell-off of state enterprises in the 1990s was conducted very largely in secret, with no public tenders and no way of knowing how bids were financed. For another, both the dictators and their crony-capitalist allies took good care to ensure that as little as possible was known about both the monopoly profits which the process allowed and the way some of these were used to support dubious regime projects like managed elections. Then there is the question of the present whereabouts of the billions and billions of dollars of ill-gotten gains — estimated at some US$11 billion in the case of Ben Ali and his family — much of which, it seems, may never be recovered in spite of the best efforts to bankers and the financial authorities in the US, Europe and elsewhere (Byrne 2012).

Turning now to the domestic assets of the ex-dictators, their families and their crony associated, information about their fate is also extremely difficult to come by. Anti-corruption commissions have been formed and great efforts made both to identify such assets and then to subject them to official confiscation. The result, it seems, has generally been their return to state hands. Only a few were then privatized, for example Buraq Airways, once owned by one of Qaddafi's wives, although on what terms with regard to its future organization — for example, to maintaining the same labor forces, the same levels of activities — is difficult to discover.[3]

For the rest, and particularly in cases where the enterprise has been reasonably well-run (for example, Ahmed Ezz's Iron and Steel Company in Egypt) one can only suppose that they are now being run by state officials, although details are again very hard to come by — certainly no transparency here.

Lastly, there is the question of the remaining state banks, used more or less as cash cows by the cronies and then, after the fall of the dictators, left full of non-performing loans which they had given, often after the most cursory examination and almost all without any tangible security. Here privatization was a difficult option given the adverse nature of their balance sheets; so a long process of internal restructuring is necessary before there can be any hope of sale.

As for the creation of a new economic order to replace the old, progress has been bogged down in Egypt and Tunisia by political disagreements, notably those between populist politicians anxious promote some species of planned development

[3]Information privately supplied by Dirk Vandewalle.

and the neo-liberal technocrats like the ex-head of Tunisia's National Bank, Mustafa Nabli, concerned with promoting investment by policies of cutting state subsidies, privatization, and balancing budget. Where such policies have also been embraced, *faute de mieux*, by a religious party containing powerful business businessmen but without a clear economic vision of its own, the ability to satisfy the demands of the unemployed by creating new state sectors is limited and, in the case of Tunisia, the cause of considerable social unrest.

Further problems have arisen from the climate of uncertainty created by the fierce determination of Egypt's prosecutors in their pursuit of cronies associated with the Mubarak regime and by the fact that the new draft constitution contains nothing about the rights of private ownership and questions concerning the use of water and the protection of the environment, making potential investors wary of committing themselves before a predictable legal structure is properly in place.

6.3. *Longer-term reform of basic institutions and their relationship with the state*

For the young revolutionaries of Tahrir and elsewhere, one of their basic aims was the root-and-branch reform of most basic institutions of the ancient regime states: the police, the educational and legal systems for example, as well as the introduction of huge projects concerned to deal with damage being done to the environment by pollution, over-use of water and so on. Unfortunately, not only would such schemes take decades to be completed but they would also cost very large sums of money, considerations that clearly make them immediately unattractive to politicians concerned with short-term electoral considerations. To make matters worse, many of these reforms are also opposed by powerful vested interests, for example, the army, the security services, and the judges in Egypt, the trade unions in Tunisia.

Hence it is no real surprise that there have been so few steps to reform the Egyptian police in spite of their gross failures at crowd control exhibited under both the Muslim Brother regime of President Mohamed Morsi (June 2012–July 2013) and now the military one of General (now Field Marshall) Abdel-Fatteh Al-Sisi that replaced it after the 'coup' of 3 July 2013. Furthermore, many of Hosni Mubarak's top officials either remained in place, like the judges who supervised the first popular elections in 2012, or have resurfaced under Sisi. Then there is the army which, whether in or out of power, has a huge set of its own interests to preserve, not just its institutional independence but also its control over sizeable economic assets, the management of which might well be at risk if they were either properly accounted for, or even worse, thrown open to the winds of international competition.

Matters have proceeded further in Tunisia where aspects of the 'deep state' proved more easy to root out. There, 40 of Ben Ali's senior officials have been put on trial and sentenced to 20 years imprisonment, including his Chief of Presidential Security Ministry and Minister of the Interior. Furthermore, an edict was passed banning senior member's of his party (the RCD) from standing in elections if they had any involvement in politics over the last 10 years.

As for Libya, there the problem of what to do with members of the Qaddafi regime has, paradoxically, been both the greatest — there being few Libyans who were not complicit with it in one way or another including the new president himself — and yet one where the purge has gone deepest. A year and half after the old regime fell, many of Qaddafi's close associates were in prison waiting for trial with lower-ranking suspects held in military detention centers as they waited for a new court system to be put in place. Nevertheless, only one person had actually been brought to trial so far, Qaddafi's former chief of external intelligence, and he still has not received a sentence.

7. Some Lessons Learnt so Far

Whether they characterize the so-called 'Arab Spring' as a revolutionary process or something less comprehensive and disturbing of the old order, most observers, for example, Mustafa Abdul-Jalil, the head of Libya's National Transitional Council, believe that it will take years to overcome what he calls 'heavy heritage of corruption and distrust' (Michael 2012). For another, as is well known, the system of constitutional democracy which is being attempted in Egypt, Iraq, Libya, and Tunisia, and which may yet be attempted in Syria and Sudan, takes many years of institutionalized accommodation supported by a wise and understanding judiciary before it can be said to achieved its aim.

Hence, the first and most significant lesson to be learn so far is certainly the importance of an agreed timetable towards the creation of a popular democracy, encouraged and supported, where possible either by the international community as represented by the United Nations, the International Monetary Fund and the World Bank, the Arab League, or the European Economic Community, or, in the case of Egypt, heavily dependent on American economic and military aid, by the United States. Moreover, such support needs to be exercised with skill and careful diplomacy with due attention to both the stick and the carrots of recognition and future rewards. So far, the Obama administration in particular has managed the process very well, preferring to give private advice to Egypt's generals rather than public admonition and making the principled decision of not threatening to cut military aid. This was perhaps inspired by historical memories of the disastrous consequences of the Eisenhower administration's decision with withdraw its promise of funding for the Aswan Dam in 1955.

Two other lessons concern the problems associated with the novel practice of a strong parliamentary democracy in which the person who controls the most seats after an election becomes the prime minister, and then the developing relationship between the prime minister, the president (as head of state) and, in Egypt, the head of the armed forces. All this is complicated enough at the best of times, for example in Lebanon, relying as it does on a mix of practice, experience and judicious accommodation. But, starting from scratch, as the Egyptians, Libyan and Tunisians have decided to do, makes it doubly complex, with the rules and relationships between the major political, as well as judicial, actors still very much a work in progress. In Tunisia and Libya, instance, there is the emergence of what looks like a Lebanese power triangle involving president, prime minister and speaker of the national assembly. And everywhere we can observe the practice of appointing a political technocrats to key ministries like finance and education.

8. A Final Question: What has been the Effect of the Spring on the Arab Monarchies and the Gulf States?

Much the same wave of excitement that toppled the North Africa dictatorship was also experienced in the two monarchical state of Morocco and Jordan, and for many of the same reasons — economic distress, unemployment, and falling middle class incomes — yet with many fewer calls for their overthrow due to the strong social base among tribal and other rural communities. Hence, by a combination of the employment of much the same security measures as failed in the republics allied to the sacking of scapegoat ministers and the promise of greater monarchical accountability, they were able to survive, even though huge economic problems remained.

As for the family monarchies in and around the Arabian peninsula, they too were briefly shaken by demonstrations of popular discontent but were generally able to weather their smaller storms by some exemplary punishments allied to large cash and other handouts from their oil-fueled reserves, as well as promoting some steps designed to increase greater popular representation at the advisory level in Saudi Arabia, Qatar, and the minority Sunni population of Bahrain. Equally worthy of note was talk, but only talk, of moving towards the more stripped-down form of monarchy found in Jordan and Morocco with succession proceeding not through the eldest fit male relative of a deceased ruler but to his eldest son.

9. Conclusion

Much has happened in the three years since the outbreak of the Arab revolts and yet in none of the states most directly involved, has anything like a working and popularly legitimate political and administrative system been created to replace the old ones. In fact, there has only been any significant process of transition in three — Egypt, Libya and Tunisia — not forgetting the gains made after the overthrow of Saddam Hussein in Iraq. Meanwhile, a number of new problems have arisen with the arrival of members of religious parties in government, the uncertainty surrounding presidential powers and pressures felt by secular liberals, women and, in Egypt, minorities, not to speak of the development of news forms of economic warfare against the state by small but intransigent groups Salafis and Jihadis.

Beyond this, certain new patterns of economic behavior can be discerned. First and foremost, the Arab Spring has been an 'Arab' economic moment in the sense of mobilizing financial resources from the rich Gulf state to provide financial assistance, under IMF guidance, to Egypt and to a lesser extent, Tunisia. It also offers more limited possibilities for greater Arab economic unity, not necessarily of the formal kind but for exploiting new forms of economic exchange as well as the type of cooperation that comes from geographical proximity such as the shared transport and electricity grids, joint steps to promote tourism and so forth. Some of these exchanges could be extended to regional or sub-regional plans to deal with the major challenges posed by declining rainfall, and diminishing food production desertification.

Acknowledgments

I have drawn largely on material to be found in Owen, R. 2012. *The Rise and Fall of Arab Presidents for Life*. Cambridge, MA: Harvard University Press. Special thanks to Malika Zeghal and Dirk Vandewalle for information provided.

References

Anderson, L. 1991. "Absolutism and resilience of monarchy in the Middle East." *Political Science Quarterly*, 106(1): 1–15.

Ayoob, M. 1995. *The Third World Security Predicament: State Making, Regional Conflict and the International System*, p. 4. Boulder, CO: Lynne Reinner.

Beau, N. and C. Graciet. 2009. *La Regente de Carthage: Main Basse sur La Tunisie*. [In French] Paris: La Decouverte.

Beinin, J. and F. Vairel. eds. 2013. *Social Movements, Mobilization, and Contestation in the Middle East and North Africa*, 2nd edn. California: Stanford University Press.

Byrne, E. 2012. "Ben Ali's family and friends." *The Guardian* (London), January 13.

Daguzan, J.-F. 2010. "De la crise economique a la revolution politique." [In French] *Magreb/Machrek*, 206: 9–10.

El Rashidi, Y. 2013. "Egypt: The rule of the Brotherhood." *New York Review of Books*, 7 February, 42–47.

Ezzat, D. 2011. "Past can't shape the future." *Al-Ahram Weekly*, May 19–25.

Fargues, P. 2012. "Demography, migration and revolt in the Southern Mediterranean." In *Arab Society in Revolt: The West's Mediterranean Challenge*, eds., Merlini, C. and O. Roy, p. 29. Washington D.C.: Brookings Institute Press.

Haddad, B. 2013. *Business Networks in Syria: The Political Economy of Authoritarian Resiliance*. California: Stanford University Press.

Heydemann, S. ed. 2004. *Networks of Privilege in the Middle East*. New York: Palgrave-Macmillan.

Karam, Z. 2012. "Ban Ki-Moon: Syria violence must end." *Huffington Post World*, January 15.

Michael, M. 2012. "Militias stymie Libya's leaders." *The Boston Globe*, February 22.

Owen, R. and S. Pamuk. 1998. *A History of the Middle East Economies in the Twentieth Century*. London: I. B. Tauris.

Pratt, N. 2007. *Democracy and Authoritarianism in the Arab World*. Boulder, CO: Lynne Rienner.

Chapter 2

UNDERSTANDING REVOLUTION IN THE MIDDLE EAST: THE CENTRAL ROLE OF THE MIDDLE CLASS

Ishac Diwan

1. Introduction

The Arab world is at a crossroads, facing enormous challenges as well as opportunities that can lead to either a gradually improving democratic path, or an authoritarian retrenchment. In the absence of an understanding of the social, political, and economic transformations that have led to the recent uprisings sweeping across the region, it will be difficult for the political analyst to try and predict the future, and for the policy analyst to provide useful advice. It will also be challenging for the multitude of new actors that have suddenly become more influential to navigate the stormy waters of the ongoing transitions.

A shared analytical frame may be emerging intuitively, but it has not yet been brought together into a coherent and logical framework. Many of the characteristics of the recent Arab uprisings are puzzling and do not fit easily with popular intellectual frames. Why did they occur at the end of 2010, when there were no apparent direct triggers such as declines in subsidies or shifts in foreign alliances, rather than some time in the 1990s when the welfare state started being rolled-back? Why did the revolutions start in Tunisia and Egypt, the countries with some of the highest economic growth in the region in the preceding few years, rather than in countries such as Syria or Yemen where the economic conditions have been more dire and political repression more severe? Why were they initiated by secularist middle class youth, the supposed beneficiaries of the modernizing republics, rather than by the long-standing Islamic opposition?

The goal of this Chapter is to develop a coherent, structural, long term account of the socio-economic and political evolution of the Arab republics that would explain both the persistence of autocracy until 2011, and its eventual collapse, in a way that is empirically verifiable.

One leading family of structural narratives focuses on a slow transition from socialism, where the roll-back of the state, which was started in the mid-1980s, ultimately led to the break-down of the social contract underlying the autocratic bargain. While such accounts cannot claim that the roll-back is the proximate cause of the insurgency given the long delay, an understanding of why (and how) transitions were delayed, which mechanisms were used by autocrats to remain in power even as market forces chipped at their authority, and which contradictions emerged in this late autocratic 'equilibrium' characterized by selective repression and cooptation, as well as cronyism, is needed to form the basis for analyzing why the system ultimately collapsed.

A second type of account puts particular segments of society — the youth, or the middle class — as the driving force for change. Two logical arguments can be made in these accounts, one that emphasizes the emancipative effects of rising education, and the other rising levels of grievances, connected with rising inequality and the lack of good jobs to match increased skill levels. These hypotheses which have been used to explain the transition to democracy in various parts of the world can be molded into consistent accounts that fit to Arab realities, but they also require empirical validation: have the opinions of these groups about the desirability of democracy changed over time? Are the youth or the middle class leading opinion change? Can the change in opinions towards democracy be correlated with either a rise in aspirations or grievances, or both?

A third type of consistent account is to view the past as a fight between secularists and political Islamic parties, which is ultimately won by the latter whose rising popularity ended up bringing them to power. But not only is this account at odds with the way the revolts unfolded — it rests on the presumption that political Islam became more popular over time, which is a proposition that needs to be tested empirically using opinion poll surveys.

Finally, a related fourth issue concerns the rationality of the will to change. An angry middle class or a generation of youth can rebel out of anger. It may be too much to ask insurgents to hold rational expectations and to rebel in order to bring about a better future. But at the very least, we would expect them to be convinced that the alternative to the existing autocratic regimes is a favorable bet, with possible outcomes that dominate the situation that they are rejecting. While it may well be that the improvements that they are seeking are not in the economic but in the social realm (i.e., liberty, agency, dignity), discussions about crony capitalism, the scarcity of good jobs, and rising inequalities would lead the analyst to at least suppose that the economic performance of the pre-revolution economic regime was also at stake. Here too, there is an area wide open for investigation — the challenge is to understand how the economic neo-liberal economic regimes of the last decade functioned and how well they performed.

As suggested above, in sifting through these accounts and fitting them into a coherent whole, some relationship with reality and verifiable facts will be important. In this Chapter, I offer contributions to this search by examining what three types of data say about important elements of such an account with a focus on Egypt: first, by looking at what standard economic data can say; second, by examining opinion survey data to gauge the desire for change and correlate it with underlying beliefs in areas such as inequality, where economic measurements suffer from well-known weaknesses; and third, but looking at corporate and stock market data carefully to test the existence and uncover the possible inefficiency of 'crony' capitalism.

The Chapter is to a large extent the summary of my recent work in the area with several co-authors. Section 2 critically reviews the theoretical models used to characterize the region in light of the stylized facts and of the more global literature on transition, and it outlines a broad framework more adapted to the conditions of the region. It argues that the uprisings should be seen as episodes where the middle class (thereafter, MC) shifted its allegiance from the autocratic to a democratic order. Section 3 examines the evidence available from opinion poll surveys on the evolution of the MC opinions relating to economics and social policies in Egypt. Section 4 examines corporate data in Egypt and finds considerable support for the thesis that cronyism was prevalent, and some support for the thesis that this was bad for growth. Section 5 concludes by summarizing the outlines of the emerging account, and outlines areas for future research.

2. Theoretical Frameworks

In this section, I review selectively the recent literature on Middle East politics, both contrasting it with the global literature on transition, and confronting it with stylized facts of the recent Middle East past. I then present the contours of the various models developed in other regions undertaking the third wave of democratization, setting up the stage for the empirical investigation of the next sections.

Discussions about the impact of oil rents or Islam on democracy have been at the heart of the analysis of the politics of the Middle East for the past two decades. The Rentier state model was developed to describe Arab development (e.g., Beblawi and Luciani 1987), and empirical work has uncovered a negative relation between oil and democracy (e.g., El Badawi and Makdisi 2012; Ross 2001) — these ideas have become influential to describe the political economy of natural resources elsewhere. Coherent game theoretical models with rational behavior and interactions between an autocrat and citizens leading to an autocratic, or elite bargain were also developed (see for e.g., Desai, Olofsgard and Yousef 2009). In these types of models, citizens surrender their political rights to autocrats in exchange for economic security. The intuitive appeal of this long honored tradition of Middle East scholarship — it goes back to Marx and Wittffogel — is that the extractive nature of oriental governance (such as in the Ottoman Empire in the past) did not allow the development of social classes that in theory, would lead to modernization. In its more recent manifestation, this literature has continued the tradition of not looking deeply at social transformations within societies, given that it is this presumed immobility that allows and reinforces the Faustian elite bargain. Since the "Presidents for Life" (in Roger Owen's terms (2012)) seemed unmovable, the analytical focus to study the effect of the major reduction in state expenditures experienced since the 1980s had rightly been placed on the various ways in which the regimes have managed to maintain themselves in power using political tools such as cooptation and repression.

2.1. *The roll-back of the state*

A look at key economic performance indicators for the Arab developing countries as a group, from 1980 to 2008, depicted in Figure 2.1, shows clearly that the roll-back of the state began more than 25 years ago. Government expenditure shot up in the 1970s on the back of rising oil wealth in the region, but they fell precipitously in the 1980s, reaching 22% GDP in the early 1990s, a low figure by international standards. The reforms in the Arab world tended to hurt the poor (subsidies to agriculture were deeply cut for example) as well as the MC (especially in lower public sector wages and a stop to hiring), and they led to protests and bread riots across the region, but fell short of leading to democratization. This period consolidated the alliances between the autocrats and elite capital. By the mid-1990s, the old social contract was already dead (Diwan and Walton 1998).

In the Latin America of the 1980s, similar structural adjustments had led to a near synchronous wave of democratization. But in the Middle East, the autocratic rulers did not open up the political space in order to reduce the social pressures stemming from the decline in economic resources. Figure 2.2, which depicts the evolution of an index of political rights (see Political Empowerment Index, Cingranelli and Richards or CIRI 1999) between 1980 and 2010, suggests that in fact the opposite happened. The region was politically less open in 2010 than in the

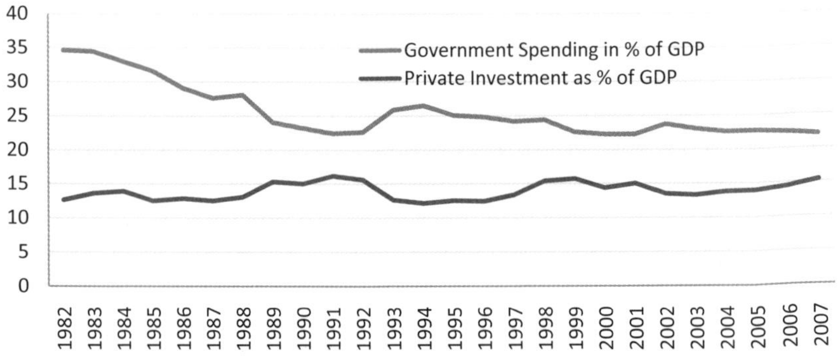

Fig. 2.1. Key macroeconomic indicators for all developing Arab countries.
Note: These are averages across all developing Arab countries.
Source: World Bank Indicators.

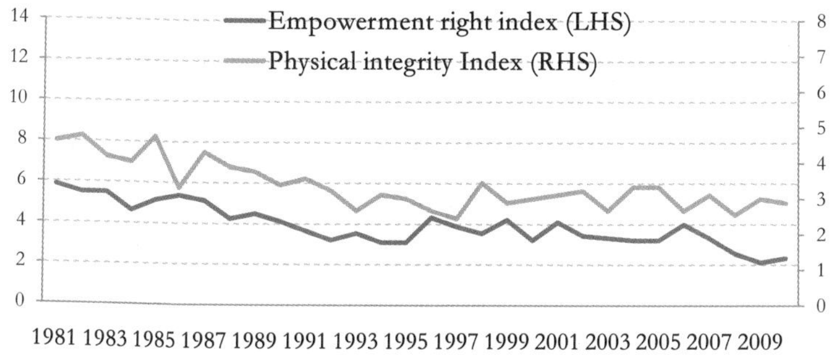

Fig. 2.2. Repression and freedom indices for all Arab countries.
Note: These are averages across all Arab countries.
Source: CIRI, Dataset.

mid-1980s, with the average score for the region falling from about 6 in 1980 to 1.2 in 2010 on a scale from 0 to 14, with 0 depicting complete dictatorship.

2.2. *Repression and co-optation*

The literature on the Middle East had described in detail how (and in some cases why) different regimes chose to respond with a different mix of cooptation and repression to maintain their control (Schlumberger 2007; Posusney and Angrist 2005). The autocrats sought to maximize the use of their dwindling assets, dividing citizens into two groups, one of which benefited from cooperation while the other was subject to repression. Figure 2.2 also depicts average levels of repression in the region, as measured by the index of Physical Integrity (also from CIRI), on a scale from 0–8 where 0 is maximum repression. Over the period, the average value of the index for the Arab countries fell from 4.5 to 2.9.

That repression has become an essential tool in the preservation of autocratic regimes since the late 1990s is also attested by the level of spending on security matters. Autocrats also sought to strengthen their coalition by co-opting the MC. Co-optation was achieved in large part through direct economic benefits in the form of subsidies for goods that are consumed relatively less by the poor, such as petroleum and energy (earlier, subsidies for small scale agriculture and for basic food items that benefit the poor had been reduced or eliminated).[1] At the same time, the fiscal regimes seem to have become more pro-rich over time: tax rates have been relatively low and generally regressive, and universal services have decayed in most countries.

While these considerations are suited for analyzing the past, they are not as useful as tools to describe the current political winds of change blowing through the region.

[1]In the last decade these subsidies grew to become about 200% the combined budget of health plus education in 2009 in Egypt, and 150% in Tunisia. The situation in Syria and Morocco is also similar. These subsidies went predominantly to the MC and the rich — in Egypt, 46% of the benefits for example accrued to the top decide in 2010 (Abouleinem *et al.* 2009).

Indeed, why did the careful balance of repression and cooptation suddenly collapse in recent years in the Arab republics? The youth bulge had actually peaked earlier, around 2000, economic growth rates were recovering from the global crisis, and subsidies were not being cut, quite the opposite. There is a rich global literature on transition to democracy which has emerged in the shadow of the 'third wave' of democratization that has engulfed Latin America, Africa, Asia, and Eastern Europe in the past two decades. They suggest several promising lines of research to understand recent change in the region. First, there are two major theories that are of interest as possible structural explanations of the social phenomena that led to the uprisings in Egypt (and elsewhere in the Arab Republics): modernization (or the rise in aspirations), and distributional conflict (or the rise in grievances). Each has a 'youth' version that has also been applied to the Arab environment, and both will be reviewed here. There are also various accounts that stress fights within the elites groups, including the army, and the role of foreign support. Finally, there are also many claims which appear in the regional literature about the role of political Islam in leading, shaping, or slowing change that need to be tested empirically. Let us review each of these ideas below.

2.3. *Modernization theory*

A popular theory, developed under the umbrella of the World Value Survey (WVS) enterprise, views democratization as a long term phenomena that is driven by social 'modernization'. Various analyses of the WVS data-sets have found that there are two main dimensions of cross-cultural variation in the world: (i) traditional values vs. secular rational values; (ii) survival values vs. self expression values. The former emphasizes modernity as a move away from religion, family ties, and deference to authority towards greater rationality, while the latter emphasizes a move away from economic and physical insecurity towards rising levels of agency, trust, and tolerance. This literature shows that greater emancipation from traditional and survival values fosters democracy. This is typically accomplished through generational replacement, with younger generations usually leading change (Tilley 2002). In the WVS sample of countries, Muslim and Arab countries tend to have the highest scores on traditional and on survival values (Inglehart and Welzel 2010). When structural variables, including connections with globalization are taken into account, one still finds that the Muslim countries of the Middle East have been lagging on this emancipation path, but much more on gender equality rather than on democratic values (Esmer 2002; Norris and Inglehart 2002), leading some authors to argue that the social dominance of Islam accounts for much of this specificity, although it is also found that higher education does have some impact in closing the emancipation gap (Alexander and Welzel 2011). In this view of the world, the current wave of democratization in the Arab world would be related to the weakening of traditional authority and religion, driven by education, urbanization, and economic growth, which would have made these societies 'ready' for democracy, and awaiting a political opportunity to coordinate social efforts towards democratization. Testing such a theory revolves around finding a rise in the support for democracy and other modern values among the educated, and possibly the youth.

2.4. *Distribution theory*

The main alternative structural theory of democratization is based on distributional conflict. In these models, the poorer segments of the population favor taxation and redistribution, which the rich oppose (see Gandhi and Przeworski 2006). As a result, there is an incentive for the rich elite to govern in an autocratic way, and for the poorer segment to attempt to take over. Starting from a socio-political equilibrium, when inequality rises, the system comes under stress. The equilibrium can shift to either a more repressive authoritarianism, or to a redistributive equilibrium.[2] In models of democratic transitions (such as those examined by Acemoglu and Robinson 2006), the distributive motive for change is expanded to endogeneize the very existence of democratic governments. When elites are confronted with mobilization from below, they can make short term concessions to diffuse the threat, but they can also be expected to default on these promises when mobilization subsides. Democratic institutions therefore, provide a means for the elite to commit credibly to a more equal distribution of income in the future (because reversals are costly) when faced with credible challenges. As a result, when low income groups mobilize in favor of redistribution, they do so by militating for a more democratic order.

In such models, there tends to be a special role for the middle class — a class that is formally defined as being simply in between the poor and the rich — which may be in the autocratic coalition in the initial autocratic equilibrium, but which can cause the equilibrium to shift by splitting away from the autocratic coalition and forming a coalition with the poor. This would tend to happen when inequalities rise in ways that make the MC become more 'like the poor'. The introduction of the MC in distributional games also reduce the incentives of the elites to fight back with more repression as they can credibly expect that the MC will moderate the demand for redistribution in the democratic equilibrium. Whether the MC exists as a self-recognized group with the ability to define and defend its interests remains of course a question that needs to be answered at the country level.

In a recent wide-ranging empirical review of the past two decades, Haggard and Kaufmann (2012), show that about half of the recent transitions are explained by distributional concerns — the other half is divided between cases where it was driven by splits within the ruling elites, and cases where elites perceived democracy to serve their own interests.

---

[2]In such models, the equilibrium will tend to shift to one with rising repression when the initial level of inequality is high (because the rich have more at stake), and to a democratic equilibrium when it is low but rising.

2.5. *What happened to inequality?*

In this account, the recent uprisings have been driven by a rise in inequality — in the countries where inequality was not large to start with (Egypt and Tunisia), the elites did not fight back (unlike what happened in Yemen and Libya, countries with larger levels of inequality). Making inequality a core driver to the understanding of the Arab Spring is tempting, as this stems from the central role of inequality in the history of the region, as it travelled from socialism and populism towards capitalism, and ended with what is commonly described today as a regime of crony and unequal capitalism, which is perceived to have generated unacceptable inequalities, directly by supporting the growth of a class of super-rich, and indirectly by being unable to create sufficient good jobs for the newly educated middle class. Admittedly, there is no direct evidence that inequality has risen sharply in the recent past in Egypt on the basis of distribution data. Generally, household surveys reveal that consumption inequality (as measured by Gini coefficients for example) has risen moderately in Egypt, from about 0.3 in the 1990s, to 0.35 in the 2000s (Bibi and Nabli 2010; Belhaj 2012). But there are two reasons to think that these statistics only describe a limited part of reality.

First, household surveys are notorious for under-counting the rich. There are many indications of a rise in the income share of the 10% richest in society, which are perceived to have benefited most from a more market oriented economy, and of the top 1%, which have benefitted most from the rampant crony capitalism of the last decade. By some estimates, the top 10% in Egypt possibly commands 30–40% GDP.[3]

Second, grievances are likely to be connected to changes in the inequality of opportunities, rather than the inequality of incomes only. Over time, the roll-back of the state had reduced the role of the state as an employer — from a height of 40% of the labor force, by 2009, only 25% of the labor force worked for the state in Egypt. Recent studies show clearly that as a result, the large waves of more educated workers (average years of education had risen from two years in the 1980 to eight years by 2009) entering the labor market were faced with an increasingly unfair situation where relationship (*wasta*) and status were more important than diplomas in landing into the good jobs. With no new jobs in the state, these new entrants had to divide themselves between the formal private sector, which did not grow in proportional terms, and where wages are higher than in the public sector, and a large and growing informal sector, where wages are lower than in the public sector (Asaad 2007). Empirical research has only recently started to focus on this type of inequality, but recent work is starting to show that unlike simple consumption Ginis, such measures show a dramatic increase in recent years.

[3]Between 1998 and 2006, GDP rose by 60% in nominal terms, while consumption stayed essentially at the same level all along the distribution according to household surveys, suggesting that large parts of the increase may have accrued to the under-counted rich, and very little has trickled down to the rest of society.

The main implication of a distributional theory of change is that as inequality rises, opinions would increasingly lean towards redistributive policies. The shift in opinions would normally be formed along class lines, but a variant would have them formed along age lines, with the youth rebelling against the older 'insiders' to change the system in their favor.

The rise in inequalities and relatively low performance of Arab economies in terms of job creation are now being related to the type of state-business relations that had developed over time in the region. The liberalization of markets in the 1990s, especially the credit markets, seems to have led to a concentration of economic power in the hands of the few firms with good connections to the state (see in particular the pioneering work in Heydemann (2004)). It may be that such forms of capitalism were not conducive to economic dynamism, and that they also biased politics. But the literature of the economic impact of the type of state-business relations that had grown in the Middle East is not developed enough to allow one to make such allegation in any convincing way. State-business relations can either support a dynamic capitalism or lead to a low equilibrium of corruption and low investment. What is needed at this stage is to study the performance of Arab capitalisms in more depth to understand their (lack of) performance. We focus on this theme in Section 4.

2.6. *Political Islam*

The set of concerns which is quite specific to the Middle East revolves around issues related to political Islam (PI). The tenets of PI include some social values which are strongly espoused by some and not by other members of society (such as beliefs related to the role of Shari'a in legislation, gender issues, and freedom of speech as it relates to the 'sacred'). PI has been in the past one of the main organized opposition movement, militating at various points in time against autocracy, secularism, unpopular foreign alliances, or corruption — and it was at times severely repressed and it operated largely outside the formal system. One view would be to read the recent political changes as a 'victory of PI'. But given the diversity of opinions within PI, this is a simplistic approach. In recent years, some groups within the broad range of parties espousing PI have moderated their messages and came to accept the democratic game. Indeed, it was only in 2004 that the Muslim Brotherhood in Egypt managed to commit publicly to abide by a constitutional and democratic system, calling for the recognition of "the people as the source of all authority", and committing itself to the principles of the transfer of power through free elections, the freedom of belief and expression, the freedom to form political parties, and the independence of the judiciary (Shahin 2005).[4] At the same time, insurgent groups have declined.

---

[4]Similar processes of moderation took place in Turkey and Tunisia. Demiralp (2009) describes the process leading to AKP's increased moderation by a combination of lessons from repression, opportunism, and the growth of a friendly MC. In Tunisia, Al-Nahda committed publicly in 1981 that: "We have no right to interpose between the people and those whom the people choose and elect" (quoted in Osman (2010)).

So the more interesting question is to figure out how political Islam has been connected to the social change leading to the uprisings? There are many possibilities. As a mobilizing force, PI can resolve coordination problems around the forum provided by mosques, as coordination is typically a central constraint in social movements. As an ideology, there are several competing narratives. PI can counter modernization with conservative values — for example on gender issues, or it can be used to neutralize distributional concerns by favoring quietism (values promoted by Sufi and Salafi groups among the poor). But it can also support middle class redistributive goals (as the Youth branch of the Muslim Brotherhood), or it can support middle class devout but economically conservative private sector oriented individuals (which seems to be the attitude of the Muslim Brotherhood). An altogether different possibility is that the moderation of PI facilitated the defection of the MC — Diwan (2012) argues that democratization was delayed in many countries of the MENA because the rise of PI, especially in its early militantist and armed fashion, scared secularists into supporting the autocratic orders, even where economic benefits fell.[5]

2.7. *Divisions among the elites*

Finally, some see the success of the uprising in Egypt in toppling the Mubarak regime as mainly driven by the support it received from the army and its Western backers. This view would suggest that the main driver was a split within the elites, especially among those supporting the group of cronies which has been in power since 2005 or so and the traditional army/security complex elites. That these actors were influential is beyond doubt, but the question is rather whether their actions were driving forces, or whether they decided to side with existing social forces for change. I do not pursue this line below, being more interested in exploring structural reasons for change, but clearly, finding little empirical support for the two main theses described above would advantage the view of a central role for the army, or for the defection of the regime's foreign supporters.

2.8. *The middle class*

Before closing this section, it is useful to characterize the MC more given that it appears to be the main competitor to the youth as the main actor for change in Egypt and the Arab republics. The emergence of a modern middle class, people who grew out of poverty thanks to public education and state jobs, was a defining element of the post-colonial Arab Republics of the 1950s, which ushered leaders such as Bourguiba and Nasser, bringing in the Attaturkian model of modernization based on

[5]Some analysts claim that state repression was used strategically to push PI into extremism. A case study example is from Egypt, where state repression increased after the election gains of the Muslim Brotherhood in the 2005 elections, when it started to appear as a credible alternative to the ruling regime. This pressure created deep divisions within the Muslim Brotherhood over whether it should abandon the political process (Osman 2010; Bubalo *et al.* 2008).

secular and nationalist ideologies. Since then, Arab autocrats have valued keeping MC-led parties in the governing 'political settlement', either within the governing coalition, or as part of the legal opposition, due to their important legitimizing role. For the Arab autocrats, losing their MC anchors is tantamount to losing all legitimacy and turning into naked dictatorships with no operational narrative. In this broader frame, the authoritarian bargain of the past decade can be best characterized as an alliance between elite capital and elements of the MC that delivered economic benefits to the coalition members, including in the form of subsidies.

There are indications that the MC has been hurt by the economic liberalizations of the 1990s, and especially by their acceleration in the 2000s. Beside the direct effect from the labor market discussed above, the interests of the MC have been hurt in many ways by the roll back of the state and the rise of neo-liberalism.[6] In addition, low public sector wages also fueled petty corruption in areas such as health and education, generating another important source of discontent. More research is needed to understand more clearly the changing welfare of the MC. In the World Values Survey data that we analyze in the next section, the survey asks respondents to identify the class they belong. This measure provides a broad, self-assessed measure of well-being that goes well beyond income in capturing life-long income, aspirations, and ownership of assets of various sorts. Comparing data from 2000 and 2008 for Egypt shows that the size of the MC has shrunk from 65% to 58% of the population in favor of the poor.[7]

But besides its size, the nature of the MC has also changed over time. Until recently, Middle Eastern scholars did not seem to believe that the MC could play an active role in leading political change. Its effective influence on policies was low as it was mainly made up of civil servants and employees of state owned enterprises, which reduced its ability to play the role of an 'autonomous actor'. A new market oriented MC rose in late 1990s in response to economic liberalization. The newcomers tended to be small merchants and industrialists, often in the informal sectors, that have benefited from the market oriented reforms, as well as the small but expanding skilled labor of the formal private sector labor market. This group has been politically more active than the old (see Nasr 2009) — for example, it played an important role in securing the success of the Iranian revolution in 1979, and the rise of the AKP in Turkey.[8]

---

[6] In Egypt, real wages in the public sector declined over time. The minimum wage, which anchors all wages, has declined from 60% of per capita GDP in the early 1980s to a mere 13% in 2007 (Abdelhamid and El Baradei 2009). This can be also seen at the macro level — by 2009, 25% of the Egyptian labor force worked for the state but earned a total wage bill of less than 9% of GDP, implying average wages were below GDP per capita, which is very low by international standards.

[7] The WVS also suggests that the average financial satisfaction of the poor deteriorated, that of the MC remained stable, and that of the rich rose during the period, further bolstering a sense of rising inequality during the period.

[8] Indeed, the AKP benefited handsomely from the alliance with the support provided to SMEs and the rise of what became known as the Anatolian Tigers, SMEs that drove growth in Turkey in the past decade (Demiralp 2009; Gumuscu 2009).

To conclude this section, let me stress the limits of the discussion above: the models presented may well be coherent, but other models will as well, and so empirical evidence needs to be looked at.

3. Attitudes Towards Democracy

I now attempt to test which of the theories described above applies best to Egypt by looking at the structure and evolution of opinions. I use the World Values Survey (WVS), which is a research project that aims to measure people's perceptions, opinions and beliefs all over the world. The survey allows us to evaluate the change in perceptions, opinions, and beliefs in a systematic way. Although the WVS encompasses opinion on a wide spectrum of issues relating to social life, such as religiosity, globalization, happiness, financial satisfaction and environment, the discussion below focuses on the questions about attitudes towards democracy, economic policies, and role of religion in politics. A relatively large sample size (about 3,000 respondents in each survey) and careful sampling methods along dimensions of urbanization, age, gender, and income allows us to exploit the micro-information contained in the database. I focus on the 4th and 5th waves of the survey, which were collected in 2000, and in 2008. The questions that I use are outlined in the Annex.

The use of opinion polls to test theories of social change needs to be justified. One can surely try to test the universal appeal of particular theories by examining cross-country variations, and indeed, many studies have attempted to do, such as Haggard and Kaufmann (2012) which was cited earlier. But clearly these approaches have their own limitations, such as the inability to find good controls, or the possibly highly contingent occurrences of change. The other alternative is to try to test these theories at a country level, using implications in terms of patterns of variations between *individuals* and between various types of sub-groups (by age, class, education, etc.). For this type of work, one actually needs to rely on opinions, since what's at stake are variables such as perceptions of inequality, preferences for democracy, or even feeling of belonging to particular social classes. For example, when considering whether revolutions are caused by changes in inequality, unless the rise in inequality is reflected in perceptions of rising inequality, it would not motivate people to rebel. Moreover, by looking at micro opinion data over individuals and over time, one should be able not just to observe the rise of 'revolutionary' fervor, but also, to pinpoint who the leading agents of change are, and possibly, what drove them to change. The theory of revolution as redistribution would suggest that the poor should be more interested in redistribution than the rich. If the reverse is observed, then we should be looking for another theory to explain change.

That the last poll we use is in 2008, two years before the uprisings raises some concerns, as opinions in 2008 may not be similar to those in early 2011. The next survey should be available in 2014, and it would be important to update this study then.[9] In the meanwhile, one can hope that the 2008 survey is representative of long term trends. But it is also important to note that the 2008 survey was taken before Egypt was hit by the global financial crisis, which led in time to a large fall in real wages (Roushdy and Gadallah 2011).

3.1. *Preference for democracy*

Let us start by looking at how preferences for democracy (PfD) evolved over the period. I construct this variable from responses to a question where respondents are asked to choose their first and second choice from a list of four options that include (i) "giving people more say in important government decisions", (ii) "maintaining order in the nation", (iii) "fighting inflation", and (iv) "protecting freedom of speech". I code the response as support for democracy when respondents rank option (i) ahead of option (ii). Because they had to make a choice, respondents tended to rank democracy lower than in other unconstrained questions that simply ask whether they like democracy — the latter are not very informative and tend to show an over-whelming support for democracy. An examination of the data reveals three striking regularities.

Let us start by contrasting the evolution of the PfD national averages in Egypt, Iran, Jordan, and Morocco, the only MENA countries covered by the WVS. While there is a remarkable shift of opinions in Egypt, with the PfD variable jumping from 24% to 52% of the population over the period, support for democracy remains relatively flat in the other countries. The comparison suggests that the uprisings in Egypt do seem to represent a deep social wave that is specific to that country. This remarkable shift of opinions can be partly explained by the high support for 'order' in 2000, when the Islamic insurgency was still strong, and to the results of the 2005 elections which saw for the first time the participation of the Muslim Brotherhood in the electoral process.[10]

Second, let us look at the PfD in Egypt according to class and age (see Figure 2.3). It is immediately apparent that the rising support for democracy is very much a class phenomena — in particular, there is rising support among the poor and the MC, but declining among the rich. The middle class seems to play a leading role, supporting democracy more than the poor (by about 10 points), with more than 50% of the class in favor. This seems to suggest that while distributional factors are at play in 2008 (with the rich broadly against democracy, as suggested by the distribution theory), modernization forces may be providing an additional push for the MC to support

[9] The sixth wave of the WVS has been collected. All data has been made public since June 1, 2014 (www.worldvaluessurvey.org).

[10] PEW surveys also collect this type of information around the world. Its first survey in Egypt in 2005 (55% in support of democracy over order) is consistent with the score of the 2008 WVS. Very few countries see scores as low as those seen in Egypt in 2000 — they include Russia, Ukraine, and Pakistan, countries where high insecurity push people to have a high preference for "order".

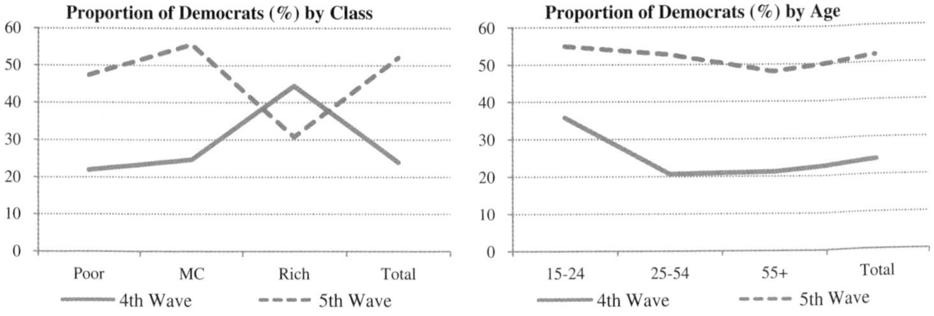

Fig. 2.3. Preference for democracy, by class and age.

democratization. There may also be factors that reduce the willingness of the poor to support a change in the status quo, such as risk aversion or ideological attitudes. These are themes and hypotheses that we will pursue further below.

Third, the youth do not seem to hold opinions in 2008 that are much different from their parents on the desirability of democracy, unlike the situation in 2000, when they were more democratic than their elders. So to the extent that the underlying forces driving opinions are connected to skilled youth unemployment, a major phenomenon for the MC, it seems that Egyptian MC parents became as unhappy as their children about the lack of job opportunities — and this pushes them to favor regime change and democracy.

It can be verified, with regression analysis, that these results are not spurious means comparisons, but that they actually do represent an association between individual characteristics. I use Logit functional forms.[11]

$$\text{Probability of support for Democracy} = f\ (\text{class dummies, age}) \tag{2.1}$$

The results, shown in Table 2.1, which were apparent in the graphs are confirmed — there is initially a strong age effect that goes away by 2008 and is replaced by a strong MC effect, which did not exist in 2000.

3.2. *Preferences for equality*

Is the rise in support for democracy connected with a change of opinions about distributional concerns? Let us look at what the survey reveals about individual preferences for equality (PfE). The related survey question asks respondents to rank (on a scale of 1 to 10) whether income inequality is good for incentives (low score), or

[11]To account for class structure I use dummies for the MC and for the Rich, relative to the Poor. The coefficient for the Rich dummy is not shown, as it does not turn out to be significant in all regressions probably bacause of the small number of observations for this class.

Table 2.1. Logit regression for preference for democracy.

Dependent variable: Preference for democracy	2000	2008
Age	−0.167***	−0.0276
	(−4.96)	(−0.95)
MC	−0.108	0.280***
	(−1.15)	(3.66)
N	2893	3050

***$p < 0.01$, **$p < 0.05$, *$p < 0.1$.

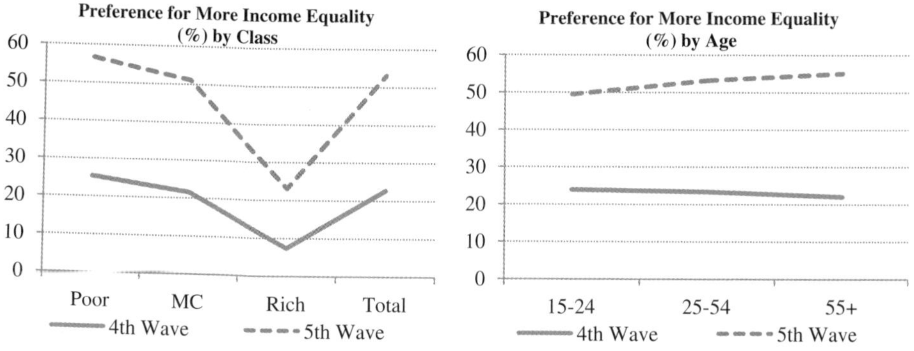

Fig. 2.4. Preferences for equality, by class and age: 2000 and 2008.

incomes should be made more equal (high score).[12] Answers to the question thus reveal opinions on how public policy should deal with inequality — at the risk of caricaturing, we can refer to people with high scores as 'leftists' and people with low scores as 'rightists'. Figure 2.4 suggests that (i) PFE monotonically decreases with class, as suggested by a distribution view of the world, and this holds in both periods. (ii) Over time, all classes move to the 'left', and (iii) that there are no important age effects. But while the increase PfD and the rising PfE happen in parallel, we still need to check whether they are connected at the individual level. Moreover, we are also interested in understanding why the poor have a high PfE and a low PfD relative to the MC. To understand how individual characteristics connect and measure the potential effects of modernization and distribution separately, I run a Logit regression, where I include education and the PfE variable plus interactive terms to discriminate between MC and poor among the 'leftists':

$$\text{Probability of PfD} = f\ (\text{education},\ \text{Pf E},\ \text{Pf E} * \text{MC}) \tag{2.2}$$

[12]In the actual survey, the scale is the reverse, but we have inverted it to ease the interpretation of the results. Note that the exact level of this indicator depends on how we code the information. Because opinions are very much clustered around the levels 1–3 in 2000, I take in the graphs any score above 3 to indicate a shift towards a preference for equality. In the regression analysis however, I code the variable in 4 levels for greater precision.

Table 2.2. Logit regression for preference for democracy.

Dependent variable: Preference for democracy	2000	2008
Education	0.163***	0.0861***
	(5.43)	(3.53)
PfE	0.0841	0.136**
	(1.46)	(0.87)
PfE*MC	−0.0343	−0.130***
	(−1.27)	(−3.51)
N	2893	3009

+PfE variable is coded at 4 levels. ***$p < 0.01$, **$p < 0.05$, *$p < 0.1$.

The results are in Table 2.2:

- Supporting the modernization thesis, we find that education fosters support for democracy.
- While the 'Left' supported democracy in 2000 as much (or as little) as the 'Right', by 2008, leftists supported democracy more than rightists, and moreover, poor leftists supporting democracy more than MC leftists (the interactive term is negative). This confirms that distributional concerns are, as suggested by theory, more important for the poor than for the middle class.

The results then suggest that there are at least two paths to democracy — going left and democratic (more intense among the poor), or going "modern" and democratic (especially among educated and richer people). It is because they are at the interception of both concerns then that the MC emerges as the main champion for democracy.

3.3. *The influence of political Islam on democratization*

What role did PI play in paving the way, or obstructing, these individual paths towards democratization? Can PI, as a movement or an ideology, explain the conservatism of the poor that was noted above (especially in 2000), or can it explain the progressivism of the MC (especially in 2008)? Or perhaps the adherents of PI are those that continued to oppose democracy in 2008? Or is adherence to PI unrelated to opinions about democracy?

To explore the drivers of public opinions towards PI, I construct the variable PI from a question where people are asked if they believe that "religious authorities provide answers to social problems" (where no = 0 and yes = 1). National averages show a decline in popular support for PI, although it remains a majority view — from 81 in 2000 to 60% of the respondents in 2008 adhere to PI as defined here. Moreover, the composition of groups along these dimensions changes massively between the two periods. In 2000, a very large 62% of the population supported both autocracy and PI, but this group shrinks to 28% in 2008. It is as if the acceptance by the Muslim Brotherhood in 2004 of the democratic rules of the game has thrown many citizens into turmoil and has confronted them with choosing new political orientations. There are two major social transformations that are apparent in the re-composition of the political field: a move towards secular beliefs (+22.6% of the population), and a move towards democracy (+26.6%). Those that were religious autocrats in 2000 'move' to become mainly PI and secular democrats in 2008 (only a few select to become secular autocrats). The shift in support for democracy then needs to be explained by composition effects and changes in preferences within groups — both of these show very large shifts. I run the following ordered Logit regression, with multiplicative effects to separate the impact of PI on the poor and the MC:

$$\text{Probability of Preferences for democracy} = f\,(\text{PI},\ \text{PI} * \text{MC}) \qquad (2.3)$$

The results in Table 2.3 confirm that adherents of PI did not support democracy in 2000 as much as secularists. By 2008, the pattern is the same, except that the MC group that espouses PI becomes, like secularists, a force for democratization. It seems as if PI acts as a conservative veil for the poor only, preventing them from expressing their class interests, but this effect does not operate among the MC after 2008, either because they are better educated, and/or because they are more likely to be influenced by more moderate parties within the PI umbrella. This supports and refines Tessler's (2012) findings that support for PI is congruent with rising support for democracy — what we find is that this applies only to the MC but that the poor who supports PI do not support democracy as much.

So overall, it seems that bringing PI into the equation reveals that rather than two, there were actually four distinct paths to democracy in Egypt (left and right secularists, and left and right Islamists), with each attracting different types of people that had left the autocratic PI mainstream orientation of 2000. Within each path, support for democracy rises, but it also faces particular types of opposition forces, resulting in different propensities to become democratically oriented within the group. It is noteworthy that four 'democratic' candidates during the first round of presidential elections in 2012 came to represent each of these views.

3.4. *Bottom line on the transition hypotheses*

The data does not support any of the youth-driven theories of change, including the youth version of modernization, and the youth version of grievances driven change.

Table 2.3. Logit regression for preference for democracy.

Dependent variable: PfD	2000	2008
PI	−0.349**	−0.246**
	(0.130)	−0.095
PI*MC	0.055	0.390***
	(0.102)	−0.097
N	2789	2976

***$p < 0.01$, **$p < 0.05$, *$p < 0.1$.

On the other hand, much of the analysis has shown that both the class based version of modernization and distribution theories draw strong support. Between 2000 and 2008, grievances increased, and the aspirations of a more educated population rose simultaneously. This concurrence explains why the MC, which is at the interception of both forces, turned out to be the main champion for democratization. In effect, if demand for democracy came in surging, it was not only for circumstantial reasons, but also because of the coincidence of large social change of the past decade, together with the rise of inequalities in the late crony capitalism phase.[13]

4. State-Business Relations and Networks of Privilege

The popular discontent that led to the uprisings can be traced to two main elements of economic policy: the roll-back of the state, alluded to above, and the consolidation of close relations between the state and particular elements of the business elites under economic liberalism. The central question of why the Arab region has under-performed in terms of job creation, given what looked on paper as impeccable market reforms, has been debated for years. Some have argued that the market reforms have not gone far enough; others, that economics had become dominated by networks of privilege (Heydemann 2004) or even crony capitalists (Sadowski 2001) with myopic short term interests that have stifled competition, innovation, and ultimately job creation. Conceptually, there is nothing intrinsically bad about close state-business relations. Khan in particular describes how industrial policy can foster accumulation and the development of new sectors, as had happened with Korea's chaebols for example (Khan 2010). To the extent that they have the right incentives to perform, close state-business relations can form the basis for dynamic capitalism and an effective state. But they can also become sources of influence, corruption, and other forms of rent-seeking that distorts economic and political incentives.

Popular perceptions of business elites have become quite negative in the region. Cronyism is now seen as the key characteristic of the economic opening that started in the 1990s and accelerated in the 2000s, and at the source of many ills including the job deficit, the rise in inequalities, and distortions to politics which has prolonged the life of the autocrats. The perceived 'corruption' of the political and business elites was a key driving force of popular discontent. For example, the Pew survey reveals that in 2010, corruption was the top concern of Egyptians with 46% listing it as their main concern, ahead of lack of democracy and poor economic conditions (Pew 2011). This is confirmed by the Transparency International ratings — Egypt moved from a rank of 70/158 in 2005 to 115/180 in 2008. We now know that this was not just about perceptions.

In both Tunisia and Egypt, the ongoing trials of leading businessmen is starting to shed light on the ways in which influence was yielded for private gains — the granting

[13]The circumstantial reasons that are often cited include the reduced Islamic militancy, the 'democratic' choice make by the Muslim Brotherhood in 2005, and the upcoming presidential election of 2014.

of monopoly rights to close associates of the rulers, the selling of public firms and land at reduced prices, and the manipulation of the financial markets for the benefits of a few insiders. In Tunisia, the Ben Ali and Trabulsi families monopolized business opportunities. Similar stories about favoritism and insiders abound in Syria, Libya, Yemen, and Algeria, where political cronies seem to control large chunks of the private sector. In Egypt, it seems that the trend was accelerated in the last decade with the 'businessmen cabinet' headed by Ahmad Nazif (2004–2011). Two iconic cases being investigated now illustrate the nature of privileges. The first is that of Ezz Steel. Ahmad Ezz, a very successful businessman who dominated the steel industry after 2000, is now accused of having lobbied on behalf of his firm on issues related to raising external tariffs to increase protection in the steel sector, as well as relaxing anti-monopoly constraints, from his position as MP and Chair of the Budget Committee in Parliament (which among other things oversees the work of the Competition Commission and trade policy), member in the very influential Policy Committee of the National Democratic Party (NDP) (chaired by Gamal Mubarak), and his position as NPD secretary for Organisational Affairs. A second example, again involved in several court cases, is that of Palm Hill Corporation, the second largest real estate developer in Egypt. The main owner of Palm Hill, Ahmed El-Maghrabi, was Minister of Housing in the Nazif Cabinet, and has been accused of exploiting his ministerial position to sell Palm Hills large tracks of land, at an exceptionally cheap price, giving his firm a large advantage over competitors.

Despite these perceptions, it may or may not be true that 'cronyism' was bad for growth and jobs. The big question that needs to be addressed then is that of the economic performance of neo-liberal economies under autocracy, relative to the counter-factual imagined by the MC then they rebelled. This is by no means an easy task. But at a minimum, one should be able to describe more objectively and quantitatively some of the characteristics of the ancient regime, and to develop a clearer sense of the impact of 'cronyism' on economic performance. This suggests three main areas for research: is there evidence of favoritism? How do the connected operate in an economy that is ostensibly liberalized and thus out of reach of governmental dictates? More ambitiously, are there objective ways of evaluating the impact of the types of state-business relations that were developed in the 2000s in the region on economic and political performance?

The literature on Arab capitalism is still in its infancy. There has been more work on Egypt (e.g., Skafianis 2003; Roll 2010), Morocco (Henry 1997), and the Gulf (Hanieh 2011), and recent work by Steve Heydeman and associates (Heydeman 2006) but essentially, it has remained difficult to get direct measurements of the extent of favoritism, and there has been no serious attempts to statistically evaluate its socio-economic impact. A recent study of the Egyptian stock market around the momentous events of 2011 (Chekir and Diwan 2012) shed some light on these issues.

The advent of the stock market is relatively recent in Egypt. The market only really took off in the last decade of Mubarak's reign, when his son Gamal Mubarak, working closely with a group of young economic experts and of ambitious businessmen, took it on himself to define a new vision for Egypt, and by doing so, started to redefine the political program of the aging ruling party. After the socialism of Nasser (1958–1968), the timid opening of Sadat in the 1980s, and the state capitalism of the first Mubarak's period up to the early 2000s, a new effort was under way to modernize Egypt's private sector — or so did the official narrative go. This effort included a push to create an internationally competitive corporate sector in the midst of a renewed effort at stabilization, prizatization, trade reforms, and at the center, the liberalization of the financial market, after a costly state financed capitalization. The period saw the emergence of a new class of capitalists backed by state favors. They were prime beneficiaries of the privatization drive and they spearheaded the development of new sectors and the modernization and expansion of old ones. The rising businessmen were well connected and some occupied important post in Government, the ruling party, Parliament, and various influential boards and Committees (Osman 2010).

4.1. *The value and nature of favors*

In our paper (Chekir and Diwan 2012), we do three things: first, we evaluate the value of connections through an event study around the time of the revolution; second, we compare the past corporate performance of connected and unconnected firms; and finally, we discuss the broader economic impact of privileges. We use publicly available database of on corporate performance and stock prices focusing on the 111-largest Egyptian companies that are traded on the Egyptian Exchange (EGX). In the study, we rely on what appears to be extensive market knowledge in Egypt of the inner working of these firms to identify 22 firms as being closely connected to the state. These firms operate in all sectors. In 2002, their size was about the same as the other firms on the exchange, but by 2010, their median size had increased to a phenomenal seven times the median of non-connected firm, while the latter has barely grown.

In conducting our event studies, we follow a well established literature (for examples see Fisman (2001) on Indonesia, Ramalho (2003) for Brazil, and Boubakri *et al.* (2008) for a global data-set). As an event study, the revolution of January 2011 presents a near perfect case. It was largely unexpected. When the stock market reopened again in February 2011, it was quite clear that these firms' high level connections had lost most, if not all, their value. As a result, the securities of all these firms must have been re-priced and indeed, the price of connected firms fell by more than those of the non connected ones. But these differences in price movement do not necessarily reflect only differences in levels of connections. They also reflect other differences, such as differential leverage to market or to revolution specific risks. We thus made two corrections, one related to the sensitivity of firms to the aggregate shock experienced by the economy, and the other, to their sensitivity to sector specific shocks connected directly to the revolution. We estimate a regression for each the event of the type:

$$\text{CAR}(i) = a + b\text{PC}(i) + c\text{SEC}(i) + x(i) \tag{2.4}$$

Where CAR is the excess return of security i,[14] PC is the politically connected firms indicator (a dummy that takes the value of zero for non-politically connected firms and 1 for politically connected firms), SEC is a vector of sector dummy variables, and x is the error term. The event window is between January 15, 2011, when the uprising started, to March 23, when the market reopened (it was closed on January 27).

The results are in Table 2.4. They confirm that connected firms have lost more value than others during these events *on account* of their connections. In particular, in the weeks following the Egyptian uprising of January 2011, the stocks of the group of connected firms fell on average by 24% on account of their connections, in addition to market-wide and sector effects experienced by all firms. This can be considered to be a lower bound of the value of connections, since after Mubarak was removed, there was still a chance that his regime will continue. Moreover, some of the privileges received by connected businessmen such as access to cheap privatization have accrued before they have floated their companies on the stock exchange.

We then looked at the corporate performance of connected firms in the five years before the revolution to ascertain directly how they may have benefitted from their connections. A large literature has looked at how firms may gain from political connections, with most studies finding strong debt effects, and to a lesser extent, tax, market power, bail-out, and state favor effects (see Cull and Xu (2005) for China, Johnson and Mitton (2003) for Malaysia, Khwaja and Mian (2005) for Pakistan, Leuz and Oberholzer-Gee (2006) for Indonesia, and Boubakri *et al.* (2008) and Faccio *et al.* (2006) for a global panel). These studies generally show that connected firms have higher leverage, pay lower taxes, have stronger market power, are bailed out more

Table 2.4. Event analysis (cumulative abnormal returns with fixed effects); ordinary least squares.

Variables	Dec 2011
Connected	−0.241***
	(0.0666)
Constant	0.188***
	(0.0276)
Observations	111
R-squared	0.173
Nbr sectors	15

***$p < 0.01$, **$p < 0.05$, *$p < 0.1$.
Source: Chekir and Diwan (2012).

[14]The CARs are based on estimation of a market model as follows $\text{CAR}(i) = R(i) - \text{beta}(i) * R_m + e(i)$ where R_m is the market return.

often, and that more of this happens in more corrupt and poorer countries. In terms of magnitudes, Faccio (2010), who looks at a global panel that includes several thousand firms in 47 countries, finds a significant leverage effect with a size of 0.03 to 0.07 (depending of strength of connection) and at up to 0.17 for Thailand and about 0.10 for Russia and Malaysia (the countries were the effect is largest), a sizable but generally not significant tax effect, and a significant extra market share secured by connected firms of about 6%. In her sample, connected firms are on average three times larger than non-connected firms.

Given data availability, we were able to investigate empirically differences in four dimensions: market shares, debt, taxes paid, and profitability. But again, these apparent differences may be due to the fact that connected firms tend to be large and that large firms enjoy special treatment by the credit market, or that they are over-represented in sectors that use up a lot of debt, or that have large returns to scale. To control for these factors, we run the following regressions:

$$\text{LHS} = f(\text{connectedness, case 30, year, sectors, error}) \tag{2.5}$$

where the LHS dependant variables are in turn the firms' debt to equity ratio (total debt to shareholder equity), market share (measured in terms of size of firm's total assets relative to the total of those in the firm's sector), tax payments, and the return on assets (measured as net income divided by the book value of assets). The results are in Table 2.5.

First, we found that connected firms had a larger market share than their non-connected competitors (an average advantage of 8% of the market). Second, we also found that they were able to borrow much more than their competitors, with an extra leverage of 25 points on average over the period, but with this advantage rising significantly over the period (they end up with an average debt to equity ratios of 1.7

Table 2.5. Panel regression for corporate characteristics (ordinary least squares with fixed effects: sectors and years).

Variables	D/E	Tax ratio	Market share	RoA
Connected	0.209***	0.00800	0.0874***	−2.103**
	(0.0571)	(0.00988)	(0.0193)	(0.888)
Large	−0.0784	0.0232**	0.0504***	2.024**
	(0.0532)	(0.00985)	(0.0195)	(0.914)
Constant	0.681***	−0.155***	0.117***	4.116***
	(0.0572)	(0.0105)	(0.0262)	(0.927)
Observations	445	428	988	566
R-squared	0.117	0.108	0.378	0.069

$^{***}p < 0.01$, $^{**}p < 0.05$, $^{*}p < 0.1$.

Note: D/E is Shareholder equity (book) minus intangible assets over total liabilities; market share is share of total assets of a firm over the total assets of all firms in the industry; RoA is the return on assets, given by profits divided by the book value of total assets; Tax ratio is tax over net income.

Source: Chekir and Diwan (2012).

compared to 0.8 for their competitors). Third, and unlike what is often claimed on the basis of occasional examples, we found no evidence that connected firms paid fewer taxes than non-connected firms, which seems to indicate that some institutions were more prone to favoritism than others. It must be noted that in all these cases, we also control for firm size, and so these effects are independent of firm size (for example, the 30 largest Egyptian firms, which belong to the "Large" group, pay more taxes, and have a larger market share on account of this size effect).

How do we interpret these findings? The banking sector was liberalized in Egypt early in the 2000s, and while banks were seeking good customers, which ended up being in large part these connected firms (at the end of the period, the 22 firms received 80% of the private credit going to the 100 firms that we analyze) they are unlikely to have been influenced by political considerations. Instead, the connected firms must have managed to expand their market share significantly due to their connections, including for example their privileged access to information, and their ability to resolve business difficulties as they arose due to their influence on the economic governance bodies, that they were able to get government contracts more easily, and that they were generally protected against predation by the bureaucracy — all cases of oiling the wheels of their businesses.

We also found that connected firms have lower profitability than non-connected firms after controlling for any size effect. We find that the non-connected firms get an extra 2% return on assets. This is a very significant finding. The main conclusion is that despite their preferential status and in some cases monopoly power, and despite their disproportional access to funds, the connected firms were not as well run as the average firm.

4.2. *Implications for the economy and polity*

It is not possible to tease from the data why the profitability of the connected firms was not higher, given the privileges they enjoyed, but we can speculate. One possibility is that they were run inefficiently (their owners and managers were selected because they were trusted rather than skilled), and their purpose was to deny the heights of the economy to potential regime opponents. Another possibility is that they 'tunneled' out their profits, partly to bankroll the ruling party, and partly to themselves — indeed, the main figures became very rich, and were the main reason for the perception of a large rise in the 1% in Egypt during this period.

It can be seen that capital flows went to relatively inefficient firms, reducing economic growth directly. During this period for example, SMEs were starved for credit, but they ended up delivering a disproportionate share of the new jobs (Assaad 2009). Moreover, it is also possible that this unfair competition reduced the dynamism of the economy as a whole. What matters most at the end is whether a dynamic form of capitalism was emerging or whether the economy was stuck in a low investment trap. That private investment in Egypt never went beyond 15% of the country's GDP, with large capital flight (Kar and Curcio 2011), militates the second interpretation, as was the stagnation of non-connected firms in our sample. This suggests that the revolutionaries must have been right to believe that a democratic regime could deliver better economic outcomes, and equally, that the new post-uprising regimes can find a lot of 'growth space' if they manage to reduce cronyism and promote a fairer and more dynamic form of capitalism.

5. Conclusions

In this Chapter, I tried to sift through theoretical and empirical considerations to piece together a coherent and empirically sound narrative of the socio-political and economic transformations that have occurred in the past few decades in the Arab Republics, and that could be useful to explain both the autocracy of the past, and the ongoing transformation.

The arguments developed above connect economic development (especially fiscal policies and the rise of crony capitalism), social change (rise in both aspirations and grievances), and political change (a more autonomous middle class splitting away from the autocratic coalition). The overall picture that emerges includes:

- The roll-back of the state in the mid-1980s, but with no democratic opening, leading to the rise of an elite capitalistic class allied with security circles, enforcing its dominance with the use of security tools to repress its opposition and economic tools to co-opt the middle class.
- The closer state business relations within a 'liberal' environment and a police state did not develop into a successful industrial policy, but rather, into an economic system of gift exchange with moderate performance, which taxed growth and thus did not create sufficient good jobs; but that also generated additional grievances by unbalancing politics, and leading to a rise in the 1%-type inequality.
- This gave rise to an autocratic, low equilibrium that lasted three decades which was supported by the West, with the MC co-opted and afraid of a takeover by political Islam, and with the poor repressed and neutralized by state-fed religious conservatism.
- Increased fiscal pressures, driven in large parts by rising subsidies and lower tax revenues led to deteriorating social services and lower public investment, further hurting the poor and the marginalized regions and leading to a rise in class identification.
- The MC evolved as a champion of change, driven by both grievances (lack of opportunities for its educated youth, and an anger for increased inequalities which it shared with the poor), and aspirations (rising education leading to increased demand for democracy, especially among the richer parts of society).
- The uprisings were not driven by increased support for PI — quite the contrary, and moreover, there was an increase democratization of PI over time.

To substantiate further such a broad account would require more research, both at the country level, and in particular areas. It must be highlighted that very little work has been done to uncover the political economy of the transformation over time of state budgets in Arab countries, and their increased regressivity. More work is also needed to understand more precisely the evolution of Arab capitalism in its varying types. Various aspects of the parallelism in the evolution of Arab countries need to be looked at carefully. In particular, the surprising coincidence in the rise of cronyism everywhere over time could be understood in relation to repression and the rise of police states, and possibly the influence of Gulf investments in the region. The recent contagion effects also need to be investigated in light of the many similarities in the structural characteristics driving change in these countries, including the evolution of PI and support from the West. This would go a long way to understand the common structural drivers, in addition to oil, and push back more forcefully essentialist arguments.

Annex

The questions from the WVS and the variables generated for the analysis are as follows:

Preference for Democracy (PfD): PfD is generated by ordering of V71 and V72. If a respondent chooses 1 in *V71* over other choices in *V72*, s/he is taken to prefer autocracy; if chooses 2 or 4 in *V71* over other choices, s/he is categorized as preferring democracy. *V71.* "If you had to choose, which one of the things on this card would you say is most important? (Code one answer only under "first choice" and one under your second choice)." *V72.* "And which would be the next most important? (1) Maintaining order in the nation; (2) Giving people more say in important government decisions; (3) Fighting rising prices; (4) Protecting freedom of speech."

Preference for Equality (PfE): We use *V116.* "How would you place your views on this scale? 10 means you agree completely with the statement on the left (*Incomes should be made more equal*); 1 means you agree completely with the statement on the right (*We need larger income differences as incentives for individual effort*); and if your views fall somewhere in between, you can choose any number in between."

Political Islam (PI): We use *V191.* "Generally speaking, do you think that the religious authorities in your country are giving adequate answers *the social problems facing our society*" (Y/N).

Socio-economic groupings: We use *V252.* "Would you describe yourself as belonging to the: (1) Upper class; (2) Upper middle class; (3) Lower middle class; (4) Working class; or (5) Lower class. Classes are redefined in the analysis as 'Rich' (1), 'Middle Class' $(2+3)$ and 'Poor' $(4+5)$."

Education: We use *V238.* "What is the highest educational level that you have attained?: (1) No formal education; (2) Incomplete primary school; (3) Complete primary school; (4) Incomplete secondary school: technical/vocational type; (5) Complete secondary school: technical/vocational type; (6) Incomplete secondary: university-preparatory type; (7) Complete secondary: university-preparatory type;

(8) Some university-level education, without degree; (9) University-level education, with degree."

References

Abdelhamid, D. and L. El Baradei. 2009. "Reforming the pay system for government employees in Egypt." *Egyptian Centre for Economic Studies*, Working Paper No. 151 (June): 10.

Abouleinem, S., H. Al-Laithy and H. Keir-el-Din. 2009. "The impact of phasing out the petroleum subsidies in Egypt." Egyptian Center for Economic Studies, Working Paper No. 145.

Acemoglu, D. and J. A. Robinson. 2006. *Economic Origins of Dictatorship and Democracy.* Cambridge: Cambridge University Press.

Alexander, A. and C. Welzel. 2011. "Islam and patriarchy: How robust is Muslim support for patriarchal values?" *World Values Research*, 4(2): 40–70.

Assaad, R. 2009. "Labor supply, employment, and unemployment in the Egyptian economy, 1988–2006." In *The Egyptian Labor Market Revisited*, ed. Assad, R., pp. 1–52. Cairo: Economic Research Forum Publications.

Beblawi, H. and G. Luciani. eds. 1987. *The Rentier State: Nation, State and Integration in the Arab World, Vol. 2.* London: Routledge Kegan&Paul.

Belhaj Hassine, N. 2012. "Inequality of opportunity in Egypt." *World Bank Economic Review*, 26(2): 265–292. Washington, DC: World Bank Group.

Bibi, S. and M. Nabli. 2010. "Equity and inequality in the Arab world." Economic Research Forum Policy Research Report No. 33.

Boubakri, N., J. C. Cosset and W. Saffar. 2008. "Politically connected firms: An international event study." Unpublished Working Paper. HEC Montreal.

Bubalo, A., G. Fealy and W. Mason. 2008. *Zealous Democrats: Islamism and Democracy in Egypt, Indonesia and Turkey.* Double Bay, New South Wales.: Longueville.

Chekir, H. and I. Diwan. 2012. Crony capitalism in Egypt. Center for International Development, Harvard University Working Paper No. 250.

Cingranelli, D. and D. L. Richards. 1999. "Measuring the level, pattern, and sequence of government respect for physical integrity rights." *International Studies Quarterly*, 43(2): 407–418.

Cull, R. and L. C. Xu. 2005. "Institutions, ownership and finance: The determinants of profit reinvestment among Chinese firms." *Journal of Financial Economics*, 78: 117–146.

Demiralp, S. 2009. "The rise of Islamic capital and the decline of Islamic radicalism in Turkey." *Comparative Politics*, 41: 315–335 (21).

Desai, R. M., A. Olofsgård and T. M. Yousef. "The logic of authoritarian bargains." *Economics and Politics*, 21(1): 93–125.

Diwan, I. 2012. "A rational framework for the understanding of the Arab revolutions." Centre of International Development Working Paper No. 237. Boston, MA: Harvard University.

Diwan, I. 2013. "Who are the democrats? Leading opinions in the wake of Egypt's 2011 popular uprisings." Boston, MA: Mimeo, Centre for International Development, Harvard University. Working Paper No. 256.

Diwan, I. and M. Walton. 1998. "Opening up and distribution in the Middle East and North Africa: The poor, the unemployed and the public sector." In *Opening Doors to the World: A New Agenda for the Middle East*, ed. Safadi, R. Cairo: The American University in Cairo Press.

El Badawi, I. and S. Makdisi. 2007. "Explaining the democracy deficit in the Arab world." *The Quarterly Review of Economics and Finance*, 46(5): 813–831.

Esmer, Y. 2002. "Is there an Islamic civilization?" *Comparative Sociology*, 1(3–4): 265–298.

Faccio, M. 2010. "Differences between politically connected and nonconnected firms: A cross-country analysis." *Financial Management*, 39: 905–928.

Fisman, R. 2001. "Estimating the value of political connections." *American Economic Review*, 91: 1095–1102.

Gandhi, J. and A. Przeworski. 2006. "Cooperation, cooptation, and rebellion under dictatorships." *Economics and Politics*, 18(1): 1–26.

Gumuscu, S. 2009. "The power of the devout bourgeoisie. The case of the Justice and Development Party in Turkey." *Middle Eastern Studies*, 45(6): 953–968 (16).

Haggard, S. and R. Kaufman. 2012. "Inequality and regime change: Democratic transitions and the stability of democratic rule." *American Political Science Review*, 106(3): 495–516.

Hanieh, A. 2011. *Capitalism and Class in the Gulf Arab States*. New York: Palgrave Macmillan.

Henry, C. M. 1997. "Crises of money and power: Transitions to democracy?" In *Islam, Democracy, and the State in North Africa*, ed. Entelis, J.P., pp. 177–204. Bloomington: Indiana University Press.

Heydemann, S. ed. 2004. *Networks of Privilege in the Middle East*. New York: Palgrave Macmillan.

Inglehart, R. and C. Welzel. 2010. "Changing mass priorities: The link between modernization and democracy." *Perspectives on Politics*, 8(2): 551–567.

Johnson, S. and T. Mitton. 2003. "Cronyism and capital controls: Evidence from Malaysia." *Journal of Financial Economics*, 67, 351–382.

Kar, D. and C. Karly. 2011. *Illicit Financial Flows from Developing Countries: 2000–2009*. Global Financial Integrity Report, January.

Khan, M. 2010. "Political settlements and the governance of growth-enhancing institution." School of Oriental and African Studies, University of London, Working Paper.

Khwaja, A. I. and A. Mian. 2005. "Do lenders favor politically connected firms? Rent provision in an emerging financial market." *Quarterly Journal of Economics*, 120: 1371–1411.

Leuz, C. and F. Oberholzer-Gee. 2006. "Political relationships, global financing, and corporate transparency: Evidence from Indonesia." *Journal of Financial Economic*, 81: 411–439.

Nasr, S. V. R. 2009. *The Rise of Islamic Capitalism: Why the New Muslim Middle Class Is the Key to Defeating Extremism*. New York: Free Press.

Norris, P. and R. Inglehart. 2002. "Islamic culture and democracy: Testing the 'clash of civilizations' thesis." *Comparative Sociology*, 1(3–4): 235–263.

Osman, T. 2010. *Egypt on the Brink: From Nasser to Mubarak*. New Haven: Yale University Press.

Pew Research Center Report. 2011. "Arab Spring fails to improve US image." Global Attitudes Project.

Posusney, M. P. and M. P. Angrist. 2005. *Authoritarianism in the Middle East: Regimes and Resistance*. Boulder, CO: Lynne Rienner.

Ramalho, R. 2003. "The effects of anti-corruption campaign: Evidence from the 1992 presidential impeachment in Brazil." MIT Working Paper.

Roll, S. 2010. "'Finance matters!' The influence of financial sector reforms on the development of the entrepreneurial elite in Egypt." *Mediterranean Politics*, 15: 349–370.

Ross, M. L. 2001. "Does oil hinder democracy?" *World Politics*, 53(3): 325–361.

Roushdy, R. and M. Gadallah. 2011. "Labor market adjustment to the world financial crisis: Evidence from Egypt." Economic Research Forum Working Paper No. 643.

Sadowski, Y. 2001. *Political Vegetables? Businessmen and Bureaucrats in the Development of Egyptian Agriculture*. Washington, DC: Brookings Institution Press.

Schlumberger, O. ed. 2007. *Debating Arab Authoritarianism: Dynamics and Durability in Nondemocratic Regimes.* Stanford University Press.
Shahin, E. E.-D. 2005. "Political Islam: Ready for engagement?" La Fundación para las Relaciones Internacionales y el Dialogo Exterior (FRIDE) Working Paper No. 3.
Skafianis, J. 2004. "The whales of the Nile: Networks, businessmen, and bureaucrats during the era of privatization in Egypt." In *Networks of Privilege in the Middle East*, ed. Heydemann, S. New York: Palgrave Macmillan.
Tessler, M. 2012. "Islam and the struggle for a political formula: Findings from the 2010–11 Arab barometer." Mimeo, University of Michigan.
Tilley, J. 2002. "Is youth a better predictor of sociopolitical values than is nationality?" *The Annals (The American Academy of Political and Social Science)*, 580(1): 226–256.
World Bank. 2009. *From Privilege to Competition.* Washington, DC: World Bank Group.

Chapter 3

THE MAKING OF THE TUNISIAN REVOLUTION

Fadhel Kaboub

1. Introduction

The 2010–2011 Tunisian uprisings that took Ben Ali, his feared security apparatus, and his Western Allies by surprise shook the world and presented many mainstream analysts and commentators with a dizzying paradox (Hibou 2011). How did this politically stable, westernized, highly educated, tolerant, and relatively prosperous society erupt into popular protests that toppled one of the strongest police states in the Arab world, and plunge the entire region into a wave of popular revolts? Only a few weeks before the uprisings began in Tunisia, the World Bank issued its 2010 Country Brief on Tunisia stating: "Tunisia has made remarkable progress on equitable growth, fighting poverty and achieving good social indicators." The report went on to argue that "Tunisia has consistently scored above its income category in the Middle East and North Africa average on most dimensions of comparative governance ranking and development indexes." Finally, it concluded with an almost congratulatory statement claiming that "Tunisia is far ahead in terms of government effectiveness, rule of law, control of corruption and regulatory quality" (World Bank 2010). All of these statements were subsequently removed from the World Bank website in the days after Ben Ali fled to Saudi Arabia.

The illusion of stability, economic prosperity, and growing liberal democracy was created by an elaborate set of smoke screens, propaganda public relations messages, data manipulations, and vicious clamp downs on dissenting opinions. However, for the average Tunisian, especially those living in the non-coastal cities and towns, the harsh socio-economic reality was as clear and palpable as could be (Bedoui and Gouia 1995). The middle class socio-economic status was sliding steadily, while the Trabelsi-Ben Ali business empire was devouring the traditional business class, alienating investors, and harassing entrepreneurs and small business owners. In 2002, *Reporters Without Boarders* ranked Tunisia 128th in its Press Freedom Index, and by 2010, the country's ranking dropped to 164 (out of 178), narrowly outranking the likes of North Korea, Cuba, Syria, and Turkmenistan.

This Chapter argues that what seemed to be an island of stability in the Middle East was in fact a ticking time bomb that was set off by Mohamed Bouazizi in December 2010. It further argues that the overthrow of the Ben Ali regime could not have taken place had it not been a leaderless revolt. As a result, the Chapter provides a critical analysis of the making of the Tunisian revolution by investigating the key factors that maintained stability, and the mechanisms that set the stage for the uprisings. In doing so, the analysis reveals the radical social transformation that took place since the early 1990s leading to the breakdown of the social contract, and the gradual drift of the middle class away from its implicit support of the Ben Ali regime. The new political landscape opens up a real opportunity for democratic transformation, vibrant civic engagement, and sustainable economic revival. Therefore, our analysis would be incomplete without a careful look at the new dynamic between the forces of political Islam, secularism, and the middle class. Finally, the Chapter closes with a summary and some concluding remarks.

2. The Inevitable Leaderless Revolt

Before January 14, 2011, many political analysts believed that dictatorships could only be brought down either by a military coup, an external intervention, or an internal challenge by a well-established political opposition with strong leadership. In other words, democratic change in the Arab world was believed to only happen in a top-down fashion because the region's culture was "not ready for democracy" (Huntington 1984; Lewis 1993; Diamond 2010). What the Tunisian revolution has demonstrated, however, is that a non-violent grassroots popular uprising can overthrow a 23-year-old dictatorship in 23 days without any support from abroad, without any connection to radical Islamic groups, and most importantly without any centralized leadership. The leaderless revolution model struck a nerve in the heart of all the dictatorship regimes in the Arab region. The main argument that we want to establish here is that the police-state nature of most of these regimes was well prepared to deal with organized opposition of all kinds (e.g., secular, religious, leftist, underground, violent, peaceful, externally-sponsored, etc.), but they were never prepared to deal with a leaderless decentralized revolt (Lynch 2012). In order to fully comprehend the birth of this phenomenon, one has to critically assess the institutional setting of the Tunisian socio-economic and political landscape that made a leaderless revolution not only possible, but also simply inevitable.

A leaderless revolt does not automatically imply lack of organization (formal or informal), but it also does not imply that it was only possible via social media and communication networks. A leaderless movement is a last resort strategy for the politically oppressed peoples of all socio-economic, religious, cultural, and political orientations. As Trotsky explained, revolution is "the forcible entry of the masses into the realm of rulership over their own destiny" (Trotsky 1932, p. 17). What brings the masses together in a leaderless movement is not class-based or faith-based solidarity but rather *political* solidarity. Socio-economic discontent is important in creating a fertile ground for uprisings, but it is ultimately *political exclusion* that drives the revolution (Goodwin 2001).

Rather than reviewing the breadth of the literature on revolutions and social movements, this article looks at the Tunisian uprisings through the analytical lens of George Lawson's theory of "negotiated revolutions" (Lawson 2005). Negotiated revolutions seek to join the international system of liberal democracies; they use non-violent means to challenge the state, they are based on the idea of liberation rather than utopia, and they aim to rectify injustices through restorative rather than punitive or retributive justice. Lawson argues that the concept of classical revolution has lost currency after the fall of the Soviet Union. Post-1989 revolutions were mainly concerned with embracing the Western free market economic model rather than overthrowing the international system and achieving a utopian social order. Therefore, post-Cold War revolutions are domestic revolts aimed at creating a liberal democracy in order to join the international system rather than fighting it. According to Lawson (2011), revolution trajectories take shape with a particular social order and are determined by three factors: state effectiveness, coercive apparatus, and the formation of a close-knit identity with the revolutionary movement (Lawson 2011, pp. 1078–1081). The following analysis will establish the transformation of the Tunisian socio-economic political landscape from one marked by a stable social contract model in the post-independence period to one marked by a corrupt and repressive plutocratic state that was disembedded from its people, and a society that, despite its socio-economic and cultural diversity, found itself increasingly united under the revolutionary 'shared identity' of the oppressed.

Like many former colonies, Tunisia's postcolonial governance inherited a top-down political system under the leadership of a charismatic independence hero. Habib Bourguiba, who declared himself 'President for Life' in 1975, was once asked about Tunisia's political system, he replied, "The system? What system? I am the system." Soon after independence in 1956, Bourguiba established a political system that allowed him and his Neo-Destour party to monopolize power and push through his modernist social and economic reforms without any meaningful political opposition. A lawyer by training, Bourguiba was a masterful negotiator and political player. He established a presidential political system in which the national assembly rubberstamped presidential decisions and provided the illusion of government accountability (Perkins 2004). A non-competitive electoral system was established to simply gauge the popularity of government policies, rather than challenge its leadership. By the early 1980s, Bourguiba was old, ill, and no longer fully in charge. Driven by paranoia, he kept shuffling and replacing his ministers fearing that some of them might get too ambitious, dare to challenge his leadership, and overthrow him. Zine El-Abedine Ben Ali was the unlikely candidate that Bourguiba picked specifically because he was the least politically savvy and least charismatic member of his government. Ben Ali was the head of Army Intelligence (1964–1974), head of

National Security (1977–1980), Ambassador to Poland (1980–1984), Interior Minister (1986–1987) and simultaneously Prime Minister for six months before overthrowing Bourguiba on November 7, 1987. Ben Ali was the exception in Bourguiba's administration; he was the only professional military person in Bourguiba's elite civilian administration of university graduates and technocrats.

Tunisia was going through a major economic crisis during Bourguiba's last years in office. The political vacuum pushed the country to the verge of collapse as the Islamists' political ambitions and rising popularity become more evident. Ben Ali ushered in the World Bank sponsored structural adjustment program, and promised to establish a pluralistic liberal democracy by abolishing life time presidency, and setting a term limit of three 5-year consecutive presidential terms. In reality, however, Ben Ali was just buying time in order strengthen his grip on the political landscape and preserve the same presidential powers granted under Bourguiba's system. He freed political prisoners and invited 16 political organizations and parties, including the banned Islamists, to join him in signing a 'National Pact' to promote national interest, stability, and democratic reforms. Ben Ali used pro-democracy and pro-human rights language to court as much support from his potential opponents as possible. He even flirted with the Islamists during his first three years in office by promising to legalize their party. This allowed him to gauge their popularity and identify their network and their supporters before launching a massive clamp down on the entire group (Erdle 2010).

The Neo-Destour party was renamed Rassemblement Constitutionel Democratique (RCD) and continued to dominate the political landscape until it was finally dismantled in the aftermath of the revolution in 2011. Ben Ali's political rhetoric encompassed and overshadowed all the progressive political messages of the opposition (i.e., human rights, freedom, democracy, gender equality, environmental sustainability, social justice, solidarity, etc.). Whatever the opposition wanted to advocate, Ben Ali was already saying and doing; or at least pretending to do. Therefore, there was no need to have an opposition. Those who understood what Ben Ali and the RCD were doing and voiced their objections were simply banned, prosecuted, or exiled. For instance, Tunisie Verte (Tunisian Green Party) was never allowed to legally operate in Tunisia (although its application was never formally rejected); instead, Ben Ali's regime approved the application of the "Green Party for Progress" which was simply the creation of the Interior Ministry. Tunisie Verte continued to struggle for legal status and to fight for ecological sustainability while being constantly harassed by the regime (Zitouni 2011). Ben Ali also portrayed himself as a patron of the Islamic faith in Tunisia by building a glorious mosque in Carthage and attending all major religious ceremonies. In addition, his son-in-law, Mohamed Sakhr El Matri, started a private Islamic radio station (Zitouna FM) and an Islamic Bank (Zitouna Bank). This was all done to counter any political challenges from Islamist opposition groups. In short, Ben Ali and the RCD made it impossible for real opposition to emerge or to exercise any meaningful influence in the political sphere. Over the years, Ben Ali continued to promote the illusion of political pluralism by increasing the number of seats reserved for the opposition parties in the national assembly, but the 'majority lists' election rules were constantly tweaked to marginalize influence of the opposition while always giving them hope for the possibility of gaining more seats in the future. Even a split within the RCD party was virtually inconceivable. Anyone suspected of having the potential to build political capital that could challenge the President was immediately moved to a less prominent position. Overall, Tunisians became cynical about the possibility of political change from within the existing electoral system, so nobody was surprised to see Ben Ali's bids for re-election winning 90–99% of the votes.

Were other non-political forces such as the national associations or the military capable of bringing about political change in Tunisia? The national associations (*association nationales*) are the corporatist organizations that represent the third most important pillar of the Bourguibist and Ben Ali forms of government (complementing the elite state bureaucracy and the ruling party). Their role is to financially co-opt the population and provide support for government policies. The most important national associations are the General Union of Tunisian Workers (UGTT), the Tunisian Union of Industrialists, Merchants, and Artisans (UTICA), the Tunisian Union of Farmers and Fisherman (UTAP), the National Union of Tunisian Women (UNFT), and the General Union of Tunisian Students (UGET). All of these associations were led by supporters of the ruling party, which often put them at odds with lower ranking members of their associations[1] (Erdle 2010; Alexander 2010a, 2010b). For instance, Abdessalam Jrad Abbassi was the Secretary General of UGTT during the 2008 Gafsa mineral field workers movement and his family also owned a subcontracting mining company that favored wage cuts and layoffs of the Gafsa miners. As a result, over the years, Tunisians grew even more cynical about the possibility of political change coming from a coalition between the national associations and the broader labor movement or civil society.

As for the military, both Bourguiba and Ben Ali always marginalized it in terms of financial resources and favored the state security forces instead (police, national guard, secret police, and presidential guard). Fearing a military coup, Bourguiba gave a room in the presidential palace of Carthage (right next to his office) to the Swiss embassy, so he could use it as a diplomatic refuge in case of emergency. Ben Ali not only continued in Bourguiba's tradition, but also strengthened the secrete service and presidential security apparatus, which employed 55,000 people. Other estimates suggest that the number was between 150,000 and 200,000 people and supported nearly 10% of the population (Erdle 2004, p. 214). May 2002 proved to be a turning point in how Tunisians felt about the possibility of change coming form the military. That was the time when Ben Ali's third consecutive term in office was due to expire, and he had to call for a referendum to amend the constitution in a way that would

[1] One noticeable exception, however, is UGTT, which often opposed the regime's harsh stance against workers, especially in the late 1970s. During the 2011 uprisings, it became evident to the UGTT leadership that the regime would become a dangerous liability in the face of popular protests.

effectively ensure his presidency for life. On May 1, 2002, a military helicopter crash killed the Army Chief of Staff, five colonels, four majors, two lieutenants, and one warrant officer first class. Virtually the entire top echelon of the military was wiped out in this mysterious 'accident'.[2] The news of the helicopter crash obliterated the last hope of the military intervening to stop Ben Ali from restoring presidency for life. On May 26, 2002, the constitutional referendum was passed with 99.5% approval, thus giving Ben Ali the green light to rule the country until 2014. Ben Ali never suspected that Rachid Ammar, the army chief of staff, a military man with no political ambitions, would refuse orders from Ben Ali's Interior Minister (Ali Seriati) to fire on protesters, and side with the protesters in January 2011.

Therefore, the Tunisian revolution had to come from a non-traditional decentralized leaderless movement. A 'leaderless' movement occurs when the population at large has literally come to a strong consensus that does not need to be broadcasted via megaphones by a set of heroic and charismatic leaders standing on stage. The message is known to, and shared by the people. Social uprisings are market by "the formation of multi-class coalitions in which diverse strands of protest are linked through decisive leadership, common ideological frameworks and shared narratives, often inspired by stories of national awakening" (Lawson 2011, p. 1080). The collective experience of the Tunisian population with the oppression and corruption of the Ben Ali regime, and the complete sense of humiliation that Tunisians were subjected to, made it unbearable for the middle class, which saw its socio-economic status and interests gradually become more aligned with that of the poor rather than the regime and its elite class supporters. This formed a large multi-class coalition against the Ben Ali regime and his security forces. Needless to say, this leaderless movement did not emerge overnight and it did rely on a large number of fearless citizen activists who played the role of catalysts in the lead up to the 2011 uprising. The Ben Ali regime was always able to handle a few activists and opposition leaders at a time. Opposition leaders can be jailed, tortured, exiled, or even killed, but a leaderless mass movement was simply undefeatable (Schraeder 2012). It was a broad-based social movement with a 'shared narrative' of being the victims of oppression, corruption, abuse, censorship, and injustice. This 'shared narrative' that sparked the uprising encompassed a number of grievances and was heard loud and clear in the popular chants of the protesters.

In addition to the palpable socio-economic daily struggles that Tunisians grew accustomed to, the WikiLeaks US diplomatic cables confirmed what many people in Tunisia had known for a number of years. The detailed description of the lavish lifestyle of the Ben Ali and Trabelsi families angered the population and increased its frustration with the increasingly oppressive, corrupt, and arrogant government. The WikiLeaks cables convinced the middle class residents of the coastal cities that they are in the same boat as the disenfranchised residents of the interior cities and towns

[2] A government investigation declared the event an unfortunate accident. Even a post-revolution military investigation has found no evidence of any wrongdoing. The accident, however, remains suspicious.

of the country. Hence it can be seen that when Bouazizi set himself afire in Sidi Bouzid, it was a symbolic culmination of a nation-wide rage against the regime. In fact, this leaderless revolt stood firmly on top of a series of smaller revolts that the Ben Ali regime managed to crush. In addition to the struggles of human rights, pro-democracy, and Islamic political activists, we should mention three significant pre-Bouazizi regional revolts that demonstrate the sense of collective struggle that Tunisians felt under Ben Ali.

First, the "October 18 Movement for Rights and Freedoms" which formed in 2005 as a broad coalition between liberals, leftists, and Islamists to protest the so-called "Anti-Terrorism Law" enacted in 2003. The law was written in a way that made it easy for the regime to prosecute dissenting views. Second, the so-called "Hunger Intifada" began on January 5, 2008 in the town of Redayef (southwest of Tunisia) and spread throughout the Governorate of Gafsa. The Gafsa mineral field is the fifth largest in the world with an annual production of 8 million tons of calcium phosphate, but suffers from severely high levels of unemployment, poverty, and environmental degradation. The main employer in Gafsa is CPG, a state-owned company that has drastically reduced its work force in the last 10 years from 15,000 to only 5,000 workers. The movement began with the group of unemployed graduates (*Uniondes diplômés chômeurs*) staging a sit-in in front of the UGTT office to protest the CPG's latest corrupt hiring practices, and to demand jobs and a commitment to regional economic development. They were soon joined by their families, the poor, women widowed by mining-accidents, and the exploited working class who set up tents in the area for the next six months. The movement was met by the iron fist of the regime, which led to the killing of two young protesters by the security forces, and the arrest of more than 200 peaceful demonstrators. Substantiated reports of torture and abuse fuelled the protesters determination. In what Amnesty International described as an unfair trial, 50 trade unionists were handed up to 8-year prison terms, and their protesting mothers, sisters, and wives were harassed, arrested, ill-treated, and imprisoned for up to one year. That is how the leaderless movement was born in Gafsa. Finally, the third pre-Bouazizi regional revolt took place in Ben Guerdane on August 9, 2010 when angry protesters clashed with the police to protest a new tax of 150 dinars on cars crossing the border with Libya. The vast majority of the Ben Guerdane population makes a living through cross-border trading with Libya. The protests spread to neighboring regions of Skhira and Feriana, and like the Gafsa 2008 events, the people of Ben Guerdane suffered ruthless treatment, arrests and abuse by the police. The unrest was so severe that Tunisia had to close the border for several days. After mediation efforts led by UGTT, the arrested protesters were released without charge, the border was reopened, but the tax levy remained in effect (Khosrokhavar 2012).

It is the culmination of all these events that initially created a sense of hopelessness in the face of injustice and abuse by the regime, then turned into a collective sense of unity in suffering, that turned into a general sentiment of fearlessness. By the end of August 2010, the leaderless revolt calling for jobs, freedom, and dignity was ripe and ready for the Bouazizi sacrifice to light the mighty spark of the Arab uprisings. Although the middle class did not take part of the initial moments of the uprisings, lawyers played a significant role in giving the Sidi Bouzid protesters legitimacy and calling on other professionals and members of the middle class to stand up against injustice. The lawyers were also able to articulate the 'shared narrative' and 'shared identity' of the multi-class diverse anti-regime social movement. Lawyers, however, were not the leaders of the movement, they were facilitators working in the same capacity as other professionals, labour activists, bloggers, human rights advocates, etc. Similarly, social media and mobile telecommunication technology facilitated the spread of information and communication within the broad-based social movement. As a result, the Tunisian uprisings do not resemble the pre-1989 revolutions of the poor and working class as theorized by Moore (1978) and Skocpol (1979). The Tunisian revolt does, however, confirm Lawson's theory of "negotiated revolutions" which are driven by the nonviolent masses and in which "the control of fervor and the dignity of protest rise above the social context defined by the old regime" (Lawson 2005, p. 490).

However, deep inside the inner circle of the Ben Ali regime, there was a radical structural transformation that took place over a 20-year period that has played a significant role in the fall of Ben Ali and the creation of a new alliance between Islamists and secular groups within Tunisia's middle class. This transformation was crucial in the formation of a socially diverse multi-class anti-regime coalition with a shared narrative and a shared identity.

3. The Transformation of Elite Power Structure

The power structure of the Ben Ali regime was initially very similar to the one set up by Bourguiba after independence; but by the early 2000s, the old Bourguibist system gave way to a mafia-like power structure centered on Ben Ali's entourage. During the Bourguiba and early Ben Ali days, however, the elite power structure was characterized by what Volker Perthes (2004) and Steffen Erdle (2004) described as three concentric circles that highlight the different degrees of influence within the Politically Relevant Elite (PRE). The inner circle comprises the core elite group that makes decisions on strategic issues. The second circle is the intermediate elite group which exerts considerable influence on issues of lesser political importance, but have little influence on strategic issues unless they are invited to contribute or are delegated some decision making powers on an occasional basis. The intermediate elite group includes the upper ranks of state bureaucracy, ruling party executives, and leading figures in the national associations. The third circle is what Perthes (2004) refers to as the "subelite" who are only capable of indirectly influencing strategic decisions, setting the national agenda, or contributing to the national discourse. This circle includes the midlevel of the above-mentioned groups, in addition to contesting elites such as independent NGOs and opposition parties. The boundaries between these three circles are permeable in a way that allows for occasional penetration of some members of the subelite into the intermediate elite, and occasionally even into the inner circle.

The regime's inner circle was composed of three distinct groups: the palace, the lieutenants, and the entourage. The palace is the President's team of political advisors, close friends, and family members. The lieutenants are Ben Ali's most important executive team, which includes the most powerful ministers (interior (security apparatus), foreign affairs, international cooperation, social affairs, and economic affaires) and the Politburo of the RCD. The entourage consisted of Ben Ali's family, his second wife's family (the Trabelsis), and the families married to Ben Ali's daughters (Chiboub, the Mabrouk, Zarrouk, and El Matri). The entourage quickly expanded to include the in-laws of the in-laws, all of whom became presidential relatives through marriage, and therefore had privileged access into the inner circle. The inner circle political elites who also preside over the RCD party structure reinforced their political capital via marital and business affiliations within the Trabelsi-Ben Ali clan (Beau and Graciet 2009).

Ben Ali's early days in power followed in Bourguiba's footsteps by playing a game of "musical chairs" that reshuffles elites to strengthen the core and minimize discontent (Owen 2012). Bourguiba, however, relied on the post-independence educated elites from the Tunis and Sahel bourgeoisie, whereas Ben Ali carefully selected apolitical technocrats who were highly qualified to execute his policy directives, but lacked social and political capital to be his political rivals. Overtime, the entourage began to dominate and overpower the lieutenants, and use the executive power of the palace to increase their economic power. The former elites became more isolated and alienated after the rise of the Trabelsi-Ben Ali clan, which had amassed a tremendous amount of wealth in a very short period and acquired a vast business empire in banking, insurance, communications, real estate, construction, transportation, retail, tourism, manufacturing, and mining. The economic power of the Trabelsi-Ben Ali clan was built under crony capitalism, which was set in motion soon after Ben Ali tightened his grip over the political landscape in 1992, and neutralized all political opposition.

In 1992, Ben Ali issued a presidential executive order mandating that all major government contract bids must go through the President's office. In the past, however, a committee of technical experts from varies ministries formed a selection committee within the auspices of the Prime Minster's office, and selected the winning bids for all major government project bids. The 1992 decision set in motion a long wave of corruption and kickbacks emanating from the President's personal office. This period also coincided with Tunisia's endorsement of the World Bank-sponsored *Mise à Niveau* policies (structural adjustment program), which mandated the privatization of several state-owned enterprises, all of which also benefitted the Ben Ali plutocracy.

The traditional business owners and entrepreneurs who lacked the proper network connections to the Trabelsi-ben Ali clan suffered severely from the new regime structure. Short of marrying into the President's family, they were often faced with three choices: sell their businesses to the clan; agree to 'partner' with them (you do the work, and they collect most of the profits), or face constant harassment by the government (tax audits, inspections, etc.) and unfair competition until being driven out of business. None of these choices were pleasant. It created a division within the Tunisian capitalist class, and further concentrated economic power with the President's entourage. The economic impact of this elite power reconfiguration was devastating because many of the former business elites who refused to join the clan (e.g., Batam, Kallel, etc.) shifted their investment in the Tunisian economy into real estate (which fuelled speculation) or moved abroad. The lack of private sector investment was fuelled by the fact that the Trabelsi business empire was there to serve the lavish life-style of the clan rather than reinvest in the companies they owned. And to top it all off, the government was reducing its investment share in GDP, which made Tunisia's job creation hopes ever more dependent on foreign direct investment (FDI), tourism, and workers remittances. Eva Bellin (2002) demonstrates how the so-called reforms of the Ben Ali era have crippled both labor and capital, which have been the social actors of democratic change in so many countries after 1989. Between 1987 and 2000, Ben Ali was able to keep the Bourguiba-style cozy relationship between his regime and the labor movement via modest concessions, as well as the traditional business elite class, which benefited from government contracts and export subsidies. However, the emergence of Ben Ali's extended family as a corrupt business empire has changed this dynamic and open the door for both labor and capital to align their interest with a diverse multi-class anti-regime social movement.

4. The Breakdown of the Social Contract

One of the most important points to understand about the making of the Tunisian revolution is the transformation of the middle class during the Ben Ali era. The rapid improvement in the Tunisian standard of living and quality of life that took place in the 1970s was suddenly brought to a halt during the 1980s economic crisis, and by the time Ben Ali took over as President in 1987, the neo-liberal economic reforms were already set in motion through a series of IMF stand-by credit agreements and World Bank loans granted in 1986–1987. Both institutions credited Tunisia's leadership for its commitment to economic reforms and its "pre-emptive SAP", which began in the 1970s *Infitah* (opening) policies (Murphy 1999, White 2001). The long-standing social contract between the government and its people became the main obstacle standing in the way of Tunisia's economic prosperity. The traditional way of viewing the state as the main agent of economic development through its protection and support of a large middle class[3] began to gradually fade away during the crisis in the 1980s. The gradual nature of this change is what kept the middle class from

[3]Tunisia invested heavily in health and education in its post-independence period because Bourguiba firmly believed that a country without any significant natural resources can only advance via its human capital. Therefore, the middle class grew during that period and became he main beneficiary of the social contract.

revolting at first, but when the economic concessions became unbearable and the heavy-handed political oppression became increasingly intolerant of economic grievances, people became increasingly cynical of government reforms, and grew fearless of its repression.

While on life-support under IMF and World Bank assistance in the 1980s, the Tunisian government had to pledge its long-term commitment to SAP and economic liberalization by making a concerted effort to privatize State-Owned Enterprises (SOEs), reduce budget deficits, tighten monetary policy, increase labor market flexibility, eliminate price controls, liberalize trade and finance, introduce currency convertibility, focus on export-led growth, and stabilize external debt. The World Bank put a lot of pressure on the Tunisian government to amend or abolish the *Code de Travail* (Tunisia's labor legislation[4]) and to replace it with a business-friendly legislation giving employers the freedom to hire and fire without restriction in order to stimulate private investment and foreign direct investment (FDI). Incidentally, much of the labor market 'flexibility' resulted in the creation of a group of subcontracting companies (mostly owned by the Trabelsi-Ben Ali clan) operating on the margins of the Tunisian labor laws and relying exclusively on "contractual" workers (*les contractuels*). Tunisia used a gradualist approach to reduce employers' social security contributions, and crafted amendments to clarify conditions and compensations for labor dismissal (Murphy 1999, p. 154). Over a 20-year period, however, those small steps amounted to significant declines in the real purchasing power and the relative bargaining position of the working class, and what used to be small acceptable sacrifices during the 1980s crisis became blatant abuse and injustice in the era of the Trabelsi-Ben Ali plutocracy.

The government was convinced that SAP would heal its ailing economy and prop the country to the level of developed nations by the turn of the century. From his first days in office, Ben Ali pushed ahead with a series of legislation to put SAP in motion. The tax system was revised and harmonized to give Value Added Tax (VAT) a more prominent role in public finance; a tax-evasion amnesty was initiated; a consolidation of tax brackets (at lower maximum rates) was introduced, soon followed by a more aggressive tax collection effort targeted to high-income earners, rental income, and business profits. New government committees were set up to study SOEs and make recommendations for privatizations, and new legislation was passed in 1989 to provide a legal framework for privatization. The government decided to keep control over strategic industries and gradually privatize SOEs that have a non-administrative character.[5] In an effort to convince the international financial institutions (IFIs) of the positive progress in the privatization drive, the government decided to begin by privatizing the most profitable (sellable) SOEs such as textile companies, hotels, and small banking subsidiaries. Other SOEs in mining, construction materials, and transportation were given Performance Contracts to

[4]See Elsafi (2006) for a detailed overview of labor law in Tunisia.
[5]See Belev (2000) for a comparative analysis of privatization policies in Tunisia and Egypt.

improve efficiency and profitability.[6] Monopolies such as transportation were partially opened to competition. By the time the Eighth Development Plan (1992–1996) came into effect, Tunisia launched its more aggressive privatization effort under financial incentives from the World Bank,[7] the European Union (EU), and USAID.[8] While this period did not witness any complete privatizations of strategic SOEs, the government consistently sold shares of SOEs through stock market floatation to induce further management transparency and scrutiny for companies such as Tunis Air, Compagnie Tunisienne de Navigation (CTN), and Société Nationale de Distribution des Pétroles (SNDP). In 1996, the Société Tunisienne d'Électricité et du Gaz (STEG) lost its monopoly over production of electricity and was required to buy from independent suppliers, but it still remained the monopoly provider of electricity to final consumers. Tunisie Telecom, the state monopoly telecom company, remained under state control and received a massive high-tech upgrade in infrastructure throughout the 1990s. In 2004, the government decided to sell a 35% stake of Tunisie Telecom, the most profitable SOE, which saw its profits hit a record high of $823 million in 2005, up 23% from 2004. The bidding euphoria began immediately with some of the top telecom companies in the world competing to win the deal. In the end, it was the UAE's Telecom-DIG that snatched the deal in March 2006 with a spectacular US$2.24 billion bid (TND3.05 billion). Starting in the mid-1990s, privatization deals and government sub-contracting became increasingly lucrative for Ben Ali's inner circle, the in-laws, and close business partners. The age of large-scale corruption emanating from the Palace of Carthage had begun.

The government efforts to boost its austerity program, reduce food subsidies, and cut the food import bill in the second part of the 1980s were upset by severe droughts and locust plagues that devastated agricultural output. This led Prime Minister Hedi Baccouche to think that perhaps Tunisia should scale back its SAP and focus on fighting unemployment and reducing external debt. He faced stiff opposition from Ismail Khelil (Governor of the Central Bank) and Mohammad Ghannouchi (Planning and Finance Minister), which ultimately led to his dismissal in September 1988, and his replacement by Hamed Karoui (former Minister of Justice) who pushed ahead with SAP despite the devastation of unprecedented floods in January 1989. Things got worse economically with the Gulf War in 1990–1991. By the end of 1990, Tunisia had lost more than $700 million from Kuwaiti (and Kuwaiti-dominated) investment funds, US financial aid, and tourism revenues. More than 200 Tunisian firms doing business with Iraq and Kuwait also faced serious setbacks during the Gulf War and its aftermath. But despite all these complications, the government was determined to continue its economic liberalization at all costs. IFIs continued their financial support through the early 1990s, austerity brought government deficits

[6]SOEs were sold to firms from countries that were 'friendly' to the regime (Qatar, Egypt, UAE, Turkey, Morocco, Libya), with direct kickbacks disbursed to Ben Ali and his cronies.
[7]Disbursement of loans became conditional upon acceleration of the privatization effort.
[8]USAID provided a $10 million grant to support further privatizations.

under control, which made Tunisia more attractive to international creditors and ushered in a series of syndicated loans and a greater appetite for borrowing, which doubled the countries external debt once every decade, reaching $9 billion in 1996, and $20 billion by 2007, with a debt service ratio exceeding 15%.

On the trade liberalization front (*Infitah* policy aside), Tunisia's free trade journey began in 1990 when the country officially joined the General Agreement on Tariffs and Trade (GATT) through which Tunisia agreed to eliminate trade barriers such as tariffs and import licenses. And in 1995, Tunisia became the first Mediterranean non-member country to sign an Association Agreement with the EU that established a schedule for gradual tariff reductions spanning from 1996–2008. In 2008, Tunisia entered the complete trade liberalization phase with the EU,[9] which represented a double challenge for the Tunisian government; on the one hand it significantly reduced tax revenues, and on the other hand put more pressure on the unemployment front due to fierce competition from the EU. This was the last nail for the coffin of Tunisia's old social contract. The gradual transformation of Tunisian government policy from a producer-state to a regulator-state (privatization of SOEs and greater private sector role in investment) has left its mark on the socio-economic fabric, thus affecting the institutional structure at the economic, social as well as political level (Ben Salah 1977). The economic liberalization brought about economic dislocation and social exclusion, which was initially absorbed by the large middle class, which saw its status slowly move closer to that of the poor while the size of the socio-economically vulnerable population steadily increased, especially in the interior of the country (Brisson and Krontiris 2012).

In Tunisian society, middle class status has been acquired primarily through education and access to government jobs. While the government continued to support education throughout the economic liberalization period, it significantly cut back on hiring. For example, some of the most representative professionals in the Tunisian middle class are schoolteachers. Primary school teachers, for instance, used to be hired at the tune of 1,000–2,000 new teachers per year in the 1960s all the way until 1990, but then began experiencing severe cutbacks with an average annual decline of 398 teachers per year between 2000 and 2005; and an average annual increase of only 45 new teachers between 2005 and 2010 (Al-Dimassi 2012, p. 140). This trend was also noticeable in a wide variety of administrative hiring practices within government ministries. The decline of the middle class status became more visible as the educated youth faced the terrible reality of unemployment after college. In 1994, the unemployment rate among college graduates was only 3.8%, and began to nearly double every five years, reaching 8.7% in 1999, then 14% in 2005, and 22.9% in 2010. The most recent statistic released in 2011 is a devastating 29.2%.

The increased burden on the middle class also came in the form of higher home mortgage rates, which are controlled by the government. Those rates went from a low 3% in the 1970s to nearly 7% in 2009. Household debt grew rapidly in the last

[9] See also Nabli *et al.* (2002) for an assessment of Tunisia's competitiveness in the global economy.

two decades to substitute for wage stagnation and compensate for the higher cost of living and reduced opportunities for government employment opportunities. The most noticeable household debt growth period occurred between 1997 and 2003. In 1997, the household debt to income ratio stood at 28.9% and rapidly increased to 43.1% in 2003. Two-thirds of the incurred debt was devoted to home mortgages, while the rest went to automobiles and other consumer household items (Al-Dimassi 2012). As a result of this household debt increase, Tunisian families grew more dependent on worker remittances from abroad, which used to finance less than 7% of household expenditures in the early 1980s, but now pay for nearly 10% of their expenditures. Therefore, the economic status of the middle class became more financially unstable at the same time that society was opening up to a hyper-consumerist western culture, which fuelled conspicuous consumption and the desire to emulate the super-rich Tunisian elite. This social transformation led to a further disenfranchisement of the poor class because it did not have access to loans from financial institutions, while the middle class was able to borrow, spend, accumulate debt, live beyond its means, and slowly slide down the financial stability scale.

It is important to point out that as the government embraced the free market policies to replace the developmental state of the 1960s, the gradual withdrawal of government expenditures has left a significant gap that was supposed to be filled by private investment. The latter, however, was driven by the excessive borrowing of the Trabelsi-Ben Ali clan, and was mostly speculative in nature and mostly directed to imports of cheap consumer goods, so it was not capable of absorbing the unemployed. In addition, the government focused on promoting self-employment and entrepreneurship through microfinancing schemes sponsored by the National Solidarity Bank, most of which contributed to the rise in indebtedness, defaults, and corruption (Hibou 2011). As a result, the government broke its economic support ties to the middle class, which grew increasingly dissatisfied with its material status but had no political recourse to express its grievances; instead the Ben Ali regime increased its oppression, and the middle class began to see its interests drift away from that of the elite, and align more with the poor, the disenfranchised, the oppressed, and the underground opposition.

As the social contract was being eroded by free market policies, the Ben Ali regime became gradually incapable of supporting the middle class, which grew increasingly dissatisfied with the rising cost of living, rising corruption, and lack of opportunities for upward mobility. Instead of compensating the middle class for the deterioration of their economic status either by increasing subsidies or increasing political concessions on freedom of speech and democratization the Ben Ali regime increased repression despite its constant rhetoric about freedom and democracy. Ben Ali could no longer claim that political repression was necessary to protect the secular middle class from the Islamists. The reaction of the Tunisian population was cynicism towards an increasingly hypocritical and repressive regime. Simultaneously, the Islamist message about social and economic justice, which used to resonate with the poor, became more relevant for the secular middle class. Therefore, in order to understand the new alliance between the Islamists and the secular/liberal middle class in Tunisia, one has to delineate the specific historical origins and evolution of political Islam in post-independence Tunisia.

5. Towards a New Liberal-Political Islam Coalition

Bourguiba's ascension to power in 1956 affirmed the dominance of the secular independence leaders over the more conservative and religious followers of his political rival Salah Ben Youssef. Bourguiba put in place one of the most progressive personal status laws (Personal Status Code) in the Arab and Islamic world, isolated religious institutions such as the Zitouna mosque from the education system, eliminated the Islamic land tenure (*hbous*) system, and banned religious courts. However, the Arab defeat in the 1967 war brought some doubt about the legitimacy of secular nationalism; and as Bourguiba shifted his economic policy toward free markets in 1970 after the socialist experiment of the 1960s, he drew increasing criticism and opposition from the secular left, which included socialists and communists who were driven by a regional current of Arab nationalism. So, in order to protect his regime in the early 1970s, Bourguiba supported a group of Islamic studies students and professors to create an organization called the Association for the Safeguard of the Quran (ASQ), which attempted to counter the rising influence of the leftist/Marxist dominated groups, especially UGTT and UGET.

ASQ was initially a non-political group of intellectuals who focused on questions of religion and culture in Tunisian society. They were educated people who grew up in religious and conservative middle class families, and felt overwhelmed by the dominance of the secular French culture that grew stronger amongst the Tunisian secular elite after independence. Some of the ASQ members had been in Syria and Egypt where they came in contact with members of the Muslim Brotherhood. A philosophy teacher by the name of Rachid Al-Ghannouchi[10] emerged as the group's leader and argued that the threat to Tunisia's Islamic and Arab heritage and cultural identity can only be stopped through political means. The ASQ focus quickly shifted away from religion and culture towards questions of economic discontent and political activism (Alexander 2012).

Several factors contributed to the rapid growth of the ASQ in the 1970s. First, several members of the Muslim Brotherhood of Egypt traveled to Tunisia after their release from jail, and many of their ideas gained currency amongst ASQ members. Second, a violent crackdown on labour activists in 1978 created a political vacuum in the opposition that the Islamists were quickly able to fill. And third, the 1979 Islamic revolution in Iran brought excitement, hope, and bigger political aspiration for Islamists across the Middle East. By the end of 1979, Bourguiba's government began

[10] Al-Ghannouchi was originally inspired by Arab nationalism, which Bourguiba vehemently rejected. Arab nationalism was an anti-colonial movement and many nationalists turned to Islamism as a form of 'authentic' anti-colonial struggle.

to crackdown on the Islamists and accused them of planning an Iranian-style violent theocracy. This was Bourguiba's way to rally support from the secular middle class against the Islamists. ASQ was quick to respond by denouncing violence and Iranian-style theocracy, and established a new organization called the Islamic Group, which was the prelude to the establishment of a political party called the Mouvement de Tendence Islamique (MTI) or the Islamic Tendency Movement in 1980. The MTI was banned and its members were arrested, prosecuted, tortured, and exiled. The violent crackdown by the government led to a few violent revenge attacks by some members of the MTI. However, all violence was vehemently denounced by the MTI, which gave it greater credibility among Tunisian society and differentiated it from other Islamists groups in the region. The MTI changed its name to Ennahdha (renaissance) during the early days of the Ben Ali regime. Ben Ali initially flirted with the Islamists giving them hope for official recognition of their party. He needed to buy time and identify their members and supporters before launching his major crackdown.

The threat of a solid Islamist political opposition was very clear for Ben Ali. In the midst of the 1980s economic crisis, Ennahdha had a non-violent democratic agenda that is based on Islamic values and is consistent with the middle class hopes for economic and social justice. In 1988, the Islamists won 85% of the vote in the student's elections, and in 1989, the Islamist ran as independents, and had a clear victory (estimated at 30–60% of the votes) over the secular opposition parties, but results were falsified in favor of Ben Ali's party. For Ben Ali the honeymoon with the Islamists was over. Ennahdha was banned for good, but its underground network of supporters and especially its fundraising for the families of jailed or unemployed members, and the widows and orphans of the party, remained a strong base for their connection to the poor, and to the secular middle class. Unlike their counterparts in Egypt, the Islamists in Tunisia were unable to form charitable organizations and clinics, but they remained active socially without getting involved in politics. However, its exiled members continued to voice their critique of the Ben Ali regime and expose its human rights violations, lack of political freedom, undemocratic practices, corruption, and poor record on economic and social justice. Ben Ali's attack on the Islamist movement meant that anyone suspected of being a member, supporter, or sympathizer would be subject to constant police harassment and would face serious economic hardship due to lack of employment opportunities. This is way the middle class often appeared to be overly secular by fear of association with the Islamist, but over the course of Ben Ali's presidency, there was a slow convergence of interests that eventually brought a larger segment of the middle class closer to the Islamist camp.

In a way, Ennahdha's political work to connect with the middle class during the 1990s and the 2000s was not any different than its message of the 1970s and 1980s. Ennahdha did not move its political and social agenda to meet the middle class position; instead it was the increasingly disenfranchised middle class (especially in the interior of the country) that gradually moved closer to the Islamist position. In addition, the advent of satellite news networks, especially Al Jazeera, played a major role in revealing the people's discontent with the Ben Ali regime and the realization that the Islamist boogeyman was in fact an illusion created by the autocratic regimes to scare the secular middle class into supporting the political status quo when in reality their best interest was more aligned with the political message of the Islamists (Ramadan 2011). The aggressive news coverage of the 2003 Iraq invasion, the second Intifada (2000–2005), the 2006 Israeli attack on Lebanon, the 2009 attack on Gaza, and the 2010 Gaza Flotilla massacre have increased the collective sense of hopelessness about the prospects of democratic change through external international pressure. As a result of all these external and internal events, it became inevitable that the Tunisian secular middle class would be in the same boat as all the other economically vulnerable and politically excluded members of society.

Though not a driving force during the December 2010 uprising, Ennahdha quickly put its political forces on the ground to take advantage of the newly opened political space and was able to make use of its fundraising capabilities and its vast network of supporters to gain sufficient clout during the 2011 elections (Bradley 2012). It is currently sharing power with a secular coalition. Today, Ennahdha enjoys a solid popular support base of 30% of the population. While sharing power with two secular political parties, Ennahdha has so far honored their commitment to human rights, freedom of speech, and other democratic values, despite some outstanding grievances related to the spinners' dossier, corruption, and security. On the economic front, however, Ennahdha suffers from a lack of imagination. Its economic plan is no different than Ben Ali's failed market-based policies, which relied almost exclusively on exports, tourism, and FDI. Both Ennahdha in Tunisia and the Muslim Brotherhood in Egypt have openly endorsed free market policies partly because they do not want to be associated with the Iranian-style socialist experience.

Ennahdha is not the only Islamist political party in Tunisia. After the fall of the Ben Ali regime, a new radical wing known as Salafists has emerged. Although very small in numbers (around 5,000 people at most), in 2011 the Salafists quickly grew in numbers and became very active, confrontational, and on several occasions violent (Pargeter 2012). They have a Taliban-type interpretation of Islam and governance. In an odd way, the Salafists are strengthening the coalition between Ennahdha and the secular parties, because Ennahdha must constantly denounce the political views of the Salafists and restate the party's commitment to democracy, women's rights, and human rights, while at the same time protect the Salafists' freedom of speech and right to engage in non-violent protests. This fragile coalition can only be stable under the following conditions. First, the Salafists must be allowed to exercise their freedom of expression in a non-violent manner, which will keep Ennahdha a relatively moderate partner for the secular political parties. Second, the youth unemployment crisis must be quickly alleviated in order to ease the burden on the middle class and relieve some of the economic inequality and social exclusion, especially in the interior of the country. Third, long overdue labor demands must be reconciled under Ennahdha's neo-liberal economic model. Fourth, the current government must maneuver foreign affairs to balance domestic concerns with international pressures and commitments especially with neighboring countries (Libya and Algeria), as well as major EU partners (France, Germany, and Italy), the United States, and the new regional foreign policy superpower, Qatar (Hroub 2012). Fifth, the new constitution which most observers believe meet the highest standards of constitutional law and democratic principles must be fully enforced by the courts and infused into every aspect of legal, political, and social life. Democracy cannot flourish without some minimal level of social and economic justice, the eradication of pervasive corruption, increased transparency in the government's economic transactions, and the institutionalization of a respected legal framework (Khosrokhavar 2012, p. 82). Failure to face these challenges may lead to a severe social and political instability, further youth uprisings, labor revolts, or even a reversal towards an autocratic system dominated by theocratic rules.

6. Conclusion

The Tunisian uprising that ousted the Ben Ali regime only lasted 23 days, however, its root causes go back several decades and are deeply entrenched into the historical evolution of Tunisia's economic, social, cultural, religious, and political fabric. The successful uprising that took place on January 14, 2011 sparked mass protests across the Middle East, but has not led to any major success stories yet. Egypt continues to struggle with post-Mubarak and post-Morsi political and economic instability. Libya suffered through a devastating civil war and is still struggling to control armed militias despite having elected a new government. Yemen still operates under the same political structure, and is facing severe internal divisions that may push the country into another civil war. Bahrain's royal family is still in power despite massive protests bringing nearly a third of its citizens into the street to face violent crackdown by security forces. And Syria is in an all out civil war with a staggering death toll of several thousand people. By comparison, the Tunisian case is a best-case scenario. However, there are many challenges that face Tunisia today and that require a careful diagnoses and thoughtful interventions.

This Chapter traced the root causes of the transformations that marked the economic, social, and political events leading up to the 2011 uprisings, with a particular emphasis on the role of the 1980s economic crisis and the role of neo-liberal reforms in ending the social contract and moving the secular middle class closer to the Islamist movement in Tunisia. Any new administration that aims to address Tunisia's pressing challenges must, therefore, avoid cosmetic changes and political rhetoric if it is serious about addressing youth unemployment, economic inequality, labor disputes, widespread corruption, social exclusion, judicial reform, religious freedom, freedom of speech, and civil rights. It is inevitable that many of the demands of Tunisian civil society cannot be achieved without an economic plan that is capable of producing large numbers of good paying jobs for the unemployed youth. However, given the fragile political and security environment in the region as well as the dire economic circumstances of Tunisia's major trading partners (such as the ongoing fiscal crisis in the Eurozone) and the global economic slowdown, it is very hard to imagine any significant improvements in export revenues, tourism, workers remittances, or FDI flows. In addition, it is unreasonable to expect domestic business investment to drive job creation in the absence of a predictable business and political environment. Therefore, the urgency of direct job creation is undeniable (Karray 2011). Tunisia must vehemently reject neoliberalism and turn toward an employment-led growth model rather than export-led and debt-driven growth models (Kaboub 2007, 2012). Direct job creation programs are not silver bullet solutions to Tunisia's economic problems, therefore they must be accompanied by a wide range of political, judicial, educational, environmental, agricultural, industrial, and trade reforms that are tailor-made to take advantage of Tunisia's existing resources and the skills of its unemployed population (Pickard and Schweitzer 2012). However, rhetorical hopes for better economic and political outcomes are dangerously misleading if one does not focus on well-targeted active labor market policies.

Acknowledgments

I am grateful to Shu-Wen Chye, Mehdi Ben Guirat, Ishac Diwan, Rana Odeh, Brendan Mark, Lena Salaymeh, Laura Venzke and two anonymous referees for their thoughtful comments and constructive criticism. This research project benefited from financial support from the Economic Research Forum and the Denison University Research Foundation.

References

Al-Dimassi, H. 2012. "The social and political significance of the middle class." In *Tunisia's Revolution: Causes, Contexts, and Challenges*, ed., ACRPS [In Arabic]. Doha, Qatar: ACRPS.

Alexander, C. 2010a. "Tunisia: The best bet." In *The Islamists Are Coming: Who they Really Are*, ed. Wright R. Washington, DC: Woodrow Wilson international Center for Scholars.

Alexander, C. 2010b. *Tunisia: Stability and Reform in the Modern Maghreb*. Washington, DC: Routledge.

Beau, N. and C. Graciet. 2009. *La Régente de Cartahage: Main Basse sur la Tunisie*. Paris, France: La Découverte.

Bedoui, M. and R. Gouia. 1995. "Patterns and processes of social exclusion in Tunisia." In *Social Exclusion: Rhetoric, Reality, Responses*, eds. Rodgers, G. and J. Figueiredo. Geneva, Switzerland: International Institute for Labour Studies.

Belev, B. 2000. *Forcing Freedom: Political Control of Privatization and Economic Opening in Egypt and Tunisia*. Lanham, MD: University Press of America.

Bellin, E. R. 2002. *Stalled Democracy: Capital, Labor, and the Paradox of State-Sponsored Development*. Ithaca, New York: Cornell University Press.

Ben Salah, A. 1977. "Tunisia: Endogenous development and structural transformation." In *Another Development: Approaches and Strategies*, ed. Nerfin, M. Uppsala, Sweden: Dag Hammarskjöld Foundation.

Bradley, J. R. 2012. *After the Arab Spring: How Islamists Hijacked the Middle East Revolts.* New York: Palgrave Macmillan.
Brisson, Z. and K. Krontiris. 2012. *Tunisia: From Revolution to Institutions.* Washington, DC: The World Bank.
Diamond, L. 2010. "Why are there no Arab democracies?" *Journal of Democracy*, 21: 93–104.
Elsafi, Z. 2006. *Labour Law* (In Arabic), Tunis: Centre de Publication Universitaire.
Erdle, S. 2010. *Ben Ali's 'New Tunisia' (1987–2009): A Case Study of Authoritarian Modernization in the Arab World.* Berlin, Germany: Klaus Schwarz Verlag.
Erdle, S. 2004. "Tunisia: Economic and political restoration." In *Arab Elites: Negotiating the Politics of Change*, ed. Perthes, V. Boulder, CO: Lynne Rienner Publishers.
Goodwin, J. 2001. *No Other Way Out: States and Revolutionary Movements, 1945–1991.* Cambridge, UK: Cambridge University Press.
Hibou, B. 2011. *The Force of Obedience: The Political Economy of Repression in Tunisia*, Cambridge, United Kingdom: Polity Press.
Hroub, K. 2012. "Qatar and the Arab Spring." *Perspectives*, 4: 35–41.
Huntington, S. P. 1984. "Will more countries become democratic?" *Political Science Quarterly*, 99: 193–218.
Kaboub, F. 2012. "From neoliberalism to social justice: The feasibility of full employment in Tunisia." *Review of Radical Political Economics*, 44: 305–312.
Kaboub, F. 2007. "ELR-led economic development: A plan for Tunisia." Working Paper No. 499, Annandale-on-Hudson, NY: The Levy Economics Institute, April.
Karray, C. G. 2011. *La Prochaine Guerre en Tunisie: La Victoire en Cinq Batailles.* [In French] Tunis, Tunisia: Cérès Editions.
Khosrokhavar, F. 2012. *The New Arab Revolutions That Shook the World.* Boulder, CO: Paradigm Publishers.
Lawson, G. 2005. "Negotiated revolutions: The prospects for radical change in contemporary world politics." *Review of International Studies*, 31: 473–493.
Lawson, G. 2011. "Halliday's revenge: Revolutions and international relations." *International Affairs*, 87: 1067–1085.
Lewis, B. 1993. *Islam and the West.* Oxford: Oxford University Press.
Lynch, M. 2012. *The Arab Uprising: The Unfinished Revolutions of the New Middle East.* New York: PublicAffairs.
Moore, B. Jr. 1978. *Injustice: The Social Bases of Obedience and Revolt.* White Plains, New York: M.E. Sharpe.
Murphy, E. C. 1999. *Economic and Political Change in Tunisia: From Bourguiba to Ben Ali.* London, UK: Macmillan Press.
Nabli, M. K., B. Mejda, B. Mohamed, M. El Abbasi, R. El Ferktaji and B. Talbi. 2002. "Trade, finance, and competitiveness in Tunisia." In *Finance and Competitiveness in Developing Countries*, eds. Fanelli, J. M. and R. Medhora. London, UK: Routledge.
Owen, R. 2012. *The Rise and Fall of Arab Presidents for Life.* Cambridge, MA: President and Fellows of Harvard College.
Pargeter, A. 2012. "Radicalization in Tunisia." In *Islamist Radicalisation in North Africa: Politics and Process*, ed. Joffé, G. New York: Routledge.
Perkins, K. J. 2004. *A History of Modern Tunisia.* Cambridge, UK: Cambridge University Press.
Perthes, V. 2004. "Politics and elite change in the Arab world." In *Arab Elites: Negotiating the Politics of Change*, ed. Perthes, V. Boulder, CO: Lynne Rienner Publishers.
Pickard, D. and T. Schweitzer. 2012. *Overcoming the Binding Constraint to Economic Growth in Post-Revolution Tunisia.* Cambridge, MA: John F. Kennedy School of Government.

Ramadan, T. 2011. *L'Islam et le Réveil Arabe.* [In French] Montreal, Quebec: Presse du Châtelet.

Schraeder, P. J. 2012. "Tunisia's jasmine revolution, international intervention, and popular sovereignty." *The Whitehead Journal of Diplomacy and International Relations*, 13: 75–88.

Skocpol, T. 1979. *States and Social Revolutions: A Comparative Analysis of France, Russia and China.* Cambridge, UK: Cambridge University Press.

Trotsky, L. 1997 (orig. pub. date 1932) *The History of the Russian Revolution.* London, UK: Pluto Press.

White, G. 2001. *A Comparative Political Economy of Tunisia and Morocco: On the Outside of Europe Looking In.* Albany, NY: State University of New York Press.

World Bank, 2010. "Country brief: Tunisia." Washington, DC: The World Bank.

Zitouni, M. 2011. *La Lutte des Verts Contre la Dictature du Géneral Ben Ali.* [In French] Tunis, Tunisia: Orbis Impression.

A TRANSITION TO DEMOCRACY?

Chapter 4

ON THE DETERMINANTS OF DEMOCRATIC TRANSITIONS

Caroline Freund and Melise Jaud

1. Introduction

In 2011, the people of Tunisia, Egypt, Libya, and Yemen toppled autocratic regimes that had governed these nations for decades. Change came suddenly in Egypt and Tunisia, while a period of conflict engulfed Libya and Yemen before new leaders were elected. The uprisings also spread to Syria where violent conflict continues and resolution remains uncertain. In contrast, the Kingdoms of Jordan and Morocco responded to demands for change with partial reform. The revolutions brought hope for democracy and prosperity in these countries, with more voice for the citizens, accountability of the government, and more opportunities for the youth. In order to understand how political systems in the region are likely to evolve, transition experiences from around the world over the last 50 years have been taken as a guide.

In this Chapter, we build a new dataset of democratic transitions and investigate the role of a host of structural, political, and societal factors on the likelihood of attempting democratic transition and after it has been tried, whether it has been successful. We pay particular attention to the role of natural resources and gender equality in education — both relevant issues for the Middle East and North Africa (MENA) region. Vast literature has emphasized the negative impact of natural resources on democracy (Acemoglu *et al.* 2004; Ross 2001). For MENA countries, an important impediment to democratization may be their oil-rich soil. Regarding the role of gender equality, there is empirical evidence that it matters for economic growth (Barro 1991; Dollar and Gatti 1999). However, its role for democracy has received little attention. For the most part, MENA countries have made considerable progress in closing gender gaps in education outcomes. Can we correlate this evolution with the recent ongoing political changes?

This Chapter has several new findings. First, the swift completion of democratic transition is by no means guaranteed, but it is doable. 90 countries have changed regimes in the last half century. Of these, nearly half the countries that have tried (46%) have succeeded and experienced a successful transition to democracy. 39% had a failed transition, and 15% moved gradually toward democracy.

The second important contribution is the strong evidence that gender equality and natural resources are important factors for the likelihood of regime change and the stability of democracy. In particular, we find that the literacy gap between women and men — the ratio of the share of women that are educated to the share of men that are educated — has a positive and significant effect on both the likelihood of transition and the likelihood of its success. It could be that societies that invest more in their whole population are inherently more democratic. Alternatively, the presence of women's voices during a transition may lead to less violence and less chance of reversal. This novel result suggests that future work should focus on identifying the precise mechanisms at play. We also find that resource-rich countries are less likely to attempt transition, and when they do they are more likely to fail. While recent gains in female literacy offer reasons for optimism for a rapid transition in the MENA countries undergoing transitions, resource-rich countries (such as Libya and Egypt) may face additional challenges.

Finally, the Chapter uncovers several additional determinants of transitions and their success. Consistent with previous studies, we find that conflict, a military government, and urbanization are factors that matter in contributing to whether a transition is smooth or not. Importantly, we find evidence of strong neighborhood effects — an attempt at transition in the region in the last two years makes all countries more likely to attempt transition; and a successful transition in the region makes other countries more likely to be successful. Thus, one successful transition in MENA can have a big impact in terms of leading to similar outcomes in other countries in the region.

Our work relates to a vast literature on the determinants and economic effects of democracy. A large number of empirical studies have investigated how democratization correlates with various economic and non-economic variables (Barro 1999). More recently several studies have tried to go beyond correlations and establish causal relationships (Przeworski *et al.* 2000; Acemoglu and Robinson 2006; Acemoglu *et al.* 2008; Epstein *et al.* 2006; Papaioannou and Siourounis 2008). However, most empirical studies either exploit changes in levels of available political freedom indicators, or construct binary indicators of political transitions from autocracy to democracy without paying much attention to the transition process itself. Different transition processes may occur under different set of conditions and may yield different economic outcomes. We contribute to the literature by constructing a new classification of democratic transitions — the successful, gradual, and failed — according to the speed, intensity, and permanency of the political reform process. This new classification allows us to examine failed versus successful transitions, and rapid versus gradual transitions.

The remainder of the paper proceeds as follows. The next section presents the data and the methodology to identify the three types of democratic transitions, successful, gradual, and failed before examining the incidence of democratic transitions in the World and MENA. Sections 3 and 4 look into the factors associated with transitions and their durability. Finally, Section 5 offers some lessons relevant for MENA and concludes.

2. What Do Democratic Transitions Look Like?

Figure 4.1 shows the evolution of the level of democracy, using the Polity IV index, between 1960 and 2010. The MENA region remained mostly untouched by the wave of democratization that was initiated in Latin America in the late 1970s, which then spread to Asia, and Southern and Eastern Europe in the 1990s, and finally to some parts of sub-Saharan Africa by the late 1990s? The Arab Spring has ignited change in the region, however there is uncertainty regarding the scope, the pace, and the durability of the political transitions.

2.1. *Identifying democratic transitions: Successful, gradual, and failed*

In this section we construct a new dataset of political transitions from autocracy to democracy. Defining democracy is a controversial methodological issue in political

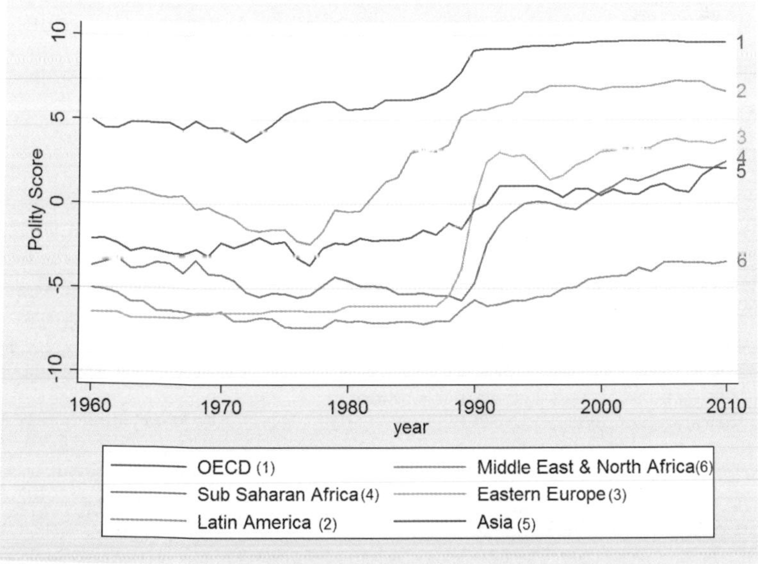

Fig. 4.1. Evolution of democracy across regions, 1960–2010.

Source: Polity IV, 2010; Statistics are computed as simple averages of the Polity score at the country level.

science. We follow the standard approach and rely on one of a handful of available measures of democracy, the composite Polity indicator from the Polity IV database (Marshall *et al.* 2010).[1] The Polity score is employed to identify three types of transitions — the successful, the gradual and the failed — based on the intensity, the speed, and the sustainability of the political reform process.[2] The sample includes 160 countries between 1960 and 2010.[3]

A successful transition is defined as a substantial rapid and sustained regime change from autocracy to democracy. A transition in time t qualifies as successful if the following conditions are met:

(i) The Polity score increased by at least 6 points over a 3-year period,
(ii) the Polity score in time t is above 5,
(iii) following transition the Polity score remains stable above 5 until the end of the time period,
(iv) the regime in place has been non-democratic for at least 5 years prior to transition.

Condition (i) ensures a sudden and substantial political-regime change. Condition (ii) marks the year of transition as the year the Polity score increased and ensures that a minimum level of democracy is reached in the first year of the transition. Condition (iii) ensures that the transition is sustained with no reversal to autocratic regime. Finally condition (iv) ensures that the transition is a regime change from autocracy to democracy and not a recovery from a previous drop in the Polity score.

A gradual transition is defined as a substantial, gradual, and sustained regime change from autocracy to democracy. A transition in time t qualifies as gradual if the following conditions are met:

(i) The Polity score increased by at least 6 points over a 4 to 15-year period,

[1]The Polity IV index attempts to capture not only outcomes but also procedural rules. It is based on three components: (i) the competitiveness of political participation, (ii) the openness and competitiveness of executive recruitment, and (iii) the constraints on the executive. It is a composite index, computed as the difference between a democracy and an autocracy score. The index ranges from -10 to $+10$ with higher values indicating higher level of political freedom. The main limitation of the index is that by construction it does not aim to classify political regimes. It remains nonetheless the democracy indicator that is most widely used with a broad time and geographic coverage.

[2]Several empirical studies construct binary indicators of political transitions from autocracy to democracy, however they incorporate limited information on the transition process itself see for example Przeworski *et al.* (1996a); Papaioannou and Siourounis (2008). In particular, unlike our classification previous classifications these studies do not explicitly account for the speed and intensity of the transition on the one hand and its permanency on the other hand.

[3]The dataset dates back to 1800. The data is used starting from 1960 to match the growth data. The data is not rectangular, as some countries were created during the time period (e.g., the former soviet bloc countries), or changed names (e.g., Czechoslovakia that split into the Czech Republic and the Slovak Republic in 1992). New states and states that changed names are treated as new countries in the analysis.

(ii) the Polity score in time $t + 15$ is above 5,
(iii) the Polity score in time t is at least 0,
(iv) following transition, the Polity score remains stable above 5 until the end of the time period,
(v) the regime in place has been non-democratic for at least 5 years prior to transition.

Conditions (i) and (ii) ensure that the change in political regime occurs over a longer time period allowing cases where the democratization process has been more uncertain, to be identified. Condition (i) also ensures that there is no overlap with the successful transitions. Condition (iii) ensures a gradual transition starts with an increase in the Polity score and marks the year of initiation of the transition. Conditions (iv) and (v) are the same as for a successful transition.

A failed transition is defined as a 'non-successful transition'. That is, at least one condition in the set of 'successful' conditions is not met. Either, the regime change is not substantial enough and a transition in time t qualifies as failed if the following conditions are met:

A {
(i) The Polity score increased by at least 3 points over a 3-year period,
(ii) the Polity score in time t is above 0 but at most 5,
(iii) the regime in place has been non-democratic for at least 5 years prior to transition.

Alternatively, the regime change is substantial but not sustained and a transition in time t qualifies as failed if the following conditions are met:

B {
(i) The Polity score increased by at least 6 points over a 3-year period,
(ii) the Polity score in time t is above 5,
(iii) following transition, the Polity score is not maintained above 5 until the end of the time period,
(iv) the regime in place has been non-democratic for at least 5 years prior to transition.

Conditions A.(i) and A.(ii) identify cases of partial transitions where limited improvement in political freedom has been achieved. There is a move away from an autocratic regime but a full-democratic regime is not reached. Finally condition A.(iii) is the same as before. Conditions B.(i)–(iv) identify cases of total but unsustained transitions. Conditions B.(i)–(iii) ensure that the transition is substantial and rapid but that the country reverts to a non-democratic form of ruling before the end of the sample period. Condition B.(iv) is the same as before. Conditions A.(ii) and B.(ii) mark the year of transition as the year the Polity score increased.

Figure 4.2 presents an example of a successful, a gradual, and a failed transition, as defined above. Lebanon in 2005 is a typical illustration of a successful transition, moving from autocratic to fully democratic within a 3-year period. In

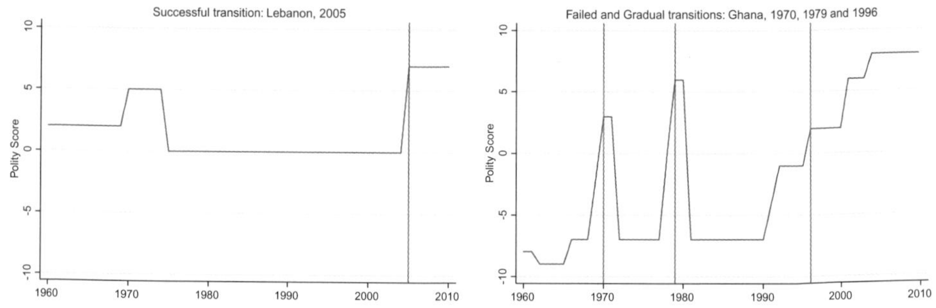

Fig. 4.2. Democratic transitions: Successful, gradual and failed.
Source: Polity IV (2010) and authors' calculations.

contrast, Ghana on the contrary experienced two failed transitions in 1970 and 1979, when the country experienced substantial but unsustained democratic regime changes. In 1996 Ghana initiated a gradual transition and democratized over an 8-year period.

2.2. *How frequent are democratic transitions?*

Our identification conditions yield 90 democratic transitions initiated between 1965 and 2005, including: 41 successful, 14 gradual, 35 failed.[4] Table A in the appendix lists all transitions by category, country, year, and non-transition countries in our sample. Of the 160 countries in the sample, 79, more than 50%, initiated a democratic transition, with 10 countries experiencing more than one transition. Initiating the transition process does not guarantee completion. More than one-third of countries that moved toward greater voice and accountability in the last 50 years (39%) have failed their transition. In 46% of the countries, democracy was consolidated swiftly, while in 15% of the countries, evolution towards democracy was gradual.

Figure 4.3 shows that a typical autocratic country has about a 3% chance of experiencing a transition at some point in any given year.[5] The world average masks important regional differences. In particular, the MENA region has recorded the lowest share of democratic transitions. Out of the 19 MENA countries in the sample, four experienced a democratic transition prior to 2010. Lebanon transited successfully in 2005 while transitions in Iran in 1997, Djibouti in 1999, and Algeria in 2004 are classified as failures.

Figure 4.4 maps the episodes of democratic transitions at the beginning and the end of the sample period. It illustrates how geographical and cultural proximity may

[4]Given the data start in 1960 and goes up to 2010, episodes in the early and late years cannot be identified because the sustainability conditions are not satisfied. In addition we exclude from the sample, countries for which we do not have 9 years of consecutive annual observations.

[5]The figure shows unconditional probabilities which calculation may be biased depending on the moment in time transitions occurred (early or late in the sample period) in the countries and whether countries experienced multiple transitions.

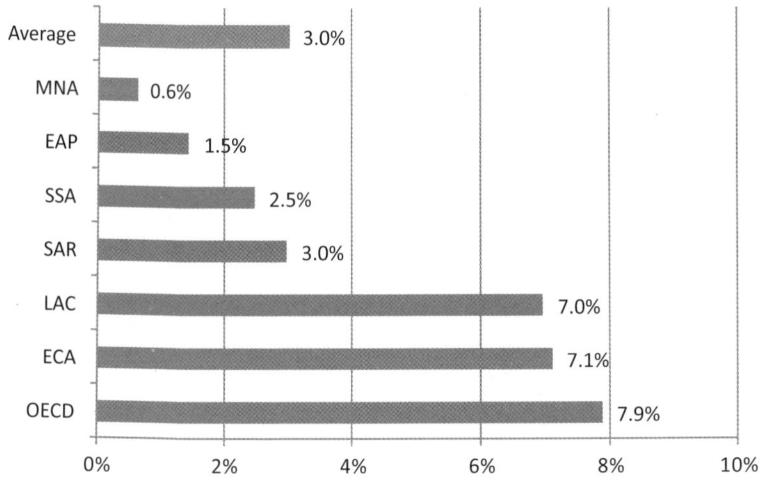

Fig. 4.3. Incidence of democratic transitions by region, 1965–2005.

Note: The average (regional) rate of incidence is computed as the ratio of the total (regional) number of transitions to the total (regional) number of potential candidates to transition. The number of potential candidates to transition is the number of country-year pairs that are under autocratic ruling and in which a transition could have occurred.

affect the way transition spreads across countries, and countries in a region tend to change (or remain unchanged) together. While most countries were autocratic in 1960, only 41 were autocratic and had not experienced an attempt at transition over the last half century in 2010. Africa is over-represented in failed transitions, while Latin America, Southern and Eastern Europe are over-represented in rapid transitions. Mainland East Asia is largely autocratic while the islands successfully evolved towards democracy. In MENA, most countries remained autocratic or failed to transition. However, recently during the Arab Spring a strong regional dynamic toward democratic change was demonstrated, with the revolution in Tunisia spreading to neighboring countries.

3. How Do Transitions Happen?

3.1. *Estimation framework*

In this section, we model the incidence of democratic transitions, that is the probability of transition from an autocracy (event = 0) to a democracy (event = 1), and test the impact of a host of factors and particularly natural resources and gender equality in education. We estimate a probit model using data until the first year the transition is observed and dropping all latter years in the sequence.[6] We restrict our

[6]In the case of countries experiencing multiple transitions, we assume that the second events are independent from the first.

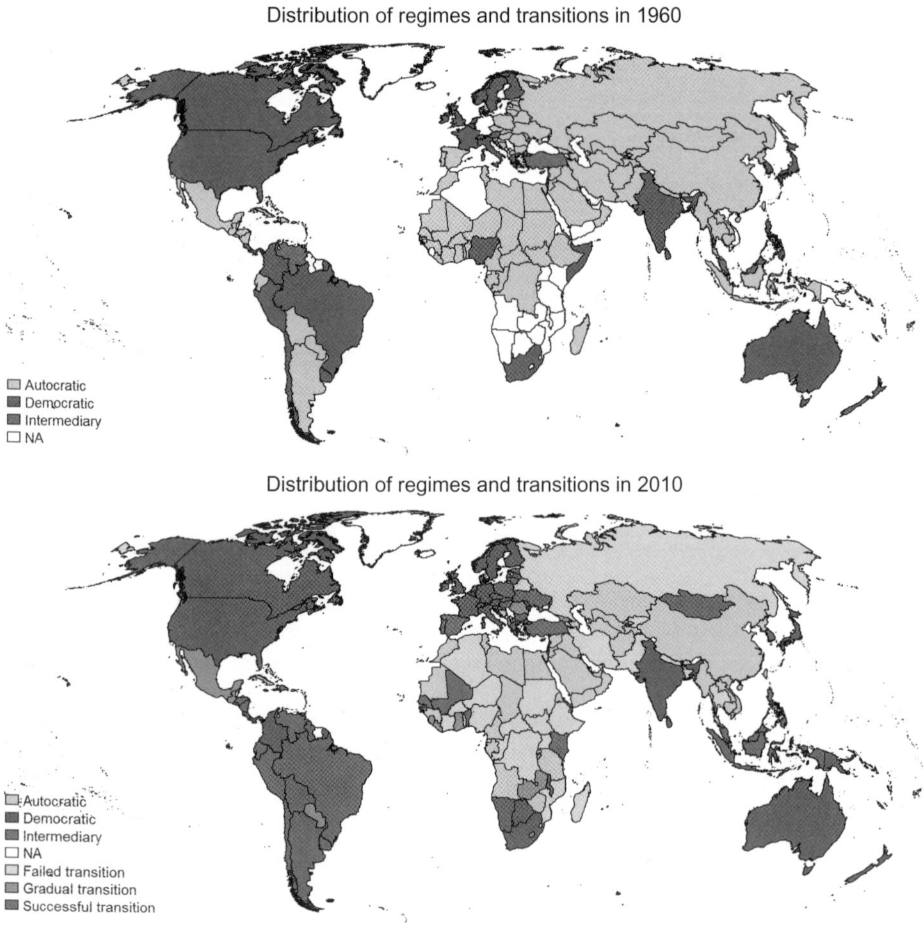

Fig. 4.4. Regimes and democratic transitions in the world, 1960–2010.
Note: NA corresponds to non-independent countries.

sample to countries that experienced a transition to democratization, whether successful, gradual or failed, and potential candidates — these include countries under autocratic ruling in which a transition could have occurred. Specifically, we estimate the following model:

$$\pi_{i,t} \equiv \Pr(Democ_{i,t} = 1) = \Pr(\alpha + \beta X_{i,t} + \eta_t + \upsilon_{i,t} > 0)$$

$$where\ Democ_{i,t} = \begin{cases} 0 & \text{if } t < T^* \\ 1 & \text{if } t = T^* \\ \text{missing} & \text{if } t > T^* \end{cases} \tag{4.1}$$

where $\pi_{i,t}$ is the probability that country i experienced a transition in year t. The variable $Democ_{it}$ is an indicator variable for country i, taking value 0 in the years prior to transition, 1 in the year of the transition (T^*), and missing values for all subsequent years. The vector X_{it} is a vector of time varying covariates including an indicator variable marking natural-resource rich countries, and a variable controlling for gender equality in education. The definitions of the controls and sources are detailed in Table B in the appendix. All specifications include a set of time effects to control for time-varying shocks that affect all countries. Finally, v_{it} is an error term. Table C in the appendix contains summary statistics for key data.

In this framework, we do not seek to establish causality. However several potential sources of endogeneity should be noted. First, there is an issue of reverse causality since transition to democracy may cause some of the covariates to vary rather than the other way round. Second, there is the potential for omitted variable bias. Other factors not controlled for in the specification may determine both the change of the political regime and the variation in some of the covariates, including economic growth, income etc. Because our model is non-linear in parameters, including country fixed effects — to control for country-specific factors affecting both covariates and the probability of transition — would creàte an incidental parameters problem. One possibility is to estimate the model using Chamberlains fixed-effects logit. However, this comes at the cost of having to exclude countries that never experienced a democratic transition from our sample. In order to limit the potential omitted variable bias, in all specifications we further include a dummy variable for colonial status, to control for colonial heritage in institutions, a dummy variable for island and landlocked countries, as the different external environment may influence the emergence of democracy in those countries.

3.2. *Empirical results*

Table 4.1 reports estimates of Eq. (4.1). We report probit marginal effects computed at means for all continuous regressors and robust standard errors clustered at the country level (in parentheses). Column (1) controls for standard socio-economic factors–industrialization, urbanization, wealth, and education — associated with democratization as proposed in the economic and political science literature (Barro 1999; Przeworski *et al.* 2000; Glaeser *et al.* 2007; Acemoglu *et al.* 2009). Our results suggest that rich authoritarian countries are less likely to transition to democracy. Put differently, dictatorships are more likely to survive in wealthy countries, perhaps because populations are more satisfied with their standard of living. However, the magnitude of the effect is small. The coefficient on *lnGDPpc* suggests that a tripling of the per capita GDP — roughly a one standard deviation change — reduces the probability of transition by 2.3 to 3.7 percentage points. This result contrasts with some previous empirical studies. Cross-sectional regression analyses have positively related improvements in per capita income to democratization (Barro 1999; Przeworski *et al.* 2000). However, this relationship does not hold once constant country specific factors are controlled (Acemoglu *et al.* 2009). We find no evidence that

Table 4.1. Determinants of democratic transitions.

	(1)	(2)	(3)	(4)	(5)
lnGDPpc	−0.023***	−0.032***	−0.032***	−0.035***	−0.037***
	(−2.915)	(−3.578)	(−3.609)	(−4.715)	(−4.370)
growthGDP	0.026	0.039	0.044	0.037	0.022
	(0.357)	(0.580)	(0.732)	(0.437)	(0.253)
urbanrate	0.123**	0.196***	0.204***	0.199***	0.194***
	(2.533)	(3.640)	(3.679)	(4.212)	(3.821)
lnpopulation	0.009**	0.010**	0.010**	0.005	0.004
	(2.373)	(2.323)	(2.450)	(1.236)	(0.937)
democratic K	0.062*	0.048	0.044	0.024	0.023
	(1.884)	(1.503)	(1.430)	(0.884)	(0.894)
polright	0.003	0.005	0.006	0.004	0.004
	(0.650)	(1.013)	(1.120)	(0.752)	(0.797)
literacyrate		0.023	−0.079	−0.065	−0.063
		(0.883)	(−1.602)	(−1.224)	(−1.269)
natressource		−0.042***	−0.039***	−0.027**	−0.026**
		(−3.084)	(−2.965)	(−2.256)	(−2.202)
FM_literacyratio			0.128**	0.126**	0.129***
			(2.320)	(2.219)	(2.577)
trade opness				−0.025	−0.026
				(−1.370)	(−1.376)
FDI				−0.275*	−0.261
				(−1.679)	(−1.640)
WTO				0.020	0.022
				(0.842)	(0.911)
war					−0.002
					(−0.190)
crisis					−0.003
					(−0.237)
Time effects	yes	yes	yes	yes	yes
Observations	964	964	869	869	869
Pseudo R2	0.100	0.122	0.122	0.122	0.122
Nb countries	84	84	79	79	79
Nb transitions	47	47	41	41	41

Note: The reported coefficients are marginal effects computed at means for all continuous regressors. Constants are not reported. Standard errors are clustered at the country level. T-statistics are in parentheses. *, **, and *** denote statistical significance at the 10, 5, and 1 percent levels, respectively.

democratization tends to follow periods of low GDP growth, the coefficient on the average GDP growth variable is insignificant.

Following Barro (1999) we control for the rate of urbanization, *urbanrate*, and the country size with the log level of the population, *lnpopulation*. The coefficient on the urbanization variable implies that a standard deviation increase in the urbanization rate increase the likelihood of transition by 4.2%. A population that is better connected and able to organize and engage in collective actions is more likely to attempt to overthrow an authoritarian regime. Previous experience with democratic institutions may affect a country's future attempts at transition (Persson and Tabellini

2009). We control for the number of years a country has been a democracy, or its democratic capital, *democracy_K*, and find a positive but not significant effect.[7] We also include as a regressor the country's level of political right, using the political right index from the Freedom of House dataset (2010). The index measures the right to participate freely in the political process and countries are graded between 1 (most free) and 7 (least free). If the presence of more political freedom motivates people to engage in collective actions that lead to new or improved democracies (Inglehart and Welzel 2005), we would expect a negative coefficient on our variable of interest *polright*. Our data does not support this hypothesis. Also, including the variable on the right-hand side allows us to control to some extent for country specific cultural features and reduce the potential country-specific omitted characteristics bias.

In columns (2) and (3) we augment specification in column (1) with our two variables of interest, natural resources and gender equality. Our sample includes 39 resource-rich countries, out of which 13 are Middle Eastern countries.[8,9] Natural resource richness stands out as an important obstacle to democratic transition, and resource-rich countries have a probability of transition 2.6 pps to 4.2 pps lower than their resource-poor counterparts. This is consistent with the literature on natural resources and accountability, which argues that less accountability is demanded from governments that do not tax the population (e.g., Acemoglu *et al.* 2004; Ross 2001).

Considering gender equality, the empirical gender and growth literature shows that gender inequality in education hurts economic growth. In column (3) we test whether it affects the probability of regime change too. We include a variable, *FM_literacyratio*, defined as the ratio of the share of women that are educated to the share of men that are educated.[10] The results suggest that gender equality in education has a positive and statistically significant effect on transition. Specifically, the gap between male and female education discourages transition and the bigger the gap the less likely you are to swiftly reach democracy. A one standard deviation increase in the ratio of female to male literates raises the probability of transition by 2.7 percent. While more research on the mechanism is needed, one possible explanation for the effect of gender equality on the political reform process may be that

---

[7]Democratic capital accumulates in years of democracy and in countries with democratic neighbors, but depreciates under autocracy.

[8]Alternatively, we run regressions using the average level of years of schooling in the population aged above 15 (Barro and Lee 2001). Results are robust and available upon request. However, the number of observations is significantly reduced. To conserve the largest sample, we report results using the literacy rate.

[9]List provided in International Monetary Fund, Fiscal Affairs Department, 2007. "Guide on Resource Revenue Transparency." Countries are considered rich in hydrocarbons and/or mineral resources on the basis of the following criteria: (i) an average share of hydrocarbon and/or mineral fiscal revenues in total fiscal revenue of at least 25% during the period 2000–2005 or (ii) an average share of hydrocarbon and/or mineral export proceeds in total export proceeds of at least 25% during the period 2000–2005.

[10]The literacy rate data is from the World Development Indicators, 2011. The World Bank. The data is linearly interpolated when missing.

democracy is about citizen's rights, and societies with education equality are effectively valuing all citizens both more highly and more equally.[11] Specification (3) is our preferred specification and is used as a basis for sensitivity checks.

In columns (4) and (5) we control for additional factors and further check the robustness of these effects. Column (4) controls for trade openness, WTO membership and FDI while column (5) controls for whether the country is in crisis (banking crisis) or at war. The coefficients on our variable of interest, *natresource*, and *FM_literacyratio*, remain statistically significant. The coefficients on the macro economic variables are not statistically significant suggesting that countries that underwent democratic transitions are on average similar to countries that did not in terms of macroeconomic conditions.

Table 4.2 augments specification in column (3) in Table 4.1 with additional controls and provides further evidence of the importance of the role of natural resources and female literacy for the democratic transition. To conserve space in Table 4.2 we only present the coefficient estimates associated with our key variables of interest, *natresource* and *FM_literacyrate*, and the additional covariates controlled for. The coefficient on the gender literacy gap variable remains positive and statistically significant in all but specification (6). In specification (6) the coefficient estimate increases and is only marginally insignificant at the 10 percent. This is likely due to a significantly reduced sample. The estimates on the natural resource variable are negative and statistically significant in all specifications, further suggesting the importance of both factors on the ability of countries to transition.

Turning to the additional covariates, in column (1) we explore the link between conflict and democratization. An attempt at transition is more likely to emerge in the aftermath of minor conflicts ($<1,000$ deaths) while large scale wars ($>1,000$ deaths) do not trigger changes in the political structure.[12,13] In column (2) we control for the form of regime in place at the time of the transition. Out of the 35 military regime countries in the sample, 23 were under military ruling in the two years preceding transition. The coefficient on the variable *military*, suggest that a military rule encourages transition.

---

[11]Alternatively, we run regressions controlling for the fertility rate of women in the population. The coefficient on the fertility rate variable is close to zero and is not statistically significant, while the coefficient on the gender gap in education variable remains positive and statistically significant, suggesting that the effect of gender equality in education on transition does not work through a reduction in the fertility of women. We do not report these results as controlling for the fertility rate in the regression drastically reduces the sample. However results are available upon request.

[12]There is a large literature that relates natural resources endowment, conflict, and democracy (e.g., Collier and Hoeffler 2004). Importantly, in our analysis the coefficients on our natural resource and conflict variables remain significant and qualitatively the same whether included separately or jointly in the regression, suggesting that the inclusion of both variables as determinants of the likelihood of transition does not bias our results.

[13]This result contrasts with previous works that suggest a negative relationship between civil strife and democracy. Such studies rely on the level of democracy rather than the likelihood of transition (Collier and Hoeffler 2004).

Table 4.2. Additional determinants of democratic transitions.

	(1)	(2)	(3)	(4)	(5)	(6)	(7)
natressource	−0.037***	−0.036***	−0.036***	−0.040***	−0.039***	−0.094***	−0.040**
	(−2.910)	(−2.802)	(−2.871)	(−2.874)	(−2.712)	(−3.574)	(−2.572)
FM_literacyratio	0.112**	0.099*	0.099*	0.130**	0.125**	0.273	0.105*
	(1.992)	(1.772)	(1.873)	(2.224)	(2.096)	(1.558)	(1.800)
conflict	0.040***	0.041***					
	(2.904)	(3.049)					
war	−0.017	−0.017					
	(−1.335)	(−1.406)					
military		0.022**					
		(2.144)					
region transition			0.004**				
			(2.287)				
leader age				−0.019			
				(−0.620)			
regime length				0.002			
				(0.246)			
youth					−0.003		
					(−0.807)		
inequality						0.001	
						(1.016)	
ethnicfract							0.045*
							(1.745)
catholicism							0.063**
							(2.292)
protestantism							0.008
							(0.098)
islam							0.028
							(1.016)
Time effects	yes	yes	yes	yes	yes	yes	yes
Observations	957	957	957	918	901	177	782
Pseudo R2	0.129	0.136	0.124	0.114	0.105	0.270	0.132
Nb countries	84	84	84	82	83	35	64
Nb transitions	47	47	47	47	45	17	41

Note: The method of estimation is Maximum Likelihood. The reported coefficients are marginal effects computed at means for all continuous regressors. Standard errors are clustered at the country level. The dependent variable is the probability that country i experienced a democratic transition in year t. Countries with less than twenty years of observation for the dependent variable are dropped from the sample. All specifications augment specification in column (3) in Table 1 with additional controls. To conserve space only the coefficient estimates associated with our key variables of interest, natresource and FM_literacyratio, and the additional covariates are reported. The constant is not reported. T-statistics are in parentheses. *, **, and *** denote statistical significance at the 10 percent, 5 percent, and 1 percent levels, respectively.

Column (3) explores the neighborhood effect of transitions. The likelihood of a country's democratization is partly dependent on external factors. In particular, there is evidence that democratizations occur in waves, with democratization in one country being favored by political changes in neighbor countries (Huntington 1991). Importantly, a favorable regional environment may influence the democratization process. To capture this influence, we consider the frequency of democratic transition in the region country i is nested in, over the past two years, *region_transition*. There is a neighborhood effect, such that an attempt at transition in the region in the last two years makes all countries more likely to attempt transition.

Column (4) explores whether the characteristics of the leader and regime in place can predict revolutions. Bueno de Mesquita *et al.* (2003) develop a game theory model where they show that old autocrats with possibly short life expectancies or newly established autocrats, who have not yet sorted out loyalties, are more likely to be overthrown. We control for the age of the leader in place as well as the time the regime has been in power. Both coefficients are statistically insignificant.

Columns (5) to (7) consider several societal factors particularly relevant to the MENA region. The uprisings in MENA were initiated by the young population. Experiences from 50 years of transitions however suggest no significant association between the size of the youth in the population and the initiation of transition (column 5). An important number of empirical studies have demonstrated the negative association between income inequality and the quality of institutions (Barro 1999; Easterly 2001). In the case on MENA countries, Diwan (2012) argues that the middle class has played a significant role in initiating transitions, and may help bring them to a swift close. We find no supportive evidence that income inequality affects the probability of transition in our sample.[14] In column (7) we examine how ethnic and religious diversity affect the democratization process. Empirical evidence is ambiguous. In particular, the heterogeneity in the population with respect to ethnicity may negatively affect democratization, as establishing a working democracy may be more difficult if different interest groups are fighting over power (Aghion *et al.* 2004). The coefficient on our ethnic fractionalization variable is positive and statistically significant at the 10%, suggesting that ethnic fractionalization promotes democratization, perhaps because democracy is the fairest way of governing rival factions. Our result contrasts with previous findings that democracy is inversely related to ethnic fractionalization (Alesina *et al.* 2003). However, unlike previous work, in this exercise we examine the impact of fractionalization on the onset of transition (whether successful or not) rather than the level of democracy.[15] Further research to better understand the mechanism at play is needed.

Finally, considering the role of religion on political structure, we control for the share of a countries population affiliated with three major religions, *catholicism*,

[14]Data for the Gini index are from the World Income Inequality Database, 2008. UNU-WIDER World Income Inequality Database, Version 2.0c. Information on income inequality, rarely reported on a yearly basis, is imputed in years with missing data between any two observations. We estimate specifications on a smaller sample of countries for which data for the Gini index is available.

[15]By and large, most of the literature on ethnicity and conflict, fails to find any significant evidence that more diverse societies are more prone to civil conflict. Rather than the diversity of ethnic groups, ethnic polarization, that is the contested dominance of one large group by another group, increases the probability of civil conflict (Montalvo and Reynal-Querol 2005). Importantly, in our analysis we control simultaneously for conflict and ethnic fractionalization. The coefficients on our natural resource and conflict variables remain significant and qualitatively the same whether included separately or jointly in the regression, suggesting that the inclusion of both variables as determinants of the likelihood of transition does not bias our results.

protestantis, and *islam*, in 1970. In our sample, 38 countries have as a dominant religion Islam, out of which 14 are transition countries.[16] While most studies find that democratization is less likely in countries where close links between the clergy and the state exist, in particular Muslim and Confucianism countries (Midlarsky 1998; Barro 1999; Ross 2001), our results do not support a significant role for Islamic values in either promoting or retarding transition.

3.3. *Robustness checks*

Table 4.3 explores the robustness of our main results on natural resources and gender equality. Table 4.3 re-estimates the effect of these two variables on the probability of transition using the specification of column 3 in Table 4.1 as our benchmark model. To conserve space we only present the coefficient estimates associated with our key variables of interest, *FM_literacyrate* and *natresource.*

It may be that the collinearity between the literacy rate and the female to male literacy ratio variables is driving our result. Column 1 tests the sensitivity of our estimates using an alternative proxy for gender equality in education, namely the

Table 4.3. Robustness checks: Determinants of democratic transitions.

	Alternative indicator for literacy gap (1)	Time and regional fixed effects (2)	Randon effects probit (3)
natressource	−0.039**	−0.033**	−0.532***
	(−2.562)	(−2.561)	(−2.787)
schooling gap	0.011*		
	(1.673)		
FM_literacyratio		0.089*	1.891**
		(1.881)	(2.073)
Observations	778	964	964
Pseudo R2	0.0929	0.151	0.0179
Nb countries	67	84	84
Nb transitions	41	47	47

Note: The method of estimation is Maximum Likelihood. The reported coefficients are marginal effects computed at means for all continuous regressors. Standard errors are clustered at the country level. The dependent variable is the probability that country i experienced a democratic transition in year t. Countries with less than twenty years of observation for the dependent variable are dropped from the sample. All specifications use specification in column (3) in Table 4.1. To conserve space only the coefficient estimates associated with our key variables of interest, natresource and FM_literacyratio are reported. The constant is not reported. T-statistics are in parentheses. *, **, and *** denote statistical significance at the 10 percent, 5 percent, and 1 percent levels, respectively.

[16] Albania, Algeria, Bangladesh, Comoros, Indonesia, the Islamic Republic of Iran, the Kyrgyz Republic, Mali, Niger, Nigeria, Pakistan, Senegal, Sierra Leone, and Sudan.

difference in years of schooling between female and male in the population aged above 15.[17] Our results are robust to using an alternative proxy for the gender gap in education. Column 2 controls for regional dynamics and include year*region fixed effects. Results are robust to controlling for year-region fixed effects. Finally, column 3 re-estimates the models using a random effects probit model to check that our results are not biased due to country-specific unobserved heterogeneity. Our results are qualitatively robust to controlling for random effects.

4. What Makes Transitions Successful?

4.1. *Estimation framework*

The factors that make democratic transition more likely to occur are not necessarily the factors that make such transitions, once initiated, more likely to consolidate rapidly into full democracies. With less than half of countries transiting swiftly to democracy, it is fundamental to understand what factors make democratic transitions successful, and more importantly do such factors affect whether they do so in a swift or gradual manner? In particular, do gender equality and natural resources also matter for the success of transitions? A number of empirical studies have considered the first question, looking into the determinants of the stability or survival of democracies (Przeworski *et al.* 1996b; Hadenius 1994).[18] However, none have looked into the second one.

We restrict our sample to transition events only and estimate a multinomial logit model to take advantage of the three distinct categories of transitions that we have identified. First, a transition is successful when a country has swiftly and permanently moved from autocracy to democracy. Second, a transition is gradual when a country has moved in steps towards a stable democracy. And third, a transition is failed when the transition is partial or temporary. This last category is chosen as the baseline category, since our interest is to model the probability of transition success whether swiftly or more gradually reached. Formally, the likelihood that country i transition is successful ($j = 1$) or gradual ($j = 2$) rather than failed ($j = 0$) is given by:

$$\frac{\pi_{i,j}}{\pi_{i,0}} \equiv \frac{\Pr(y_i = j)}{\Pr(y_i = 0)} = \exp(\alpha_j + \beta_j X_i' + u_i)$$
$$\text{where } j = \begin{cases} 1 & \text{if transition is successful} \\ 2 & \text{if transition is gradual} \end{cases} \tag{4.2}$$

[17]Data on years of schooling are from Barro and Lee (2001).

[18]In their 1996b paper, Przeworski and co-authors examine the relationship between economic performance, and the stability of democracy using a dataset covering 135 countries between 1950 and 1990.

The vector X_i' includes the set of controls included in Eq. (4.1) taking value the year of the transition. Table D in the appendix contains summary statistics for key data. Finally, u_i is an error term.

4.2. *Empirical results*

Table 4.4 presents the multinomial estimates for specifications that replicate those in Table 4.1. The reported coefficients are marginal effects computed at means for all regressors and robust standard errors clustered at the country level (in parentheses). The results suggest that our main variables of interest, natural resource and gender equality also matter for the success of the transition.

Results from the basic specification are reported in columns (1) to (3). The results suggest that affluence makes transition more likely to consolidate into democracies in the aftermath of transitions. The magnitude of the effect is considerable; in the sample a country moving from the median to the 75th percentile of the per capita income distribution increases the likelihood of completing transition by 35 percentage points.[19] However, in columns (4) and (5) after controlling for other macroeconomic variables, such as trade openness, FDI and WTO membership, the coefficient estimates become insignificant. This is most probably driven by the sample composition rather than an omitted variable bias.[20]

Countries with abundant natural resources are less likely to democratize, and when they do they are also less likely to succeed and more likely to evolve towards a gradual transition than resource-poor countries. However, the coefficients on this variable increase in magnitude but loose significance on the reduced sample once we control for macroeconomic conditions. One of the most robust findings is that gender equality in education also matters for a successful democratization. Greater female participation during transitions may produce a less violent revolution and it may be that more female involvement in the post-transition government brings more cooperation.

Table 4.5 reports the multinomial estimates for specifications replicating those in Table 4.2. The effect of natural resources and gender equality are robust to the inclusion of additional covariates. In most specifications the coefficients estimates on both variables remain of expected sign and statistically significant.

Turning to the additional covariates, in columns (1) and (2) we examine the effect of conflict and military involvement on the resolution of transitions. One may expect that the challenge of rebuilding the state may be arduous in countries where change involved conflict. This does not seem to be the case. Domestic conflict has no impact on completion of the democratic transition. As seen previously, military rule makes a

[19]This is roughly equivalent to a country moving from the median level of income in the lower middle income group to median level of income in the upper middle income group, that is, tripling the value of per capita GDP from $2,630 to $7,950.

[20]If we re-run specification (1) and (2) on the sample of specification (3) the coefficient on the per capita income variable are not significant anymore. Results are available upon request.

Table 4.4. Determinants of democratic success: Successful, gradual, and failed.

	(1)		(2)		(3)		(4)		(5)	
Transition to	Succ	Grad	Succ	Grad	Succ	Grad	Succ	Grad	Succ	Grad
lnGDPpc	0.352***	−0.091*	0.324*	−0.006	0.336*	−0.011	0.022	0.002	0.031	0.002
	(4.412)	(−1.916)	(1.925)	(−0.073)	(1.789)	(−0.127)	(0.072)	(0.290)	(0.094)	(0.299)
growthGDP	0.604	−0.843	0.490	−1.361	1.607	−1.335	−0.869	−0.036	−1.334	−0.019
	(0.382)	(−0.955)	(0.252)	(−1.332)	(0.729)	(−1.135)	(−0.168)	(−0.360)	(−0.243)	(−0.354)
lnpopulation	−0.057	−0.062	−0.054	−0.125***	−0.085	−0.138**	−0.192	−0.007	−0.202	−0.006
	(−0.928)	(−1.451)	(−0.569)	(−2.638)	(−0.727)	(−2.307)	(−1.366)	(−0.448)	(−1.465)	(−0.443)
urbanrate			0.043	−0.722*	0.128	−0.713	2.406	−0.025	2.467	−0.02
			(0.051)	(−1.843)	(0.134)	(−1.519)	(1.018)	(−0.395)	(0.985)	(−0.397)
democratic K			0.904	(0.919)	1.011	−1.095	−0.529	−0.007	−0.573	−0.01
			(1.200)	(−1.017)	(1.149)	(−1.082)	(−0.441)	(−0.392)	(−0.429)	(−0.350)
polright	−0.083	0.015	−0.031	−0.019	−0.013	−0.007	0.25	−0.004	0.269	−0.003
	(−0.885)	(0.200)	(−0.336)	(−0.298)	(−0.135)	(−0.118)	(1.410)	(−0.491)	(1.560)	(−0.480)
literacyrate			0.139	0.24	−1.889	−0.45	−3.673*	−0.038	−3.659*	−0.032
			(0.270)	(1.013)	(−1.539)	(−0.972)	(−1.763)	(−0.435)	(−1.794)	(−0.427)
natresource			−0.508**	0.285**	−0.523**	0.319**	−1.036	0.013	−1.055	0.011
			(−2.457)	(2.183)	(−2.395)	(2.275)	(−1.519)	(0.459)	(−1.580)	(0.449)
FM_literacyratio					2.615**	0.846	6.594**	0.042	6.598**	0.035
					(2.036)	(1.521)	(2.424)	(0.435)	(2.423)	(0.436)
trade opness							−0.414	−0.015	−0.546	−0.013
							(−0.518)	(−0.448)	(−0.742)	(−0.446)
FDI							6.532	0.197	6.79	0.212
							(0.392)	(0.393)	(0.380)	(0.363)
WTO							0.079	−0.001	0.124	−0.001
							(0.195)	(−0.322)	(0.282)	(−0.294)
war									−0.001	0.002
									(−0.002)	(0.253)

(*Continued*)

Table 4.4. (*Continued*)

	(1)		(2)		(3)		(4)		(5)	
Transition to	Succ	Grad	Succ	Grad	Succ	Grad	Succ	Grad	Succ	Grad
Observations	81		74		74		53		53	
Pseudo R2	0.252		0.352		0.393		0.556		0.559	
N countries	77		70		70		50		50	
N Succ.	39		34		34		23		23	
N Grad.	14		14		14		10		10	
N Failed	14		14		14		10		10	

Note: The method of estimation is Maximum Likelihood. The reported coefficients are marginal effects computed at means for all continuous regressors. Standard errors are clustered at the country level. The dependent variable is the probability that country i experienced a successful or gradual democratic transition rather than a failed transition in year t. The baseline category is the failed transitions. Countries with less than 20 years of observation for the dependent variable are dropped from the sample. The constant is not reported. T-statistics are in parentheses. *, **, and *** denote statistical significance at the 10 percent, 5 percent, and 1 percent levels, respectively.

Table 4.5. Additional determinants of democratic success: Successful, gradual, and failed.

	(1)		(2)		(3)		(4)		(5)		(6)	
Transition to	Succ	Grad	Succ	Grad	Succ	Grad	Succ	Grad	Succ	Grad	Succ	Grad
natressource	−0.543**	0.323**	−0.244	0.010*	−0.016	0.001	−0.952***	0.374*	−0.601***	0.485**	−0.612**	0.392*
	(−2.525)	(2.142)	(−1.145)	(1.780)	(−0.063)	(0.142)	(−3.098)	(1.690)	(−2.760)	(2.415)	(−2.059)	(1.723)
FM_literacyratio	2.675**	0.812	3.804***	0.027	3.199**	0.001	3.400**	0.932	2.219	0.801	3.236**	0.715
	(2.080)	(1.334)	(2.665)	(1.339)	(2.315)	(0.157)	(2.251)	(1.141)	(1.643)	(1.214)	(2.267)	(1.259)
conflict	0.156	0.100	0.347	0.003								
	(0.710)	(0.852)	(1.478)	(0.810)								
war	−0.213	−0.020	−0.086	0.000								
	(−0.700)	(−0.099)	(−0.264)	(0.072)								
military			−0.467**	−0.006								
			(−2.325)	(−0.984)								
military after			−0.334	−0.122*								
			(−0.749)	(−1.866)								
success region					0.420*	0.005						
					(1.527)	(0.158)						
leader age							−0.201	−0.311				
							(−0.235)	(−0.595)				
regime length							0.210	0.163				
							(1.075)	(1.512)				
presidential									−0.802*	−0.108		
									(−1.942)	(−0.540)		
proportional									0.008	0.081		
									(0.039)	(0.524)		
ethnicfract											0.766	−0.489
											(1.462)	(−1.359)
Catholicism											0.713*	−0.208
											(1.677)	(−1.044)
Protestantism											1.052	−0.219
											(0.838)	(−0.404)
Islam											0.472	−0.412
											(1.114)	(−1.537)

(*Continued*)

Table 4.5. (*Continued*)

	(1)		(2)		(3)		(4)		(5)		(6)	
Transition to	Succ	Grad	Succ	Grad	Succ	Grad	Succ	Grad	Succ	Grad	Succ	Grad
Observations	74	74	74	74	77	77	61	61	74	74	74	74
Pseudo R2	0.477	0.407	0.477	0.477	0.473	0.473	0.537	0.537	0.488	0.488	0.446	0.446
N countries	70	70	70	70	71	71	57	57	70	70	70	70
N Succ.	34	34	34	34	35	35	27	27	34	34	34	34
N Grad.	14	14	14	14	14	14	13	13	14	14	14	14
N Failed	14	14	14	14	14	14	13	13	14	14	14	14

Note: The method of estimation is Maximum Likelihood. The reported coefficients are marginal effects computed at means for all continuous regressors. Standard errors are clustered at the country level. The dependent variable is the probability that country i experienced a successful or gradual democratic transition rather than a failed transition in year t. The baseline category is the failed transitions. Countries with less than 20 years of observation for the dependent variable are dropped from the sample. All specifications augment specification in column (3) in Table 3 with additional controls. To conserve space only the coefficient estimates associated with our key variables of interest, natresource and FM_literacyratio, and the additional covariates are reported. The constant is not reported. T-statistics are in parentheses. *, **, and *** denote statistical significance at the 10 percent, 5 percent, and 1 percent levels, respectively.

transition more likely to occur; however, a successful transition is less likely when a military regime is present. In addition, the coefficient on the indicator variable *military_after* taking value 1 if the country was ruled under a military regime in the year or any of the two years following transition — is negative and statistically significant. This suggests that the prolonged involvement of the military in the aftermath of transitions raises the likelihood of failure.[21] Interestingly macro-economic conditions other than natural resources do not affect the likelihood of transition nor the likelihood of consolidation.

Column (3) provides evidence of a neighborhood effect for transition durability too. A successful transition in neighbor countries in the region makes other countries in transition more likely to rapidly consolidate democracy. Column (4) controls for the age of the leader and the regime. These variables are not statistically significant. The form of democracy, notably the constitutional arrangements put in place in the aftermath of transitions, also has important consequences for the sustainability of such transitions (Myerson 1999; Persson 2005). Column (5) includes two indicator variables presidential and proportional, taking value 1 if the electoral system introduced following transition is presidential and proportional respectively. Countries that reform into a parliamentary system, where the legislature elects the chief executive, are on average more likely to transit to a successful democracy than countries that reform into a presidential system. The results show no evidence that countries where legislators are elected on a proportional representation basis have higher chances of successful democratic change.[22] Lastly, establishing a working democracy may be more difficult if different interest groups are fighting over power. The fall of a dictator may allow underlying socio-ethnic conflicts repressed till then, to come to the fore. Column (6) shows little evidence that the outcome of past transitions is associated with the ethnic or religious composition of the population, though there is some positive effect of Catholicism.

5. Conclusion

In this Chapter we investigate the causes and consequences of political transitions, but unlike previous studies we account for differences in the process of transition itself. We construct a new dataset of 90 political transitions between 1960 and 2010, and categorize them into three types, the successful, the gradual and the failed based on the speed, intensity and permanency of the political reform. While each transition is unique, examining the 90 episodes of transitions worldwide offers some

[21]The Hadenius and Jan Teorell (2007) regime type classification which we rely on, makes democracy and military exclusive regimes by definition. So the correlation with the military-after variable is mostly by construction mostly but not entirely. In fact there are instances of failed transition coded as 'Democracy' following transition (e.g., Peru after 1979) and instances of successful transition coded as 'Military' in the first years following the year of the transition e.g., Honduras in 1982.

[22]The electoral system is a proportional representation if candidates are elected based on the percent of votes received by their party.

insights into what MENA countries can expect politically and economically as they democratize.

First, these experiences provide a cautionary tale for the region. An initial move towards democracy does not guarantee success. Indeed, more than one-third of countries that tried in the last 50 years failed to transition.

Second, the Chapter uncovers several important determinants of transitions and their success. We find strong evidence that gender equality in education, natural resources, conflict, a military government, and urbanization are important factors for the likelihood of regime change and the stability of democracy. Economic development and recent gains in female literacy offer reasons for optimism for swift transition in the MENA transition countries, while resource-rich countries may face additional challenges.

Third, one success can have a big impact on others. Tunisia started the revolution and fits well many of the above categories — low natural resources, high female literacy, and a parliamentary system.[23] The spillover effect from attempting transition has already been realized. More importantly now, if democracy is durable in Tunisia, our results suggest that it will have positive implications that extend well outside its borders.

[23]The new post-transition constitution of Tunisia provides for a semi-presidential system of government.

Appendix

Table A. List of transitions and non-transitions, 1960–2010.

Successful Democratic Transitions		Gradual Democratic Transitions		Failed Democratic Transitions		Intermediary Regimes	Always Democratic Regimes	Always Autocratic Regimes
1 Argentina	1983	1 Albania	1990	1 Algeria	2004	1 Fiji	1 Australia	1 Afghanistan
2 Benin	1991	2 Burundi	2001	2 Argentina	1973	2 Malaysia	2 Austria	2 Angola
3 Bolivia	1982	3 Comoros	1990	3 Bangladesh	1991	3 Solomon Islands	3 Belgium	3 Azerbaijan
4 Brazil	1985	4 Ghana	1996	4 Burkina Faso	1978	4 Turkey	4 Botswana	4 Bahrain
5 Bulgaria	1990	5 Guatemala	1986	5 CAF	1993	5 Venezuela, RB	5 Canada	5 Bhutan
6 Cape Verde	1991	6 Guinea-Bissau	1994	6 Congo, Dem. Rep.	2004		6 Colombia	6 Bosnia and Herzegovina
7 Chile	1989	7 Lesotho	1993	7 Congo, Rep.	1992		7 Costa Rica	7 Cambodia
8 Cyprus	1969	8 Liberia	1990	8 Cote d'Ivoire	2000		8 Denmark	8 Cameroon
9 Dom Rep.	1978	9 Mexico	1988	9 Djibouti	1999		9 Finland	9 Chad
10 Ecuador	1979	10 Paraguay	1989	10 Ecuador	1968		10 France	10 China
11 El Salvador	1984	11 Romania	1990	11 Ethiopia	1993		11 Germany	11 Cuba
12 Greece	1975	12 Sierra Leone	1996	12 Ghana	1970		12 India	12 Egypt, Arab Rep.
13 Guyana	1992	13 Zambia	1991	13 Ghana	1979		13 Ireland	13 Equatorial Guinea
14 Honduras	1982			14 Guatemala	1966		14 Israel	14 Eritrea
15 Hungary	1990	New Independent States		15 Haiti	1994		15 Italy	15 Gabon
16 Indonesia	1999	14 Georgia	1990	16 Haiti	2005		16 Jamaica	16 Guinea
17 Kenya	2002			17 Iran, Islamic Rep.	1997		17 Japan	17 Iraq
18 Korea, Rep.	1988			18 Madagascar	1991		18 Mauritius	18 Jordan
19 Lebanon	2005			19 Mozambique	1994		19 Namibia	19 Kazakhstan
20 Malawi	1994			20 Nepal	1990		20 Netherlands	20 Korea, Dem. Rep.
21 Mali	1992			21 Niger	1991		21 New Zealand	21 Kuwait
22 Mongolia	1992			22 Nigeria	1979		22 Norway	22 Lao PDR
23 Nicaragua	1990			23 Nigeria	1999		23 Papua New Guinea	23 Libya
24 Panama	1989			24 Pakistan	1973		24 Sri Lanka	24 Mauritania
25 Peru	2001			25 Pakistan	1988		25 Sweden	25 Morocco
26 Philippines	1987			26 Peru	1979		26 Switzerland	26 Myanmar
27 Poland	1991			27 Sudan	1965		27 Timor-Leste	27 Oman
28 Portugal	1976			28 Sudan	1986		28 Trinidad and Tobago	28 Qatar
29 Senegal	2000			29 Thailand	1969		29 United Kingdom	29 Rwanda
30 Spain	1978			30 Thailand	1978		30 United States	30 Saudi Arabia
31 Uruguay	1985			31 Uganda	1980			31 Swaziland
New Independent States				New Independent States				
32 Croatia	2000			32 Armenia	1991			32 Syrian Arab Republic
33 Czech Rep.	1990			33 Belarus	1991			33 Tajikistan
34 Estonia	1991			34 Kyrgyz Rep.	2005			34 Tanzania
35 Latvia	1991			35 Russian Fed.	1992			35 Togo
36 Lithuania	1991							36 Tunisia
37 Macedonia	1991							37 Turkmenistan
38 Moldova	1993							38 United Arab Emirates
39 Slovak Rep.	1990							39 Uzbekistan
40 Slovenia	1991							40 Vietnam
41 Ukraine	1991							41 Yemen, Rep.

Note: The year of transition is reported next to the country. The non transitioning countries are either stable democracies (30), stable autocracies (41) and intermediary status countries (5). Intermediary countries are countries that have experienced several transitions and reversals over the sample period. When countries experienced several democratic transitions, we consider each transition as a distinct event if there is at least a five year gap between the end of the previous transition and the start of the next one. Countries that experienced several failed transitions include, Ghana in 1970 and 1979, Haiti in 1994 and 2005, Nigeria in 1979 and 1999, Pakistan in 1973 and 1988, Sudan in 1965 and 1986 and Thailand in 1969, 1978. Argentina in 1973 and 1983 or Peru in 1980 and 2001, experienced failed then successful transitions.

Table B. Variables definition and source.

Variable	Description	Source
I. Democracy data		
Polity2	The combined Polity score is the difference between the democracy and autocracy indicator. This is an additive twenty-one-point scale (−10;10).	POLITY IV
II. Factors affecting democratic transitions and their rapid completion		
GDPpc (log)	Natural logarithm of real GDP per capita based on purchasing power parity (PPP). Data are in constant 2005 international dollars.	WDI 2011
growthGDP	Average country GDP growth computed over the previous 6th, 5th and 4th years.	WDI 2011
urbanrate	Share of the country total population living in urban agglomerations of more than 1 million.	WDI 2011
lnpopulation	Natural logarithm of a country's total population.	WDI 2011
democracy K	Democratic capital computed by Persson and Tabellini (2009).	Persson and Tabellini (2009)
polright	The extent of political rights in a country as calculated by Freedom House. Coded from 1–7 (7 being the worst). We take the average in the 6th, 5th and 4th years.	Freedom House 2010
literacyrate	Literacy rate, adult total (% of people ages 15 and above).	WDI 2011
natresource	Indicator variable taking value 1 for countries classified according to the IMF as resource-rich countries.	IMF (2007)
FM_literacyratio	The ratio of female to male literacy rate in the adult population (15–64). The literacy ratio is calculated using interpolated data. Data are interpolated using Stata's ipolate function.	WDI 2011
trade openness	Export+Imports as a share of GDP (%)	WDI 2011
FDI	Foreign direct investment, net inflows (% GDP)	WDI 2011
WTO	Indicator variable taking value one if country is a member of the World Trade Organization, and 0 otherwise.	WTO
war	Indicator variable taking value one if country was engaged in a war (conflict with at least 1000 battle related deaths in a given year), and 0 otherwise.	PRIO/Uppsala 2010
conflict	Indicator variable taking value 1 if the country was in civil war in any of the previous two years. The underlying data used is the Intensity of civil war, coded in 3 categories 0-No civil war 1-Minor–between 25 and 999 battle related deaths in a given year. 2-Major–at least 1,000 battle related deaths in a given year.	PRIO/Uppsala 2010
military	Indicator variable taking value 1 if the regime type of the country in question was military in any of the previous two years.	Hadenius and Teorell (2007)

(*Continued*)

Table B. (*Continued*)

Variable	Description	Source
military after	Indicator variable taking value 1 if the regime type of the country in question was military the year of the transition or any of the following two years.	Hadenius and Teorell (2007)
N region transition	Number of transitions of any type (as defined by the authors) that occurred in the region the country in question is nested in, in the year or any of the previous two years.	Authors' calculations
Success region	Indicator variable taking value 1 if the region the country in question is nested in, experienced at least a successful transition (as defined by the authors), in the year or any of the previous two years.	Authors' calculations
leader age	Age of the chief executive.	PRIO/Uppsala 2010
regime length	Number of years the chief executive has been in office, prior to the transition.	DPI 2010
presidential	Indicator variable taking value 1 if the electoral system in place in the country in any of the two years following the transition, is presidential.	DPI 2010
proportional	Indicator variable taking value 1 if the electoral system is proportional, that is if candidates are elected based on the percent of votes received by their party.	DPI 2010
youth	Share of the population that is aged between 15 and 34 years old.	WDI 2011
inequality	Gini index	WDI 2011
ethnicfrac	The index of ethnic fractionalization of a country, constructed as one minus the Herfindahl index of the share of the largest ethnic groups.	Montalvo and Reynal Querol (2005)
catholicism	The share of the population in each country that was catholic in 1970.	World Christian Encyclopedia
protestantism	The share of the population in each country that was protestant in 1970.	World Christian Encyclopedia
islam	The share of the population in each country that was Muslim in 1970.	World Christian Encyclopedia
III. Economic development and economic policies during transition		
GDPpc growth	Real per capita GDP growth is defined as the annual logarithmic change of real per capita GDP from t-1 to t. Data are in constant 2000 dollars.	WDI 2011
government spending	General government final consumption expenditure (percent of GDP)	WDI 2011
interest rate	Deposit interest rate (percent)	WDI 2011
inflation	Log((100+annual inflation(percent))/100)	WDI 2011
export growth	Exports of goods and services annual growth (percent)	WDI 2011
FDI	Foreign direct investment, net inflows (BoP, current US$) deflated using GDP deflator.	WDI 2011
quality of regulation	The indicator measures quality of the credit, labor and business regulation, coded from 0 to 10 (0 is the worst).	Economic Freedom of the World 2010

Table C. Descriptive statistics: Determinants of democratic transitions.

Variable	Obs	Mean	St. Dev	Min	Max
transition	869	0.05	0.21	0	1
lnGDPpc	869	7.77	1.17	5.51	11.15
growthGDP	869	0.03	0.06	−0.21	0.37
urbanrate	869	0.42	0.21	0.05	0.98
lnpopulation	869	15.95	1.55	12.76	20.99
democratic K	869	0.07	0.15	0	0.83
polright	869	5.62	1.10	2	7
literacyrate	869	0.64	0.23	0.09	1.00
natresource	869	0.50	0.50	0	1
FM_literacyratio	869	0.73	0.21	0.11	1.15
schooling gap	778	0.12	0.39	0	2.08
trade opness	869	0.71	0.40	0.09	2.46
FDI	869	0.02	0.06	−0.11	0.79
WTO	869	0.28	0.45	0	1
war	869	0.12	0.32	0	1
crisis	869	0.16	0.36	0	1
colony	869	0.90	0.30	0	1
island	869	0.03	0.16	0	1
landlocked	869	0.26	0.44	0	1
conflict	957	0.27	0.44	0	1
military	957	0.38	0.48	0	1
region transition	957	2.74	3.51	0	14
leader age	918	4.04	0.22	2.94	4.52
regime length	918	2.06	1.01	0	3.83
youth	901	34.43	2.72	27.15	45.86
inequality	177	40.62	10.47	20.69	62
ethnicfract	782	0.52	0.29	0.032	0.96
catholicism	782	0.21	0.28	0	0.96
protestantism	782	0.06	0.08	0	0.30
islam	782	0.44	0.41	0	1

Table D. Descriptive statistics: Determinants of democratic success.

Variable	Obs	Mean	St. Dev	Min	Max
transition	74	0.84	0.72	0	2
lnGDPpc	74	7.81	1.09	5.58	9.66
growthGDP	74	0.02	0.04	−0.09	0.14
urbanrate	74	0.45	0.20	0.08	0.87
lnpopulation	74	16.16	1.38	12.78	19.17
democratic K	74	0.09	0.15	0	0.83
polright	74	5.79	1.01	3	7
literacyrate	74	0.70	0.26	0.09	1.00
natresource	74	0.27	0.45	0	1
FM_literacyratio	74	0.80	0.22	0.27	1.15
trade opness	53	0.52	0.26	0.15	1.58
FDI	53	0.01	0.01	0.00	0.06
WTO	53	0.18	0.38	0	1

(*Continued*)

Table D. (*Continued*)

Variable	Obs	Mean	St. Dev	Min	Max
war	74	0.14	0.34	0	1
colony	74	0.85	0.36	0	1
island	74	0.07	0.25	0	1
landlocked	74	0.24	0.43	0	1
conflict	74	0.32	0.47	0	1
military	74	0.42	0.50	0	1
military after	74	0.12	0.33	0	1
success region	77	0.76	0.43	0	1
leader age	61	4.02	0.21	3.40	4.47
regime length	61	1.66	1.13	0	3.56
presidential	74	0.84	0.37	0	1
proportional	74	0.22	0.41	0	1
ethnicfract	74	0.51	0.26	0	0.93
catholicism	74	0.37	0.39	0	0.97
protestantism	74	0.06	0.08	0	0.30
islam	74	0.19	0.30	0	0.99

Acknowledgments

We would like to thank Aart Kraay, Philip Keefer, Daniel Kaufmann, Ishac Diwan, Olivier Cadot, Richard Damania, Ernest Sergenti, Maya Eden, two anonymous referees and participants of the 2012 World Bank Economist Forum and seminar at the World Bank for very helpful comments and suggestions. The views expressed here are those of the authors and do not necessarily represent the views of the World Bank, its Executive Board or member countries. All remaining errors are ours.

References

Acemoglu, D., J. A. Robinson and T. Verdier. 2004. "Kleptocracy and divide-and-rule: A model of personal rule." *Journal of the European Economic Association*, 2(2–3): 162–193.

Acemoglu, D. and J. A. Robinson. 2006. *Economic Origins of Dictatorship and Democracy.* New York: Cambridge University Press.

Acemoglu, D., S. Johnson, J. A. Robinson and P. Yared. 2008. "Income and democracy." *American Economic Review*, 93(3): 808–842.

Acemoglu, D., S. Johnson, J. A. Robinson and P. Yared. 2009. "Reevaluating the modernization hypothesis." *Journal of Monetary Economics*, 56: 1043–1058.

Aghion, P., A. Alesina and F. Trebbi. 2004. "Endogenous political institutions." *Quarterly Journal of Economics*, 119(2): 565–613.

Alesina, A., A. Devleeschauwer, W. Easterly, S. Kurlat and R. Wacziarg. 2003. "Fractionalization." *Journal of Economic Growth*, 8(2): 155–194.

Barro, R. 1991. "Economic growth in a cross section of countries." *Quarterly Journal of Economics*, 106: 407–443.

Barro, R. J. 1999. "The determinants of democracy." *Journal of Political Economy*, 107: 158–183.

Barro, R. J. and J. Lee. 2001. "International comparisons of educational attainment: Updates and implications." *Oxford Economics Papers*, 3: 541–563.

Collier, P. and A. Hoeffler. 2004. "Greed and grievance in civil war." *Oxford Economic Papers*, 56: 563–595.

Collier, P. and A. Hoeffler. 2005. "Resource rents, governance, and conflict." *The Journal of Conflict Resolution*, 49(4): 625–633.

de Mesquita, B., A. S. Bruce, R. M. Siverson and J. D. Morrow. 2003. *The Logic of Political Survival.* Cambridge, Massachusetts: MIT Press.

Diwan, I. 2012. "Understanding revolution in the Middle East: The central role of the middle class." Mimeo.

Dollar, D. and R. Gatti. 1999. "Gender inequality, income, and growth: Are good times good for women?" Policy Research Report On Gender and Development Working Paper Series, No. 1. Development Research Group/PREMN, The World Bank.

Easterly, W. 2001. "The middle class consensus and economic development." *Journal of Economic Growth*, 6: 317–335.

Epstein, D. L., R. Bates, J. Goldstone, I. Kristensen and S. O'Halloran. 2006. "Democratic transitions." *American Journal of Political Science*, 50(3): 551–569.

Freedom House. 2010. "Freedom in the world: Political rights and liberties 1972–2010." Freedom House, New York. Dataset available online at: http://www.freedomhouse.org/ratings.

Freund, C. and J. Mélise. 2013. "Regime change, democracy and growth." CEPR DP9282.

Glaeser, E., G. Ponzetto and A. Shleifer. 2007. "Why does democracy need education?" *Journal of Economic Growth*, 12(2): 77–99.

Gleditsch, N. P., P. Wallensteen, M. Eriksson, M. Sollenberg and H. Strand. 2002. "Armed conflict 1946–2001: A new dataset." *Journal of Peace Research*, 39(5): 615–637.

Hadenius, A. 1994. "The duration of democracy: Institutional vs. socio-economic factors." In *Defining and Measuring Democracy*, ed. Beetham, D. London: Sage.

Hadenius, A. and Jan Teorell. 2007. "Pathways from authoritarianism." *Journal of Democracy*, 18(1): 143–156.

Huntington, S. P. 1991. *The Third Wave: Democratization in the Late Twentieth Century.* Norman: University of Oklahoma Press.

Inglehart, R. and C. Welzel. 2005. *Modernization, Cultural Change and Democracy: The Human Development Sequence.* Cambridge, UK: Cambridge University Press.

Marshall, M. G., T. R. Gurr and J. K. Jaggers. 2010. *Polity IV Project: Political Regime Characteristics and Transitions, 1800–2004 Dataset Users' Manual.* Center for Global Policy School of Public Policy, George Mason University, Arlington, VA.

Midlarsky, M. 1998. "Democracy and Islam: Implications for civilizational conflict and the democratic peace." *International Studies Quarterly*, 42: 485–511.

Montalvo, J. G. and M. Reynal-Querol. 2005. "Ethnic polarization, potential conflict and civil wars." *American Economic Review*, 95(3): 796–816.

Myerson, R. B. 1999. "Theoretical comparison of electoral systems." *European Economic Review*, 43: 671–697.

Papaioannou, E. and G. Siourounis. 2008. "Economic and social factors driving the third wave of democratization." *The Journal of Comparative Economics*, 36: 365–387.

Persson, T. 2005. "Forms of democracy, policy and economic development." The National Bureau of Economic Research Working Paper No. 1117.

Persson, T. and G. Tabellini. 2009. "Democratic capital: The nexus of economic and political change." *American Economic Journal Macroeconomics*, 1: 88–126.

Przeworski, A., M. Alvarez, J. Cheibub and F. Limongi. 1996a. "Classifying political regimes." *Studies in Comparative International Development*, 31(2): 1–37.

Przeworski, A., M. Alvarez, J. Cheibub and F. Limongi. 1996b. "What makes democracies endure?" *Journal of Democracy*, 7(1): 39–55.
Przeworski, A., M. Alvarez, J. Cheibub and F. Limongi. 2000. *Democracy and Development*. Cambridge, UK: Cambridge University Press.
Ross, M. L. 2001. "Does oil hinder democracy?" *World Politics*, 53(3): 325–361.

Chapter 5

ISLAMISTS IN POWER? INCLUSION, MODERATION, AND THE ARAB UPRISINGS

Jillian Schwedler

1. Introduction

Political inclusion is a major concern for democratizing states. Among the many groups excluded and repressed by the former regime, which should now be included? Which should be excluded? And who decides? With the extraordinary events of the Arab uprisings that began in 2011, a wider range of political actors than ever before have become directly engaged in debates and processes of political transition. The new political institutions, however, remain unstable and the distribution of power between them unclear. This represents an exciting, historic, and democratic moment, even if the fate of some of those transitions remains uncertain. To be sure, a broadly inclusive reform process is necessary and desirable for meaningful democratic governance. But at a practical level, many citizens have real concerns that their recent extraordinary successes following decades of suffering and struggle against autocracy will be hijacked. They fear, among other scenarios, that fringe groups might take their countries in directions they do not support, and ignore the revolutionary demands for substantive economic as well as political reforms. Among the greatest of these fears is that incipient democratic processes will create openings for non-democratic actors to establish new non-democratic regimes, or for old regimes to re-establish themselves in new guises.

As political transitions unfold in many parts of the Middle East, one central question concerning political participation has moved to the center of many debates: will widespread inclusion of groups pressure those with more radical views to moderate their positions and their actions in order to better compete within a real democratic political field? For groups to effectively compete in electoral processes and win votes, they must appeal to a wide range of voters, thus pushing them closer to the center of the political spectrum than they might have been in non-democratic settings. This dimension of political reform is relevant for groups across the political spectrum. The question, in short, is whether political inclusion leads to moderation, and if so, how?

This inclusion-moderation hypothesis, long debated with respect to the inclusion of Islamist parties into state-dominated processes of limited political liberalization in the Middle East, has new importance today as even many regimes that did not see revolutionary mobilization explore the possibilities of democratic reform. In some cases entirely new sets of institutions are being established, while in other cases existing institutions are being reformed to allow for greater participation and, possibly, an increased role for elected assemblies in actual governance. Within these varied political contexts, a wide range of Islamist groups have gained considerable power through elections in Tunisia, Egypt, and Libya, and they have clearly emerged as the strongest (and best funded) opposition groups in Syria's civil war. Even in states that have not seen major mobilizations, such as Kuwait, Jordan, and Morocco, Islamist actors are pushing for greater voice as regimes struggle to pre-empt revolutionary sentiment through limited state-led political reforms.

In this Chapter, I review the central arguments of the inclusion-moderation hypothesis, including competing explanations and the range of mechanisms that scholars identify as at work. Then I examine how the different institutional contexts of the post-Arab uprisings may demand a re-examination of some of the arguments about inclusion and moderation.

2. Inclusion and Moderation

Questions about the political inclusion of Islamist groups have been made explicitly (e.g., Norton 1995) and implicitly (e.g., Anderson 1997) for decades. In recent years, a range of scholars working largely from a social movement perspective have expanded the discussion on the effects of inclusion and exclusion of diverse Islamist parties within a range of regime types and widely varied institutional contexts (Hafez 2003; Wickham 2004; Caldwell 2006; Clark 2006; Schwedler 2006; Bayat 2007; Turam 2007; Browers 2009; Ashour 2009; Wegner and Pellicer 2009; Yadav 2010; Tezcur 2010; Clark 2010; Schwedler 2011).

The term 'Islamist' refers to highly diverse groups that advocate social, political, and economic reform through the application of Islamic teachings to all aspects of life. Most states in the Middle East have long had a range of organizations that fit these criteria, including charitable societies and legal or quasi-legal political parties, as well as underground movements that sometimes employ political violence (often directed at non-democratic regimes), to name just a few. Because many of these groups are well established, having functioned both above and below ground for decades, one should not be surprised to see them quickly emerge as strong voices when non-democratic regimes initiate political openings or, especially, when parts of the old regime entirely collapse. Indeed, in many states, one group or party is effectively the 'only game in town' in terms of political opposition precisely because authoritarian regimes have for decades quashed other oppositional movements.

In some parts of the Middle East — notably in Turkey, Tunisia, Syria, and to a lesser extent Egypt — secular groups have been relatively more tolerated than religious groups given the regime's strong secular identity. In other parts of the region — notably Jordan, Morocco, Lebanon, and Yemen — Islamist groups have been more tolerated for a variety of historic reasons. It is therefore unsurprising that groups with the longest history and most established institutional and communal roots are able to mobilize more quickly and effectively in a changing institutional context. Because many Islamist groups, particularly branches of the Muslim Brotherhood, have been operating for decades with varying degrees of legality in large parts of the Middle East, they have been at the center of scholarly debates about inclusion and moderation. However, it is equally important to recognize that these debates are equally relevant to thinking about the trajectory of liberal, leftist, and other conservative movements within their political contexts.

What is moderation, and how can it be measured? In broad terms, moderation entails a process of change that might be described as movement along a continuum from radical to moderate, whereby a move away from more exclusionary practices (of the sort that view all alternative perspectives as illegitimate and thus dangerous) equates to an increase in moderation. The literature on moderation — while using a variety of related terms — dates back decades and has focused on groups spanning the political spectrum, from socialist and Catholic parties in 19th and early 20th Century Europe (e.g., Przeworski and Sprague 1986; Kalyvas 1996) and in contemporary Latin America (Mainwaring and Scully 2003), to the attention of Islamist political participation in the Muslim world. Most of these theoretical models emphasize the ways in which structural openings and constraints provide incentives for previously excluded groups to enter the system and play by the rules of the game, rules that are set and controlled by incumbent regimes (Schwedler 2011). This process is captured in the idea of what Samuel Huntington called a "participation/moderation tradeoff," a sort of "democratic bargain" (1993, p. 169) in which opposition groups become eligible to take advantage of political openings only once they have "modified their demands and moderated their tactics" (p. 165). This process typically involves

> their agreeing to abandon violence and any commitment to revolution, to accept existing basic social, economic, and political institutions, ... and to work through elections and parliamentary procedures in order to achieve power and put through their policies (p. 170).

The central dynamic of the inclusion-moderation hypothesis is that political actors will become more moderate if they are allowed to participate in legitimate competitive political processes, such as democratic elections, a free civil society, legal protests and demonstrations, and so on. They become more moderate largely because it is pragmatic to do so, as it increases one's chance of appealing to a wider constituency and thus gaining a larger share of power. This hypothesis mirrors the idea that political exclusion drives actors to the extremes by providing few alternatives. A key dimension of the hypothesis therefore relates to the institutional context within which groups choose to participate (or attempt to participate, as is often the case in non-democratic contexts). While political exclusion forces opposition groups to take their activities underground, political inclusion provides a wide range of actors with a spectrum of opportunities, even in quasi-authoritarian contexts in which incumbent regimes have no intention of allowing pluralist and democratic practices to really emerge. Even so, in such an inclusive context, incentives for moderation will include a relative lessening of state repression targeted at oneself (because one is able to function and advocate specific political reforms legally and openly), the opportunity to openly mobilize a broader support base, the ability to debate issues openly and in public, and so on. These institutional incentives, therefore, should lead actors to choose moderation in order to attract a wider following as well as to facilitate cooperation with other political actors to achieve common goals. As we will see below, complications emerge not only when institutional settings are controlled by an authoritarian regime, but also when the institutions themselves are in flux and the rules of the political game are themselves the object of the power struggle.

The main caution about the inclusion-moderation hypothesis in any context relates to what scholars call the paradox of democracy: the idea that democratic processes might empower non-democratic actors to reverse those openings — perhaps permanently. Acting as a 'wolf in sheep's clothing', a group might present itself as committed to the democratic process only to abandon that stance once it has gained enough power democratically to overturn the democratic system entirely, or at least to alter the processes to insure their ongoing influence in the real functioning of power. When the system itself is in flux, as is the case in post-revolutionary settings, there may be even fewer mechanisms to insure that groups must moderate in order to participate. Thus in terms of the real advancement of democracy, a recurring question about expanded political inclusion therefore concerns the possibility that elections could empower a group with no commitment to democratic norms, or that a system in flux could allow a group to entirely hijack the process of designing new institutions through non-democratic means.

Until recently, questions of political inclusion in the Middle East all concerned political openings introduced by non-democratic regimes that showed little if any intention of relinquishing any real power, despite what they said. Jordan's King Abdullah II, like his father before him, has repeatedly declared his commitment to democratization but has held the reigns of power tightly, focusing on limited electoral reform while retaining the right to appoint and dismiss cabinets without parliamentary input. As noted below, the Arab uprisings may be pushing states like Jordan to move toward more substantive reforms. Nevertheless, these processes are carefully managed from the top. If the legal opposition (parties, civil society organizations, etc.) begins to push too hard for more substantive reforms or a share of real power, the regime will typically respond by introducing new 'legal' constraints or a revised electoral law, calling for a national dialogue, and otherwise employing a 'bait and switch' tactic of continuing to talk about democratic reforms while seeking ways to constrain the opposition and preserve the regime. Historically, the institutional contexts of these limited political openings have been largely stable, even if the regimes were facing pressures for reform as a result of popular protest (often in response to economic crises). In such cases, the legal opposition would have only limited opportunities to challenge the regime's power, as the regime itself remained in place to control the political openings through a variety of channels, including absolute control of the many security agencies. At the same time, the logic of the inclusion-moderation hypothesis holds that opposition groups participate in elections in the hope of increasing their political power even though regimes seek to prevent precisely that outcome. The new political context of the Middle East since the onset of the 2011 uprisings has altered this balance, however, as regimes in Tunisia, Egypt, Yemen, and Libya are engaged in substantive reform processes — even while some of those overseeing the transitions are unsurprisingly maneuvering to insure their own centrality in the 'new' regimes. Before examining the implications of these changing institutional contexts, I will first further unpack the dynamics of the inclusion-moderation hypothesis as explored in the literature, which has until now focused on regime-led openings within broadly stable contexts.

As suggested by the paradox of democracy, of central concern for debates about moderation is the possibility that a group could adopt what might be called 'behavioral' moderation without substantive 'ideological' moderation. That is, it may behave as if it were committed to respecting pluralist and democratic political processes, but continue to hold core commitments that run counter to democratic norms. Behavioral moderation may well be desirable on its own, particularly in stable institutional contexts. But when institutions are in flux or when institutional checks are not well established to prevent a single-party takeover, the underlying commitments of political actors become extremely relevant. It is therefore ideological moderation that concerns us most — the idea that inclusion may be a way of moderating radical political actors in ways that lead to their substantive commitment to an inclusive, democratic means of bringing about political, social, or economic reform. How can inclusion bring this result?

One of the most important effects of political inclusion is that it creates strong incentives for various groups to cooperate with each other, even if only at a tactical level. In this regard, the political openings of much of the Middle East in the early 1990s — all of which saw significant reversals over the next decade — have all led to expanded instances of cooperation between Islamists and their historic ideological rivals, notably communists, socialists, and liberals (Schwedler 2006; Clark and Schwedler 2003). This development is remarkable, and would have been unthinkable just a decade earlier. Following the emergence of extremist Islamists in Egypt in the 1970s, and particularly following the Iranian revolution of 1979 and the assassination of Anwar Sadat in 1981, leftist and progressive groups viewed Islamists as regressive fundamentalists whose political programs were patently anti-modern. In the earlier, middle decades of the 20th Century, Arab nationalist movements advocating anticolonialism and a secular modernity were opposed by conservative Islamist groups, many of which supported like-minded conservative monarchies who were equally unsettled by radical nationalist movements.

By the late 1990s however, political circumstances had shifted enough that Islamists were forging tentative relations with leftists and liberals around issues of common interest. In Egypt the middle-generation of Islamists in the Muslim Brotherhood increasingly sought to cooperate with their generational cohort within other political trends (Wickham 2002; Stacher 2009), just as younger Brotherhood members found that they shared many goals and values with young liberal bloggers (Lynch 2007). Similarly in Jordan, members of the Muslim Brotherhood and the closely associated Islamic Action Front party have since the early 1990s coordinated and cooperated with some (but not all) former political rivals. In addition to parliamentary cooperation, these groups work together around issues such as mounting demonstrations against the US war in Iraq, opposing Jordan's peace treaty with Israel, and filing lawsuits against increased restrictions on freedoms of expression. Even in Yemen, whose 1990 unification and democratic 1993 parliamentary elections stunned the region as well as the world, some Islamist trends explored links with socialists by the late 1990s and later formalized this cooperative relationship in the establishment of the Joint Meetings Party, an opposition bloc that played a significant role in the 2011 protests in Yemen (Browers 2007). In the early 1990s, Palestine's Hamas cooperated with the Marxist Popular Front for the Liberation of Palestine, and Lebanon's Hizbullah has shown willingness to cooperate with a wide range of groups, including the rival Shi'i group, Amal, as well as various Sunni Muslim and Christian groups.

2.1. *The limits of inclusiveness*

Clark identifies an important caveat about the widespread emergence of cross-ideological cooperation in the Middle East (2006). She notes that cooperation does not emerge around 'red-line' issues for Islamists, particularly those for which they believe Islamic law offers no ambiguity (such as the appropriate social role of women). Yet while cooperation may be limited to issues of common purpose, the trend toward such engagement and coordination marks an extraordinary development in the political practices of Islamist groups. Political inclusion itself cannot be expected to always lead to such cross-ideological cooperation, but it is undoubtedly responsible for creating the institutional incentives for diverse groups to even consider cooperating with other groups (Clark 2010). In this regard, the willingness to cooperate with formerly shunned groups (and sometimes sworn enemies) is a form of moderation that is an important effect of inclusion through a changed institutional environment. When political institutions create incentives for cross-ideological cooperation, groups will explore that range of possibilities in ways they never would have under a fully exclusive system. This effect can be realized not only in meaningful democratic systems, but also through controlled political openings launched by non-democratic regimes.

But is this merely behavioral moderation, and not ideological moderation? If a group holds a relatively closed worldview that precludes the legitimacy of alternative views, the core question is whether inclusion can create or at least encourage ideological moderation in the sense of opening the possibility for a group to see validity in the views of others, or at the very least see legitimacy in their right to hold alternative views. Given that one can never know 'what is in the heart' of anyone else, can we know with confidence whether a group has become more moderate ideologically? Even more, can we ever know with certainty whether moderation is a result of political inclusion? I argue that the incentive structure of inclusive political institutions and processes, even in less-than-democratic contexts, are necessary but insufficient to consistently produce ideological moderation. Here, several issues are at play.

First, we should recognize that many of the more 'moderate' Islamists have always been relatively moderate. Most Muslim Brotherhood branches, for example, have never taken up arms against the incumbent regime, and the few that have done in the past so have rejected that route for decades. Brotherhood members from Egypt, Jordan, and Palestine took up arms in support of Palestinians in the 1930s and 1940s, but have mostly eschewed violence against their own regimes. Even in Egypt, where the Muslim Brotherhood formed a militant cell in the years before the overthrow of the monarchy by the Free Officers in 1952, the Brotherhood members who turned to violence in the 1960s and later did so by breaking away to form new organizations, as the mother organization continued its stance of non-violence.

In many countries, Islamists have even been staunch allies of regimes, particularly in the face of secular nationalist movements in the 20th Century. Thus while Nasser imprisoned thousands of Brotherhood members in the 1950s and 1960s, the monarch in Jordan enjoyed the support of the Brotherhood while it struggled against militant leftists and nationalists. Thus for relative moderates such as the many branches of the Muslim Brotherhood, processes of political inclusion provide them with greater visibility and more incentives to mobilize a following. But deciding to function within a legal institutional framework (such as forming a legal political party) may not signal ideological change as much as internal reorganization to fulfill the needs of a formal party that aims to participate in elections and an elected parliament.

As a political strategy, one would certainly want to encourage inclusion as a means of elevating moderate actors on the political scene, and to deny radicals a large support base by provide alternative voices working within the system. This points to a more indirect route to overall moderation of a particular context, and not necessarily of a single group. That is, regardless of whether groups become *more* moderate as a result of inclusion, the encouragement of inclusion may discourage radicalism in a way that produces an overall political *effect* of more moderation in a given political field. Radicals may remain, but their constituency is diminished as people turn to support legal, moderate alternatives that were previously unavailable. The logic of this dynamic is going to depend considerably on the individual institutional contexts. If most constituencies are relatively centrist in their views (with centrist being contextually defined), then political groups vying for a large constituency will also likely pull in that direction. If, however, extremist groups appear to have a large constituency, the incentives to moderate toward the center may be diminished. In this sense the effect of moderation may have less to do with a single group's orientation than with the structure of the broader political spectrum.

This insight is relevant to thinking about cases such as that of the Wasat party in Egypt, a moderate group from the early 2000s that included former members of the Muslim Brotherhood who allied with other actors to form a centrist Islamist party (though it never received a license to operate legally under Mubarak's rule). The group may not have become more moderate over time so much it distanced itself from groups that held less moderate views. As noted, we saw in the 1990s many Islamists beginning to participate in regime-controlled pluralist processes who were never really radical in the first place, not to mention that they were never really opponents of the regime. This is the case of Jordan and Yemen, where Islamist party leaders were long allied with each ruling regime, sometimes very closely but always united against leftist and secular 'threats' to social order. While we should not mistake the moderate behavior of these groups as having mechanistically resulted from inclusions — particularly to the extent that they were never radical in the first place — we can nonetheless trace empirically the ways in which they are engaging in more pluralist and inclusive practices of the sort that we would recognize as moderate. And we can establish that the elevation of relative moderates can have an isolating effect on radicals, thus producing an overall effect of moderation within the political sphere.

Secondly, the empirical challenge of discerning when a group has undergone substantive ideological moderation (as opposed to having adopted strategic behavioral moderation without any corresponding ideological change) is not as hopeless as it might seem. I argue in my 2006 book that we can identify change in policies that might fairly be considered ideological moderation if we look to internal party debates and documents rather than relying on public statements alone. Given the extent to which democracy has become the dominant language for political legitimacy on a global scale, we should not be surprised to see virtually every political movement, party, and regime — save perhaps North Korea, the Taliban, and al-Qaeda — making at least *some* claims of commitment to democratic norms and practices. Our problem is to determine when groups have made substantive commitments that align with shifting goals. In this regard, looking at internal debates reflects the issues with which a group is struggling to grapple substantively. If an Islamist party struggles with how — indeed, whether — it can justify particular dimensions of democratic participation in terms of its broader ideological commitments, we can confidently say that it has evolved ideologically when those internal policy commitments have shifted toward more inclusivity and tolerance of alternative views.

This process unfolded with the Islamic Action Front in Jordan in the 1990s. As I detail in my 2006 book, the Muslim Brotherhood leaders within the party first struggled with whether participation in democratic institutions could be justified on

Islamic grounds, and they decided it could be justified with reference to notions such as *shura* (consultation) and *ijma* (consensus). But that decision led the newly established (in 1992) Islamic Action Front to face practical questions about whether to cooperate with ideological rivals, such as communists and socialists, on issues of common interest. The justification for democratic participation rendered the acceptance of other actors as legitimate; did this mean that leftist ideologies were legitimate? Again the party debated the issue internally, and the consensus was that cooperation was acceptable as long as the leftists themselves were good Muslims and their leftist views were only political orientations. Redline issues continued to emerge (Clark 2006), but cooperation with former rivals was substantively justified as a result of the group's early internal debates about the legitimacy of democracy (Schwedler 2006). Similar effects have been seen in Turkey, Morocco, and Egypt (Brown *et al.* 2006; Abdelrahman 2009; Cavatorta 2009; Brownlee 2010; Wegner and Pellicer 2009).

Over time, such a series of internal debates may — but will not necessarily — lead to fundamental shifts in ideological commitments in ways that can be recognized and indeed measured as increased moderation. Inclusion was essential to provide the changing institutional context and thus political logic that led Islamists, like the Muslim Brotherhood in Jordan, to debate whether they could justify participating in the new pluralist processes. But the internal debates themselves were key to the production of more moderate positions. In cases such as Yemen, no similar internal debates led to substantive shifts in ideological commitment that were shared across the party leadership, let alone its membership.

3. The Record of Islamist Participation

As noted, questions of political inclusion have had import for a wide variety of states in the Middle East well before the 2011 Arab uprisings. Islamist groups as varied as Hamas, Hizbullah, and the various branches of the Muslim Brotherhood emerged as strong contenders in local, municipal, and national elections. Islamists have participated widely in pluralist and democratic contests — where incumbent regimes are typically the greatest obstacles to real democratic reforms — in states as diverse as Algeria, Egypt, Jordan, Kuwait, Lebanon, Morocco, Palestine, Turkey, and Yemen.

The empirical record on Islamist participation in elections is very clear: by far most Islamist parties win significant but seldom majority blocks in parliament the first time they field candidates. A share of 20–40% of the seats is not atypical, and that outcome should be expected given their existing networks and often well-established presence in various communities nation-wide (Kurzman and Laqvi 2010). Far more interesting however, is that these parties fairly consistently lose seats in subsequent elections: the slogan "Islam is the Solution" — under which many Islamist parties campaigned in the 1990s — becomes empty rhetoric when party representatives are unable to effect significant change. Constituencies hold candidates responsible for delivering goods and services as well as policy reforms, and the ineffectiveness of parliamentarians is recorded in subsequent polls. Islamist parties thus typically win big the first time around but lose seats subsequently.

There are exceptions to this trend, but the most notable (in Palestine and Lebanon) emerge in extraordinary political contexts. Until the 2011 uprisings, political openings were always initiated by the incumbent regimes — whether a monarchy as in Morocco and Jordan or a republic as in Egypt and Yemen — that were facing domestic pressures of various sorts. Many, for example, sought to distract their citizens or subjects from dismal economic conditions and/or to curry favor with western donors. Lebanon's Hizbullah has done well at the polls in part because it has provided considerable services to the south of the country during and after the long civil war (when the state was without a functioning government), and in part because of its steadfast opposition to continued Israeli occupation of Lebanese lands. Hizbullah has never won a majority block in part because Lebanon's parliamentary seats are allocated along confessional lines — the assembly is equally divided between Muslim and Christian seats, and even the Muslim seats are subdivided in ways that would prevent the emergence of a large Hizbullah block. Even so, Hizbullah's popularity has never been attributable exclusively to popular support for its domestic policies or programs.

In Palestine, the Hamas victory of February 2006 also took place under exceptional circumstances. The vote was more of a rejection of Fatah than an expression of support for Hamas, and those two political trends represent the only two games in town. Palestinians live under a highly repressive military occupation, and without a functioning state of their own. In this context, the success of Hamas at the polls should not be read as a sign of overwhelming support among Palestinians for an Islamist agenda, and even less as evidence that Islamist groups elsewhere may soon sweep their own polls. Since that time, Hamas has effectively provided Palestinians in Gaza with political leadership while Fatah has done the same for Palestinians in the West Bank; the political reality of a divided state struggling under crippling occupation renders a comparison of Hamas with the performance of other 'Islamist' group extremely difficult.

Jordan provides a case that is much more typical. In 1989, members of the Muslim Brotherhood participated in Jordan's first full elections for its National Assembly since the suspension of the constitution and the imposition of martial law in 1967. Although at the time political parties remained illegal and thus Islamist candidates were all officially independents, Muslim Brotherhood members won 22 of 80 seats (27.5% of the assembly). Combined with 12 seats won by independent Islamists, the Muslim Brotherhood dominated block controlled 40% of the seats. During the next round of elections in 1993, their share decreased to 17 seats. They led a boycott (with leftist and liberal parties) of the 1997 elections, but in 2003 they again won 17 seats, though the assembly had been expanded to 110 seats. In the 2007 contest, the group won only six seats, although accusations of electoral fraud rang forth from many quarters and the results were likely illegitimate. As a result of the ability to participate under what they deem a fair electoral law, the Brotherhood boycotted (with some but not all other opposition parties) both the 2010 and 2013 contests. Yemen's Islamist Islah party has faired similarly, with an initial impressive showing in 1993 (winning the second largest block with 62 of 301 seats) but winning steadily fewer seats in subsequent contests (Schwedler 2006).

Of course, the full story for the declining parliamentary seats for Islamists often has to do with how regimes manipulate the electoral system and sometimes even the polling itself to produce the desired results. As noted, the manipulation of the system is undemocratic but unsurprising when incumbent regimes oversee democratic openings that they do not wish to see diminish their power. But with the 2011 uprisings, the institutional context and the ability of regimes to control the processes have dramatically changed. Often for the first time ever, Islamists, like all political groups, have participated in elections that have been substantively meaningful for political governance.

4. Changing Institutional Dynamics

Most of the aforementioned debate has focused on the inclusion-moderation hypothesis in the context of regime-initiated political openings, where the goal for the regime is to incorporate opposition movements into the system without ever losing control of that process. In short, existing regimes seek to strategically introduce limited democratic processes without substantively reforming the system into a democracy. They want moderation not because it is more conducive to democracy, but because it weakens challenges to their own authority. The regime sets the rules of the game, and its ultimate commitments have less to do with advancing real democracy than with deflating challenges to the regime. Even while regimes face pressure for reforms, the state institutions are stable and remain firmly under regime control.

While opposition groups in these contexts recognize that most regimes have no intention of ceding power, their decisions about whether to participate hinge on whether the potential gains of participation outweigh the costs. Regime-led democratic openings in much of the Middle East have, for decades, been characterized by these cat-and-mouse games, with Islamist groups playing the role of the most powerful opposition to existing regimes. In Egypt, the regime was never able to crush all of its Islamist groups, though the relatively moderate Muslim Brotherhood was tolerated to a greater extent than were the more radical (and militant) Gamaa Islamiyya and Jihad al-Islami. In Tunisia and Syria, strong challenges by Islamist groups led to the virtual defeat and exile of those movements, although neither entirely disappeared, with both reemerging during and following the uprisings. Even in cases in which Islamists and regimes have a history of alliance and cooperation, as they have had in Jordan and Yemen, regimes have sought to limit the influence of Islamist groups, which have sought to gain a foothold and expand their influence without overtly threatening the regime itself.

With the Arab uprisings, however, the institutional contexts are suddenly in flux, throwing the logic of controlled inclusion and thus moderation into question. Like other groups, Islamist groups have strongly asserted themselves, particularly in Tunisia, Egypt, and Syria. In the ongoing civil war in Syria, the opposition remains highly fragmented but the long-repressed Muslim Brotherhood has emerged as one of the opposition's most powerful factions; even more, most armed opposition groups there claim some ties to Islamist groups or networks outside of the country, relying heavily on the latter for financial support. In a context of continued political violence, the inclusion-moderation hypothesis has little immediate relevance (though it will certainly become important in any post-Assad Syria, whenever that may emerge).

Scholars have long acknowledged that political strategies and processes vary significantly under changing institutional contexts. Exploring the inclusion-moderation hypothesis in such contexts, Stathis Kalyvis has argued that one obstacle faced by religious groups in democratizing contexts is whether they can signal to other groups their commitment to honor democratic outcomes and uphold democratic norms (2000). The ability to make credible commitments is much easier when a religious group is characterized by the presence of a strong institutional hierarchy, as in the case of political parties in Europe connected to the Catholic Church. Kalyvas draws a comparison to the Islamic Salvation Front (FIS) in Algeria in the early 1990s, which has no comparable institutional hierarchy. He concludes that Islamist groups are unable to make credible commitments in absence of such a strong centralized institution, and thus are unlikely to be equally successful and convincing others of their commitment to moderation (which for Kalyvas equates to democratization). While Kalyvas draws attention to important dimensions of politics under a changing institutional context, the comparison might be a bit misplaced. His conclusion that Islamist parties cannot make credible commitments due to the lack of a centralized power hierarchy is based on a faulty comparison; that is, Islam is not compared to Christianity — which, like Islam, as a religion does not stipulate any particularly power structures — but to the Catholic Church, an historically evolved institution that is not characteristic of all of Christianity. Nevertheless, the attention to the importance of institutions — whether of a particular party or of a broader institutional context — draws our attention to factors currently at play in the Middle East since the Arab uprisings.

Thus the importance of institutional context noted in the literature on the inclusion-moderation hypothesis remains unchanged, but the particular ways in which institutions do or do not encourage moderation have changed. That is, the logic of the specific configuration of the institutional openings and the relationship of the regime to the various challengers gives way as outcomes become less certain and the possibilities for opposition to fundamentally reshape the system expand. If democratic institutions are quickly adopted and largely adhered to — two very big 'if's — then the logic of the inclusion-moderation hypothesis remains: building political alliances and expanding political constituency matter for governance today as well as for insuring subsequent electoral victories. The logic of the political parties literature in democracies takes hold, so that parties successful in the long term must pull to the center and learn how to function within a pluralist system (Downs 1957; Michels 1962; LaPalombara and Weinner 1966); social movement theorists have explored a similar dynamic (Piven and Cloward 1977).

The case of Turkey raises interesting questions about institutional dynamics that extend beyond the formal political sphere and into the structure of the field of opposition. Murat Somer has recently argued that what matters for moderation is not only the institutional openings that provide incentives for opposition groups to moderate, but also whether those groups seek to forge a new democratic 'center' or whether they choose instead to ally with the existing, non-democratic political center. As Somer argues, "Turkish democratization began [in the 1920s] with a moderation of authoritarian-secular actors, but generated only a semi-democracy because the changes were not institutionalized through explicit and formal compromises to produce a fully democratic center" (2013, p. 1). Similarly, Turkey's Islamists became more moderate in the 1990s and 2000s, but they likewise compromised with the semi-democratic center and thus failed to realize a fully democratic system when it was possible. This analysis underlines the insights on Turkey by other scholars (Turam 2007; Tezcur 2010) who caution that the inclusion-moderation hypothesis should not be immediately associated with democratization, and that questions of moderation are relevant to a range of political actors, including secular actors, and not only to religious ones.

What all of these cases emphasize, however, is that changing institutional contexts can significantly shape the effects of inclusion on moderation. We should be cautious in extending the logic of the inclusion-moderation hypothesis mechanistically from case to case, as even top-down openings vary considerably in ways that affect moderation. But these systems in flux also provide some exciting opportunities to text, refine, expand, or reject portions of existing scholarship.

5. Impact of the Arab Uprisings

In Tunisia and Egypt, the inclusion-moderation hypothesis continues to have immediate relevance, although the uncertainty of the new institutional context — particularly whether the new democratic institutions will become stabilized and secure — raises questions about longer-term challenges. In addition, each has also seen the emergence of an extremist Islamist party that creates additional incentives against moderation. In both of those states, a range of Islamist actors have emerged as among the most important political actors of the transition period. Notably, in neither case were Islamist groups central to the uprisings themselves. In post-Ben Ali Tunisia, the formerly banned and exiled an-Nahda (Renaissance) party won the largest bloc of the October 2011 parliamentary elections, subsequently holding numerous ministries and even the office of the prime minister. In Egypt, the Muslim Brotherhood won the largest bloc of the new parliament elected in late 2011, and

Brotherhood member Muhammad Mursi emerged victorious in Egypt's first truly free presidential elections in Spring 2012. What can the inclusion-moderation hypothesis lead us to expect in these uncertain institutional settings, where substantive political reform is actually on the table?

As noted, the experiences of Islamists in regime-controlled elections brought strong showings in first elections, and that pattern has continued in the elections held post uprisings. The inclusion-moderation hypothesis would predict that popular support for Islamist parties would diminish in coming years as they struggle to address complex and difficult economic crises and deal with other social and political problems, including the demands of overseeing the first years of a new regime. If the pattern holds in the post-uprising contexts — particularly if the new democratic institutions are stabilized — they will also be forced to appeal to a wider audience and to work cooperatively with political actors of other ideological orientations. In this sense we are witnessing real world 'tests' of the inclusion-moderation hypothesis, but past cases suggest that it may take years to meaningfully assess the results.

In the meantime, we can reflect on the relative differences of institutional contexts. Whereas the earlier inclusions were managed by stable regimes in firm control of the political institutions, the political openings in Tunisia, Egypt, and Libya are unfolding amidst substantive struggles over the new political institutions. The overall logic of moderation may prevail during elections and in the immediate months that follow, when winning large blocks may require appealing to a wider constituency. But between elections, when debates over the role of the judiciary, the substance of the constitution, the independence of oversight institutions and so on are in full force, incentives for cooperation with other actors may be less than the inclusion-moderation hypothesis would imagine, if the possibility for plowing ahead without a diverse coalition might reasonably be successful. If moderation is not the most viable path for increased political influence, groups may instead seek to steel their own constituencies and claim a mandate based on a plurality support, even as others object that new institutions were adopted undemocratically, without consensus or cooperation. Here it seems that the real question may not be whether the inclusion-moderation hypothesis holds during transitions themselves, but whether groups that control large constituencies have already adopted democratic norms to which they will adhere, or whether the seductive pull of a monopoly over power will lead them to push for the state of their dreams.

Another dimension relevant to moderation may be significantly changed in unstable transitional contexts as compared to stable, regime-managed political openings: the broader configuration of the field of political actors. In regime-managed openings, the rules of the game are established from above and a move toward the center entails a move toward a regime-led game. But in transitional contexts, by comparison, the poles of power are unstable and can shift quickly. In such cases, the logics of cross-ideological cooperation, to give one example, may no longer hold, particularly outside of the context of pluralist elections. As others (Tezcur 2010; Somer 2013) and I have argued, we should be cautious about correlating moderation with democratization, as the former may be understood in relative terms while the latter entails a substantive set of norms as well as procedures.

For the region's moderate Islamist parties, the most salient features of this dynamic entail whether the group faces strong challenges from either the left or right. In much of the region, leftist and liberal parties have proved stronger than one might have imagined prior to the Arab uprisings. Tunisia's first free elections saw the Islamist an-Nahda movement win a plurality, but the next nine parties to win seats were all leftist or secular. In this context, an-Nahda has worked with these other parties, even coordinating so that the number two and three winners would hold the offices of president and speaker of the assembly, while an-Nahda would put forth a candidate for prime minister. In Egypt, by contrast, leftist and liberal parties have proven much less adept at mobilizing supporters at the polls.

6. New Challenges from the Margins

In Tunisia and Egypt, parties more conservative than the moderate Islamists have emerged to alter the political field and pull the debate to the right. These conservative Salafi groups have increasingly asserted themselves in these states, emerging from formerly quiescent movements to form legal political parties and to compete in elections. Winning sizable percentages of the vote, they have also pressured more moderate Islamists to prove their Islamist credentials. The Salafist Nour Party in Egypt holds 20% of the parliamentary seats, although the Muslim Brotherhood, with 40% of the seats, may share the view of the Supreme Council for the Armed Forces as well as secular and liberal parties that growing Salafi influence would be a serious setback for the new state. In Tunisia, Salafis have challenged the ruling Islamist an-Nahda movement to counter their aggressive advocacy for gender segregation, full veiling of women, and the introduction of other conservative Islamic social practices. An-Nahda movement has been put in an awkward position, but has only tepidly pushed back against the Salafi pressures.

Will these Salafi actors begin to moderate if they continue to participate in series of elections? Will they begin to explore cooperation with other actors, even non-Islamist actors, to achieve their goals? The immediate prospects seem unlikely. The Salafist goal seems largely aimed at pressuring more moderate Islamists to *not* moderate as much as they might, or as much as they already have. If this remains the case, the result may not be so much a challenge to the inclusion-moderation hypothesis as an articulation of its limits with regards to ideological moderation in a particular field of political contestation. At the same time, more moderate Islamists operating for the first time in a political context not dominated by an incumbent regime, may feel the pull not to the center but toward more conservatism, particularly if Salafi parties continue to command respectable showings at the polls. Indeed, the latter's success has effectively shifted the political 'center' to the right. In such contexts, it may be the leftist and secular groups that find themselves pulled by the logic of moving toward a more religious 'center', in ways that require them to 'moderate' their secular views.

7. Conclusion

As is evident by now, there is no single logic to the inclusion-moderation hypothesis; indeed, unpacking its many dimensions suggests that it is less of a single hypothesis than a series of propositions about the relationship between institutional constraints, the structures of a field of political contestation, and the normative commitments of individual and group actors. If the Arab uprisings produce substantive democratic institutions that stabilize over the next few years, the inclusion-moderation hypothesis will certainly prevail, as it does in other pluralist and competitive institutional arrangements.

But until then, the individual and specific institutional settings of each case — including who is contenting for power and what the broader spectrum of challengers looks like — will likely structure the incentives of political actors more powerfully. As events in the Middle East continue to unfold, these sets of questions are likely to remain as central to the actors struggling to shape the political futures of their countries as they are to scholars of moderation and political change in general.

Acknowledgments

I am indebted to many people for their careful reading of this article as well as my other writings on the inclusion-moderation hypothesis. Those who have followed my work over the years will recognize the evolution of my thinking in response to their pointed critiques; the remaining failings are certainly due to my own refusal to take every piece of advice. For this article, I am particularly indebted to Ishac Diwan for his careful reading of multiple drafts, and to the anonymous reviewers who urged me to broaden my focus and more directly address the impact of changing institutional contexts on the logics of moderation.

References

Abdelrahman, M. 2009. "'With the Islamists? Sometimes. With the state? Never!': Cooperation between the left and Islamists in Egypt." *British Journal of Middle East Studies*, 36(1): 37–54.

Anderson, L. 1997. "Fulfilling prophecies: State policy and Islamist radicalism." In *Political Islam: Revolution, Radicalism, or Reform?* ed. Esposito, J. L., pp. 17–39. Boulder: Lynne Rienner.

Ashour, O. 2009. *The De-Radicalization of Jihadists: Transforming Armed Islamist Movements.* New York: Routledge.

Bayat, A. 2007. *Making Islam Democratic: Social Movements and the Post-Islamic Turn.* Palo Alto, CA: Stanford University Press.

Browers, M. L. 2009. *Political Ideology in the Arab World: Accommodation and Transformation.* New York: Cambridge University Press.

——— 2007. "The origins and architects of Yemen's joint meeting parties." *International Journal of Middle East Studies*, 39: 565–586.

Brown, N. J., A. Hamzawy and M. Ottaway. 2006. "Islamist movements and the democratic process in the Arab world: Exploring the gray zones." Carnegie Working Papers No. 67.

Brownlee, J. 2010. "Unrequited moderation: Credible commitments and state repression in Egypt." *Comparative Studies in International Development*, 45(4): 468–489.

Caldwell, C. 2006. "After Londonistan." *The New York Times Magazine*, June 25, pp. 40–47, 62, 74–75.

Cavatorta, F. 2009. "Divided the stand, divided the fall: Oppositional politics in Morocco." *Democratization*, 16(1): 137–156.

Clark, J. A. 2010. "Threats, structures, and resources: Cross-ideological coalition building in Jordan." *Comparative Politics*, 41(1): 101–120.

——— 2006. "The conditions of Islamist moderation: Unpacking cross-ideological cooperation in Jordan." *International Journal of Middle East Studies*, 38(4): 539–560.

Clark, J. A. and J. Schwedler. 2003. "Who opened the window? Women's activism in Islamist parties." *Comparative Politics*, 35: 293–313.

Downs, A. 1957. *An Economic Theory of Democracy.* New York: Harper and Row.

El-Ghobashy, M. 2005. "The metamorphosis of the Egyptian muslim brothers." *International Journal of Middle East Studies*, 37(3): 373–395.

Hafez, M. 2003. *Why Muslims Rebel: Repression and Resistance in the Islamic World.* Boulder: Lynne Rienner.

Huntington, S. 1993. *The Third Wave: Democratization in the Late Twentieth Century.* Norman, OK: University of Oklahoma Press.

Kalyvas, S. 1996. *The Rise of Christian Democracy in Europe.* New York: Cambridge University Press.

——— 2000. "Commitment problems in emerging democracies: The case of religious paries." *Comparative Politics*, 32(4): 379–398.

Kurzman, C. and I. Naqvi. 2010. "Do Muslims vote Islamic?" *Journal of Democracy*, 21(2): 50–63.

LaPalombara, J. and M. Weinner. eds. 1966. *Political Parties and Political Development.* Princeton: Princeton University Press.

Lynch, M. 2007. "Young brothers in cyberspace." *Middle East Report*, No. 245 (Winter): 20–28.

Mainwaring, S. and T. Scully. eds. 2003. *Christian Democracy in Latin America: Electoral Politics and Regime Conflict.* Palo Alto, CA: Stanford University Press.

Michels, R. 1962 [orig. pub. 1915]. *Political Parties: A Sociological Study of the Oligarchical Tendencies of Modern Democracy.* New York: Free Press.

Norton, A. R. 1995. "The challenge of inclusion in the Middle East." *Current History*, 94: 1–6.

Piven, F. F. and R. A. Cloward. 1977. *Poor People's Movements: Why They Succeed, How They Fail.* New York: Vintage.

Przeworski, A. and J. Sprague. 1986. *Paper Stones: A History of Electoral Socialism.* Chicago: University of Chicago Press.

Schwedler, J. 2011. "Can Islamists become moderates? Rethinking the inclusion-moderation hypothesis." *World Politics*, 63(2): 347–376.

Schwedler, J. 2006. *Faith in Moderation: Islamist Parties in Jordan and Yemen.* New York: Cambridge University Press.

Somer, M. 2013. "Moderation of religious and secular politics, a country's 'centre' and democratization." *Democratization*, 20(2): 1–24.

Stacher, J. 2009. "The brothers and the wars." *Middle East Report*, No. 250 (Spring): 2–9.

Tezcur, G. M. 2010. *The Paradox of Moderation: Muslim Reformers in Iran and Turkey.* Austin: University of Texas Press.

Turam, B. 2007. *Between Islam and the State: The Politics of Engagement.* Palo Alto, CA: Stanford University Press.

Wegner, E. and M. Pellicer. 2009. "Islamist moderation without democratization: The coming of age of the Moroccan party of justice and development?" *Democratization*, 16(1): 157–175.

Wickham, C. R. 2004. "The path to moderation: Strategy and learning in the formation of Egypt's Wasat party." *Comparative Politics*, 36(2): 205–228.

Yadav, S. P. 2010. "Understanding 'What Islamists Want': Public debates and contestations in Lebanon and Yemen." *Middle East Journal*, 64(2): 199–213.

ARAB CAPITALISM IN CRISIS

Chapter 6

DETECTING CORRUPTION AND EVALUATING PROGRAMS TO CONTROL IT: SOME LESSONS FOR MENA

Jeffrey B. Nugent

1. Introduction

In view of (1) the very uncertain policy and institutional environments lying ahead for MENA countries, especially of those going through rather fundamental economic and political transitions, (2) the importance of predictable futures to business firms and households, and (3) the relevance of corrupt acts as a means of reducing uncertainty about the future institutional environment, corruption is likely to pose a serious challenge to the quality of governance and economic success throughout much of the MENA region for some time to come. Moreover, unacceptably high levels of corruption at the highest levels of government have been cited as one of the main causes for the revolutions that have taken place between 2010 and 2012 in several MENA countries. For this reason, controlling corruption deserves priority attention. But, since it varies in form and seriousness from place to place, to know how best to attack corruption in any particular country it is imperative to learn where it is most serious, and either its determinants or at least the circumstances that are most closely linked to it.

One mean of identifying areas in which corruption seems to be most endemic would be to conduct comprehensive reviews at the country level of national legislation and related enforcement for dealing with corruption. Such reviews should be able to identify areas in which national laws and/or their enforcement are lagging behind those of other countries and/or of regional and international standards in anti-corruption efforts. An important mechanism for doing just this is the United Nations Convention against Corruption (UNCAC), initiated in 1996 and officially signed in the UN General Assembly in 2003 by 140 countries. Its importance can be attributed to the fact it is the first legally binding system for committing countries to anti-corruption measures and holding individual countries to live up to the international standards set by UNCAC.

Unfortunately, to date such assessments have been completed in only a few MENA countries and those completed assessments are not yet available to researchers and the general public. All MENA countries should allow this to happen as soon as possible. In the meantime, in what follows we attempt to make use of some scattered information from existing surveys.

First in Table 6.1, we provide country-specific scores on various alternative indexes of freedom from corruption from three different sources identified in the table. Each such source uses a different scoring system but in each case, a higher number indicates that corruption is perceived to be a less serious problem. Generally speaking, these sources rely heavily on investor opinions and reports. Perhaps as result of this, with the possible exception of the International Country Risk Guide's (ICRG) score for Iraq in 2009, the scores from the different sources are fairly consistent. At present, Qatar, UAE, Jordan, Kuwait, Bahrain, Oman, and Turkey seem to be among the least serious corruption, and Iraq, Libya, Lebanon, Iran, Sudan, Syria, and Yemen among the countries with the most serious corruption problems. The table, however, reveals two rather alarming findings:

(1) In recent years, at least, no MENA country comes even close to the freedom from corruption score of Singapore which has colonial, historical and some geographic characteristics not unlike some of the smaller MENA countries and which has long been held as a model by at least one of them (Bahrain).
(2) With the possible exception of Egypt and especially Turkey (which improved substantially on all three indexes), virtually every MENA country with comparable scores in both 1990 and a more recent year experienced a substantial decline in at least one of its freedom from corruption scores. The indexes show that the averages for MENA as a whole also declined whereas the already high scores for Singapore increased further on two of the three indexes.

While Table 6.1 alerts us to the apparently growing seriousness of the corruption problem in most MENA countries, a low freedom from corruption index tells us nothing about where in the country to look for that corruption, such as problematic sectors or types and sources of the corruption. One small step in that direction is taken in Table 6.2 which shows the percentages of firms saying they would be expected to give gifts to officials for each of 10 different purposes as well as the size of the gift for securing a government contract and the percentage of firms identifying corruption as a major constraint. These percentages are computed from data taken from the most recent World Bank's Enterprise Surveys (between 2006 and 2011). Such information is available for only nine MENA countries plus the West Bank and Gaza and nearby Mali and Mauritania. While several MENA countries have lower percentages of firms responding positively to these questions than those responding in all survey countries combined (labeled 'All' in this table), it should be considered

Table 6.1. Indexes of freedom from corruption MENA and Singapore compared.

	ICRG		Heritage Foundation			Transparency International		
	1990	2009	1990	2009	2014	1998	2011	2013
Algeria	3.9	1.5	50	30	28.7	2.6[a]	2.9	3.6
Bahrain	2	2	70	50	49.4	6.1[a]	5.1	4.8
Egypt	2	2	30	33	28.6	2.9	2.9	3.2
Iran	3	2	n.a.	25	34.4	3.0[a]	2.7	2.5
Iraq	2	4.4	n.a.	n.a.	13.7	2.2[a]	1.8	1.6
Jordan	3.8	3	n.a.	47	45.6	4.7	4.5	4.5
Kuwait	3	3	70	43	43.5	5.3[a]	4.6	4.3
Lebanon	1	1	50	35	24.5	3.0[a]	2.5	2.8
Libya	1	1.5	10	25	19.3	2.1[a]	2	1.5
Morocco	3	3	50	35	33.3	3.7	3.4	3.7
Oman	3	2.5	70	47	48.2	6.3[a]	4.8	7.8
Qatar	2	2.5	90	60	72.4	5.6[a]	7.2	6.8
Saudi Arabia	2	2	70	34	43.7	4.5[a]	4.8	4.6
Sudan	2	1	n.a.	30	9.8	2.3[a]	1.6	1.1
Syria	2	2	n.a.	24	n.a.	3.4[a]	2.6	1.7
Tunisia	3	2	50	42	39.2	5	3.8	4.1
Turkey	2	2.5	10	41	44	3.4	4.2	5
UAE	3	2.5	90	57	66.4	5.2[a]	6.8	6.9
Yemen	3	2	10	25	19.4	2.6[a]	2.1	1.8
MENA Average	2.46	2.23	51.42	38.5	31.9	4.1	3.72	3.8
Israel					59.3	7.1	5.8	6.1
Singapore	5	4.5	90	93	91.2	9.1	9.2	8.6
USA					72	7.5	7.1	7.3

Notes: (1) [a]indicates data is from 2003, the earliest year possible from this source n.a. indicates data not available
Sources: for ICRG: ICRG International Country Risk Guide: www.prsgroup.com/icrg.aspx; for Heritage Foundation: http://www.heritage.org/explore; for Transparency International: http://www.cpi.transparency.org/cpi20112011/results

that few such surveys have been undertaken in high income countries where corruption is generally low. The countries where the surveys have been undertaken are with a few exceptions limited to developing and transition countries in which corruption is generally quite serious. Yet, from the most comprehensive indicator given in the final column of the table, the only MENA country with a lower than average 'percent of firms identifying corruption as a major constraint' is Morocco. The overall MENA average of such scores is over 20% higher than that of the world as a whole. Once again, corruption seems to be most common in Yemen, Syria, West Bank and Gaza, Lebanon, Algeria, and Iraq. The value of the gift required to secure a government contract relative to the value of that contract is highest for Egypt, followed closely by Lebanon, Yemen, and Syria. Over 90% of the firms in Egypt and Lebanon and about two-thirds of those in Syria and Yemen say that gifts are necessary to obtain government contracts.

These results, therefore, would seem to identify the countries and sources or types of corruption that would seem more serious and thus deserve priority attention in the

Table 6.2. Percentages of firms responding positively to questions in enterprise surveys about corruption.

Economy	Year	Percent of firms expected to give gifts to public officials "to get things done"	Percent of firms expected to give gifts to get an operating license	Percent of firms expected to give gifts to get an import license	Percent of firms expected to give gifts to get a construction permit	Percent of firms expected to give gifts to get an electrical connection	Percent of firms expected to give gifts to get a water connection	Percent of firms expected to give gifts in meetings with tax officials	Percent of firms identifying the courts system as a major constraint	Bribery index (% of gift or informal payment requests during public transactions)	Percent of firms expected to give gifts to secure government contract	Value of gift expected to secure a government contract (% of contract value)	Percent of firms identifying corruption as a major constraint
All		25.7	15.2	14.4	23.1	16.0	15.4	15.7	19.1	15.1	23.9	2.3	36.1
EECA		24.9	14.3	16.7	25.3	13.0	10.5	14.2	20.6	14.9	18.0	1.5	34.5
MENA		37.0	16.5	22.9	25.1	22.0	14.4	23.4	28.2	20.4	37.9	3.6	56.5
SSA		36.2	20.1	16.3	25.9	21.6	21.5	18.3	14.8	18.7	35.0	3.3	37.5
Algeria	2007	66.6	7.3	34.9	12.0	13.2	7.5	15.0	29.3	14.2	34.8	4.1	64.3
Egypt	2007	6.5	11.7	10.1	6.1	13.1	9.2	23.8	17.2	22.1	92.4	9.2	59.3
Egypt	2008	15.2	13.4	20.0	40.0	31.1	27.8	5.3	6.5	6.6	32.0	1.2	45.2
Iraq	2011	31.8	24.2	41.0	29.1	48.7	17.3	29.1	14.0	33.8	31.0	1.8	62.3
Jordan	2006	18.1	3.1	1.3	11.8	8.8	4.5	0.9	16.6	1.8	2.3	0.1	40.7
Lebanon	2009	22.9	12.5	0.0	27.5	8.9	9.1	19.2	40.2	17.2	97.7	8.8	66.5
Morocco	2007	13.4	0.0	20.0	15.3	5.0	4.2	10.7	30.1	8.4	6.4	0.3	27.3
Mali	2010	19.4	42.4	35.2	39.9	39.5	40.2	20.2	15.9	23.4	22.8	2.5	24.8
Mauritania	2006	82.1	33.2	32.8	53.0	39.9	76.4	48.2	10.8	46.6	76.2	8.1	17.1
Syria	2009	83.8	25.2	25.2	25.8	28.5	9.3	61.0	60.8	34.3	66.4	7.2	67.1
Turkey	2008	18.0	10.7	0.3	14.0	3.1	3.9	4.0	19.8	5.8	23.1	2.3	42.3
WB and Gaza	2006	13.3	1.6	2.9	2.6	7.1	5.9	2.7	17.1	2.5	4.7	0.5	66.5
Yemen	2010	68.2	60.8	61.1	62.3	46.2	44.1	66.7	39.0	65.2	66.2	8.3	68.3

Notes: EECA represents Eastern Europe and Central Asia, MENA = Middle East and North Africa, SSA = Sub Sahara Africa

Source: World Bank: Enterprise Surveys; available online at http://www.enterprisesurveys.org.

attempt to reduce corruption. For example, corruption in obtaining government contracts would seem to deserve priority attention in Egypt, Lebanon, Yemen, and Syria. On the other hand, corruption with tax officials would seem to be most serious in Syria and Yemen. The percentage of firms saying that firms are expected to give gifts to get an operating license in Yemen is far higher than that in any of the other countries or regions. Iraq and Yemen would seem to deserve priority for dealing with corruption in getting access to electrical connections and Syria priority for corruption by users of courts. In the case of 'speed money' or 'the need for firms to give gifts to public officials to get things done,' as shown in the table, this is again a very pervasive problem for firms in Syria, Yemen, and Algeria but not in the other countries. Naturally, answers to such a question do not identify the exact reasons lying behind affirmative answers in these cases but regulations and the delays in getting things done in relation to these regulations would seem like good candidates. To the extent that this is true, and perhaps similarly for many of the other columns in the table, the culprit may be the cumbersomeness of regulations of the type indicated, be it getting a license of a particular type or gaining access to electricity or water.

Unfortunately, not all questions on gifts were asked in all surveys. Table 6.3 presents the answers to somewhat similar questions from the Enterprise Survey for Egypt for 2006 but with an added item, namely payments to labor administrators (representatives), normally the employees of the Ministry of Labor who are responsible for worksite inspections concerning labor laws and regulations. Note from the first column of this table that almost 85% of Egyptian firms reported the need to make such payments, slightly higher even that the percent indicating the need to make gifts to tax officials. The remaining columns of this table do a little more detective work showing how these percentages vary by location and ownership of the firms. With respect to location, industrial zones are often looked at as convenient places for firms to locate to make it easier to gain access to the services they need. Note, however, that in this case the average percentage of firms located inside these zones making gift payments to officials are in many cases higher.[2] A shortcoming of Tables 6.2 and 6.3, however, is that, because they do not give the magnitudes of these payments, they do not necessarily translate into the overall cost to the firm of total gifts.

Closely related to the questions given in Tables 6.2 and 6.3 is the question posed to each sampled firm in most of these Enterprise Surveys concerning the relative importance (usually on a 0–4 scale) of a particular "obstacle" to the current operations of this firm's business. Among the obstacles firms were asked to evaluate are: access to telephone lines, to land, to electricity, to licenses and permits, or to finance, crime, competition from the informal sector, political instability, labor regulations, tax rates, tax administration, inadequately educated workforce, and finally corruption. Given the extent to which corruption is seen to be pervasive in most MENA countries from Table 6.1, we attempt to make use of the firm-specific responses to

[2]None of these differences, however, is statistically significant.

Table 6.3. Percentage of Egyptian firms giving gifts to officials by location and owner.

		Location		Ownership			
Purpose of gift to officials	Overall	Outside of zone	Inside industrial zone	Domestic	Arab	Foreign	Government
Customs for Imports	12.5	11	17	11.6	33.3	32.1	16
Registration	10.6	12	7.1	11.1	0	10.7	2
Obtain License	15.9	15.4	17.3	16.3	27.8	17.8	6
Obtain Contract	9.6	9.2	10.6	9.7	5.5	3.6	10
Tax Administration	84.2	82.5	86.9	83	91.8	83.6	94.8
Labor Representative	84.6	83.1	90.4	84.7	90.7	82.1	94.2
General	14.9	15.4	13.6	15.4	11.1	17.8	6

Note: N (the number of respondents in the survey) = 985.
Source: Enterprise Survey of Egypt for 2006.

these questions to link the various more specific problem areas (obstacles) of firms to the firm-specific evaluation of the relative importance of corruption. Relatively complete responses to the relevant questions on the obstacles including the corruption obstacle are available for the eight MENA countries listed in Table 6.4 and for some 45 non-MENA countries. In the case of Syria we make use of two different surveys (those of 2003 and 2009) since both were based on reasonably large numbers of firms and were taken with a considerable number of years apart, potentially allowing us to detect possible changes in the determinants of corruption between the two years.

In Table 6.4, for each of these countries and a pooled cross section of countries as a whole we present the results of regressions of the following form:

$$\text{CORRUPT}_i = \alpha + \beta_{jk}\text{OBST}_{ik} + \gamma_{ij}X_{ij} + \varepsilon_i \qquad (6.1)$$

where for each country CORRUPT_i represents the importance of corruption as an obstacle to the current operations of establishment i, OBST is the vector of $k = 14$ other subjective indexes of the degree of severity of each of the obstacles identified above, and X_{ij} represents the vector of $j = 12$ other controls (for location, size, ownership, age, technological characteristics, the perceived consistency of government policy, unionization and use of an external auditor identified in the top portion of the table), and ε represents the error term. The values of the constant terms are not included in the table.

In the top part of the table are the parameter estimates and statistical significance levels of the various controls and in the bottom part of the table are those for the various aforementioned obstacles to doing business. In both parts of the table, one can see some heterogeneity in the direction of the effects from one country to another, but also some general patterns. For example, in the top half of the table, location in the capital city tends to be more positively related to CORRUPT and both size and age of firm and government ownership are negatively related to CORRUPT. Firms with external auditors, however, are likely to have significantly higher CORRUPT scores in Egypt, Jordan, Morocco, and Turkey but lower ones in Algeria. Of

Table 6.4. OLS regression results : Dependent variable the importance of corrution as an obstacle to the firm's business.

Country Year	Algeria 2002	Egypt 2004	Jordan 2006	Lebanon 2006	Morocco 2004	Oman 2003	Syria 2003	Syria 2009	Turkey 2005	45 Countries including Non-MENA
Control Variables										
Capital City		0.063**	0.024		−0.028			0.209*	0.244***	0.121**
Multiplant	0.042				−0.292*		−0.004		−0.004	0.424***
Size		−0.178**	0.01	−0.019	0.018	0.031	0.05	−0.209	−0.084	0.054***
Foreign 1	−0.164	0.323	0.053	0.532	0.146	−0.241	0.002	0.15	−0.371*	−0.082**
Foreign 2	−0.004	−0.116	−0.442	0.157	0.235	−0.299	1.31	0.064	−0.789*	−0.16**
Government	−0.176	−0.373	0.127		−1.048	0.177		0.34	−0.028	−0.361**
Age of Firm	−0.009**	−0.002	−0.008	−0.002		−0.013*	0.005	−0.006	−0.003	0
Quality Certificate		0.016	0.231	0.064	0.078		0.205	−0.04	−0.052	−0.019
New Technolgy		−0.018		0.108	0.046	−0.415*	−0.358**		−0.145**	−0.097***
Email	−0.051	0.476***	−0.134	−0.026	−0.112	−0.216	0.956**	0.066**	0.2*	0.027
Website	0.037	0.09	−0.335	−0.187	0.093	0.19	−0.582	−0.214	−0.031	0.026
Capacity Utilization	0.001	−0.006**	−0.001	−0.004*	−0.001	−0.002	−0.003		−0.002	−0.001**
Age of Exporting	0.01*	0.005			−0.006	−0.019	−0.035**	0.018**	0.004	
Consistent Government Regulations	−0.15***		−0.227***	0.011	−0.034			−0.091	−0.048**	−0.018***
Union Percent	−0.001	0.001	−0.007*	−0.002	0.001		0		0.001	−0.001***
External Auditor	−0.228**	0.301**	0.456**	0.016	0.412***	0.066	−0.012	0.129	0.141*	0.013
Obstacles to Business (Strength)										
Telephone	0.009	0.092	0.031	−0.022	−0.035	0.131*	0.152**	0.029**	0.003	0.222***
Electricity	0.036	0.014	0.25***	0.094*	0.029	−0.007	0.112**	0.023**	−0.037	−0.014**
Transport		0.034	−0.121*	−0.077	0.062	−0.078	−0.033	0.012	0.022	0.091***
Land	−0.016	−0.032	0.064	0.052	−0.024	0.015	0.116**	0.08**	−0.009	0.136***
Tax Rates	0.02	0.014	0.072	0.022	−0.016	0.022	−0.081	−0.018	0.12**	0.003
Tax Administration	0.150***	0.068*	0.132**	0.153**	0.068**	0.106*	0.135**	0.089**	0.031	0.123***
Customs	0.024	0.056	−0.011	0.036	0.035	0.017	0.051	0.156	0.061**	0.16***
Labor Regulations	0.06	0.057*	0.045	0.064	0.212***	−0.042	0.137**	0.011**	−0.045	0.005

(*Continued*)

Table 6.4. (*Continued*)

Country Year	Algeria 2002	Egypt 2004	Jordan 2006	Lebanon 2006	Morocco 2004	Oman 2003	Syria 2003	Syria 2009	Turkey 2005	45 Countries including Non-MENA
Education/skills of workers	0.023	0	−0.077	−0.002	0.048	0.053	−0.075	0.056	0.034	0.025**
Licenses, Permits	−0.021	0.067*	0.028	0.045	0.157***	−0.004	0.241***	0.052***	0.032	0.035**
Access to Finance	0.015	0.071**	−0.015	0.053	0.013	0.099*	0.04	0.025	0.017	−0.183**
Political Instability	0.301***	0.264***	0.282	0.187***		0.085	0.161**	0.069**	0.027	0.013**
Crime			0.207	0.231***	0.512***	0.506***		0.089	0.512***	0.059***
Informal Sector	0.167**		−0.074	0.144***	0.073	0.162***	0.099*	0.096*	0.19***	−0.013
N	530	905	348	353	834	283	319	493	1139	408,297
R2 (Adjusted for degrees of freedom)	0.276	0.168	0.421	0.368	0.47	0.489	0.278	0.265	0.47	0.362

particular importance may be the fact that firm perceptions concerning the consistency of government regulations are significantly negatively associated with CORRUPT in most of the countries where this question was asked (Algeria, Jordan, Syria (2009), and Turkey). This could be interpreted to reflect that corruption tends to be more serious in environments where firms are led to believe that the regulations are not consistent across time and areas of the economy, perhaps prompting a firm to bribe officials to gain greater assurance about its own treatment and the future stability of such treatment.

More important, however, are the parameter estimates for the different obstacles to doing business in the bottom part of the table. Most of these relate to specific types of regulations or access to public sector supplied services. With the minor exception of access to transport (which has a coefficient −0.121 which is significant at the 10% level in Jordan, there are no cases of the seriousness of these obstacles being negatively related to CORRUPT and at least one country for which the association is positive and significant for each of the other obstacles. Not surprisingly, the largest number of MENA countries (seven) with significant positive associations with CORRUPT is for tax administration. But, the obstacles for political instability, crime and the informal sector have positive and significant parameter values for five MENA countries while those for labor regulations and licenses and permits are positive and significant for three countries. The only other obstacle without a positive and significant relation to CORRUPT in at least one country is access to an educated and skilled workforce (which is hardly a service directly supplied by government).

While we can certainly not claim that these relationships demonstrate causality from these other obstacles to CORRUPT, it would generally seem more plausible that the direction of influence is more from them to CORRUPT rather than the other way around. In any case, it is those firms reporting greater problems with tax administration, political instability, crime, "unfair" competition from the informal sector, labor regulations, and licenses and permits that subjectively rate corruption to be more serious than those for whom these obstacles are less severe. While the coefficient for crime on CORRUPT tends to be larger than those for the other obstacles (especially in Morocco, Oman, and Turkey), one should probably not make too much of this since for this obstacle reverse causality from CORRUPT to crime may be quite plausible.

In any case, the positive and significant relationships revealed in the obstacles portion of Table 6.4 may well serve as additional signals as to areas on which the individual MENA countries might do well to focus in their anti-corruption activities. For example, despite the previously stated qualification for the magnitude of the coefficient of crime on CORRUPT, attempts to identify further the reasons lying behind this relation deserve serious scrutiny in every country where this relationship could be estimated. Similarly, the results of the relation between tax administration and CORRUPT would seem to suggest that all countries included in the table except Turkey might do well to investigate corruption in tax administration. The results also suggest that all countries except Oman and Turkey could do well to do the same with policies and other changes that might influence perceptions of political instability. Similarly, all countries except Jordan and Morocco could benefit from carefully investigating the various kinds of regulations giving rise to informality and making firms which do abide by the regulations feel that competition with firms in the informal sector represents a serious obstacle to their business. The activities in enforcing labor regulations and in granting licenses and permits for various activities would seem to deserve priority attention in Egypt, Morocco, and Syria (though note that in the 2009 Enterprise Survey this association has seemingly disappeared). Access to electricity would seem associated with corruption in Jordan, Lebanon and Syria and also access to telephone lines in Oman and again until recently in Syria. The findings for access to land obstacle would seem to indicate that the process of gaining access to land could be a source of corruption only in Syria.

The above analysis is based on those rather explicit forms or manifestations of corruption between identifiable agents and their clients. But beyond this, there is another category of corruption that is especially hard to identify but can be measured at the country level in terms of balance of payments. Global Financial Integrity (a program of a US-based NGO, the Center for International Policy) has been measuring illicit financial flows worldwide since 2000 based on data and methods first developed by The International Monetary Fund and The World Bank. They use two different methods to construct measures of these illicit financial flows. The first method known as, Gross Excluding Reversals (or GER) has been in use for some time and derives from the over-invoicing of imports, and under-invoicing of exports, a common method of sending capital out of developing countries illegally. The second method, based on the change in external debt (CED), net FDI inflows, the current account balance(CAB) and the change in international reserves (ΔR), is measured by: (CED + net FDI) − (CAB + ΔR). The terms inside the first parentheses represent the country's source of funds during a specific period and those inside the second parentheses represent the use of funds. The two sets of computations can be carried out for each country over time and compared with each other as well as each of these across countries. When the recorded uses of funds outweigh the sources of funds from the country's international accounts, it implies illicit outflows of funds. These outflows presumably reflect illegal transfers and other unrecorded transactions.

Actually, for MENA countries, the computations of Global Financial Integrity reported in Kar and Freitas (2011) show that, while the first measure (GER) proves to be a major source of illicit capital flows for China and other developing countries of Asia and Africa, it is actually not very important in MENA, constituting no more than 4% of the total of the two measures for this region. However, the CED–based calculations revealed this source of capital outflows to be unusually large (those accumulated over the 2000–2009 period are valued at US $1.33 trillion) and growing over time. Despite a sharp decline in the level of these outflows in MENA during the year 2009 due to the financial crisis, MENA's share in the world total in 2009 was 18.6%, a share that was higher than all regions except Asia. The growth of the illicit financial outflows by this method in real terms over the period 2000–2009 for the world as a whole was 10.2% whereas for MENA it was 19.6%, only slightly lower than that of Africa. It was noted that most of these illicit capital outflows in MENA were in the oil exporting countries, indeed with Saudi Arabia, UAE, Kuwait, and Qatar being ranked the 4th, 6th, 7th, and 12th largest in the world in terms of the accumulated flows over the period 2000–2008. While these flows reflect unrecorded transactions that cannot easily be tied to certain types of agents, as Kar and Freitas (2011) noted, it seems due to the incomplete accounting of transactions between oil producers and host country governments.

2. Model of Principal and Agent

Now that there is at least some, albeit admittedly crude, evidence on at least some of the various determinants or types of corruption, we turn to identifying possible ways of dealing with them. As has been noted by many analysts in the past, one can obtain at least an intuitive understanding of the essential features of the forces giving rise to corruption as well as potentially useful insights into how to deal with it from the perspective of a simple principal-agent analysis. The following simple account illustrates this.

The principal (the president, a governor or minister) hires an agent to collect taxes, provide *client firms* with licenses to operate, construct, buy land or imported machinery or raw materials and provide *client households* with access to electricity, jobs, health facilities, food subsidies or schools. Both agents and clients are assumed to make rational choices as to whether to be honest or corrupt based on the expected benefits and costs of each alternative. The agent's reward for being honest and avoiding the temptation to be corrupt is the utility obtained from his base salary (S) plus that obtained from the moral satisfaction of (or reputation for) being an honest person (M), i.e., $U\ (S, M)$. On the other hand, the agent's benefit of being corrupt depends on the size of the bribe B, the probability of being caught accepting the bribe (p), the fine (in monetary or utility terms) imposed if caught (F), and the loss of M, i.e., $U(S + B\ (1\text{-}pF))$. In turn, the size of the bribe B may depend on the extent of the benefit that the client might derive from the exchange. Thus, if markets were highly competitive and hence the benefit that the client firm might obtain from an additional license to produce, or that a client household might obtain from access to a special health facility were very small, B would presumably be small as well. The overall benefit to the corrupt agent would be $U(S + B)$ if not caught receiving a bribe and U(S+B –F) if caught. The rational agent will choose to be honest only if $U(S, M) > U(S + B)$ (1-p) F. Clearly, the higher is S and M for given p and F, the more likely the agent will be honest. So too, the agent will be more likely to be honest, the lower the bribe (B) and the higher the probability of being caught taking a bribe (p).

Knowing this, and assuming that the principal was interested in limiting corruption in government, the principal may want to choose among several options according to the benefits and costs of each. These options might well include: (1) offer the agent a high S, (2) offer moral training so as to raise $U(M)$, (3) increase his monitoring of the agent to increase the probability of detection of a corrupt agent

(p), and (4) raise the fine F, or (5) any combination of (1)–(4). The particular action (if any) chosen by the principal would presumably depend on the costs to the principal as well as the benefits anticipated from each of these actions in terms of both his own distaste for corruption and any threats to his continued term as principal that might arise from adverse sentiment of the public with the appearance of corruption. It is quite possible that some of the constraint-relaxing benefits that his client might extract from the corrupt agent could be welfare-increasing for the public. It is also quite possible that each of the aforementioned alternative actions that the principal might take (higher S, training for M, etc.) might be subject to diminishing returns. If so, a combination of such actions might be optimal, rather than any single most cost-effective method.

As experience in MENA has shown, principals are not necessarily free from corruption, and indeed the magnitude of the corruption from which they benefitted has constituted one of the several major motives for the revolutions that have comprised the "Arab Spring". In any such case, the principal could be thought of as an agent with monopoly power, so that the same framework could be applied to the case of a principal extracting corruption payments directly from the clients.

The more ambiguous the rules that the principal asks the agent to administer and enforce and hence the more discretion that is given to the agent, the more likely the agent will be able to obtain a larger bribe and avoid being caught violating the rules. Ambiguity in the rules, therefore, will increase the incentive for the agent to be corrupt. By the same token, the agent, either independently or in collusion with the principal, may try to design or amend the rules in such a way as to make them more ambiguous and serve as a magnet for rent-seeking behavior on the part of clients. The above four examples of actions that might be taken to reduce corruption could be supplemented by a variety of complementary activities. For example, Lambsdorff and Nell (2005) advocates that the bribe givers are also penalized (indeed more severely than the bribe takers if the bribe is rewarded with a favor) and further that some agents be induced to fail to deliver on the expectations of a benefit in return for their bribe, both actions intended to discourage clients from approaching agents for favors.[3]

Political and other institutions can also play an important role in determining the particular way in which principals, agents and their clients interact. For example, principals may be more likely to exercise greater monitoring over their agents when they are being encouraged to do so by international agencies or foreign donors upon which they may depend. They also may be more likely to do so in democratic contexts in which incumbent corruption-ridden regimes may be voted out when citizens feel adversely affected by corruption. Likewise, it may be easier to detect

[3]The reasons for this is their belief that major social cost arises from distortions to competitive resource allocation that would result from the agent delivering on the request of the rent-seeking client and that any agent that reneges after not delivering the favor to the client is already likely to be in danger of retaliation by the client.

corruption in countries characterized by freedom of the press and other media. So too, honest agents and clients might be more likely to 'blow the whistle' on their corrupt counterparts the more that they feel protected by whistle blower protection measures and honest well-functioning and independent courts.

Given the obvious plausibility of several of the aforementioned policy actions that might be taken to limit corruption, for several of these possible options there has emerged a considerable literature on the experience to date. In Section 3, we take up a number of the proposed actions, one at a time, drawing primarily on empirical analyses and especially recent experimental evidence.

3. Methods of Fighting Corruption and Relevant Evidence

From the insights of the principal-agent model and related literature on corruption, in this Section we consider ten different common proposals for fighting corruption. Several of them may be considered naïve and there is no claim that the list is exhaustive. The 10 anti-corruption actions are:

(1) Limiting the size of the public sector and privatization,
(2) stimulating competition and openness,
(3) decentralizing the government,
(4) simplifying regulations, limiting variations over time and space, and lessening the room for discretion and ambiguity in program rules and increasing transparency and information,
(5) raising the salaries (both present and future) of the agents (bureaucrats),
(6) increasing the extent and adequacy of monitoring agents and clients,
(7) firing and replacing the endemically corrupt agents,
(8) establishing an anti-corruption agency,
(9) allowing free access to media and creating an effective and free press, and
(10) making greater use of international standards.

In several cases, various complementary measures are identified that could make the particular action under consideration more likely to succeed. As a result, in effect, the list of policy actions goes beyond the ten mentioned above. For each of the ten proposed actions, some relevant evidence is cited.

3.1. *Limit the size of the public sector and privatize*

Since much of the corruption that households and business firms are concerned with involves the government, a common view of businessmen and the general public is that corruption increases with the size of the public sector. The larger the public sector, the more bureaucracy is likely to invade the private space of households and business firms and the more permits and regulations that are likely to be required. This view is buttressed by the idea that services provided by the government are less likely to be priced by the forces of supply and demand and hence when priced too low, they may have to be rationed. Clients with close connections to either the principal or agents may like this. To maximize the rents and bribes that they may be able to collect, agents may deliberately distort rules and regulations.

This rationale leads to policy proposals that corruption can be and should be reduced by reducing the size of the government sector. This would seem especially relevant in MENA countries where governments often play a larger role in the economy than in other countries at their respective income levels. Methods of accomplishing this might include reducing the share of government expenditures in GDP (LaPalombara 1994), reducing the share of state-owned enterprises in both investment and non-agricultural GDP (Elliott 1997), privatization, or more generally minimizing the scope for "grabbing hand" in the economy (Shleifer and Vishny 2002). Nevertheless, as the experience with massive and very rapid privatization in transition countries showed, the process was often characterized by large scale corruption. The MENA region has had the experience of a number of substantial privatizations. It might be useful to search for evidence of diminished or increased corruption resulting from privatizations in individual countries.

3.2. *Increase competition and openness*

Closely related to the rationale for privatization and reducing the size of the public sector is that of decreasing the incentives for rent-seeking behavior (Krueger 1974). Means of accomplishing this would include greatly reducing licensing, non-tariff barriers and the incentives to create monopoly power (Klitgaard 1988) and more generally opening up each product market to competition by deregulating product markets and liberalizing trade (Ades and Di Tella 1997, 1999; Gerring and Thacker 2005), and committing to international trade liberalization agencies like the WTO and IMF which also provide enforcement (Sandholtz and Gray 2003) with respect to each of several dimensions of openness to trade (Sachs and Warner 2001).

3.2.1. *Decentralize government*

Instead of the excessive size or competition-reducing character of government, another common complaint in developing countries in general and MENA countries in particular is the high degree of government centralization, with all key decisions being made by centralized ministries or even higher level decision makers. Since these central decision makers are far from the problems of households and businesses in different parts of the country, decentralization is seen as a possible way of aligning incentives of government with the needs and capabilities of its citizens, thereby limiting the need for getting around the misaligned incentive system through corruption and bribes. This would suggest that, in small countries or in large countries with more decentralized government, citizens may be in a better position to monitor their governments and thereby control corruption than those in large countries with centralized government administrations.[4]

3.3. *Simplify regulations, lessen discretion and ambiguity in program rules and increase transparency and information*

Still another popular fix for corruption is to limit the complexity, quantity, time and cost of regulations. Some at least crude indications of the link between regulations and corruption for MENA countries was presented in Section 1. Corruption was seen to be related to those obstacles to business having to do with tax regulations, labor regulations and product and process regulations in the form of permits and licenses. It is both the number or regulations and their complexity and ambiguity that matter. The more steps involved, the more costly they are in time for both clients and agents and the more willing firms are to pay 'speed money' to speed up the processing.

Naturally, regulations can provide benefits such as protection from a variety of dangers (to health, accident and so on) but Broadman and Recanatini (1999) and Djankov *et al.* (2002) have provided evidence suggesting that rent-seeking effects (e.g., corruption, creation of barriers to competition) seem to vastly outweigh the benefits to safety, health and other conditions. On the other hand, deregulation of safety, building codes, financial regulations and so on has often resulted in calamities. So, what to do? One useful approach seems to be eliminating ambiguity and the scope for discretion by the potentially corrupt agent, such as by unifying rates on taxes and customs duties and eliminating vagueness in the rules while not eliminating them.[5] Another complementary approach is to raise transparency regarding the existing rates and rules, not only about taxes and tariffs but also about government decisions and programs. In situations where information about service availability or the means of gaining access to public services is limited, such services can more easily be diverted from the poor (their intended users) to the elites with better informational access. Hence, in such situations lack of transparency about regulations and programs can give rise not only to corruption but also to greater inequality. Publicizing the programs and regulations in a simple way through open village meetings, local newspapers, mailed and emailed announcements can help

---

[4]Empirical evidence in favor of this policy approach has been provided by Root (1999) and Fisman and Gatti (2002), although Knack and Azfar (2003) and Shleifer and Vishny (1993) suggested that when the size of the bribe would be endogenously determined by the individual agents, they would not be likely to take into consideration externalities such as the effect of their bribe setting on the revenues to be captured by other agents.

[5]Impressive evidence in support of this approach was provided by Gatti (1999) and Lambsdorff and Cornelius (2000).

mitigate the capture of such programs and regulations by the rich, including public sector officials.[6]

Another demonstration of the relevance and importance of information availability for controlling corruption is provided by Yang (2005). In this case, information in the form of pre-shipment evaluations of imports (PSI) was provided by a private firm to each of 19 different countries at some time between 1980 and 2000. The information supplied by the private firm was the appropriate trade classification and tariff code number applied for each shipment of imports in the country of origin (i.e., the exporting country). PSI programs do not replace local customs officials in the importing country, but the availability of this information was shown to limit the extent to which an individual customs official would depart from that classification and associated tariff rate supplied by the PSI, and would solicit bribes from the clients. The cross-country panel results in the study showed that, on average, tariff revenues increased by somewhere between 15 and 30% in the first five years after the introduction of the PSI programs and that the revenue gains were 2–3 times as large as the costs.[7]

3.4. *Raise the salaries (both present and future) of the bureaucrats*

As noted in Section 2, many economists and administrators have derived from the principal-agent model the policy prescription that, when the salaries of the agents are low, e.g., near subsistence, and hence bureaucrats may be virtually forced to accept

[6]Reinikka and Svensson (2004, 2005) documented the success of an information campaign in Uganda in the late 1990s which called for attention to the rules that were used by the government in allocating funds to individual public schools. Prior to the information campaign none of the relevant decision makers at the local school and village level knew that each local school was entitled to funds from the central Ministry of Education depending strictly on the number of students in the school and given per student. As a result, neither the teachers nor parents (who were paying most of the costs) nor even the school administrators were aware that they were almost invariably not receiving the funds to which they were entitled and which were in fact disbursed by the Ministry. After this was discovered, a public sector tracking survey (PETS) was undertaken to measure the extent to which each school was actually receiving the disbursements to which it was entitled. Rather shockingly, the survey's results showed that less than 13% of the funds allocated actually reached the schools. This angered members of the local parent teacher associations (PTAs), teachers and others. It led to a newspaper campaign carrying reports about the diversion of funds and the subsequent indictments of numerous officials, but above all, about the information on what the rules were. Another PETS study was done after the information campaign, in this case also collecting information about access to newspapers and rules of the grant program and even about the means by which such information became available. The results showed that by then the percent of disbursed funds had risen to more than 80%, with larger increases in the poorer school districts than in the better off ones demonstrating that the information program was both corruption-reducing and equity-increasing. A two-step estimation procedure was used, the first stage for information access (instrumented by distance to a place where newspapers were delivered) and the percentage of disbursed funds actually received by each school in the second stage.

[7]Notably, Yang went to some effort to distinguish the PSI treatment effects from other simultaneous changes in tax collection elsewhere in PSI-treated countries which might have reflected the influences of other policy or program changes, but found that none of these factors influenced the results. The evidence showed that PSI both decreased undervaluation of import values and reduced the coefficient of variation of the classification differences. For additional corroborative evidence of the effects of PSI information programs in a more experimental setting, see Yang (2006).

bribes to survive, agent salaries should be increased. Empirical evidence on this, however, is quite mixed. Van Rijckeghem and Weder (2001) made use of data on the wage rates in government relative to those in manufacturing from a cross section of 31 low income countries to show that countries with relatively higher government salaries tended to have lower corruption (measured by the ICRG's corruption index) but that the effect was rather small. While the authors attributed this to the higher opportunity cost of being detected as corrupt when salaries are high relative to when they are low, they admitted that alternatively this could be due to the perception of fairness as might well be the case when the increase in wage rates is viewed as correcting a previous inequity with respect to the pay of others. The opportunity cost explanation was also confirmed in a laboratory setting by Abbink (2004). On the other hand, Grindle (1997) reported the results of a study across some 29 organizations and countries in which it was shown that, by itself, higher wages did not improve performance unless a corruption-free culture and leadership was first established through training and leadership in reducing corruption. (Bridi 2010).

Barr *et al.* (2004) applied the salary-raising experiment to a different setting, an experimental one involving both health workers who had an opportunity to embezzle some funds and monitors (either elected or appointed) whose task was to prevent them from doing so in Ethiopia. They found (1) that health workers with higher salaries embezzled less, but once again only slightly less and, (2) that monitors facing elections were more diligent in monitoring than appointed ones. Abbink and Ellman (2004) added some wrinkles to the analysis, showing that, if an intermediary is requested by the donor to help in getting the resources to the poor in the community, the benefits of the monitor being elected tended to disappear because of collusion between the intermediary and community elite.[8]

Since the threat of future fines and loss of salary could play an even more important role in the decision of agents to be honest or corrupt, the prospect of higher future salaries of bureaucrats could be even more important than the level of current ones. Mayors of cities often have higher salaries than others in government and average citizens. As a result, Ferraz and Finan (2011) argued that when audits were conducted to detect possible misuse of funds by the mayors, those mayors with the possibility to remain in power at least one more term would have greater incentive to avoid misuse of funds than mayors without that possibility. To test this hypothesis, the authors made use of data from such audits to compare the extent of

[8]Other circumstances may affect the effectiveness of wage increases to agents in diminishing corruption. Di Tella and Schargrodsky (2003), e.g., investigate the effects of higher wages on the extent of corruption in the procurement of material supplies by hospitals in Buenos Aires in two different time periods: first, during a time in which there was a big crackdown on paying excessive prices and then again some time later. Immediately after the crackdown on such corruption when monitoring was at its maximum, hospital purchase prices were reduced by 15% but with no difference between the hospitals receiving the higher pay treatments and the untreated ones. On the other hand, somewhat later, when such monitoring was less intense and the price reductions were no longer as large, hospitals treated with the higher wages were associated with a significant reduction in prices compared to the untreated ones, indeed the changes reflecting a wage elasticity of prices paid of more than −0.2.

missing funds between those Brazilian cities with first term mayors who were eligible for an additional term and those where they were already in their last terms. The finding was that there were 27% less misappropriated funds in those cities where the mayors could run for an additional term. Further, they showed that these effects were greater in those communities where information access was weakest and judicial punishment for embezzled funds was lower. Hence, these results suggest electoral rules could be particularly important when other conditions for dealing with corruption are especially weak and in those MENA and other countries moving toward democracy at local and national levels.

A quite common form of dereliction of duty, and perhaps corruption, is absenteeism from work without good reason. This is a particularly serious problem in India. Duflo *et al.* (2012) report the results of a randomized experiment in which teacher's pay was changed to reward presence in the classroom in randomly selected subset of sample schools. Apparently, monitoring was quite good as it was, so that, even without extra monitoring tools, teachers with the incentivized pay schedules had average absence rates only half those of the non-incentivized teachers (which were 42%). Moreover, when more intensive monitoring (with photograph verification) was added to the higher pay treatment, there was no additional increase in teacher attendance. Perhaps even more importantly, the authors also showed that student test scores increased over time in those schools with the incentivized pay schemes.

Another issue in the design of incentive pay schemes to reduce corruption or increase performance is whether the incentives should be on a group basis or an individual basis. One can easily think of reasons (such as peer pressure) which might favor group-based incentives but on the other hand the group system could also lead to greater free-riding and hence lower effectiveness. Muralidharan and Sundaramian (2009) compared the effectiveness of these two types of pay incentives in improving student test scores in government-run rural primary schools in India. They found statistically significant positive effects of approximately equal magnitude for the two incentive types in the first year of operation but by the second year the group incentive seemed to be less effective in raising test performance than the individual one.

Naturally, in evaluating the effects of wage incentives for teachers designed to improve student performance, e.g., student test scores, attention should be given to the extent to which teacher and student efforts are merely diverted from another dimension of performance to test scores via "teaching to the test." Indeed, Glewwe *et al.* (2010) reported the outcome of a study showing that student performance increased as a result of the incentives only on those specific measures on which the incentive pay program was concentrated.

3.5. *Increase monitoring to detect corruption*

As indicated in the previous section, higher wages to agents are unlikely to reduce corruption very substantially without effective monitoring and enforcement. Olken (2007) reported the outcome of an ingenious way of finding out how best to do this in the context of over-invoicing of reimbursable costs on Indonesian village road projects. Villages were eligible to propose local road projects for funding and when their projects were selected, the projects were assigned to village teams which bought the materials, hired the labor and other inputs to complete the projects. The teams then reported costs to the funding agency for reimbursement. These reports with receipts were subject to a randomized auditing procedure, which in principle could result in someone being indicted for overbilling. Whereas in the baseline only 4% of the executed projects were audited, after treatment in one group of villages all projects were audited. Corruption, measured as the gap between the expenditures reported for each project and the estimates of an independent engineer in the treated group of villages was reduced on average by 8% (or by one third of the average gap of 24% of total cost in untreated villages). The author also reported the outcome of some alternative treatments. In one treatment in which the local citizens were empowered to do the monitoring instead of the central auditor, this had the effect of reducing the more easily observed over-invoicing of labor costs, but these benefits were small relative to the total costs. In another treatment, anonymous comment forms were distributed to the local citizenry which allowed the local citizens to express their concerns without fear of reprisal from the powerful elites. In this case, two different means were used for distributing the forms to the citizens, namely, neighborhood leaders and school children. The largest reduction in over-invoicing was obtained when the forms were distributed by the school children because when distributed by the leaders, the forms were distributed primarily to those closely related to the elite.

In another study making use of the variation in misuse of funds across Brazilian municipalities Ferraz and Finan (2008) showed that conditional on the number of fund use violations, those mayors whose cities were audited prior to an election were less likely to be reelected than those audited after the election. As Olken and Pande (2011) noted, this demonstrates an important complementarity among monitoring activities, information availability and electoral accountability. The effectiveness of monitoring can be increased when information about the outcome of such monitoring is made available prior to election.

Since monitoring is costly, an important practical issue is the choice of what to monitor. Shleifer and Vishny (1993) develop a very simple model for helping to answer that question. Their analysis focuses on the incentives of the agents offering a particular permit and those of their customers and the role of competition among both agents and customers. Competition among agents is likely to increase the ability of agents to price discriminate so as to maximize their revenues (and perhaps be able to bribe the top tier of government for the job). Competition among the customers for the permits is also important. The keener the competition becomes, the more it will push up the demand for permits and the bribe price. But whether or not this happens depends on the payment (if any) that the government gets for the issuance of the permit by the corrupt agent. If he can avoid having to pay anything to the government for selling the permit to his customer, the profit maximizing interests of the corrupt agent and the customer are aligned (but at the expense of the government), since the customer can get the permit at a price below what he would otherwise have to pay had the agent paid the stipulated price to the government. Otherwise, the corrupt agent will charge the customer a price above that which would maximize the agent's own profits but thereby introducing a built-in conflict between the agent and his customer. The absence of such a conflict would mean that it would be in neither the agent's nor the customer's interest to turn the other to the authorities. The stronger the competition for permits, the more this corrupt system would continue to spread. As a result, priority should be given to monitoring the payment of the permit fee of the agents to the government, rather than their illegal receipt of bribes.

An equally important issue in the case of monitoring is the way in which the permit-granting agents are organized. Typically many different permits are required to start a business, e.g., a building permit, a health permit, a labor permit, permits to obtain electricity and water, an investment permit, and property rights permit of some sort. Since the services provided from all these permits are complementary, the pricing of each exerts external effects on the value of the other. Again under endogenous bribe or fee-setting, Shleifer and Vishny (1993) demonstrates that, if this were done independently by each agent, the bribe prices might well be set so high as to make the activities economically infeasible. On the other hand if they were provided in a single one-stop shop, the prices of the different permits would be lower and coordinated in such a way that social welfare (agents plus customers) would be maximized. Further, if competition among the providers of each different service/permit is fostered (as in a federalist system), this may minimize the bribes but not the fees for the government as long as these payments are properly monitored.

3.6. *Rotate, fire, and replace the endemically corrupt agents*

From the principal-agent problem and the actions identified above, taking away the salary and imposing a steep fine on the corrupt agent would be another and rather straight-forward strategy for lowering the incidence of corruption. However, this may not be appropriate or feasible under weak monitoring and enforcement. In particular, the principal may have little evidence of corruption on the part of an individual agent, just overall indications of leakage of funds and anecdotes about corruption. So what can be done under such circumstances?

Abbink (2004) investigated in his computer laboratory an action that had been introduced by the German government a few years earlier, namely, the regular rotation of staff in corruption-prone activities. He did this by investigating the outcome of dictator-type sequential transfer games between individual agents and clients over a sequence of 30 sequential plays of the game. The key feature was that in one experimental group each pair played each sequential game with the same partner whereas in the other group the pairs were rotated at each stage. When the pairs were rotated, the average bribe was reduced by almost 50% relative to that when the pairs remained the same throughout the plays. Moreover, the likelihood of a bribe was reduced by about two-thirds.

In practice, however, staff rotation alone may be less productive. For example, if nothing is done except for the agents being replaced by similar ones and then they once again repeat their interactions, the same behavior may arise with the new agents as long as the clients are still interested in getting favors from the agents. A common response to this situation is to supplement staff rotation with providing 'moral training' for the new agents. However, Lambsdorff (2007, pp. 55–56) cites an account of this supplementation being put into practice in Tanzania: it did not work. All that happened was that the clients made use of those same dismissed agents they had learned to trust; in this case as middlemen between the new agents and the clients, but with the same corruption-induced distortions on resource allocation.

Sometimes the collective firing of existing corrupt agents has been accompanied by their replacement by a very different set of agents, e.g., with a new set of experienced agents from another country with no links whatsoever to existing clients. The new hires may have worked with NGOs or other organizations outside the government. Such an approach was somewhat successful with respect to customs agents in Indonesia. Yet, Bridi (2010) reported that since employing outsiders is very expensive and eventually the government needs to reinstate a national staff the benefits are unlikely to be lasting. This was true of Mozambique in part because there was little transfer of knowledge from the foreign staff to the nationals at the time of returning the operation to government officials.[9]

3.7. *Establish a high profile anti-corruption agency*

Several countries (e.g., Hong Kong, Singapore, and Botswana) have received attention for having introduced — with considerable fanfare — high-level anti-corruption agencies that have been deemed very successful (De Speville 1995; Doig and Riley 1998; Quah 1989, 2000).[10] The creation of these agencies has been said to send a message to both agents and clients in the home country as well as abroad, the principals' (renewed) commitment to fighting corruption. Huther and Shah (2000), however, suggested that these agencies work best in countries where they are needed the least, i.e., in countries with relatively low corruption and other strong governance institutions. Moreover, Pope (2000) showed that in other countries with greater corruption and poor governance, the creation of such agencies has been much less

[9]As suggested in Policy Suggestion 3.3 above, with or without collective firing and replacement, a more productive complement may be to provide greater transparency in all the actions taken. Among such measures would be to require that all the transactions between individual agents and clients be recorded digitally as well as computerizing information on total revenues collected by agents during a particular shift, day or type of client and to make it publicly available. As Bridi (2010) explained, the client will be less inclined to pay bribes not only because of the greater risk of getting caught but also by virtue of seeing that others are paying the full amount of the taxes and that the tax revenues are being channeled into their provision of infrastructure and other public goods desired by the client.

[10]Note from Table 6.1 above that Singapore has for many years now been among the least corrupt countries in the world (No. 5 in the world in the Corruption Perception Index of Transparency International 2011). Hong Kong was No. 12 and Botswana No. 32 in the same index. This placed Singapore and Hong Kong as the top two rated countries in Asia and Botswana as the top country in Africa.

successful. One way in which they fail is by having incomplete support from various parts of government and the private sector. When this is the case, those benefitting from corruption can usually find some basis for discrediting the new agency and hence setting back its mission, perhaps forever.

In an interesting attempt to compare the effectiveness of high level anti-corruption agencies with other anti-corruption strategies such as new laws and signing onto international conventions in the transition countries of Central and Eastern Europe, Rousso and Steves (2006) showed that anti-corruption agencies were on average perhaps slightly more effective, though not in a statistically significant way because of the limited number of observations and the time period under study.[11] In the conclusion, Rousso and Steves (2006) draws the following inferences from the experience with Anti-Corruption Agencies: (1) the effects of such actions take time to become effective, (2) they will not be effective if they are not sustained, (3) they are more likely to be successful the more well-coordinated they are within the country and the more they involve NGOs.

3.8. *Grant freedom of the press and media access*

Another implication easily derivable from the principal-agent problem outlined above, and an immediate derivative of Policy Suggestion 3.4 above, concerning the importance of simplifying regulations and providing information and transparency for reducing corruption, is the usefulness of granting freedom of the press and of media access. Indeed, one interesting finding from the Rousso and Steves (2009) study mentioned in the previous paragraph was that the only variable with a statistically significant negative effect on at least one corruption measure was an index of Media Freedom (from Freedom House). Their analysis treated media freedom as a control variable having only a direct effect on the change in corruption, whereas one might also think that there could be an indirect effect by making some of the other actions more transparent to the public at large.

More generally, among institutional factors that could be expected to deter corruption which have received empirical support from cross-country empirical analyses, the negative effect of various measures of press freedom on corruption has been found quite consistently. (Adsera *et al.* 2000; Lederman *et al.* 2001; Sung 2002; Brunetti and Weder 2003; Besley and Prat 2006) Press freedom may act to reduce corruption through several channels. One is by simply exposing corruption; then, once corruption has been detected, a free press can damage the reputations of the corrupt agents, and further it can pressure governments to enforce the penalties on the corrupt agents and reveal the extent of their diligence in trying to detect corruption. Naturally, freedom of press and media access could be expected to diminish the incentive of agents to be corrupt and increase the interest of the principal in dealing with corruption.

---

[11] This was done by quantifying the cross-country relation between anticorruption measures of different types in one period to changes in various bribe intensity measures in a subsequent period.

Yet, especially since press freedom and media access might be deemed to be more effective in democratic countries with well-educated populations than in autocratic ones. And since autocratic regimes tend to have more corruption and less educated populations, an important issue is whether the causality in this relation goes from lack of press freedom to corruption or the other way around. Since most of these studies are based only on cross section analysis, most are potentially vulnerable to both omitted variable biases and reverse causality.

In an especially impressive paper, Brunetti and Weder (2003) tried to tackle this problem by using an instrumental variable approach and panel data. They instrumented press freedom in several alternative ways: (1) by a measure of the level of political rights (2) with an index of democracy and (3) by the fraction of the country's population which adhered to the Protestant religion and spoke a European language. The key characteristic of a valid instrument is of course that it has a significant effect on the variable instrumented but *no* effect on the dependent variable (in this case the average score of the corruption index produced by the ICRG) *other than* that through the variable instrumented (press freedom). While the authors pointed to a previous study by Ades and Di Tella (1999) showing that political rights had no significant effect on corruption, they offered no formal test results to support their claim there was no direct influence in this case. What they did, however, was to conduct a number of sensitivity tests showing the results, even with respect to magnitudes, to be quite robust to the use of different measures of both corruption and press freedom, to the inclusion of alternative control variables, time periods and estimation procedures (OLS, TSLS, Ordered Probit, and panel estimates with and without fixed effects). In particular, they showed that an increase in press freedom from the average score to highest value would increase freedom from corruption from its cross-country mean to about 30% above this level, irrespective of choice of sample, specification, measures, and estimation procedure. While their analysis did not include access to cellphone, Facebook, Twitter or other technologies which would seem increasingly important in recent years, they found virtually equal effectiveness in almost every component of the press freedom index they used (the absence of newspaper censorship, the independence of newspapers, independence of book publishers, and independence of broadcasting).

Nevertheless, the interdependency between press freedom and these other institutional measures led Lambsdorff (2007, p. 46) to suspect that increasing press freedom, by itself at least, would be insufficient to significantly reduce corruption. Of particular relevance here is the quality and independence of the judiciary.[12] It is not always the case that everything in the press is true and hence inaccuracies, especially about corruption, can be misleading. If libel charges can be filed by individuals and

[12]Lambsdorff (2007) cites a study by Voight *et al.* (2004) indicating that *de facto* judicial independence may be more important than *de jure* judicial independence, but suspecting that the lack of a significant relation between *de jure* judicial independence and corruption could be due to reverse causality, i.e., where corruption is rampant it leads to laws and regulations strengthening the judiciary's hand in dealing with the issue.

groups which feel that they have been incorrectly blamed for corruption, the press will have an incentive to be truthful. However, if the judiciary is corrupt, inefficient or not independent of the executive and legislative branches of the government officials can easily discredit the press or prevent it from being aggressive in its investigation of corruption and other issues.

3.9. *Make greater use of international standards and monitoring*

While monitoring would seem to be one of the most important means of both detecting and reducing corruption, monitoring can be very costly and in many cases very difficult to accomplish even with the best of intentions. Yet, it is important not to lose sight of the fact that international organizations and institutions can also be called into the fight against corruption in any particular country. Such institutions provide useful standards which can enhance transparency in transactions of all kinds, both commercial and governmental. These international agencies or conventions can either monitor directly or, more commonly, train nationals in how to organize anti-corruption activities, identify existing laws and regulations that may allow corruption to flourish and point to other activities and institutional mechanisms that could be used to advantage in the fight against corruption.

In that respect, at the beginning of Section 1, we already identified the United Nations Convention Against Corruption (UNCAC) as a major international institution that could be put to good use. By the end of 2011, 158 countries had ratified this convention, but several countries in the MENA region, such as Oman, Saudi Arabia, Sudan, and Syria, had not yet done so. This convention includes chapters specifying various means of dealing with corruption, such as those concerning prevention, criminalization and law enforcement, international cooperation, asset recovery, technical assistance and perhaps most importantly monitoring each country's compliance to UNCAC standards. Several regional organizations have been organized to coordinate monitoring efforts in their respective regions, to provide the training needed to assure the validity of the monitoring and to translate the findings of shortcomings into remedial actions. The Arab Governmental Expert Group (AGEG) is the relevant organization for Arab countries, set up by the UNDP's Regional Program on Governance for the Arab Region (UNDP-POGAR). Arab nationals with experience in these activities were nominated by their governments and appointed to AGEG which has already carried out several region-wide training programs and then subsequently assisted others at the national level to help conduct the self-assessments mandated by UNCAC. These self-assessments are carried out in three stages. First, a country does its own self-assessment, then it is subjected to a desk review by all relevant organizations within the country and eventually as amended and supplemented it goes to a full, formal evaluation by an outside committee of evaluators from two different countries. Jordan and Algeria were the first two MENA countries to go through such reviews.

As Repucci (2009) indicated, the assessments in these countries demonstrated rather clearly the importance of broad participation and coordination among as many relevant public agencies and NGOs as possible. This study also identified the learning benefits derived from these first self-assessment exercises for subsequent exercises in Kuwait, Iraq, Morocco, and Yemen. Several of them were especially innovative, Kuwait's being the first in the world to have formally involved NGOs, and Morocco's for the breadth of ministries and other agencies engaged in its self-evaluation process. Early experience in the MENA region and elsewhere is generally said to have demonstrated how important it is to involve NGOs and the private sector, especially in those countries where governments are not strongly committed to anti-corruption activities and the goals of UNCAC. In any case, even if initially less than perfect, these self-evaluations should be of great use in identifying problem areas, encouraging greater monitoring of corruption and stronger coordination among government agencies in assessing penalties, coordinating actions and strengthening enforcement against corruption. Comparisons over time should also yield lessons on actions that work and actions that do not.

But there are many other international agencies and conventions that could also be important. For example, the aforementioned study on corruption changes in 26 transition countries by Rousso and Steves (2006) created an index of participation in such conventions based on seven different conventions involving different aspects of the fight against corruption such as civil and criminal law, anti-bribery , anti-corruption , money laundering and so on. Recall also that their regressions showed at least some indication that countries whose indexes of participation in these conventions increased tended to have larger declines in their corruption measures than did other transition countries.

One important international organization that can help or even force countries to improve monitoring of corruption, introduce a wide variety of policies designed to lower the incentives for corruption and to undertake new anti-corruption measures is the International Monetary Fund (IMF). Wolf and Gurgen (2002), for example, pointed to a number of actions with respect to corruption that the IMF had pushed on borrowing countries in their stand-by agreements with the IMF as well as in other programs. This was subsequent to the IMF adopting a new set of guidelines on governance issues in 1997 which also called for technical assistance from the World Bank on how best to deal with corruption. They provided many examples of specific IMF programs in specific countries that pushed anti-corruption actions like those identified in the preceding subsections.

In fishing, an industry of some importance to a number of MENA countries, there are several international standards which MENA countries might do well to sign onto, especially given how poor the information on various aspects of fishing is and how much illegal fishing seems to take place. Information on the management of fisheries, number of fishing boats with licenses, government expenditures on fisheries, fisheries agreements with other countries,[13] and transparency in policy making are

[13]According to Standing (2011), some of these agreements are with European Union (EU) countries but even in these cases, the EU refuses to make these agreements public, compounding the degree of secrecy in the industry.

all very weak. Though seriously understudied in most regions where it has been investigated such as in Asia and Africa (Standing 2011), revenues have been shown to be seriously underreported and the embezzlement of these revenues and license fees to be quite serious (Tsamenyi and Hanich 2009; Standing 2011). A study commissioned by the British aid agency Department for International Development (Marine Resources Assessment Group or MRAG 2005) documented the extent to which the lack of transparency in fishing had resulted in illegal fishing. But there are international conventions that could help and others that could be developed. For example the FAO has developed an international agreement on port state measures to prevent, deter and eliminate illegal fishing as well as the Global Record, an ambitious protocol in which every fishing vessel in the world would be assigned an ID number, and information on vessel characteristics, ports used, inspections, and catches would be recorded and made publicly available.

Of all the industries in the world, the one which has been associated most strongly with corruption is the oil industry (e.g., Hsieh and Moretti 2006; Ross 2012). This is attributed to several factors. One is the lack of transparency in relations between the producers of oil and host governments on the one hand (which involve licensing, exploration, development, production, trade and transport through refining and marketing) and the distribution of those revenues among citizens in general, users of oil and the welfare of those living in the areas near the production sights. This was reflected by the fact that as discussed in Section 1 it was the oil exporting countries of MENA that were ranked so high in terms of illicit capital outflows through the CEB method used by Global Financial Integrity reported by Kar and Freitas (2011). Another problem associated with oil exporting countries is excessive economic volatility (Gelb and Associates 1988) which can lead to very serious inefficiencies in resource allocation as well as to alternating cycles of inflation and unemployment. For the latter problem and following the lead of Norway, Sovereign Wealth Funds have become an important institutional mechanism for pulling out revenues during boom times for use during bad times and more importantly by future generations after oil reserves have been used up. Even here, however, inter-country comparisons of sovereign wealth funds have generally shown the operations of those in MENA countries to be much less transparent than those of Norway and others. Given the importance of oil and gas and other natural resource industries in the MENA region, the ability to make use of sector-specific international standards for dealing with corruption and other problems in this sector could be of great use to citizens of MENA countries. Le Billon (2011), among others, has identified a number of such mechanisms, divided into the different kinds of functions served, namely, (1) contract and revenue transparency, (2) certification, and (3) broader governance standards.

With respect to contract and revenue transparency the aforementioned Extractive Industries Transparency Initiative (EITI) is perhaps the most impressive initiative available, though still only in its early stage of development. Participation in EITI is voluntary. To gain compliance status a government must first gain candidate status. Then, on the basis of annual reports submitted, it has two and a half years to achieve compliance status from the EITI Board. To achieve compliance status a government must require firms operating in the industry to publish their payments to governments and the latter must publish what they receive from the companies with which they deal and provide an independent audit to reconcile differences. EITI compliance also requires that civil society should be involved in the design, monitoring and evaluation of the audits. According to EITI's website, at present 13 countries have achieved compliance status and 21 others have achieved candidate status. Only two MENA countries have achieved either of these (Iraq as a candidate and Yemen as a compliant country, although Yemen's compliance status has been suspended because of concerns that the involvement of civil society with respect to the auditing process was inadequate). While EITI participation may be a step in the right direction as far as disclosure and transparency are concerned, there remain loopholes. The EIYI doesn't require publication of expenditures by firms which could be another way for funds to disappear and to get into corrupt hands, it doesn't require sufficient detail in the accounts that governments and firms must submit and until recently at least its civil society engagement requirement is too vague. There seems to be no evidence that compliance status has yet lowered corruption. But the main problem is that governments and firms have preferred keeping their accounts hidden so as not to tip off competition, and existing EITI members have resisted making the requirements for compliant status more stringent (Le Billon, 2011).

Another initiative with promise in this area is the Dodd-Frank Wall Street Reform and Consumer Protect Act turned into law in July 2010 in the United States. Among the financial reforms required by this act is disclosure of payments by issuers of financial instruments in resource extraction industries to the SEC of the US this would include payments made by the firm and by any of its subsidiaries to a foreign government. The SEC, however, has not yet issued its final guidelines and US oil companies have objected that drafts of this treatment would be discriminatory since it would apply only to those firms regulated by the SEC and by their greater stringency of its disclosure requirements relative to those of EITI. However, since a number of other countries with financial markets in which oil and other natural resource firms are involved are currently considering similar developments, the discrimination critique could be weakened over time.

Since eventual success in reducing corruption through any of these international initiatives is likely to hinge on the effectiveness of the involvement of civil society in these audits and processes, however, to accomplish this may require major improvements in a much broader set of governance institutions.

4. Conclusions

In Section 1 we provided various kinds of data measuring the extent of corruption in MENA countries relative to other regions. Two alternative data sets were presented, first, survey-based data reflecting the opinions based on a variety of sources suggesting a number of specific types and sources of corruption, and second, aggregate statistical data calculating illicit financial flows calculated as a residual from the recorded international transactions.

Data from both sources indicates that a couple of decades ago, corruption was less serious in MENA than in most other regions of developing countries. On the other hand, the data also indicated that corruption in MENA has been on the rise and that in some respects MENA seems to stand out for having more corruption than other regions of developing countries, and much higher corruption than the world average in general.

On both dimensions of corruption we have seen much variation across countries. From the survey-based data sources on both firm and household levels and for most types or forms of corruption, countries like Syria, Egypt, Morocco, and Tunisia would seem to be countries where corruption is most evident and serious while the oil exporting countries of the GCC would seem to be among the most corruption-free. On the aggregate measure of illicit financial flows, however, the picture is reversed with several GCC countries having some of the largest illicit flows in the world, in some cases despite their small size, with little evidence of such problems in other MENA countries.

To a great extent, these inter-country, cross-corruption type differences are explainable. First, in terms of regulations of international trade, finance, and product markets, the non-oil countries are more heavily regulated than the oil exporting countries. Second, as suggested by the principal agent model of Section 2, even though there are regulations in countries of the GCC, because government salaries and fringe benefits are extremely high, there is little incentive for bureaucrats to be corrupt. This may not be the case in the non-oil countries with large, poorly paid bureaucracies. Third, as indicated in Subsection 3.9 above, the monopolistic and secretive character of oil operations, the non-transparent relations with host governments (some with royal families in which it may be difficult to distinguish between private and public accounts), and the rather dominant role of oil in the GCC countries makes them especially susceptible to unrecorded transactions and therefore illicit financial outflows.

For identifying corruption within MENA, Section 1 pointed to a variety of types of surveys that can and should be used to further pinpoint where specific types of corruption occur. These surveys can also monitor changes over time as might be relevant in evaluating the effects of various anti-corruption programs and strategies. In Section 3 above we have identified a wide variety of policies and programs that might be taken against corruption, reviewing evidence from different countries around the world of the degree of success that various countries have had in implementing them. Clearly, local circumstances are very relevant so that any claims that 'one size will fit all' with respect to anti-corruption programs should be viewed with great skepticism.

It is our hope and recommendation that the designers and evaluators of anti-corruption efforts will take advantage of the methods noted in the cases referred to in the studies for measuring specific types and sources of corruption and for evaluating the effectiveness of various alternative programs to reduce it. Indeed, given the growing importance of corruption in MENA, and the extent to which its persistence seems to have been an important trigger for the Arab Spring, existing governments, donors, and research networks like the ERF would do well to initiate anti-corruption programs and related research activities taking advantage of these studies and methods. Many of these are designed to deal with specific types of corruption.

Yet, there are apparently two other activities at the government or international levels that will also be essential for success in dealing with corruption in MENA countries. First, MENA governments should participate largely, and more effectively and openly, in the United Nations Convention Against Corruption (UNCAC) and in Arab Governmental Expert Group (AGEG) activities fostered by the United Nations Development Program. As noted in Subsection 3.9, the first of these is a potentially important way of very comprehensively identifying corruption and weaknesses in existing means of detection and reduction. Yet until recently — as the end of 2011 at least — Oman, Saudi Arabia, Syria, and Sudan had not yet ratified this convention and thereby failed to take advantage of the self-assessment and review mechanisms it afforded. Even among the signatories to UNCAC, not all have made use of the training and related assessment mechanisms of AGEG. In view of the large size of the public sector in most MENA countries and the understandable desires of the private sector for stable policy and regulatory regimes, it will be very important to have the private sector better represented in these activities, perhaps through NGOs.

Second, given the importance of illicit financial outflows in the GCC countries, and the vulnerability of oil revenues to these illicit outflows, further activities to control illicit financial outflows in oil and other natural resource exporting countries in the region would seem warranted. Such activities are especially needed given the apparent desire for secrecy by each government and each oil country. Again, as indicated in Subsection 3.9, each resource exporting country would be advised to sign onto the Extractive Industries Transparency Initiative (EITI) initiated by former British Prime Minister Tony Blair and to go through the steps needed to become compliant with the standards that have been established under that initiative. These include requiring all firms operating in these industries to publish their payments to governments, and governments to provide a full account of what they receive from the firms. Taking advantage of this mechanism and going on to investigate discrepancies could go a long way toward reducing the enormous illicit financial outflows that currently exist in GCC countries. Beyond this, the international community can be useful in forcing all firms wishing to have shares traded in the stock exchanges to publish the sources of their oil and all other payments to host countries. Such efforts would have the additional and very desirable effect of increasing the transparency of budgetary policies, consequently encouraging the use of fiscal rules that could greatly reduce the volatility and pro-cyclicality of government spending in natural resource exporting countries, since excessive volatility is a well-known cause of slower growth in the long run.

Acknowledgments

I would like to express my appreciation for the research assistance of Rose Gauthier and to comments and suggestions from Ragui Assaad, Mine Cinar, Ishac Diwan, Heba Handoussa, Rob Jenson, Daniel Kauffman, and other participants in the Annual Conference of the Economic Research Forum in Cairo, Egypt, March 2012.

References

Abbink, K. 2004. "Staff rotation as an anti-corruption policy: An experimental study." *European Journal of Political Economy*, 20(4): 887–906.

Abbink, K. and M. Ellman. 2004. "The donor problem." University of Pampeu Favra Economics Working Paper 796.

Ades, A. and R. Di Tella. 1997. "National champions and corruption: Some unpleasant interventionist arithmetic." *Economic Journal*, 107: 1023–1042.

Ades, A. and R. Di Tella. 1999. "Rents, competition and corruption." *American Economic Review*, 89: 982–994.

Adsera, A., C. Boix and M. Payne 2000. "Are you being served? Political accountability and quality of government." Inter-American Development Bank Research Department Working Paper 438.

Barr, A., M. Lindelow and P. Serneels. 2004. "To serve the community or oneself: The public servant's dilemma." World Bank Policy Research Working Paper 3187.

Bertrand, M., S. Djankov, R. Hanna and S. Mullainathan. 2007. "Obtaining a driver's license in India: An experimental approach to studying corruption." *The Quarterly Journal of Economics*, 122(4): 1639–1676.

Besley, T. and A. Prat. 2006. "Handcuffs for the guiding hand? Media capture and government accountability." *American Economic Review*, 96(3): 720–736.

Bridi, A. 2010. "Corruption in tax administration." Transparency International U4 Anti-Corruption Research Centre. U4 Expert Answer (Janaury). Available online at http://www.u4.no/ publications/corruption-in-tax-administration/.

Broadman, H. G. and F. Recanatini. 1999. "Seeds of corruption. Do market institutions matter?" World Bank Policy Research Working Paper 2368. Washington, DC: World Bank.

Brunetti, A. and B. Weder 2003. "A free press is bad news for corruption." *Journal of Public Economics*, 87(7–8): 1801–1824.

De Speville, B. E. D. 1995. "The experience of Hong Kong in combatting corruption." Second Integrity in Government Seminar Amman, Jordan, 16–17 December.

Di Tella, R. and E. Schargrodsky. 2003. "The role of wages and auditing during a crackdown on corruption in the city of Buenos Aires." *Journal of Law and Economics*, 56: 269–288.

Djankov, S., R. La Porta, F. Lopez-de-Silanes and A. Shleifer. 2002. "The regulation of entry." *The Quarterly Journal of Economics*, 117(1): 1–37.

Doig, A. and S. Riley 1998. "Corruption ad anti-corruption strategies:issues and case studies from developing countries." In *Corrution and Integrity Improvement Initiatives in Developing Countries*, ed. United Nations Development Programme, pp. 45–62. New York: United Nations Publications.

Duflo, E., R. Hanna and S. Ryan. 2012. "Monitoring works: Getting teachers to come to school." *American Economic Review*, 102(4): 1241–1278.

Elliott, K. A. 1997. "Corruption as an international policy problem: Overview and recommendations." In *Corruption and the Global Economy*, ed. Elliott, K. A., pp. 175–235. Washington, DC: Institute for International Economics.

Ferraz, C. and F. Finan. 2008. "Exposing corrupt politicians: The effects of Brazil's publicly released audits on electoral outcomes." *The Quarterly Journal of Economics*, 123(2): 703–745.

Ferraz, C. and F. Finan. 2011. "Electoral accountability and corruption: Evidence from the audit reports of local governments." *American Economic Review*, 101(4): 1274–1311.

Fisman, R. and R. Gatti. 2002. "Decentralization and corruption: Evidence across countries." *Journal of Public Economics*, 83(3): 325–345.

Gatti, R. 1999. "Corruption, and trade tariffs or a case for uniform tariffs." World Bank Policy Research Working Paper 2216. Washington, D.C.: World Bank.

Gelb, A. and Associates. 1988. *Oil Windfalls: Blessing or Curse?* New York: Oxford University Press.

Gerring, J. and S. Thacker. 2005. "Do neoliberal policies deter political corruption? " *International Organization* 59: 233–254.

Glewwe, P., I. Nauman and M. Kremer. 2010. "Teacher incentives." *American Economic Journal: Applied Economics*, 2(3): 205–227.

Grindle, M.S. 1997. "Divergent cultures? When public organizations perform well in developing countries." *World Development*, 25(4): 481–495.

Hsieh, C. R. and E. Moretti. 2006. "Did Iraq cheat the United Nations? Underpricing, bribes and the Oil for Food Program." *The Quarterly Journal of Economics*, 121(4): 1211–1248.

Huther, J. and A. Shah. 2000. "Anti-corruption policies and programs: A framework for evaluation." World Bank Policy Research Working Paper 2501. Washington, D.C.: World Bank.

Kar, D. and S. Freitas. 2011. *Illicit Financial Flows from Developing Countries Over the Decade Ending 2009.* Washington: Global Financial Integrity.

Khan, M. H. 2006. "Determinants of corruption in developing countries: The limits of conventional analysis." In *International Handbook on the Economics of Corruption*, ed. Rose-Ackerman, S., pp. 216–244. Cheltenham: Edward Elgar.

Khan, M. H. and K.S. Jomo, eds. 2006. *Rents, Rent-Seeking and Economic Development: Theory and Evidence in Asia.* Cambridge, UK: Cambridge University Press.

Klitgaard, R. 1988. *Controlling Corruption.* Berkeley: University of California Press.

Klitgaard, R. 1991. *Adjusting to Reality: Beyond 'State versus Market' in Economic Development.* San Francisco: International Center for Economic Growth.

Knack, S. and O. Azfar. 2003. "Trade intensity, country size and corruption." *Economics of Governance* 4(1): 1–8.

Krueger, A. O. 1974. "The political economy of rent-seeking society." *American Economic Review*, 64: 291–303.

Lambsdorff, J. G. 2007. *The Institutional Economics of Corruption and Reform.* Cambridge, UK: Cambridge University Press.

Lambsdorff, J. G. and P. Cornelius. 2000. "Corruption, foreign investment and growth." In *Africa competitiveness report 2000*, eds. Schwab, K., L. Cook, P. Cornelius. J.D. Sachs, S. Sievers. and A. Warner. Cambridge, Massachusetts: Harvard University Press.

Lambsdorff, J. G. and M. Nell. 2005. "Let them take gifts and cheat those who seek influence." Passauer Diskussionpapier, Volkswirttschaftliche Reihe Diskussionsbeitrag v-41–05.

LaPalombara, J. 1994. "Structural and institutional aspects of corruption." *Social Research*, 61(2): 325–350.

Le Billon, P. 2011. "Extractive sectors and illicit financial flows: What role for revenue governance initiatives?" Transparency International U4 Anti-Corruption Research Centre. U4 Issue No 13 (November). Available online at http://www.cmi.no/publications/file/4248-extractive-sectors-and-illicit-financial-flows.pdf

Lederman, D. N. Loayza and R.R. Soares 2001. "Accountability and corruption: political institutions matter." World Bank Working Paper 2708. Washington, DC: World Bank.

Leite, C. and J. Weidemann. 1999. "Does Mother Nature corrupt? Natural resources, corruption and economic growth." International Monetary Fund Working Paper 99/85 (July).

Mauro, P. 1995. "Corruption and growth." *The Quarterly Journal of Economics*, 110(3): 681–712.

Mauro, P. 1997. "The effects of corruption on growth, investment, and government expenditure: A cross-country analysis." In *Corruption and the global economy*, ed. Elliott, K. A., pp. 83–108. Washington, DC: Institute for International Economics.

Marine Resources Assessment Group (MRAG). 2005. "Review of impacts of illegal, unreported and unregulated fishing in developing countries." London: Marine Resources Assessment Group.

Muralidharan, K. and V. Sundaramian. 2009. "Teacher performance pay: Experimental evidence from India." National Bureau of Economic Research Working Paper 15323.

Olken, B. 2007. "Monitoring corruption: Evidence from a field experiment in Indonesia." *Journal of Political Economy*, 115(2): 200–220.

Olken, B. A. and R. Pande. 2011. "Corruption in developing countries." National Bureau of Economic Research Working Paper 17398.

Pope, J. 2000. "The Transparency International Sourcebook 2000." In *Confronting Corruption: The Elements of A National Integrity System*, ed. Pope, J. Berlin: Transparency International.

Quah, J. T. 1989. "Singapore's experience in curbing corruption." In *Political Corruption: A Handbook*. New Brunswick, eds. Heidenheimer, A. J., M. Johnson. and V.T. Levine, pp. 841–853. New Jersey: Transaction Books.

Quah, J. T. 2000. *Confronting Corruption: The Elements of a National Integrity System.* Berlin: Transparency International.

Reinikka, R. and J. Svensson. 2004. "Local capture: Evidence from a central government transfer program in Uganda." *The Quarterly Journal of Economics*, 119(2): 679–705.

Reinikka, R. and J. Svensson. 2005. "Fighting corruption to improve schooling: Evidence from a newspaper campaign in Uganda." *Journal of the European Economic Association*, 3(2–3): 259–267.

Repucci, S. 2009. "Maximizing the potential of UNCAC implementation: Making use of the self-assessment checklist." Transparency International U4 Anti-Corruption Research Centre. U4 Issue No 13 (January). Available online at http://www.cmi.no/publications/file/3484-maximising-the-potential-of-uncac-implementation.pdf.

Root, H. 1999. "The importance of being small." Center for International Studies Working Paper 99–13. Los Angeles: USC.

Ross, M. L. 2012. *The Oil Curse: How Petroleum Wealth Shapes the Development of Nations.* Princeton: Princeton University Press.

Rousso, A. and F. Steves. 2006. "The effectiveness of anti-corruption programs: Preliminary evidence from the post-communist transition countries." In *International handbook on the economics of corruption*, ed. Rose-Ackerman, S., pp. 247–277. Cheltenham: Edward Elgar.

Sachs, J. and A. M. Warner. 2001. "The curse of natural resources." *European Economic Review*, 45: 827–838.

Sandholtz, W. and M. Gray. 2003. "International integration and national corruption." *International Organization*, 57(4), 761–800.

Sayan, S. 2009. "Institutions and economic performance in the MENA region: Editor's introduction." In *Economic Performance in the Middle East and North Africa: Institutions, Corruption and Reform*, ed. Sayan, S., pp. 1–12. London: Routledge.

Shleifer, A. and R. W. Vishny. 1993. "Corruption." *The Quarterly Journal of Economics*, 108(3): 599–617.

Shleifer, A. and R. W. Vishny. 2002. *The Grabbing Hand — Government Pathologies and Their Cures.* Cambridge, Massachusetts: Harvard University Press.

Standing, A. 2011. "Making transparency work in Africa's marine fisheries." Transparency International U4 Anti-Corruption Research Centre. U4 Issue No 11 (October). Available online at http://www.u4.no/publications/ making-transparency-work-in-africa-s-marine-fisheries/.

Sung, H.-E. 2002. "A convergence approach to the analysis of political corruption: A cross-national study." *Crime, Law and Social Change*, 38(2): 137–160.

Tsamenyi, M. and Q. Hanich. 2009. "Managing fisheries and corruption in Pacific Island fisheries." *Marine Policy*, 33: 386–392.

Ul Haque, N. and R. Sahay. 1996. "Do government wage cuts close budget deficits: The costs of corruption." *IMF Staff Papers*, 43(4): 754–778.

Van Rijckeghem, C. and B. Weder. 2001. "Bureaucratic corruption and the rate of temptation: Do wages in the civil service affect corruption, and by how much? " *Journal of Development Economics*, 65(2): 307–321.

Voight, S., L. Feld and A. van Aaken. 2004. "Power over prosecutors corrupts politicians: Cross-country evidence using a new indicator." University of Kassel Working Paper.

Wolf, T. and I. Gurgen. 2002. "Improving governance and fighting corruption in the Baltic and CIS countries: The role of the IMF." In *Governance, Corruption and Economic Performance*, eds. George, T. A. and S. Gupta. pp. 538–64. Washington, DC: International Monetary Fund.

Yang, D. 2005. "Integrity for hire: An analysis of widespread customs reform." *Journal of Law and Economics*, 51(1): 25–57.

Yang, D. 2006. "The economics of anti-corruption: Lessons from a widespread customs reform." In *International Handbook on the Economics of Corruption*, ed. Rose-Ackerman, S., pp. 512–541. Cheltenham: Edward Elgar.

Chapter 7

ENHANCING COMPETITION IN A POST-REVOLUTIONARY ARAB CONTEXT: DOES THE TURKISH EXPERIENCE PROVIDE ANY LESSONS?

Izak Atiyas

1. Introduction

The purpose of this Chapter is to explore the possible role of the regulatory environment in enhancing competition in the post-revolutionary Arab societies, drawing on the experience of Turkey in the last decade. The pre-revolutionary regimes in these countries are often perceived to entail a distorted form of competition where firms with political connections have the upper hand, and where profitability results not from productivity but from privileged access to scarce resources controlled by the political authority or from politically established barriers to competition. It is well accepted that long-term growth, on the other hand, requires a system where creative destruction can work its way. This requires a policy and regulatory framework that constrains political authority in a way such that it limits arbitrariness and discrimination in policy toward firms and ensures more equal access to politically controlled resources. The regulatory framework needs to also redirect public authority to address various market failures so as to reduce barriers to entry, and, in particular, prevent anti-competitive behavior and foreclosure by dominant firms. More generally, transition to a more competitive environment requires institutional measures to ensure that state power is used to maximize citizens' welfare rather than the welfare of state elites and/or their constituencies.

This Chapter will provide a review of these institutional measures. These measures — or new rules of the game — include remedies such as privatization, delegation of authority (in particular to relatively independent regulatory agencies), a competition law and its enforcement, liberalization, stakeholder participation in governance and monitoring, and open and non-discriminatory procedures for public procurement. The remedies also include forms of public-private participation schemes in order to attract private capital to finance the provision of public services, especially in infrastructure. In this Chapter, these remedies will be referred to as the competition-enhancing reform package.

Significant variability across different jurisdictions notwithstanding, it would be fair to say that this reform package has gained global acceptance over the last three decades. Several developments have been instrumental in this. One important factor has been technological change, in particular the emergence of the possibility of introducing competition to industries that had until then, been organized as state monopolies, for example electricity and telecommunications. The possibility of introducing competition did not mean that anti-competitive behavior no longer posed problems. The need to constrain anti-competitive behavior created a necessity for a new regulatory framework so that new entrants could have a chance of survival and gain market share. Another widespread reason was the desire of many governments to reduce the burden of infrastructure investments on the public budget and attract private investments instead. Although this 'public finance' motivation for the reform package has been underlined for emerging economies, the literature suggests that it was an important consideration in the case of developed economies as well. A parallel development has been a tendency to seek contractual forms to shift the provision of various public services from within agencies of central or local governments to the private sector, in the hope that competition would enable the provision of these services more efficiently. International organizations such as the World Bank and the International Monetary Fund (IMF) expressed dissatisfaction with the performance of public enterprises, and the political mood in some countries reflected a similar disappointment and saw privatization as a solution.

These components of competition/liberalization, private participation and privatization were emphasized to different degrees in different jurisdictions. Hence the overriding concern in the European Union (EU) as a whole has been competition/liberalization, as well as the formation of a single market, and the emphasis on privatization has differed significantly across member states. The privatization component was emphasized in many World Bank and IMF programs in developing and transition countries, partly reflecting the ideological shifts in the post-1980 environment, and partly reflecting the need to generate public revenues to help resolve fiscal and financial crises. It would be fair to say that the reform package and especially its privatization component are being subject to a more critical assessment now.[1]

An important political dimension of the reform package has been the delegation of substantial regulatory rule-making and enforcement power from ministries and ministerial departments to what have been called independent regulatory authorities (IRAs). Several normative and positive explanations have been advanced for this transfer of power, including the insulation of the regulatory process from short term

[1] See, for example, Roland (2008) on privatization in general and Estache *et al.* (2009) for reform in utilities.

political influence, deployment of mechanisms of credible commitment to reduce fears of expropriation, ensuring that state intervention is implemented in a non-discriminatory manner and without favoring firms with political connections, and enhancing the state's ability to attract the necessary human capital for complex regulatory tasks. Delegation of rule-making authority to IRAs was also meant to reduce the discretionary powers of the political authority and attain a more rule-based and transparent framework for economic policy.

The Chapter will use Turkey as the main example from which useful lessons can hopefully be learnt. The country is an interesting example because it has adopted many elements of the reform package in the last two decades or so. Hence one can ask: to what extent have these institutional changes produced the desired results? Have adoption of new laws and establishment of IRAs really created a more competitive environment? Or were these changes merely cosmetic? It is hoped that a critical review of Turkey's experience may provide lessons about the likely outcomes of similar institutional changes elsewhere.

The Chapter is organized as follows: Section 2 will review the content and institutional set-up of a competition enhancing reform package, Section 3 will present an overview of the Turkish experience. On the basis of that experience as well as suggestions from the literature, Section 4 will discuss some tradeoffs and challenges in pursuing reform, and Section 5 will conclude.

2. A Competition Enhancing Reform Package

The adoption of the elements of the competition-enhancing reform package in most developing countries in the 20th Century occurred as part of a transition from an economic policy regime where the state played a direct role in allocating resources to one where the market mechanism was given a more prominent role. From a normative point of view this required a new system of rules, or an overall regulatory framework to ensure that the market mechanism worked properly and that various forms of market failures were addressed.

2.1. *The content*

In most countries, at the heart of this new regulatory framework lies competition law which applies across industries a set of rules that outlaws anti-competitive agreements among firms and prevents dominant firms from exercising market power in an abusive manner. The main logic and language of competition law has also been more or less applied to other industries previously organized as public monopolies and which have been liberalized to allow entry by new players and where market structure makes it especially easy for incumbent players who own or control the basic infrastructure facilities (such as transmission and distribution networks, or fixed or mobile telecommunications infrastructure) to foreclose markets to these new players. However, in these so-called network industries competition law has been seen as insufficient to ensure effective competition and most countries have enacted sector-specific regulations that constrain the behavior of incumbents in an *ex-ante* manner and that ensure new players non-discriminatory access to network facilities.

In industries where the service in question does not allow meaningful competition among multiple service providers and where it is desired that the private sector play an active role in the provision of the public service in question, mechanisms have been developed to ensure that the concession in question is awarded to those private players who are most fit. Hence the logic of competition has also been extended to public procurement. As stated by one observer "the main principle in public procurement is to facilitate open and non-discriminatory competition with free entry" (Limi 2011, p. 121). This is probably an over-simplification, since from the government's perspective the procurement process starts with a decision about whether to produce the service in question in-house or whether to engage the private sector in its provision. This is then followed by an ownership decision: should the assets be owned by the government or the private sector, and if by the latter, for how long? Still, it would not be a mistake to state that the logic of a competitive process has become more prominent in the search for desirable mechanisms of procurement. In particular, designing procedures that are 'open and non-discriminatory' has become an important principle that guides governments.

2.2. *The institutional setup*

Replacing direct and often discretionary state control with new forms of control through rules and procedures corresponds to a major realignment in the structure of the state and in the way state power is deployed. What made this restructuring even more drastic has been the specific institutional form that has accompanied it. In most countries adoption of the reform package has been accompanied by the establishment of IRAs which have been delegated the power to design and implement many of these new rules and procedures. Competition laws are enforced through independent agencies almost everywhere in the world, and IRAs have been established for network industries and other industries where market failures are apparent such as financial markets and banking industries and even other areas where governments interact with the private sector such as public procurement.

The literature has identified a number of reasons behind this delegation of authority:

(1) Independence from the political realm is necessary so that regulatory objectives are differentiated from other political objectives. For example, the regulation of prices to contain monopolistic abuse should not be contaminated with other objectives such as the fight against inflation (Ugaz 2002). Overall, price stability is more effectively attained through other (monetary and fiscal) policies.
(2) Efficient regulatory decisions can require a long-term outlook and politicians often have shorter term horizons (Ugaz 2002).

(3) An independent body, relative to a ministry directorate, is more effective at providing regulatory credibility and commitment. Both are necessary to reduce the risk of expropriation in general but also specifically to reduce the risk of discrimination in favor of politically connected investors. Delegating the power of regulatory authority to an IRA that is not under the direct control of the political authority may be an effective institutional measure to generate this credibility.

(4) Sector specific regulation often requires expert skills that may be difficult to attract within the confines of current personnel regime and pay scales of the public administration. Relatively independent bodies may be established with their own personnel policies.

In what sense are IRAs supposed to be independent? First they are expected to be independent from politicians. The literature has emphasized a number of formal conditions, discussed below, that characterize political independence, but it is also emphasized that these *de jure* conditions do not in themselves ensure *de facto* independence. Independence also refers to independence of IRAs from the firms that they regulate or other interest groups that have a stake in regulation. The term 'capture' is often used to refer to influences by various players that make regulatory activity produce results that are different from those that serve the public interest, whichever way the latter is defined. Estache and Wren-Lewis (2010a) distinguishes between *capture of decisions* and *capture of information*, where the former refers to interest groups' direct influence on decision makers and the latter to ability to withhold information and prevent it from being disclosed so as to appropriate information rents. They also distinguish between *ex-ante* and *ex-post* capture: *ex-ante* capture refers to interest groups' efforts to influence laws and regulations whereas *ex-post* capture occurs within the existing legal framework (e.g., effort to inflate costs to get higher rates).

In reference to formal conditions of political independence the literature emphasizes the following (e.g., Thatcher 2011). First, independence means that the IRA can act without the approval of the ministry and that the ministry cannot overturn a regulation or decision handed over by the IRA. It also means that if the politicians want to change the behavior or the aim of IRAs, they have to do this by enacting laws rather than issuing instructions. Second, regulators cannot be dismissed by ministers at will, except on the basis of wrongdoing or incapacity. Typically regulators are appointed (or in some jurisdictions elected) for a fixed term. Whenever regulators are run by boards rather than a single director, there are often recommendations that board members should be appointed in a staggered manner. The third condition emphasized in the literature is financial independence. This usually means that the budget of the authority should not be at the discretion of the government. This condition is often implemented through earmarked taxes or special revenues earmarked to the agency such as license fees or penalties. Of course, even when these conditions are met, politicians may affect regulatory decisions through various means. For example, since in many jurisdictions appointment of regulators is a political process, this may give politicians the opportunity to appoint individuals who are likely to have similar preferences or who are more susceptible to influence.

IRAs are not meant to be completely independent from the political realm; after all their creation is a political act (often a constituting piece of legislation). The general formulation is that the determination of policy is carried out in the political realm and the task of the IRA is to design, implement, and enforce the secondary legislation through which the policy is realized. Independence from the political realm also does not mean that IRAs are not accountable. Again, the literature lists a number of measures to ensure accountability. A classic list is provided by Smith (1997, p. 1):

- Rigorous transparency — including open decision-making and publication of decisions and the reasons for those decisions
- An appeals process
- Scrutinize the agency's budget, usually by the legislature
- Prohibit conflicts of interest
- Subject the regulator's conduct and efficiency to scrutiny by external auditors or other public watchdogs[2]

These can be taken as the basic measures to ensure the independence and accountability of IRAs. The institutional design of IRAs contains additional variables or dimensions that need to be decided on and how variations along those dimensions are likely to affect IRAs' performance has been a subject of debate. These dimensions will be discussed in the next section.

3. The Experience of Turkey

Turkey's transition to a market oriented policy regime started in the 1980s. Before that Turkey pursued a model of import substitution industrialization with widespread state intervention through direct production and various forms of price controls, subsidies, and directed credit. The economic presence of the state notwithstanding, however, the role of the private sector was important. In fact, the objective of state intervention was partly to help develop private industry, and private industry did develop albeit in a highly concentrated, oligopolistic and internationally uncompetitive manner.

Hence when Turkey started to move towards a more market oriented economic policy regime in the 1980s, there was already a relatively developed private sector led by diversified holding companies owned by dynastic families. Most of these holding companies actually developed starting in the 1950s. This followed a move from a single party to a multi-party regime — a decision taken in 1945 — and in the

[2]Indeed the Turkish experience provides compelling examples about how these elements may make a crucial difference in the performance.

election in 1950 the opposition won with a landslide and there was a change in the government. In any case, although not independent of the state and possibly highly dependent on it for capital accumulation as well as critical inputs, by the 1980s the private sector in Turkey was an important locus of economic and social power.[3]

3.1. *From discretionary capitalism to institutional reform*[4]

In the 1980s, barriers to international trade and finance were reduced or removed, so were controls on domestic financial markets and more specifically on the banking system. However during the 1980s and 1990s, governments in Turkey did not show a deep interest in developing a solid legal and regulatory framework for a market economy.[5] This was especially true for the financial markets. The liberalization of the capital account itself was carried out without the approval of the central bank (and against warnings that liberalizing international finance under conditions of macro-economic instability was not a good idea). The banking sector expanded rapidly without an effective system that would ensure that excessive risk-taking would be curtailed. This was especially relevant given the availability of arbitrage opportunities provided by borrowing in foreign currency and investing these funds into domestic assets, especially government securities bearing high real interest rates, reflecting some sort of collusion between the banking industry and fiscally profligate governments (Alper and Onis 2004). The weakness of regulation of the banking system not only encouraged excessive risk-taking, but also allowed several cases of gross corruption where banks assets were siphoned off by bank managers and owners (Atiyas and Emil 2005). Along with deterioration of public finances, the weaknesses in the banking system was among the primary triggers of the financial crisis of 2000–2001.

Attempts to privatize state assets were undertaken through half-baked laws and often through decrees with the force of law. Governments basically tried to give substantial discretion to the executive or to specific agencies controlled by the executive, on the procedures and methodologies to be followed in the privatization process; in effect, they would have allowed governments to pursue privatizations in unaccountable and un-transparent ways. Most of these efforts were met by annulments by the Constitutional Court, in most cases on the grounds that the laws or decree-laws effectively transferred legislative authority to the executive: in other words, the Constitutional Court demanded that details of the procedures to be followed during privatizations, the options available regarding privatization methods and the like should be explicitly stated in the law and should not be left to the discretion of the executive. In short, then, given a choice between rules versus discretion, the governments of 1980s and 1990s were clearly in favor of discretion.

Throughout the 1990s there were attempts to pursue privatizations or private participation in telecommunications and electricity without first establishing a

[3]Ersel (2012).
[4]This section borrows from Atiyas (2012).
[5]An important exception is the enactment of a competition law, see below.

regulatory framework to contain the exercise of monopoly power or to ensure the development of competition. With regards to the energy sector, governments tried to attract private capital through various contractual schemes entailing[6] monopoly rights and government take or pay guarantees. Some of these contracts were awarded without a competitive tender procedure. These contracts have been later investigated by the High Court of Accounts and criticized for high costs, possible irregularities and incompatibility with competitive markets (Atiyas 2005). The contingent fiscal liabilities generated by these contracts also caused concerns.

What happened in the fiscal area in the 1990s can be best characterized by fragmentation and disintegration. The political science literature on Turkey has emphasized the importance of populism and patronage in political competition. In terms of fiscal policy, this means that the use of public resources to nurture political support is a central instrument of political competition. This puts pressure on public finances and creates a strong tendency to generate public deficits. Towards the end of 1990s, budget 'unity' broke down completely: there were various forms of off-budget expenditures, especially through state-owned banks in the form of support for agriculture and small enterprises. The real magnitude of these quasi-fiscal expenditures and their implied burden on the budget and public debt were at the time not shown in official statistics and disclosed to the public. It is generally accepted that hidden public debt also played an important role in the events leading to the crisis of 2000–2001.[7]

Overall, then, it can be said that while the scope of state intervention decreased in the 1980s and 1990s relative to the previous few decades, this period was nevertheless characterized by discretionary rather than a rule based policy environment. There were important initiatives during this period which were exceptions to this characterization. The first was the establishment of the Capital Markets Board (CMB) in 1982 to develop and regulate securities markets in Turkey. The CMB was the first independent regulatory authority (IRA), and, as discussed by Atiyas and Ersel (1994), it was evident that, since it entailed delegation of significant rule-making authority away from the government and ministries, it represented a counter-example to the centralization of policy making authority that characterized most of the 1980s and 1990s. One possible explanation for this move is the rapid and uncontrolled growth of non-bank financial institutions from 1980–1981, which subsequently resulted in the "bankers' crisis" of 1982, and lead to a loss of popular confidence in the non-bank financial system. CMB was seen as necessary to restore the confidence without which capital markets could not develop. The development of capital markets was seen in turn as a necessary component of the economic transformation the country was going through in the post-1980 period.

[6] These were schemes involving Build Operate Transfer, Build Operate Own and Transfer of Operating Rights.

[7] One could say that emergence of corruption in the financial sector and the disintegration of fiscal institutions were expressions of a more general institutional decay going on in the country. This was reflected in the emergence of para-military illegal gangs whic pursue murders on behalf of the state or the overall Susurluk scandal involving the close relationship between the state and organized crime.

The second initiative was the enactment of a competition law in 1994 and the establishment of the Competition Authority in 1997. These moves can be explained by Turkey's commitments under the Customs Union with the EU in 1996. Indeed, as will be discussed in more detail below, the path towards EU accession (as well as pressures from international agencies such as the IMF and the World Bank) played major roles in the evolution of Turkish economic institutions.

The program that was launched after the crisis of 2000–2001 entailed a number of significant institutional measures. In a way, the program adopted the 'second generation reforms' proposed by international organizations such as the IMF and the World Bank, but by and large the reforms also coincided with those that Turkey had to pursue as a country in the process of accession toward membership to the European Union. Many of these reforms which were part of the recovery program launched in 2001 were adopted without much change and even extended by the AKP government that came to power after the elections of 2002.

One of the most important steps undertaken in the reform program was to introduce independence of the central bank. A supportive fiscal policy stance played an important role in the success of monetary policy. A Public Financing and Debt Management Law adopted in 2002 subjected all central government borrowing and guarantees to strict rules and imposed reporting requirements on all debts and guarantees. The Public Financial Management and Control Law passed in December 2003 consolidated all fiscal operations of the government in an integrated general government approach, from the preparation to the closing stages of the budget. It also envisaged a three-year budget framework. These are measures that substantially improve fiscal control and transparency of the budget process. To the extent that any expenditure has to be executed within an established budget process and in a transparent manner, and therefore would be scrutinized by the public, it can be said that these measures also limit the discretionary powers of the executive. Overall the governments in the post-crisis era have been very successful in implementing a large fiscal adjustment even though observers have identified a significant number of slippages in the implementation of the new fiscal framework (Dedeoglu 2010).

Another critical dimension of the post-crisis program was strengthening the supervision and regulation of the banking system. The Banking Regulation and Supervision Authority (BRSA) was established in 1999 but its powers were significantly increased after the crisis. It has engineered a massive recapitalization of the banking system and has earned a reputation for being a strong regulator, a sharp contrast with the weak regulatory environment in the previous two decades. Tight regulation of the banking system is generally seen as a major factor behind the resilience of the financial sector in Turkey during the 2008–2009 global crisis.

Regarding competition proper, as mentioned above, a Competition Law, modeled after that of the EU, was already enacted in 1994 as part of a Customs Union with the EU. The Competition Authority is recognized to be a professionally competent and relatively independent agency, not only by domestic stakeholders, but by international peers as well (OECD 2005). The decisions of the Competition Board are required to be publicly available and published with justifications, which increases the transparency and accountability of the agency. This may have created an added source of discipline that has improved its performance. Maintaining independence may have also been easier due to the fact that it functions across many industries and does not deal in a continuous manner with a specific enterprise or groups of enterprises, a situation that could have facilitated capture.[8] This does not mean that there are no shortcomings: there are instances of favoritism towards state owned enterprises, inconsistencies in decisions across cases or over time, insufficient or sometimes deficient economic analysis, excessive formalism and the like. Nevertheless these shortcomings do not change the basic fact that overall the agency's decisions are seen to be free of systematic bias and they meet a minimum level of quality, at least relative to the rest of the RAs in Turkey.

In the area of privatization, by the end of the 1990s the legal infrastructure was almost complete. In effect, the executive had been forced to reduce the degree of administrative discretion and establish more transparent and accountable procedures for privatization. In addition, as discussed below, by 2001 legal regulatory frameworks were also established for the deregulation and privatization of industries which were hitherto dominated by public monopolies, namely telecommunications and energy. While privatization revenues generated until 2000 were below $9 billion, more than $30 billion has been raised between 2001–2010 (Onis 2011). Among privatized assets were large enterprises in industries such as petrochemicals, petroleum refinery, telecommunications, electricity distribution, banking, and alcohol and tobacco products.

Overall, privatizations in Turkey have been revenue-driven. The problem with revenue-driven privatizations is that the governments may overlook competition problems or indeed may endow enterprises to be privatized with monopoly rents in order to increase privatization revenues. The Competition Authority has been involved in the privatization process and has been able to influence some privatization transactions to ensure that measures are undertaken to reduce competition problems that may arise once assets are turned over to private ownership. For example during the privatization of Turk Telekom the Competition Authority has required that the provision of internet services be organized as a separate legal entity and that the cable TV infrastructure be separated from Turk Telekom. More recently, the Competition Authority has prevented investors from owning both gas and electricity distribution companies in the same region. The idea here was that under separate ownership gas and electricity distribution companies may enter each other's business areas and thereby give rise to a competitive process, whereas placing them under the ownership of a single investor will prevent the development of this form of competition. In tradable industries such as cement as well, the Competition

[8]One should point out that most observers single out another important factor that may help explain the degree of professionalism of the Competition Authority: the high quality of the bureaucrats who were initially appointed as line managers and who have shaped the emerging culture of the agency.

Authority has taken decisions that has influenced privatization outcomes and have prevented the sale of enterprises to groups whose purchase of these assets would have created or enhanced dominance.

In industries characterized by natural monopoly segments such interventions by the Competition Authority have limited influence on market outcomes; ultimately the evolution of market structure depends on the existence and effective implementation of a regulatory framework that protects competition, ensures access to network facilities by new entrants, presents exclusionary and discriminatory behavior by incumbents, etc. As discussed below, these competition-enhancing aspects of institutional change in industries characterized by competition problems have not been very strong in Turkey.

In the telecommunications industry, at the risk of oversimplifying, the story is one of substantial capture by the fixed line incumbent operator. The Telecommunications Authority (now the Information and Communications Technologies Authority, ICTA) was established in 2001 and Turk Telekom was privatized in 2005. Privatization has possibly resulted in a significant increase in productivity of Turk Telekom: employment was reduced by almost 50% after privatization, reflecting the extent of politicization and over-employment under state ownership. However, Turk Telekom maintains dominance in the broadband internet services market (over 90% market share) as well as long distance and International calls markets (more than 50% market share). Until very recently Turk Telekom was protected from competition by high interconnection rates, delays in the licensing of new entrants, delays in the introduction of services that would allow new entrants greater command over the range of services that can be provided over the fixed line network. To most observers, these outcomes reflect Turk Telekom's influence over the Ministry of Transport and by consequence, over the IRA. While the telecommunications laws contained standard measures that have ensured ICTA's *de jure* independence, the authority's de-facto independence was significantly curtailed (Atiyas and Doğan 2010).

However, the stance of the ICTA in the mobile industry provides and interesting contrast. Compared to the fixed segment the ICTA has adopted a more competitive stance in the mobile segment, as reflected, for example, in interconnection rates which have been quite low by international standards. Atiyas and Doğan (2010) argue that this may reflect the fact Turk Telekom's subsidiary is a new entrant in the mobile telecommunications markets. The interesting point here is that, if the ICTA's more aggressive pursuit of competition in the mobile industry can indeed be explained by political economic factors, this stance was carried out through the established rules of the game (i.e., lower interconnection rates) rather than by more coarse and discretionary interventions. In other words, the ICTA's tendency to favor Turk Telekom was curtailed by the new rules and had to be mediated by an overall more competitive stance. This suggests that perhaps the new rules did have some bite after all.

In the electricity sector the restructuring process in Turkey started with the adoption of the Electricity Market Law in 2001 which envisaged unbundling of distribution, transmission and generation assets, establishment of non-discriminatory access to the transmission and distribution networks and the formation of Energy Market Regulatory Authority (EMRA), the IRA responsible for electricity, natural gas, and oil industries.

The electricity restructuring process has been driven by privatization. Privatizations themselves have been structured so as to generate maximum possible revenues for the government. As a result, competition and consumer welfare has taken a secondary role, since there is a danger that high purchase prices will eventually reflect themselves in higher consumer prices. Privatizations have been delayed significantly, and privatization of generation assets, where productivity increases are most likely to occur as a result of competition, has not even started. Hence, in fact, 10 years after the launch of the restructuring process, the extent of competition is still limited to about one quarter of generation capacity, the rest of the capacity being either under non-competitive contracts inherited from the past, or under government ownership. Moreover, the government is still perceived to be quite active in setting some of the retail prices while in principle this should be under the authority of the EMRA.

It should be stressed that it is not government ownership of these assets that prevents the development of competition: there are examples of countries where governments own significant parts of generation assets but still have competitive markets. What Turkey could have done is to horizontally break up and corporatize these assets, place them under competent management and give them the mandate of behaving in a competitive manner. The primacy of privatization as the driving force of the restructuring process has precluded this option.

These problems notwithstanding, the restructuring model *has* been successful in attracting new investments in capacity by the private sector without any non-competitive contracts, of the order 3–4000 MW each year since 2008. This is largely due to the fact that under the new model a wholesale market was established where prices are determined by supply and demand. In effect, the establishment of a wholesale market meant that the government relinquished a significant tool that could in principle be used for expropriation or favoritism.

In the area of procurement, Turkey has adopted a Public Procurement Law (PPL) in 2002, largely modeled after the EU Public Procurement Directives. Again, the accession process has been an important motivation in the adoption of the Law, and ostensibly in the many amendments that have been implemented since then. The PPL permits domestic preferences; there is a price advantage of up to 15% for domestic contractors offering domestic products. In procedures for contracts below the thresholds, contracting authorities may restrict participation to Turkish companies. The number of amendments since has been high, and as reported by SIGMA (2008) “some of these amendments were introduced on an ad hoc basis by individual ministries and Parliamentarians rather than as part of an overall government strategy. These amendments have introduced exemptions that had not been envisaged under the acquis communautaire." Importantly, private sector utilities (in the water, energy, transport and telecommunications sectors) are not covered in the PPL. The PPL also established a Public Procurement Authority. SIGMA's (2008) assessment of the PPA was that it was a "stable and strong institution. It has already largely contributed to the establishment of a modern public procurement system and, in general, has the capacity to implement procurement legislation effectively." Recently investigations were launched against some PPA staff and a member of the Board on the grounds that they have accepted bribes from business people and engaged in corruption in close to 100 public tenders.

In most cases discussed above, the delegation of regulatory authority to a relatively independent agency resulted in an overall increase in the transparency of the policy making process. Even though there are variations across IRAs, they generally work in a more transparent manner relative to ministries: putting draft regulations up on websites for public consultation has become routine. To different degrees, the decision making processes of IRAs are bound by procedural rules that are encoded in regulations; such rules reduce discretion and enhance predictability. The Competition Agency and the ICTA are required to provide justifications for their decisions. Requiring IRAs to provide justifications for their decisions makes a major contribution to transparency and accountability and makes judicial reviews more effective and credible. Even though implementation differs across agencies (more effective implementation in the case of the Competition Authority), this requirement allows stakeholders to be more demanding in terms of transparency.

There is one area where developments regarding transparency and accountability have been in the reverse direction, and that is the case of the Housing Development Administration (TOKI). TOKI is directly attached to the Prime Ministry. It builds public housing with the collaboration of private contractors. It has free access to public land and wide discretionary powers over land that is under its control. Construction activities of TOKI are exempt from the Public Procurement Act; TOKI is also exempt from the Public Financial Management and Control Law. It has been reported that its assets have reached about 2% of GDP, though financial information about its activities is hard to find because of lack of financial reporting.[9] While most of the IRAs reported above are audited by the High Court of Accounts (Sayıştay), which reports to the Parliament, TOKI is audited by the High Audit Board (Yüksek Denetleme Kurulu), which is attached to the Prime Ministry, implying that the financial transactions and activities of TOKI are not being audited by an independent body. It is also known to be an efficient developer and has built over half a million residences, 85% of which consists of social housing. In short, TOKI has the ability to manipulate land rent in a highly discretionary and non-transparent manner meanwhile supporting a network of construction companies.

[9]See Atiyas (2012) for more details.

3.2. *Assessment*

The review presented above suggests a number of comments. The first has to do with the role of crises. The fact that economic crises facilitate or sometimes trigger a process of economic policy reform has been emphasized frequently in the literature and in that sense Turkey is no exception. It is interesting to note that central bank independence, regulation of the banking system and measures that enhanced the controllability of the budget figured prominently in the aftermath of the crisis of 2000–2001 as these were among the most problematic areas prior to the crisis. The second aspect that needs to be emphasized is the role of international agencies and especially of the European Union. The IMF and the World Bank played a significant role in the adoption of the reform laws in many areas including telecommunications and electricity, but the prospect of membership to the EU played a crucial role: it increased acceptance of and created legitimacy for reform and at the same time it vastly reduced transaction and bargaining costs among stakeholders in Turkey by providing templates of what was largely perceived as best practices in a wider range of areas including telecommunications, energy, competition law, banking and public procurement. Third, it is clear that the Turkish experience towards a more rule-based policy environment has been an uneven process. Even though most IRAs were given formal independence, *de facto* independence varied significantly across agencies. Still, even in cases where independence was more nominal than real, the mere existence of a new set of rules and formal institutional arrangements seems to have helped these industries to become more competitive. This is suggested by the experience in the mobile industry and wholesale electricity markets mentioned above.

While this Chapter has emphasized the institutional dimensions of enhancing competition, the Turkish experience does underlie the importance and complementarity of the broader economic policy framework. After all the institutional and competition enhancing measures described above were undertaken in an environment of more or less liberalized product and financial markets, a process that started in the 1980s. Liberalization of domestic markets was complemented by liberalization of foreign trade and international finance. As examined in Atiyas and Bakış (2013, 2012), however, both labor productivity and total factor productivity increased faster in the 2000s relative to the 1980s and 1990s, perhaps reflecting improvements both in the institutional environment and macroeconomic stability in the last decade.

Finally, it is not yet clear whether the emergence of these institutions represents a new equilibrium and whether they are compatible with the underlying political institutions in Turkey. The important role of the perspective of EU accession was mentioned above. This perspective has been weakening in recent years and it remains to be seen how this will affect the conduct of economic policy in Turkey. Recently there are signs that the government may be considering steps that will reduce the powers of IRAs. The government recently passed a decree law which authorized ministries to 'inspect' the activities of agencies associated with the ministries. The decree law gives ministries the authority to harass agencies by subjecting them to inspections. These inspections would concentrate primarily on procedural and not substantial issues. More importantly, ministries still cannot overturn IRA decisions. However, it is very possible that this power to inspect will be used to curtail the de-facto independence of IRAs. In addition, several members of the governing party and the Prime Minister have been quoted in the press complaining about the excessive authority of the IRAs and the fact that they lack political accountability.

4. Evaluation: Trade-Offs and Challenges of Enhancing Competition

This section will discuss some elements and tradeoffs that need to be considered in the design and implementation of a competition-enhancing reform program. It will try to draw on lessons from theory, the Turkish experience, and empirical studies.

4.1. *A brief review of empirical evidence*

Empirical evidence on the role of IRAs on economic outcomes generally focus on infrastructure industries. There is quite a bit of evidence that there is a positive correlation between the presence of an independent regulator and sectoral performance. Many studies focus on the telecommunications industry. In a widely cited paper, Wallsten (2001) examines the effect of privatization and regulation in the telecommunications industry of 34 African and Latin American countries. He finds that privatization in the presence of an independent regulator is positively correlated with telecom performance measures such as connection capacity, penetration, and labor productivity. Privatization alone, however, is associated with few benefits, and is negatively correlated with connection capacity. A positive correlation between the presence of an independent regulator and sector performance, especially penetration, has been found in other studies as well, see Estache and Wren-Lewis (2009, 2010b) for reviews. The impact of IRAs however does depend on the details of the regulatory framework. For example Estache and Rossi (2005) focus on the electricity industry and finds that privatization with the existence of an independent regulator utilizing incentive regulation is associated with higher efficiency relative to firms under public ownership. By contrast, the efficiency of privatized firms under rate of return regulation is not significantly different from those of the public firms. More recently, Cambini and Rondi (2011) look at investment rates of utilities in Europe and find that regulatory independence has a positive effect on investment.

Another way in which the presence of an IRA may affect economic outcomes is that they may reduce transactions costs. Guasch, Laffont and Straub (2007, 2008) find that the existence of an independent regulator decreases the extent of renegotiation of concession contracts in the water and transport sectors. The reason could be that the presence of a regulator may have improved the contract design to begin with, which in turn would reduce future conflicts. Also, under the presence of a regulator, disputes may be handled within the regulatory framework, with no need to change the initial contract.

There is also some evidence on factors that influence the degree of formal independence of regulatory authorities. In a recent study using data from 175 IRAs worldwide from seven industries, Hanretty and Koop (2012) find that independence is more likely or higher in utilities and financial markets. Independence is positively associated with 'replacement risk' which captures the frequency with which governments are replaced with governments with different partisan compositions. In countries where replacement risk is high and consequently policies may change frequently, delegation may enhance policy stability, which will have a positive effect on investments. Independence is also negatively associated with the number of veto players in the political system. This is captured, for example, by the number of parties in government, the number of constitutional bodies that may influence policy (such as the number of legislatures), the degree of homogeneity of parties in the parliament, etc. The reasoning behind the negative correlation is that the higher number of veto players may be a functional equivalent of more independence in delegation, because more veto players make policy changes and reversals more difficult, reducing the need for independence of IRAs. These results in general provide support to theories that see delegation to IRAs as a solution to regulatory credibility and risk of expropriation.

A few studies attempt to measure the association between formal and *de facto* independence, but here the problem is that measuring the degree of *de facto* independence on a consistent basis across countries is very difficult. In the limited number of studies on Europe, the relation between formal and *de facto* independence is found to be weak. Given this weak relationship, the fact that many studies have found a positive relation between the presence of an independent regulator and economic performance mentioned above is interesting.

There is also evidence that the regulatory environment interacts with other characteristics of the political environment. One important variable in that regard is the extent of corruption. Wren-Lewis (2011) examines the impact of corruption on the efficiency of electricity distribution companies in Latin America and the Caribbean but this paper also examines whether that impact depends the institutional environment, namely ownership of the distribution assets and the establishment of IRAs. The theoretical analysis shows that corruption should have a negative effect on efficiency. The impact of degree of independence of the agency, however, depends on the relative corruptability of agencies versus politicians. For the specific case of electricity distribution companies in Latin America and the Caribbean, Wren-Lewis (2011) finds that the overall degree of corruption does indeed have a negative impact on the efficiency of distribution companies. Moreover, the presence of an IRA significantly reduces this effect. Privatization is also found to lower the negative effect of corruption on efficiency, but this finding is not robust to controlling for the endogeneity of ownership.

4.2. *The politics of enhancing competition*

Institutional reform has a basic paradox: important elements of the competition enhancing reform package entails delegating substantial discretionary authority from the ministers and agencies that they control to IRAs. Assuming that the IRAs are more independent then ministerial departments, the delegation therefore entails significant dispersion of previously centrally held political power. Hence while delegation is partly to ensure that regulatory decisions are insulated from political influence the paradox is that at the same time, this act of delegation itself is a political act. The question is: when is such delegation in the interests of those who currently hold political authority? That is, when is delegation incentive compatible with political power?

Both the theory and empirics behind IRAs suggest a few answers to this question: an important dimension of the act of delegation is an increase in regulatory credibility and a decrease in expropriation risk. This suggests that governments will be interested in delegating if they have a strategic interest in attracting private capital, both domestic and foreign. This may be true for several reasons. The cost of public finance or the existing level of public debt may be high. Or governments may be interested in allocating public funds primarily to social sectors such as education, health, poverty alleviation or even support for SMEs, and rely on private investment for infrastructure industries. Hence the 'public finance' motive for liberalization would also favor the creation of a competitive environment. Even there the political elite always have the alternative of striking special deals with individual investors and share monopoly rents. The cost of that would be slower growth, so governments under a popular mandate and political pressure to deliver high growth would have better incentives to create a competitive environment. In addition, enhancing the competitive environment would also create a more conducive setting for the growth of small and medium enterprises. For these reasons, one might think that post-revolutionary Arab societies would contain the correct political incentives for improving the level of competition.

Another possibility is that governments may be interested in encouraging the competitive process in some industries while continuing to regulate the creation and distribution of rents in others. This seems to be part of the story behind the experience in Turkey. It seems that the government opted in favor of competition in tradable sectors as well as (at least to a degree) in electricity and telecommunications while continuing to play a much bigger role in construction and urban development.

Assuming that those who hold political power are convinced of the necessity of reform, one still has to consider the issue of broader popular political support. The global experience seems to suggest that public support for the adoption of a regulatory reform program is not a major constraint. Assuming that the reforming government is willing and has a winning coalition in the legislature, the adoption of the program can only be hindered through popular discontent expressed through mass protests that create political instability and perhaps violence. This is not likely to occur save for a few components or instances such as privatization that is expected to create substantial unemployment, which is an eventuality that may generate substantial resistance from labor and trade unions. It should be possible and relatively easy to deal with this problem by including in the reform program well designed labor adjustment programs that aim at compensating the losers. With significant expected productivity increases from privatization, financing such programs should not be that difficult.[10] Privatization has other potential political hazards that the literature has identified, these will be mentioned below. The rest of the regulatory reform program is not likely to generate significant political sentiments that would result in mass protests.

Popular support for the sustainability of the program is a different game because in the medium term popular opposition and discontent cannot be disconnected from electoral politics; if there is popular discontent with the program then the opposition may win elections on an anti-reform program and the program may be reversed. In the medium term the main means through which popular support can be maintained seems to be through successful implementation of the regulatory reform program: if public services are successfully provided and if access to services is successfully enhanced, this should be an important factor that ensures public support. In any case, over the medium term one should expect a positive concordance in the sense that successful reform would generate its own political support. But this potential of positive concordance also suggests a constraint: the reform has to deliver over a reasonable time frame if it is going to be politically sustainable. This can be called the deliverability constraint. Note that while partly a technical issue, a high level of delivery also hinges on ability to curb capture and corruption.

Political support for the reform as well as the degree of success in implementation is also related with the way in which reform is carried out. In many developing countries regulatory reforms are adopted during or immediately after major economic crises, often as part of conditionality imposed by multilateral organizations such as the World Bank and the IMF. As discussed above, this was certainly the case in Turkey (Ozel and Atiyas 2011) for telecommunications and electricity. This is often done without much discussion and in a top down manner. Laws are typically prepared by relatively small teams of believers, with little or no public consultation. In fact, the Turkish experience suggests that the reforming team often carries out its work in secrecy exactly because of fear of resistance from the rest of the political (and bureaucratic) elite. This is expedient in the short run: if the government has a majority in the enacting body, swift adoption is assured. The Turkish experience also suggests that lack of wider ownership creates major hazards over the medium term which also hurts the deliverability constraint. This works in various ways. First, secrecy and bypass create resentment, and resentment of the bureaucracy creates resistance and hurts implementation. More importantly, bypass also prevents the establishment of a common understanding about the objectives of the program and more importantly how the various parts of the program fit together. For example restructuring in the electricity industry is quite a complicated project consisting of multiple dimensions. Consistency among these dimensions is hence a must. However,

[10] After the privatization of Turk Telekom, the incumbent telecom operator in Turkey, employment was reduced by almost 50%. This did not create an uproar thanks to a program that gave options to workers either to opt out with a hefty severance pay or find employment elsewhere in the government.

in the case of Turkey it took a tremendous amount of time for the bureaucracy (and even the private sector) to really understand the different dimensions of the restructuring process. This has resulted in faulty designs of incentive mechanisms and very long delays in implementation.

4.3. *The role of privatization (vs. liberalization)*

The Turkish experience suggests that the role of privatization in curbing inefficiency and capture in industries where competition is limited or non-existent was exaggerated. The literature suggests that (under contractual incompleteness) relative to private ownership, public ownership performs better for allocative efficiency and worse for productive (or cost) efficiency (e.g., Schmidt 1996). Hence regulators and policymakers face a trade-off. In the case of Turkey, electricity distribution suffered from high electricity losses and theft. They are being privatized and their tariffs are subject to incentive regulation with loss targets. If companies can decrease losses to levels beyond the targets, their profits increase. This is a potentially high powered incentive to cut costs, but the obvious welfare loss is the surplus that is captured by the distribution companies. This is a clear example of the efficiency-rent extraction trade-off discussed in the literature on regulation under asymmetric information (e.g., Laffont and Tirole 1993).

Martimort and Straub (2009) also suggest that collusion between regulators and private firms may lead firms to appropriate a larger share of increases in efficiency in the form of higher prices, especially for firms in sectors involving large fixed costs and requiring high mark-ups to cover total costs (such as water, roads, port, and airport construction). The authors suggest that this result may explain the widespread dissatisfaction with privatization in Latin America even though many studies find that privatization leads to efficiency increases.

This is not meant to suggest that the public finance justification for privatization (i.e., privatization to raise revenues) may not be justified under certain circumstances. The purpose here is to suggest that, absent competition, the benefits of privatization may be exaggerated and that under certain circumstances it is worthwhile to think of alternatives, especially public management reform, corporatization, etc.

4.4. *Separation of powers and the special role of a competition authority*

In the literature on regulation under asymmetric information, one way to ensure that the (non-benevolent) regulator acts in the public interest is to make the payments made to the regulator contingent on the report that the regulator provides to the government on the costs of the firm.[11] As emphasized by Dal Bo (2006), making

[11] The non-benevolent regulator is modeled as the middle layer of the three-layer principal agent hierarchy with a (benevolent) government at the top, a firm with private cost information at the bottom, and the regulator. The regulator obtains a private signal about the cost of the firm and reports that to government. However, the firms can bribe the regulator into reporting false information, or claiming to have generated no information.

contingent payments to regulators is not a realistic option. An alternative proposed by Laffont and Martimort (1999) is the separation of regulatory powers. The Turkish experience actually seems to support this suggestion.

In Turkey the competition authority and sector-specific regulators have quasi-concurrent powers over anti-competitive behavior in the regulated industries. Of course, the existence of concurrent powers is likely to increase regulatory uncertainty whenever the respective agencies reach conflicting verdicts on specific issues. Separation of powers may also lead into inter-agency conflict and push agencies into a power struggle to maximize their jurisdiction. It may also induce firms in the regulated industries firms to abuse the separation of powers by picking and choosing agencies so as to maximize the likelihood of a favorable decision. In the Turkish case, the degree of regulatory uncertainty has been reduced through a division of labor that has emerged over time: the competition authority has come to limit its intervention into areas of market behavior that are not directly regulated by the sector-specific agencies. This of course reduces the welfare enhancing impact of separation of powers, but this loss of impact can partly be compensated by vesting the competition authority with a strong advocacy role. Under an advocacy duty, the authority submits its opinions in areas where it has no direct jurisdiction. It turns out that such opinions can have a critical role in increasing the overall transparency and accountability of the regulatory system.

Note that even when regulatory agencies are not corrupt, sector specific regulators and the competition authority may legitimately have somewhat different preferences: for example, electricity or telecommunications regulators may have an interest in network expansion and they may attach a lower weight to the development of competition in their respective industries. A critical dimension of the separation of powers problem is to place the authority to regulate mergers and acquisitions under the competition authority. Mergers and acquisitions potentially play a critical role in the evolution of market structure and are critical determinants of the degree of competition in the medium and long term. Undue increase in concentration raises the likelihood of anti-competitive behavior and it becomes much more difficult to protect consumer welfare through conduct remedies. Regulating mergers gives the competition authority the power to prevent increases in concentrations that are likely to lessen competition.

An important dimension of regulating concentrations is the role of the competition authority in privatizations. As mentioned earlier, a critical danger of privatization in concentrated or monopolistic industries is to turn public into private monopolies. The incentives of governments (especially the Treasury or the Ministry of Finance) during privatization are towards raising maximum revenues to the detriment of developing competition. This would not only run counter to the agenda of developing competition but would also represent a big threat to generating political support for the reform agenda. The Turkish experience suggests that engaging the competition authority in the privatization process may be an effective way to decrease the likelihood that public monopolies are turned into private monopolies.

The competition authority in Turkey has taken critical decisions during the privatizations in infrastructure industries such as electricity, telecommunications and transport (ports) as well as in tradable industries that have helped reduce (to some extent) the creation of private firms that hold excessive market power.

One important detail in this regard is that normally competition laws do not empower competition agencies to prevent ownership changes that *do not increase* the degree of concentration or dominance in the market. So normally a competition agency would not be able to prevent the purchase of a monopoly by a private investor that does not have a prior presence in a specific industry. The Turkish Competition Authority has gone out of its way to usurp that power through a communiqué, and for reasons that are hard to understand, this (albeit welfare enhancing) transcendence has not been legally or politically challenged. It may be wise to actually endow the competition authority with such power in the laws that form the legal basis of privatizations.

4.5. *Empowering consumer groups*

In environments where the risk of capture of the IRA by the firms that it is supposed to regulate is relatively high (or where the information advantage of the regulated firm is relatively high) one remedy that has been proposed is to develop publicly funded consumer advocacy groups. Besides compensating for the threat of capture by firms, establishing publicly funded (*but not controlled*) consumer advocacy groups may help with generating political support for the sustainability of the reform program. Consumer advocacy groups may also help create a wider base of legitimacy for the reform program and help with the objective of creating new sources of social and political power. But one should also note that this requires education, expertise, and active media etc. The literature suggests that such initiatives may be effective. There is empirical evidence, cited in Dal Bo (2006) that in the US regulated prices are lower in states where there are consumer advocates.

4.6. *Selection of regulators*

There is evidence cited in Dal Bo (2006) that the method of selection of regulators may have an impact on regulatory outcomes. For example, some studies show that when the regulators are elected, or appointed by legislators, or when executive appointments require legislative approval, regulated prices tend to be lower, possibly reflecting the influence of consumers. It should be pointed out that most of these studies are on the US and may be less relevant for countries with parliamentary systems, especially when the government parties also hold majorities in the parliament. What is not clear in some of this research is whether electoral influence works through incentives or through selection of different types of regulators. Besley and Coate (2003) explores the following idea: When regulators are appointed by the executive, sensitivity of regulatory policy to voter preferences is dimmed because "regulatory policy becomes bundled with other policy issues that the appointing politicians are responsible for." By contrast, when regulators are elected, their stance on regulation is the only salient issue so that the electoral incentive is to run a pro-consumer candidate. They find evidence that support the idea that elected states are more pro-consumer in their regulatory policies in that they allow less pass-through of fuel costs to electricity prices. Overall, these studies suggest that elected regulators are more pro-consumer. Of course, this does not immediately suggest that from a social welfare point of view this is a better design because it may reflect populism and lower than optimal prices, possibly endangering future investments. On the other hand, in environments where capture by regulated firms is the more powerful distortion, elected regulators may be a welfare-improving remedy.

In any case, obviously the preferences of the board or the directors play a crucial role in the performance of the agency. This, in turn, means that the procedure set for the appointment of the regulatory agency is very important as well. Often, regulators are appointed either by the executive or the legislature. In parliamentary systems, separation of powers is weak so the executive branch of the government often has ultimate influence on the appointments. While from a social welfare point of view, one would desire that people who are appointed would be types who would protect the independence of the agency and who would try to encourage decisions that would maximize a well accepted measure of welfare (say, total or consumer surplus). Above all, this would require people with competence and integrity. It is very difficult to find procedural ways to reduce the influence of the executive so as to increase the quality of appointments. Perhaps a better way to improve the quality of appointments is to increase the transparency of the appointment process. For example, both the executive and the opposition can have the right to nominate candidates, information about whom can be made public before the executive makes its final choices. In addition, the opposition may have the right to question the candidates in hearings held at the relevant parliamentary committee. Under such a procedure, the executive would still have the final choice, but may have to better justify its choices.

5. Conclusion

This Chapter has drawn from the experience of Turkey to discuss various changes in the regulatory environment that can be instrumental in enhancing competition in post-revolutionary Arab societies. Presumably the enhancement of competition entails a transformation from a regime where profitability relies on special political connections to one where success is predominantly driven by productivity. This in turn requires a policy and regulatory framework in which the political authority is constrained in its ability to discriminate among firms on the basis of political connections.

Establishing a non-discriminatory policy and regulatory framework often entails institutional remedies whereby substantial amount of decision and rule making authority is delegated to agencies that are relatively independent from the government and individual ministries. The Chapter has discussed the objectives and characteristics of this delegation, the nature of the independence and other dimensions such as accountability and transparency.

The Chapter has also reviewed the experience of Turkey where such delegation has occurred in the last decade or two, albeit imperfectly and in a way that is non-uniform across sectors. Even in its imperfect form, and where *de facto* independence of the new agencies is questionable, it has discussed examples where the new rules of the game did have some bite in limiting the extent of capture. It has underlined the particular importance of the role of crises, international organizations and the perspective of accession to the EU. Moreover, it has discussed that in the case of Turkey enhanced transparency and accountability in some sectors occurred simultaneously with increased discretion in others. The jury is still out, however, on whether the new institutions will survive political dynamics where the EU anchor is becoming weaker.

There is quite a bit of evidence that the presence of IRAs especially in infrastructure industries is associated with better performance. The presence of IRAs also seem to moderate the negative impact of corruption on efficiency. There is also evidence that independence of IRAs is higher in environments predicted by theory, that is environments where political 'replacement' risk is higher and the number of veto players is lower. A final verdict is yet to be spelled out but the Turkish experience as well as the empirical evidence suggests that institutions that enhance competition may play a role in creating an environment that is more conducive to investment and growth.

Acknowledgments

I am grateful to Ishac Diwan and participants at the Pre-Conference Workshop on "The Political Economy of Arab Awakening", held in Cairo in March 2012, for their comments. All remaining errors are mine.

References

Alper, C. E. and Z. Onis. 2004. "The Turkish banking system and the IMF in the age of capital account liberalization." *New Perspectives on Turkey*, 30: 25–55.

Atiyas, I. 2012. "Economic institutions and institutional change in Turkey during the neoliberal era." *New Perspectives on Turkey*, 47: 45–69.

Atiyas, I. 2005. *Elektrik Sektorunde Serbestlesme ve Duzenleyici Reform.* [In Turkish] Istanbul: TESEV Publication.

Atiyas, I. and O. Bakış. 2013. "Aggregate and sectoral TFP Growth in Turkey: A growth accounting exercise." Tusiad-Sabanci University Competitiveness Forum REF Working Paper No 2013-1.

Atiyas, I. and O. Bakış. 2012. "Structural change and industrial policy in Turkey." Paper prepared for the ERF Workshop on Structural Transformation and Industrial Policy in Selected Mena Countries, September 30.

Atiyas, I. and P. Doğan. 2010. "Glass half empty? Politics and institutions in the liberalization of the fixed line telecommunications industry in Turkey." In *Understanding the Process of*

Economic Change in Turkey: An Institutional Approach, eds. Cetin, T. and F. Yilmaz. pp. 261–283. New York: Nova Science Publishers.

Atiyas, I. and F. Emil. 2005. "Political economy of governance failures, crises and opportunities for reform." Published as Chapter 4 of *Turkey Country Profile*, Cairo: Economic Research Forum.

Atiyas, I. and H. Ersel. 1994. "The impact of financial reform: The Turkish experience." In *Financial Reform — Theory and Experience*, eds. Caprio, G., I. Atiyas and J. Hanson. New York: Cambridge University Press.

Besley, T. and S. Coate. 2003. "Elected versus appointed regulators: Theory and evidence." *Journal of the European Economic Association* 1(5):1176–1206.

Cambini, C. and L. Rondi. 2011. "Regulatory independence, investment and political interference: Evidence from the EU." EUI Working Papers RSCAS 2011/42.

Dal Bo, E. 2006. "Regulatory capture: A review." *Oxford Review of Economic Policy*, 22(2):203–225.

Dedeoglu, E. 2010. "How does the fiscal rule work? First the public financial management system shall be adapted to fiscal rule." TEPAV Policy Note 2010-15.

Ersel, H. 2012. "Politico-economic development of Turkey and the transformation of political Islam, 1950–2010." Paper presented at the Economic Research Forum Pre-Conference workshop on the Political Economy of Arab Awakening. Cairo, Egypt.

Estache, A., A. Goicoechea and L. Trujillo. 2009. "Utilities reforms and corruption in developing countries." *Utilities Policy*, 17: 191–202.

Estache, A. and M. A. Rossi. 2005. "Do regulation and ownership drive the efficiency of electricity distribution? Evidence from Latin America." *Economics Letters*, 86(2): 253–257.

Estache, A. and L. Wren-Lewis. 2010a. "What anti-corruption policy can learn from theories of sector regulation." GRASP Working Paper 6.

Estache, A. and L. Wren-Lewis. 2010b. "On the theory and evidence of regulation in network industries in developing countries." In *The Oxford Handbook of Regulation*, eds. Baldwin, R., M. Cave and M. Lodge. pp. 371–406. Oxford, UK: Oxford University Press.

Estache A. and L. Wren-Lewis. 2009. "Toward a theory of regulation for developing countries: Following Jean-Jacques Laffont's lead." *Journal of Economic Literature*, 47(3): 729–770.

Guasch, J. L., J. J. Laffont and S. Straub. 2007. "Concessions of infrastructure in Latin America: Government-led renegotiation." *Journal of Applied Econometric*, 22(7): 1267–1294.

Guasch, J. L., J. J. Laffont and S. Straub. 2008. "Renegotiation of concession contracts in Latin America: Evidence from the water and transport sectors." *International Journal of Industrial Organization*, 26(2): 421–442.

Hanretty, C. and C. Koop. 2012. "Measuring the formal independence of regulatory agencies." *Journal of European Public Policy*, 19: 198–216.

Limi, A. 2011. "Public procurement: Learning from the experience of developing countries." In *Emerging Issues in Competition, Collusion, and Regulation of Network Industries*, ed. Estache, A. London, UK: CEPR.

Laffont, J. J. and D. Martimort. 1999. "Separation of regulators against collusive behavior." *Rand Journal of Economics*, 30(2): 232–262.

Laffont, J. J. and J. Tirole. 1993. *A Theory of Incentives in Procurement and Regulation.* Cambridge, MA: MIT Press.

Martimort, D. and S. Straub. 2009. Infrastructure privatization and changes in corruption patterns: The roots of public discontent. *Journal of Development Economics*, 90: 69–84.

Organisation for Economic Co-operation and Development (OECD). 2005. *Competition Law and Policy in Turkey.* Paris: OECD.

Onis, Z. 2011. "Power, interests and coalitions: The political economy of mass privatization in Turkey." *Third World Quarterly*, 32(4): 707–724.

Ozel, I. and I. Atiyas. 2011. "Regulatory Diffusion in Turkey: a Cross-sectoral Assessment?" In *The Political Economy of Regulation in Turkey*, eds. Çetin, T. and F. Oğuz, pp. 51–74. New York: Springer.

Roland, G. 2008. *Privatization: Successes and Failures*. New York: Columbia University Press.

Schmidt, K. M. 1996. "The costs and benefits of privatization: An incomplete contracts approach." *Journal of Economics, Law and Organization*, 12(1):1–24.

SIGMA. 2008. *Turkey Public Procurement Assessment May 2008.*

SIGMA. 2009. *Turkey Public Procurement Assessment May 2009.*

Smith, W. 1997. "Utility regulators: The independence debate. Public Policy for the Private Sector." December, Note 127, 9–12, Washington D.C: World Bank.

Thatcher, M. 2011. "Risks of capture and independent regulatory agencies in network industries in Europe: A political and institutional analysis." In *Emerging Issues in Competition, Collusion, and Regulation of Network Industries*, ed. Estache, A. London: CEPR.

Ugaz, C. 2002. "Consumer participation and pro-poor regulation in Latin America." WIDER Discussion Paper No. 2002/121.

Wallsten, S. 2001. "An empirical analysis of competition, privatization, and regulation in Africa and Latin America." *Journal of Industrial Economics*, 49: 1–19.

Wren-Lewis, L. 2011. "Do infrastructure reforms reduce the effect of corruption? Theory and evidence from Latin America and the Caribbean." University of Oxford Department of Economics, Discussion Paper Series No 576.

LESSONS FROM ELSEWHERE

Chapter 8

POLITICAL AND ECONOMIC DEVELOPMENTS IN TURKEY AND THE TRANSFORMATION OF POLITICAL ISLAM (1950–2010)

Hasan Ersel

1. Introduction

Islamic-rooted Adalet ve Kalkınma Partisi (AKP, Justice and Development Party),[1] as a result of its spectacular victory in general elections held on November 3, 2002, secured a strong majority in the parliament and formed a single-party government.[2] There is no doubt that the ongoing AKP experiment is one of the most important episodes in Turkey's political history. It also created considerable controversy among observers in Turkey. Some observers considered it a surprising result open to unpredictable political developments, while others interpreted it as a manifestation of the advancement in the maturity of Turkish 'democracy'. A major reason behind these widely diverging views lies in the fact that, although Turkey has made significant achievements (see Table 8.1) since 1950, it is still neither a 'developed economy' nor a 'liberal democracy'.

Most observers of Turkey's political and economic development agree that Turkey evolved from a backward, closed agrarian economy into an open economy with a significant industrial base capable of exporting a diverse set of products to a large number of countries between 1946 and 2010. Simultaneously, the Turkish political system was transformed from a single-party regime into a functioning multi-party

[1]The list of abbreviations is given at the end of the Chapter.

[2]Although the AKP received only 34.3% of the votes, it won 66% of the seats in the parliament. This was mainly due to the undemocratic nature (such as 10% election threshold at the national level) of existing election laws, enacted under the earlier military regime.

Table 8.1. Turkey: Main socio-economic indicators.

	1950	2010
Per Capita GDP (TL, in 1998 constant Prices)	314	1448
Foreign Trade/GDP (%)	9	39
Agriculture's share in GDP (%)	41	12
Urban population as % of total	19	71
Illiteracy Rate (%)	68	6

Source: Turkish Statistical Institute (http://www.turkstat.gov.tr).

'electoral democracy'.[3] On both democratization and development fronts, Turkey's performance was neither exceptionally successful nor did it follow a stable trajectory. During this episode, Turkey encountered several economic crises[4] and four *coup d'états* that disrupted the working of the multi-party regime.[5] Nevertheless, Turkey was able to return to its long term path which can be broadly defined as 'democratization' plus 'private sector led growth'. Presently Turkey is classified by The Economist Intelligence Unit as a 'hybrid regime', i.e., it is two grades below 'full democracies'. According to Freedom House, Turkey is considered only as a 'partially free' country. The World Bank on the other hand, classified Turkey in 'upper middle income countries', and not in developed economies.[6]

The purpose of this Chapter is to examine the historical developments that led to the emergence and rise of the Islamic-rooted AKP in Turkey.[7] The methodology adopted is based on the assumption that the political and economic state of a society can be represented by its political institutions and economic structure (e.g., the organization of production, investment, and distribution). The analysis and explanation of political economic development of a country, therefore, requires one to examine changes in these two dimensions.[8] Most political and economic systems are subjected to various types of shocks which may change the trajectory of the system for good, or its effect may be temporary. For example a shock may reverse the

[3] 'Electoral democracy' is one of the terms used to describe 'hybrid regimes' that exhibit some characteristics of liberal democracies (such as the recognition of the importance of the elections is determining the political preferences of the people) but may fail to satisfy fully some of its other dimensions (such as political pluralism, equality before the law, civil liberties, human rights, and elements of civil society outside the government.) In Özbudun (2011), it is argued that 'electoral democracy' is a suitable term to describe Turkey's political regime. See Morlino (2009) for a more general discussion of hybrid regimes.

[4] Major crises that affected Turkey's course of development were 1958, 1978, 1994, 2000, and 2008.

[5] Between 1950 and 2010, there were four *coup d'etats* launched by the armed forces: 1960, 1971 ('coup by memorandum'), 1980, and 1997 ('post-modern').

[6] Turkey was one of the few countries that spent 50 or more years in the 'lower-middle-income' cluster before 'graduation' according to Felipe *et al.* (2012, p. 22).

[7] For a comprehensive survey of the political role of Islam in the late 19th and early 20th Centuries in the Ottoman Empire, see Karpat (2001). Recent developments in political Islam in Turkey attracted attention of many researchers both in Turkey and abroad. See, for example, Hale and Özbudun (2010); Tuğal (2009); Turam (2007); Yavuz (2003, 2006, 2009) and references given in these works.

[8] This approach is developed and discussed in Acemoglu *et al.* (2005); Acemoglu and Robinson (2006).

democratization process and the country may end up with a long enduring authoritarian regime.[9] An external shock however may adversely affect the economic performance of the country only for a few years. Then the economy recovers and goes back to its past development path.[10] Turkey, offers an interesting case study for examining the long-term effects of such shocks on a political and economic system.[11]

In the following sections (Sections 2–7), political and economic developments between 1923 and 2002 are summarized. Section 8 is devoted to the analysis of the AKP era, and some lessons that can be drawn from Turkish experience are given in the last section.

2. The Single-Party Regime and *Étatism* (1923–1945)

The Republic of Turkey[12] inherited a war-torn economy from the Ottoman Empire with extremely weak physical and human capital bases. In the political sphere, the clear choice of the founders was a single-party regime which was "*...westernist, and secularist in its outlook, authoritarian in its style of governance and etatist-nationalist in its strategy of development*" (Sunar 2004, p. 122) (italics my own emphasis). These major characteristics of the single-party regime, although exhibited some variations in time, remained almost unchanged until the end of the Second World War (WWII).

The new state faced the twin problems of nation building and economic development, and therefore primarily engaged in establishing its core political and economic institutions until 1939. During this period, a series of reforms were undertaken aiming the transformation of the backward, predominantly agricultural society into a modern one. The outbreak of WWII effectively halted the reform efforts. Between 1939 and 1945, the main concern of the government was to keep Turkey out of war and it was occupied with managing the war economy. The regime was successful in the first aim and this was achieved through a well orchestrated diplomatic strategy supported by the full mobilization of an army of approximately one million. Inevitably, the latter factor exerted enormous strains on the economy and led to severe problems such as shortages, soaring black markets, and decline in economic activity (Pamuk 1991).

In the economic sphere, on the other hand, the founders' choice was in favor of 'private sector led development'. The government, even before the official announcement of the nature of the political regime as a republic, invited representatives of all economic interest groups to discuss the economic system of the

[9]For example, in Brazil, the military coup that overthrew President João Goulart (1919–1976) on March 31, 1964, led to the establishment of an authoritarian regime that survived until March 15, 1985.

[10]Turkey's experience with the financial crisis of 2008 can be considered as an example. Turkey was severely affected by the global crisis starting from the last quarter of 2008, but recovered rather quickly in 2010.

[11]For a through analysis political developments in Turkey, see Kalaycıoğlu (2005). See also Öniş and Şenses (2007), for an illuminating approach to political economy of the development process in Turkey.

[12]The Republic of Turkey (Turkey for short) was founded on October 29, 1923.

country. The meeting was held in Izmir (February 17–March 4, 1923). The participants of the conference, besides emphasizing the vital importance of economic development, agreed that the country needs a 'mixed economic system', where private sector activity should be supplemented by the public sector. Turkey's initial experience with liberal policies favoring private sector continued until the Great Depression in 1929. Between 1923–1929, although the economy exhibited sizeable growth by integration to the world economy through agriculture and trade, the progress of industrialization was disappointing (Keyder 1981). The weakness of the economy and the limitations of the private sector led development strategy became apparent after the 1929 crisis which led to a sharp decline in agricultural prices, deterioration in the current account balance and foreign exchange shortage. These developments led the authorities to adopt a new policy framework, *étatism*, that relies considerably more on the public sector for capital accumulation and industrialization, without abandoning the regime's commitment "to the capitalist system and to the principles of free enterprise and private property..." (Hershlag 1968, p. 69).[13] During the WWII period, Turkey like many other countries, had to rely extensively on governmental interference in economic life. Therefore, it can safely be argued that *étatism* survived until the end of the WWII and the system, once more, gradually shifted back to private sector led development from 1946 onwards.

3. Transition to Multi-Party Regime (1946–1950)

The general parliamentary election held on July 21, 1946 is considered as the end of single-party regime in Turkey, as the newly established[14] Demokrat Parti (DP, Democrat Party), gained sizeable number of seats (61) in the parliament and formed a group.[15] The Cumhuriyet Halk Partisi (CHP, Republican People's Party), that ruled the country during the single-party era, won an overwhelming majority (397 seats) and sustained its dominance. Four years later, however, the DP won the May 14, 1950 elections and came to power with a strong majority in parliament. Turkey, therefore, made the first major democratic breakthrough in the Middle

[13]Okyar (1965) defended the view that étatism was Turkey's policy response the Great Depression. Birtek (1985), on the other hand, argued that "...*Etatism should be seen as the double response of a historically specific polity: first to the World Depression and secondly to the developments in the Turkish economy in the years 1923–1930*" (italics my emphasis). Birtek's position seems to be shared by most researchers. For detailed analyses of étatist policies see Hershlag (1968, pp. 61–127), Boratav (1981), Hansen (1991, pp. 319–337), and Pamuk (2000).

[14]It should also be pointed out that, the DP was not the first opposition party that was founded in Turkey. During the single-party era, two failed attempts were made (in 1924 and 1930) to set up a second party. Both of these political parties did not have the chance to participate in elections. In contrast, Milli Kalkınma Partisi [National Development Party], which was established on September 5, 1945, participated in few elections and did not achieve much success. The party, nominally, survived until May 28, 1958. For a detailed account of the transition to multi-party system, see Koçak (2010, 2012).

[15]The 1946 general election was far from being a fair one. The 'open vote, secret classification' rule, widespread intimidation, and the absence of judicial oversight led it to be labeled as a 'dubious election'.

East, in 1950, dropping its single-party, military authoritarian system for a free-wheeling, two-party, contested democracy. It did so at a time when it was "still largely agrarian, with a small middle class and high level of illiteracy" (Waterbury 1994, p. 24).

This major change in the political institutions was initiated by the CHP and the transition to multi-party regime was rather smooth.[16] Nevertheless, this outcome was neither due to an easily discernable single factor that triggered the process, nor was it the result of a well-thought and executed plan. As was stressed by Özkurt (2007) and, notably by Koçak (2010, pp. 13–16), the transition process was unpredictable; its outcome was far from certain and "the probability of reversal was not negligible". President and CHP's chairman İsmet İnönü's positive approach to such a transition was not shared by many of his party members. On the other hand, as is convincingly demonstrated by Koçak (2010, 2012), it is not possible to delineate a single major factor to explain this dramatic decision that led to a fundamental change in the country's political institutions. It seems that a multitude of domestic developments (e.g., erosion of the credibility of the CHP due its authoritarian stance, its handling of the economic difficulties of the war years, its failure in dealing with corruption) alienated the CHP from the masses and also led to creation a strong opposition even within the party cadres. In the international sphere in 1945, Turkey found itself in near-isolation since the country did not actively participate in the Allied effort during WWII and, worse, it faced a serious threat from the communist Soviet Union. These developments may have hence induced the political authority to adopt an authoritarian stance in order to enhance the credibility of Turkey in the eyes of western democracies. Finally, it should also be emphasized that, despite its eventual failure, the multi-party regime of Second Constitutional Era (1908–1918) was still remembered by a considerable number of intellectuals

Although, the establishment of multi-party (*de facto* two-party) system was a major step forward, it was hardly a breakthrough towards a liberal democracy. The spectrum of political views that was allowed to be represented by political parties was extremely narrow. Parties that represented the political left (broadly defined to cover not only communist parties but social democratic ones as well), minorities, and religious views were effectively banned. In other words, only those political parties that reflected the differences among the ruling elite were allowed.[17] Despite these deficiencies it should be admitted that the multi-party regime, by bringing in competition to the political arena, led to a major change in the status of the masses: from

[16]On Turkey's transition to multi-party regime see, for example, Karpat (1959), Ahmed (1993, pp. 102–109), Kalaycıoğlu (2005, pp. 67–74), Özkurt (2007), and notably Koçak (2010, 2012).

[17]Turkey's relations with the West this did not create this situation. Such a 'quasi-democratic' regime was quite acceptable for the Western democracies (USA and Western Europe) which tolerated the pro-West right-wing dictatorships of Portugal (of António de Oliveira Salazar) and Spain (of Francisco Franco). In fact Portugal, under the Salazar regime, became a founding member of NATO.

being mere observers of the political decision making process, to being active participants who express their demands and influence some political outcomes.

Evidently such a starting point inevitably had a long and enduring negative effect on the development of democracy in Turkey. Existing political parties agreed on outlawing the political left but followed a different route on channeling religious views and demands to the political arena. Both the CHP and the DP agreed to relax the rather stringent conditions that were imposed to establish secularism. The first signal was given by the CHP government on November 25, 1948, when religion was included in primary school curriculum as an elective course 'upon popular demand'. Since its establishment, on the other hand, the DP distinguished itself from CHP's 'assertive secularism' and came close to the 'passive secularism'.[18]

The envisaged transition identified the political parties as necessary institutions for collecting and transmitting people's political views and demands. However, in practice the system did not encourage, and even hindered, the development of civil society institutions. This remained a major factor that adversely affected the democratic development of the country.[19]

Turkey however started to change its economic development strategy well before the 1950 elections.[20] Abandoning *étatism* was, to a considerable degree, the result of the demands stemming from those groups that had accumulated significant wealth, especially during the WWII years. The changing world environment, notably the increased influence of the US, was also instrumental in shifting to a strategy of private sector led growth. The signals for liberalization of the foreign trade and the foreign exchange regime were also made clear in the post-WWII years: on September 7, 1946 Turkey launched its first official devaluation as part of a policy package which aimed at partially liberalizing its foreign trade. This was done to make it eligible for IMF membership and integrate its economy to the changing world environment.

[18]The twin concepts of 'assertive' and 'passive' secularism are introduced and discussed in Kuru (2006, 2007) and, notably, in Kuru (2009, Chapter 1). Assertive secularism aims at privatizing and individualizing religion and limiting (even banning) its visibility in the public sphere. In contrast, passive secularism, emphasizes state neutrality towards various religions and allows public visibility of religion. In Kuru and Stepan (2012b), it is pointed out that secularism can be fruitfully decomposed into more categories by introducing a second dimension that distinguishes 'separationist' and 'respect all, support all' type secular approaches.

[19]Özbudun (2012, pp. 82–87) discusses the development of 'organized pluralism' in Turkey. In Özbudun (2012, p. 87) it is argued that "*some of the principles of the founding philosophy of the Turkish republic are hardly favorable to the development of a truly pluralist and consensual democracy*" (italics are my emphasis).

[20]On this point see Owen and Pamuk (1998, pp. 104–106). The views of the US administration are best presented in controversial, albeit evidently influential, report published as Thonburg, Spry and Soule (1949). For a critical evaluation of the changes in policies during 1946–1950 period, see Yalman (2009, pp. 176–197).

4. Infancy Phase of the Multi-Party Regime — Failure on Both Fronts (1950–1960)

The DP came to power with a strong majority after parliamentary elections held on May 14, 1950 and remained in power for a decade. Since the most of the cadres of the DP were recruited from the CHP (with some holding high political and/or administrative positions during the single-party era)[21] they were quite experienced in working with the bureaucracy and were familiar with the macro-governance issues. The DP however did not have a well-defined agenda in developing democracy in Turkey.[22] After the elections, the government devoted most of its energy to defend its own position rather than undertake political reforms to promote democracy. The DP's relatively 'liberal' political stance faded away in time and the regime, starting from 1954, and notably after 1957, gave signals of shifting towards an authoritarian one. However, this tendency never reached the stage of blocking parliamentary and local elections. Although there were some significant irregularities, two general elections took place under the governments formed by the DP.

During its tenure, the DP remained faithful to its original stance concerning the status and the role of the religion in society which was close to 'passive secularism'. The DP era, on the other hand, was infamous for introducing populism to Turkish political life. Although 'clientelism' and 'patronage'[23] were not new to Turkish political life, both gained momentum during the DP's tenure.[24] These maladies of the infancy period of multi party democracy, though changed in form and intensity, continued to be effective in the later years.

The DP's economic program was not that different from the policies followed by the CHP between 1946–1950, with the exception of its stronger emphasis on agricultural development and import liberalization[25] (Owen and Pamuk 1998, pp. 106 110). Import liberalization led to a considerable increase in consumption standards, notably in urban areas.[26] Favorable weather conditions and strong external demand due to the Korean War boom enabled the economy to attain exceptionally high growth performance between 1950 and 1953. Mechanization in

---

[21]For example, the DP's chairman Celal Bayar previously served first as the Minister of Economy (1932–1937) and then as Prime Minister (1937–1939).

[22]The DP's strategy, in the words of Sunar (2005, p. 123), was "to underplay cultural modernization, emphasize development and to hitch the hitherto frustrated energies of social groups to the party so as to take on bureaucracy in a drive for party supremacy."

[23]These concepts and their significance are discussed in Sayarı (2011). See also Keyman and Öniş (2007, pp. 90–91) for the endurance of clientelist-patronage politics. According to Sunar (2004, p. 126), "DP's strategy was to incorporate the middle class peasantry and urban middle commercial groups into a patronage front — a front that would be held together by state assisted capitalist growth."

[24]One of the catchphrases used by the DP was "We will create a millionaire in every district".

[25]The governmental decree dated August 10, 1950 considerably liberalized the import regime. This move was also supported by changes in Turkish legislation to promote foreign direct investment by a law enacted on August 1, 1950 (amended extensively by a new law enacted on January 18, 1954.).

[26]For an evaluation of the economic development and policies during the DP era, see Hansen (1991, pp. 338–351). Long-term agricultural development in Turkey is discussed in Pamuk (2008).

agricultural practices led to creation surplus labor in the rural areas and triggered mass migration to cities. This process started a rapid and disorganized, almost chaotic, urbanization and changed the socio-economic structure of the country. The DP's agriculture-based development strategy also led to an increase in income in rural areas and to an expansion of domestic market.

The course of events were reversed in 1954 as the agricultural production suffered severely from draught and as external terms of trade sharply turned against Turkey. The country, especially after 1957, faced increased inflation rates and severe current account deficits.[27] The failure of the economic program, eventually forced the government to change some of its policies. One early victim was its import liberalization (Hershlag 1968, pp. 178–184).[28] This was followed by a series of policy measures that changed the government's market oriented approach into an interventionist one. Faced with a major economic crisis in 1958, the government was forced to devalue the Turkish lira at an unprecedented rate of 72.5%.[29] Under strong pressure by the Organization for European Economic Co-operation, as well as individual countries such as Germany, the government had to accept a very stringent stabilization program on August 4, 1958.[30]

When one considers the period of 1950–1960 as a whole, it is evident that the DP failed to fulfill its own agenda of moving Turkey towards liberalization both in political and economic spheres. The DP's idea of relying on private sector was not systematically aimed at creating a competitive market economy.[31] Instead, the DP had to resort heavily on public funds to support private sector development. This policy, when combined with the clientelism and patronage, not only negatively affected the political environment, but also led to the creation of an inefficient private sector whose survival critically depends on support from the government. Turkey's first experiment with the multi-party system was haltered when a *coup d'etat* was launched on May 27, 1960.

[27] See Owen and Pamuk (1998, pp. 106–110). The inflationary effects of the DP's agricultural support policy is discussed in Akyüz (1973, pp. 172–180).

[28] This policy change started as early as in September 1953 when the government took its first measures to end liberalization in foreign trade and exchange rate regimes.

[29] This figure is based on comparison of official exchange rates before and after the devaluation. In practice, the official exchange rate lost its relevancy well ahead of these decisions as Turkey was already in a multiple exchange rate system. The share of transactions on official exchange rate was negligibly small. When the relative importance of the transactions under each exchange rate is taken into account, devaluation rate was much lower.

[30] See Kruger (1974, pp. 29–116) for a detailed analysis of the economic developments and the stabilization program between 1953 and 1960. See also Hansen (1991, pp. 338–351).

[31] It should, however, be pointed out that this does not mean that the DP did not make any attempt to improve the institutional base of the market system. For example, the corporate law (Law No. 6762) was accepted on June 29, 1956. This law, with some revisions, remained in effect until 2012. However, DP governments were reluctant to develop an institutional infrastructure (for securing macroeconomic stability, competition, property rights, conflict resolution etc.) which was required for a well-performing market system.

5. Multi-Party Regime on a Fragile Path

The first *coup d'etat* in Turkey in 1960, led to a new constitution which was a reaction to the problems encountered during the 1950–1960 period. The constitution was based on the idea of establishing a set of institutions, such as the senate (upper house), the constitutional court and the state planning organization to secure and strengthen the rule making and enforcing capability of the system through the enhancement of checks and balances. It was hoped that the framework would prevent anti-democratic forces from becoming effective and that it would also put an end to economic populism by containing the choices of governments within the rational boundaries of economic policy making.

The achievements of this framework were, at best, moderate. First of all, the constitution, on the one hand, in line with the aspirations of the society, established some institutions to secure political liberties.[32] On the other hand, it legitimized the military tutelage that constituted a basis for future military interventions to civilian political life. Secondly, there is no doubt that the planned development strategy, which was institutionalized by the constitution, considerably improved the technical quality of the economic policy making process in Turkey. However, in contrast to initial hopes, its effect in containing populist/clientelist tendencies of the politicians was quite limited.

From a political point of view, 1960–1980 was a difficult period; full of uncertainties, political conflicts and violence (notably in the 1970s), and three *coup d'etats* (1960, 1971, and 1980). However when one looks back the following points seem to be relevant for Turkey's future political and economic development:

(i) Almost all players in the political arena accepted 'electoral democracy' as a given.[33] However, the same players were not that enthusiastic in introducing political institutions of liberal democracy. Almost all attempts towards democratization hence stemmed from newly emerging civil society institutions, which were mostly ignored by the mainstream political actors or, occasionally, silenced by force.

(ii) Starting from early 1960s, Turkey experienced coalition governments that introduced a new dimension to political competition. Between 1961 and 1979, Turkey had 10 coalition governments (and one minority government).

(iii) Adalet Partisi (AP, Justice Party) which replaced the DP followed the tradition established by the latter. It was a pro-private sector and a 'passive secular' political party. This party was in power for most of the 1961–1979 period, either as part of a coalition government or alone.

---

[32] The liberal political environment of the early 1960s was short lived. The erosion of political liberties in the following years was institutionalized by changes in the legislation after the 1971 *coup d'etat.*

[33] This statement holds true even for the military that launched three *coup d'etats.* Turkey returned to electoral democracy soon after each coup. Nevertheless, military tutelage remained strong not only during this period, but until 2011.

(iv) In the 1970s, politically effective Islamic parties were established.[34] In 1973 elections the Milli Selamet Partisi (MSP, National Salvation Party) was able to make a strong debut by obtaining 11.9% of the votes and securing 48 seats in 550 seat parliament, but it failed to repeat the same performance in 1977 elections. Its share in votes declined to 8.5% and the number of seats it gained halved. During this period, however, for the first time in Turkey's history, an Islamic party participated in a coalition government. The coalition government formed by a social democratic CHP,[35] and the Islamic MSP on January 26, 1974 established a new era in Turkish politics.[36] In this coalition government the MSP held the deputy prime minister post and several ministerial positions (including important ones such as the Ministry of Industry and Technology). Sharing the responsibility of the government under rather difficult conditions (the First Oil Crisis in 1973 and the events in Cyprus that eventually led to Turkey's military intervention in 1974) enabled the MSP to get acquainted with governance issues and helped the public understand the MSP's political stance.

(v) Europe became increasingly more influential in Turkish political life. Turkey's desire to be part of European Community (later European Union) and its strong economic ties with the European countries increased sensitivity to issues raised by European institutions, especially those related to human rights, democratization, and civil society development.

(vi) Starting from the early 1960s, Turkey adopted an import substituting industrialization strategy. Although this inward-oriented development policy worked reasonably well for some time, its shortcomings became visible towards the end of the 1960s. It gradually transformed/degenerated into an unsystematic protection policy that sustained the monopoly power of the incumbents with a strong anti-export bias. As a result, Turkey found itself in balance of payments difficulties that reached crisis levels towards the end of the 1970s.

(vii) During this period, Turkey's domestic market grew rapidly. In response to it, industrial companies established relations with small business out of metropolitan areas to expand their sales networks. On the other hand, in order to

[34] The first Islamic party, Milli Nizam Partisi (National Order Party), established by Necmettin Erbakan in 1970 was short lived. The party was banned in 1971 and was immediately replaced by Milli Selamet Partisi (MSP, National Salvation Party), founded, again, by Mr Erbakan. The MSP survived until the *coup d'etat* in 1980.

[35] After its defeat in 1965 elections, the CHP radically changed its political stance and openly identified itself as a party at 'the left of the center'.

[36] Formation of the CHP–MSP coalition government was *de facto* recognition of the passive secularism by the CHP. On the other hand, it also helped the MSP to integrate itself to the political system. In fact, after the dissolution of the CHP–MSP coalition, the MSP joined two other coalitions led by the center-right AP in 1975 and 1977.

promote industry beyond the traditional industrial centers governments launched programs to support small and medium enterprises (SMEs).[37]

(viii) Turkey began to send guest-workers abroad in 1961.[38] The main attraction center was Germany. The visible contribution of guest-workers was their remittances that helped Turkey to deal with its balance of payments problems. These workers also kept in close contact with their families in Turkey, and new consumption patterns arose in rural areas of the country as a result, which in turn contributed to an increased demand for domestic consumer goods industry. A much more important long term contribution of guest-workers was their role in indirectly exposing the people in the rural areas of Turkey to social and political rights and democracy practiced in Europe.

(ix) During this period Turkey also faced serious economic difficulties. The country was severely hit by the first (1973) and second (1979) oil shocks. Turkey's oil bill sharply increased and the demand for its exports declined. The 1974 Cyprus conflict and the US arms embargo that followed also contributed to Turkey's economic problems. Between 1977 and 1980, the Turkish economy stagnated, inflation soared up, and balance of payments difficulties intensified.[39] At the same time, domestic political tensions increased and political violence reached unprecedented levels.

On January 24, 1980 the ruling coalition government led by the AP, announced a radical program to change Turkey's economic strategy from import substituting industrialization to export led growth. In order to implement this transformation the program envisaged liberalization in trade and finance, and the privatization of state owned enterprises. Domestic political developments, however, prevented the government to implement its program. On September 12, 1980 the military launched a *coup d'état*, to apparently end the bloodshed and political chaos. The parliament was dissolved, all political parties were abolished and civil society institutions were prevented from functioning. The military junta, decided to leave the management of the economy to technical experts and invited Turgut Özal, the architect of the

---

[37]This idea was first explored during the 1960s in forming 'workers cooperatives' to be financed by the savings of Turkish workers abroad. A revised and elaborated version of the project was promoted by the CHP in the 1970s under the name of 'popular sector', i.e., small and medium sized industrial companies which were owned either by workers or by a group of local shareholders. The achievements were, at best, modest. Many companies failed due to politically motivated choices concerning output mix, technology and location; mis-management and lack of qualified work force. However, this approach served to change the business mentality in the small cities/towns in Anatolia and encouraged local residents to establish new SMEs. In fact, during this period and especially in 1980s there was a significant increase in the number of small and medium sized commercial firms. It should, however be pointed out that since the whole approach was based on allocating public funds (through specialized state owned development banks) it also strengthened the culture of clientelism and patronage.

[38]Between 1961 and 1979, 878, 949 Turkish citizens left the country to become migrant workers in various European countries, mostly in Germany (Aydaş *et al.* 2004, Appendix 1).

[39]The rather unfavorable developments in the global economy in the late 1970s should also be taken as an important factor in explaining the deterioration of Turkey's economic performance.

"January 24 Program" to assume the responsibility of its implementation as deputy prime minister. The military junta, by crushing all democratic institutions, cleared the way for the implementation of the program without any effective opposition and the social costs of the program were easily enforced on the public.

The 1980 *coup d'etat* was a major shock for Turkey. The military junta stayed in power for almost three years and this led to drastic changes within political and economic institutions. During this period Turkey suffered from political repression, arbitrary arrest, imprisonment without trial, torture, and other severe human rights violations. A new constitution was prepared under the military rule and was put to a national referendum on November 7, 1982 and approved by an overwhelming majority. However one year later, despite the junta's animosity, a newly established party, Anavatan Partisi (ANAP, Motherland Party), under the leadership of former deputy prime minister Tugut Özal, won the elections with a large margin and secured a comfortable majority in the parliament that enabled it to form a single-party government. ANAP's single-party governments remained in power until 1991.

6. Towards an Open Market Economy

The ANAP identified itself as a successor of the DP-AP tradition in Turkey's politics. From the very beginning the ANAP claimed to represent different political groups ranging from traditional center-right to nationalists and Islamists, i.e., a large coalition of political groups spanning center-right of political spectrum.[40] The ANAP governments prioritized economic issues and notably aimed to transform Turkey into a market oriented open economy. During this period Turkey continued to implement its reform program by liberalizing its trade, financial system, and capital movements.[41] They emphasized the development of Turkey's relations with other countries, particularly in the Middle East. On the other hand, the ANAP governments paid special attention to develop relations with Europe and applied for a full membership to the European Economic Community on April 14, 1987. The ANAP was more vocal and considerably more consistent than its predecessors with its 'passive secular' stance. The ANAP's policies solidified the foundation of Islamist parties. During its tenure, in response to rising domestic and foreign pressures established the Ministry of Human Rights, the ANAP repealed the articles of the penal code that severely restricted activities of politically left and religious groups in 1991. However, the ANAP preserved the undemocratic 1981 constitution, political party, and election laws that were introduced by the military regime. The political coalition that gave support to the ANAP and its policies remained strong until the 1987 elections, but its power, especially after losing 1991 elections, eroded.

[40] In this sense ANAP can be compared with Japan's Liberal Party in the post-WWII era.

[41] For an analysis of Turkey's trade liberalization, see Togan (1994). Financial liberalization is examined in Atiyas and Ersel (1994), and capital (finance) account liberalization in Ersel (1996).

The ANAP, after some delay, took the issue of re-regulation seriously and changes were made in legislation to strengthen regulation and supervision in banking and newly emerging capital markets, allowing the central bank to act more independently in designing and implementing monetary policies. The ANAP's pro-market stance did not rule out government support for the private sector. On the contrary, ANAP governments resorted to generous and widespread incentives to promote exports and investments. This approach, besides fueling clientelism and political patronage, also led to considerable waste of resources through corruption (as in the case of imaginary exports) and through supporting inefficient activities.[42]

During this period export oriented business flourished and spread all around the country. Some SMEs located out of the main industrial zones began to engage in export business, notably with neighboring countries. Although the high hopes of creating industrial centers that produced goods to be exported in the smaller cities in Anatolia were not fully realized, some SMEs were able to exploit this opportunity and expand their business. On the other hand, entering a much more competitive export business environment influenced the business practices of SMEs and, indirectly, contributed to social change in those parts of the country.

The ANAP was quite tolerant to political competition within the limits of existing legislation. During the 1980s the 'social democratic' Halkçı Parti (HP, Populist Party) and its successor Sosyal Demokrat Halkçı Parti (SHP; Social Democrat Populist Party) represented main opposition. In 1983, Islamist Refah Partisi (RP, Welfare Party) was founded and became a third voice in parliament. The ANAP's dominant position in the center-right remained unchallenged until the ban on the political activities of the political leaders of the pre-1980 *coup d'etat* era was lifted on September 6, 1987.

7. The Years of Macro-Governance Failure (1990s)

Although the reform process continued until 1991, the successive ANAP governments started to suffer from 'reform fatigue' as early as 1987.[43] The general elections held in 1991 ended the ANAP's rule. The party never recovered in the following years and this led to the creation of a big vacuum in Turkey's political arena.

The 1990s can be characterized as years of macro-governance failure. During this period, succeeding coalition governments not only shied away from the undertaking reforms but were incredibly ineffective in dealing with country's economic and political problems. Notable in this context was the Kurdish problem that became a major issue in the early 1980s, before reaching levels of armed conflict and high casualty rates. No ruling government was able to find a democratic way to make progress in solving the political, social, and economic problems that eventually led to

---

[42] In Ersel and Filiztekin (2008) it is shown that investment incentives during this period, to a large degree, failed to achieve their intended objectives.

[43] In 1987 Turkey had general parliamentary elections and for the first time, the ANAP was challenged by a populist center-right political opposition that threatened its secure position.

this conflict. Instead, its very existence was used frequently as an excuse for not undertaking further structural reforms. In the economic sphere, the incompetence of governments became visibly clear when the 1994 crisis was triggered by severe policy mistakes of the ruling parties in power then. The crisis weakened the economy and led to considerable erosion in the credibility of economic policies. Turkey's domestic instability did not help when the country had to deal with the East Asian and Russian crises of 1997 and 1998 respectively.

During the 1990s, the Islamic RP played a significant role in Turkish political life. In the 1995 elections, RP obtained 158 seats in the parliament after getting 21.8% of the total votes. In 1996 RP formed a coalition government and its chairman, Necmettin Erbakan, became Turkey's first Islamic prime minister.[44] Unfortunately, it triggered a harsh and anti-democratic response of the military and in 1997 the so-called 'post-modern coup' was staged.[45] As a result of this military intervention, the RP had to leave the coalition government which it was heading[46] and became banned by the constitutional court in 1998.

The political and economic instability of the 1990s dragged Turkey into a major crisis in 2001. The severity of the crisis[47] went beyond the imagination of the authorities and compelled them to launch a radical, comprehensive and costly stabilization and structural reform program in 2001.[48] The program was explicitly targeted at improving public finances, restructuring the financial sector, and enhancing the regulatory capabilities of the state. For the first objective, a sizeable primary surplus in the budget was targeted and privatization was sped up and its proceeds were allocated to debt reduction. On the reform side, the program aimed at overhauling the regulatory system, accelerating privatization, and enhancing policy implementation capabilities of the authorities. The program was carefully designed, reforms were well sequenced, and a timed, successful communication strategy was launched. These factors contributed to the credibility and the success of the program,[49] but were not sufficient in preventing enormous vote shifts that punished all political parties that participated in political decision making in the 1990s, including the members of the coalition government that launched the economic recovery program and reforms. The three parties that formed the last coalition government of the 1990s ended up with no seats in the newly elected parliament.

[44]Mr Erbakan previously served as deputy prime minister in the coalition governments in the 1970s.
[45]The 1997 military intervention was not a coup in the traditional sense. The military used the threat of launching a coup to achieve its aim.
[46]Foreseeing the ban of RP by the constitutional court, RP supporters established Fazilet Partisi (FP, Virtue Party) in 1997.
[47]In 2001 Turkey's GDP declined 7.6% during a period of three quarters, unemployment numbers increased to around a million, and inflation and public sector deficit increased sharply.
[48]The program was labeled as "Strengthening the Turkish Economy—Turkey's Transition Program".
[49]As can be expected, the 2001 program drew attention of many researchers. See for example Öniş and Şenses (2009) and references therein.

The crisis itself and the measures taken to put the economy back on track had profound effects on the behavior and expectations of all economic agents. First, dangers of economic instability were clearly appreciated by all economic agents, large or small. Second, it was also realized that under such circumstances, the 'mother state' is neither capable of preventing crises nor able to protect economic agents, i.e., the era of protectionism was over.[50] Understandably, that led to a consensus among all economic agents in prioritizing 'economic stability' over all other economic targets and shaped the political choices of the society. The 2000–2001 crisis, therefore, led to the consolidation of the liberalization process. First, the fiscal crisis of the state curbed the public sector's protective capabilities. Second, the disillusionment with the political authorities' performances as well as its bureaucracy's capabilities, notably, in the second half of the 1990s, led to a dramatic change in the business community's risk perception and in their expectations from the political authority. The fiscal crisis of the sate effectively curtailed the practice of socialization of private risks through government intervention. The business community, therefore, became increasingly more risk averse, and as a result, stability became a major and common concern. This development was one of the factors that contributed to rise of political conservatism, and indirectly, allowed the private sector to gain more autonomy from the government.

8. Conservative AKP and Its 'Reformism'

The elections that were held on November 3, 2002 swept a newly established (in 2001) Islamic-rooted AKP, to power.[51] Although its founders were politically active in previous Islamic parties (MSP, RP, FP), the party itself was not a linear extrapolation of them in terms of its political stance and strategy. They challenged the views of the old guard and openly demanded radical changes in the party's political strategy and party structure. Upon their failure in convincing the FP delegates to the necessity of such changes, they left the FP in 2000 and later founded AKP. From the very beginning, AKP stressed its difference from its predecessors and even labeled itself as a 'Conservative Democratic' party.[52] The founders of the AKP, obviously, aimed at establishing AKP as a party of the masses, and not only a party of the

[50]Individually insignificant agents (SMEs, workers and small farmers) suffered most from the economic crisis and they were not part of the beneficiaries of the bail-out mechanism introduced by the 2001 program. On the other hand the authorities did not intend to bail-out all individually significant agents (banks, corporations). Based on a social benefit/cost calculation this facility was offered to a subset of such economic agents. Therefore, it can still be argued that the second effect was significant for all economic agents.

[51]For a systematic analysis and evaluation of the historical developments that led to creation of AKP, its party structure, and major challenges it faced when it came to power, see Hale and Özbudun (2010).

[52]When one takes into account the differences between the old guard and the 'reformers', AKP's effort to differentiate itself from previously established Islamic parties is understandable. Nevertheless, it is not clear whether the rather ambiguous use of the term 'conservative democrat' serves the purpose. For a review of the concept and interpretation of it in the context of the AKP, see Akdoğan (2006).

deeply religious segment of the society. Their emphasis was strongly on human rights, democracy, and on a 'free' market system. In contrast to the MSP/RP tradition, the AKP was careful not to be identified as anti-Western. Therefore AKP, despite its common intellectual roots with previous Islamic parties, was, in fact, more akin to the ANAP of the 1980s.

The 2002 election results were, in a sense, surprising.[53] A major and historically specific factor behind the rise of the AKP in 2002 general elections was the demise of the center-right parties, ANAP and DYP. Their dramatic failure in almost all aspects of macro governance during the 1990s wiped out their credibility in the eyes of their supporters. The AKP filled this vacuum by addressing concerns and demands of these groups and gained their trust.[54] In other words, the AKP following the ANAP's experience in the 1980s was able to form a large coalition of political groups under its umbrella. After coming to power, the AKP made two important moves that strengthened the public's confidence in its programs. They were:

(1) The decision to strengthen Turkey's relations with Europe, notably by seriously pursuing its EU membership project and committing itself to development of human rights in Turkey. The AKP continued the political reforms started by the previous coalition government, and introduced legislation to amend constitution and the penal code according the EU criteria.
(2) The decision to continue to implement the IMF-supported stabilization and restructuring program which was launched in 2001 by the previous coalition government. With this move, the AKP made its commitment to market economy and distinguished itself from the previous Islamic parties that were ambiguous on the role the market system and the economic functions of the state.

8.1. *Intellectual roots of the AKP and changes in socio-economic environment*

The AKP's major success was not the introduction of a new way of thinking to Islamic political society in Turkey. On the contrary, the AKP was successful in closely observing/analyzing the changes already taking place in the Islamic political society, its articulation to the system and in systematically adjusting its agenda accordingly. Since the early 1950s this segment of the society gradually integrated itself with the economic system, probably in a much more profound way than what was observed in political arena. The process started with provincial merchants and businessman; but later due to industrialization and rapid urbanization, Islamic political society became significantly more visible in large cities through the presence of businessmen and workers. Under neoliberal policies of the 1980s, especially as a

[53] For an evaluation of the 2002 general elections, see Özel (2003); Öniş and Keyman (2003). See also Çarkoğlu and Kalaycıoğlu (2007, pp. 112–213) for a detailed analysis of voting behavior in 2002 elections.
[54] The AKP's success drew attention of many researchers and presently there is voluminous literature that examines various aspects of this party. See, for example, Yavuz (2006, 2009); Hale and Özbudun (2010).

result of the country's focus on export industries, some of these small business found ways to expand their activities and became part of the market economy. In other words, the changing socio-economic structure of the country and their increasing dominance of the market system not only integrated these people to the system by redefining their roles in economic and social life, but also fundamentally changed the composition and intensity of their socio-economic demands.[55]

The MSP/RP tradition hardly paid attention to these developments. Both parties were strongly 'anti-Western', and they therefore opposed Turkey's membership to NATO, its attempt to join the EU and Turkey's customs union agreement with the EU.[56] The MSP and RP were also very critical of the practice of democracy and secularism in Turkey. Although they refrained from advocating an autocratic regime based on *sharia* law, their views were still hardly compatible with the concept of pluralistic society. On the economic front the MSP and RP were strongly in favor of industrialization. Although they also claimed to be pro-private sector, in practice, their economic policies relied heavily on government intervention and public control.[57] Towards the end of 1990s, these views lost considerable credibility in the eyes of the Islamic political community and RP's failures in addressing macro-governance issues, became increasingly more disappointing for its supporters.

The need for a new approach was first addressed in the FP's program. The party's approach to the core problems such as the roles of market economy, secularism, and the EU (in fact to the West in general) was much more positive than its predecessors.[58] However, the FP leadership's effort to reconcile the views of the old guards and reformers failed, and the latter group left the party; the AKP was founded by those politicians.[59] The AKP made considerable effort to distinguish itself from other previous Islamic parties by elaborating and integrating this new thinking into its political program. In doing so, the AKP benefited considerably from the experiences of the ANAP in the 1980s. In fact, the AKP's program, in terms of its political philosophy and also in its pragmatism, resembles the ANAP's program of the 1980s more than the MSP/RP approach.

Occasionally it is claimed that the AKP represents the interests of small businesses. This view, at best, is misleading. It is obvious that, like all political

[55]As shown in Tuğal (2009) the change in the socio-political views of the Islamic political society continued after the AKP came to the power. Increasingly, they became favoring participating in democratic life and the market economy. This development led to a more open expression of religiosity and social conservatism.

[56]Turkey's customs union agreement with the EU came into effect on January 1, 1996.

[57]The RP's attempt to formulate its alternative economic system proposal, which was called "Just Economic Order" was an intellectually weak and inconsistent document. It fell well short of satisfying even the party followers.

[58]For a more detailed discussion, see Hale and Özbudun (2010, pp. 1–19).

[59]Some examples include Abdullah Gül (current president as of 2014), Recep Tayyip Erdoğan (current prime minister as of 2014) and Bülent Arınç (current deputy prime minister as of 2014) among others. These individuals, besides their long political careers in Islamic Parties, also assumed responsibilities in political decision making at national and local levels and/or served in bureaucracy.

parties, the AKP have no choice but to be sensitive to the demands of small businesses, which directly affects the well-being of a large part of society.[60] Secondly, surveys clearly show that AKP's supporters are scattered to almost all segments of the society, including incorporated business, workers, farmers, and bureaucracy. Thirdly, such a claim is based on the assumption that small businesses constitute to a homogenous group of politically effective actors. In fact, in 2009, only 12.4% of small firms (i.e., those that employ less than 20 persons) were operating in manufacturing sectors. The rest is scattered in diverse activities in trade and service sectors. Small firms hire 39.6% of paid workers (1.1 paid workers per firm) and produce only 27% of the total value added. It is true that since the 1970s almost all governments engaged in the SME[61] development, particularly in manufacturing. Although significant developments concerning SMEs took place, as a group, they still fall short of what the title of 'Anatolian tigers'[62] brings to mind.[63] On average, the SMEs lack minimum economic scale, are technologically backward, and financially weak. As observed during the 2001 and 2008 crises, small firms are also vulnerable to macro shocks; their importance stems not their economic power, but their fragility.[64]

8.2. *Stability over everything else: The AKP era*[65]

When it came to power, the AKP chose to continue with the 2001 program and it stood by the IMF's policies. Although this choice surprised some observers, it was

[60] In 2009, 5.3 million people were working for small firms as paid workers or otherwise.

[61] It should be pointed out that the term SME is a broader concept and covers not only small firms but also medium size enterprises, which are, in general, qualitatively quite different. In Turkish statistics SMEs are defined as firms that employ less than 250 persons. Nevertheless small firms constitute 98.6% of this group. See Özar (2009) for a comprehensive analysis and evaluation of SMEs in Turkey.

[62] 'Anatolian tigers', a title which lost its popularity in recent years, was actually reflecting the, mostly unfilled, hopes of policymakers that considered SME development a convenient way of spreading industry to smaller towns, bringing in dynamism that is required to compete in export markets and creating employment. The outcome was considerably less than expected. Most of the small firms were not sufficiently competitive, failed to enhance their productivities (see Filiztekin and Tunalı 1999), and were financially weak.

[63] Another term which is used in connection with the SMEs is the "Islamic Capital". As is pointed out in Hoşgör (2011) such a labeling is both confusing and misleading. First of all, what is meant by "Islamic Capital" is not clear. If it is used to identify the religious beliefs of the major shareholders (in most instances sole owner) of the SMEs, indeed, it may hold not only for almost all SMEs but also for many large companies in Turkey. It is merely an expected result in 99.5% Muslim society. On the other hand, the significance of "Islamic Capital" as an economic category is, at least, ambiguous. If it is meant that such enterprises constitute a "sub-economy", it is not supported by the observations of most researchers. On this point, see Demir *et al.* (2004); Tuğal (2009); Hoşgör (2011). In fact, most of the SMEs engage in doing business with large establishments either by joining their distribution networks or as providers of intermediate goods for them. On the other hand, major external financing sources of the SMEs are trade credits (notably from larger establishments) and commercial bank credits, generally in that order.

[64] A small subset of the SMEs (mostly medium sized), were indeed, successful in expanding their business and in finding export markets. For an account of the success stories of the SMEs see Taymaz *et al.* (2008).

[65] See Öniş (2012) for a critical examination of the political economy of the AKP era.

rational from the AKP's own political perspective. First of all, after the 2001 crisis, political and economic stability became almost the only issue on which a consensus could be reached among all economic decision makers. The AKP's approach to this issue was based on two assumptions. The first is that a single-party government can establish and sustain political stability. Although faced with strong political resistance, this assumption was, in general, satisfied. The second is the existence of a stable political and economic environment will help a country achieve fast growth. This assumption, although more controversial than the first, held some ground during the 2003–2008 period. The alignment of policies with the IMF, in this context, played the role of an anchor and, therefore, increased the chance of implementation of the policy measures and positively contributed in establishing their credibility in the eyes of, notably foreign, economic agents. The AKP, throughout its tenure, courageously continued to implement tight fiscal policies which gave some support to the Central Bank's anti-inflationary monetary policies.

On the reform side, remaining urgent reforms were mostly required as necessary conditions for Turkey's accession to EU. The EU-accession process, therefore, became a historically important event that positively affected Turkey's efforts to restructure its political and economic institutions in the post-2001 period. The so-called negotiation process for Turkey's accession to the EU is in fact a partially sequenced reform program structured over 35 *'acquis'* chapters. It was comprehensive and had aims at establishing and/or restructuring political and economic institutions compatible with the Copenhagen political and economic criteria, necessary for EU membership. The EU conditionality, although frequently counted as a second anchor along with the IMF's, is in fact qualitatively different from the latter as it established a path for the creation of 'inclusive' political and economic institutions in Turkey.[66] The EU-negotiation process, until 2006, was a major encouraging factor behind the AKP's reformist approach, but its role was almost reversed in the following years.[67] The apparent increase in the opposition to Turkey's EU membership in the European countries, coupled with the relatively high social and political costs of the remaining reforms, disheartened the AKP government to retain its initial reformist stance.

8.3. *The 2008–2009 crisis and its aftermath*

Turkey began to feel the negative effects of global crisis in the fourth quarter of 2008. It soon became apparent that Turkey was one of the worst hit countries in the world.

[66] See Hoekman and Togan (2005) for a comprehensive discussion of the structural issues related to the EU negotiations process.

[67] For a comprehensive discussion of the impact of the EU on Turkey's reform efforts, see Keyman and Öniş (2007, pp. 25–138). See also Muftuler-Bac (2005) for the analysis of the stimulation of EU candidacy on Turkey's political and legal reforms.

Its GDP declined consecutively for four quarters.[68] The total loss was 7.9% of the GDP and around one million people lost their jobs.[69] All economic decision makers (large and small firms, and individuals) reacted strongly towards the shock. Banks immediately curbed their credits and incorporated businesses reduced their output, investments, and employment. Workers and small businesses, on the other hand, were affected rather adversely through job losses and widespread bankruptcies. The AKP government was quite late in realizing the exceptional nature of the crisis and the seriousness of its possible effects. When it decided to act it had two options: the first was to launch a fiscal stimulus program as many developed countries did but face the risk of the negative implications of the deterioration in public finances. The other was to stick to the existing policy that focused on stability. The AKP government chose the latter and it worked reasonably well for the short period.

By sticking to its stabilization objective, the AKP government was able to contain the uncertainty perceived by the private agents which strengthened its policy credibility.[70] The economic activity, after a near free fall in 2009, recovered quite rapidly and helped Turkey's external credibility. However it soon became clear that this growth performance was unsustainable. Current account deficit, after a sharp decline in 2009, increased to 6.4% of the GDP in 2010 and shot up to alarming level of 10% of the GDP in 2011. The government was compelled to take measures to reduce growth rates, contain inflation, and search for ways to implement long neglected structural reforms.

9. Conclusion

Using the terminology of Acemoglu and Robinson (2012), Turkey's political and economic development between 1946 and 2010 can be considered as a transition from a predominantly "extractive" political and economic system towards to a more "inclusive" one. Despite its significant achievements, the process did not end Turkey's democratic deficit problem[71] and the country still has a long way to become a developed economy. No doubt the nature and speed of transition can be partly

[68]Since these quarters are distributed over two years (2008, 2009), the annual figures hide the actual scale of the shock.

[69]The 2008 crisis was more severe than the one the country faced in 2001. In 2001 the GDP declined over a period of three quarters with a total income loss of 7.6% and an increase of unemployment numbers, again, close to one million.

[70]The election result indicates that AKP's heavy emphasis on stability was appreciated by the public. AKP's vote share increased to 46.6% in 2007 and to 49.8% in 2011. With this performance the AKP, after the DP in the 1950s, became the second party in Turkey that had won three consecutive general elections. It is also the first incumbent party in Turkey's history that increased its vote share in two succeeding elections.

[71]For a critical evaluation of the state of democracy in Turkey see the European Commission report on Turkey (2012).

explained by factors that are specific to Turkey. Nevertheless, in the light of the discussion above, it is possible to draw the following lessons from it:

(1) Under certain circumstances, institutional reforms can be launched by the ruling political authority and act as a catalyst for a transition process. Turkey's transition to multi-party regime (1946–1950), and to market based economy (1981–1991), are examples of such transitions.

(2) Consolidation of the new institutional structure is possible only if the likelihood of reversal reform decisions ceases to be a major concern of the society. Turkey's experience indicates that the elimination of an effective threat of a military take-over played a significant role in consolidating electoral democracy. Similarly, considerable advancement was made in consolidating market economy only after all economic agents realized that the policy options to socialize private risks are no longer available for governments.[72]

(3) It is utterly unrealistic to assume institutional changes take place along a smooth path without any resistance. On the contrary, it is an unstable process full of uncertainties. Therefore governments cannot avoid paying attention to ensure stability while undertaking institutional reforms. The AKP's experience indicates obtaining stability may gain priority over other concerns and even stop the progress of any reform efforts.

(4) Turkey's experience indicates that, although a multi-party regime can establish and sustain an electoral democracy, it may fail to evolve into a liberal democracy. In order to achieve the latter, all parties that represent widest spectrum of political views should be allowed to compete and the system should be open to 'partially overlapping institutions', i.e., political parties and civil society institutions, to participate in political process. Turkey has only recently and partially reached the stage of satisfying these two conditions.

(5) Achieving a 'private sector led growth path' is a complex and uncertain process. First of all, it requires the development of private sector institutions (private property, corporate sector, governance capabilities etc.). This requires sizeable accumulation of capital (both physical and human) and, in general, it is achieved under the umbrella of state protection. Although protective policies may be effective in expanding the private sector, they also may work against the aim of establishing the 'private sector led economy'. Under a protective system private agents may not feel necessary to develop their capabilities in undertaking the risks of their actions. In other words, policies to socialize private risk do not serve the purpose of creating a private sector autonomous from of government. On the contrary it leads to a system dominated by clientelism and patronage, which negatively affects efficiency and competitiveness. This latter effect feeds

[72]For example, in Turkey, the financial crisis of the state in 2001 effectively made protectionist/clientelist policies infeasible. Imposing a hard budget constraint on government (such as aligning a stance with the IMF) and increases the opportunity cost of such policies at best.

the demand for protectionism and works against the prospect of establishing liberal democracy.[73]

(6) Electoral democracy, despite its limitations, is still important as it offers channels for communication, establishes forums for public discussion, and creates opportunities to reconcile conflicting views. This is particularly important when there are significant changes in the social and political views of different social groups. In Turkey, integration of small businesses to the system played a significant role in changing the views of Islamic political society. The working of the electoral democracy, on the other hand, played a significant role in the convergence of conflicting views on the social and political roles of religion towards 'passive secularism'. In fact, this process, besides reducing social tension over this issue, also led to an increase in social support behind the idea of secularism.

(7) It cannot be denied that in today's globalized environment, external factors play a role in influencing developments of its political economy. These factors should neither be ignored nor exaggerated. For Turkey, Europe's role in influencing the course of developments cannot be sidelined. Nevertheless, its contribution to Turkey's institutional development efforts was secondary.

List of Abbreviations

AKP: Adalet ve Kalkınma Partisi (Justice and Development Party)
ANAP: Anavatan Partisi (Motherland Party)
AP: Adalet Partisi (Justice Party)
CHP: Cumhuriyet Halk Partisi (People's Republican Party)
DP: Demokrat Parti (Democrat Party)
DSP: Demokratik Sol Parti (Democratic Left Party)
DYP: Doğru Yol Partisi (True Path Party)
FP: Fazilet Partısı (Vırtue Party)
MHP: Milliyetçi Hareket Partisi (Nationalist Action Party)
MNP: Milli Nizam Partisi (National Order Party)
MSP: Milli Selamet Partisi (National Salvation Party)
RP: Refah Partisi (Welfare Party)
SP: Saadet Partisi (Felicity Party)

Acknowledgments

I am grateful to Ishac Diwan for his continuous support, and for his exceptional tolerance. I also would like to thank Tuncer Bulutay, Ziya Öniş, Şevket Pamuk, Subidey Togan as well as two anonymous referees for their comments and suggestions.

[73]This point may explain why Turkey stuck with a protectionist regime for almost a half century, until it became infeasible due to the fiscal crisis of the state in 2001.

References

Acemoglu, D., S. Johnson and J. A. Robinson. 2005. "Institutions as the fundamental cause of long-term growth." In *Handbook of Economic Growth, Volume 1A*, eds. Aghion, P. and S. N. Durlauf, pp. 385–472. Amsterdam, North Holland: Elsevier.

Acemoglu, D. and J. A. Robinson. 2006. *Economic Origins of Dictatorship and Democracy.* Cambridge: Cambridge University Press.

Acemoglu, D. and J. A. Robinson. 2012. *Why Nations Fail — The Origins of Power, Prosperity and Poverty.* New York: Crown Business.

Ahmed, F. 1993. *The Making of Modern Turkey.* London: Routledge.

Akdoğan, Y. 2006. "The meaning of conservative democratic political identity." In *The Emergence of a Modern Turkey-Democracy and AK Party*, ed. Yavuz, M. H., pp. 49–69. Salt Lake City, Utah: The University of Utah Press.

Akyüz, Y. 1973. *Money and Inflation in Turkey (1950–1968).* Ankara, Turkey: Faculty of Political Sciences Publications.

Atiyas, İ. and H. Ersel. 1994. "The impact of financial reform: The Turkish experience." In *Financial Reform: Theory and Experience*, eds. Caprio Jr., G., İ. Atiyas and J. Hanson, pp. 103–139. Cambridge, Cambridge University Press.

Aydaş, O. T., B. Neyaptı and K. Metin-Özcan. 2004. "Determinants of workers remittances — The case of Turkey." *Emerging Markets Finance and Trade*, 41(3): 53–69.

Birtek, F. 1985. "The rise and fall of étatism in Turkey, 1923–1950." *Review*, 8(3): 407–38.

Boratav, K. 1981. "Kemalist economic policies and étatism." In *Atatürk the Founder of a Modern State*, eds. Kazancıgil, A. and E. Özbudun, pp. 165–190. London: C. Hurst.

Çarkoğlu, A. and E. Kalaycıoğlu. 2007. *Turkish Democracy Today-Elections, Protest and Stability in an Islamic Society.* London: I.B. Tauris.

Demir, Ö., M. Acar and M. Toprak. 2004. "Anatolian tigers or Islamic capital: Prospects and challenges." *Middle Easten Studies*, 40(6): 166–188.

Diamond, L., M. F. Plattner and D. Brumberg. eds. 2003. *Islam and the Democracy in the Midddle East.* Baltimore and London: The Johns Hopkins University Press.

European Commission (EC). 2012. "Turkey 2012 progress report." European Commission Staff Working Document No. 336, October 10.

Ersel, H. 1996. "The timing of capital account liberalization — The Turkish experience." *New Perspectives on Turkey*, 15: 45–64.

Ersel, H. and A. Filiztekin. 2008. "Incentives or compensation? Government support for private investment in Turkey." In *Industrial Policy in the Middle East and North Africa*, ed. Galal, A., pp. 35–50. Cairo: The American University in Cairo Press.

Felipe, J., A. Abdon and U. Kumar. 2012. "Tracking middle income trap — What is it, who is in it, and why?" Lévy Economics Institute, Working paper No. 715, April.

Filiztekin, A. and I. Tunalı. 1999. "Anatolian tigers — Are they for the real?" *New Perspectives on Turkey*, 20: 77–106.

Hale, W. and E. Özbudun. 2010. *Islamism, Democracy and Liberalism in Turkey.* Abingen Oxon: Routledge.

Hansen, B. 1991. *Egypt and Turkey.* Oxford: Oxford University Press.

Hershlag, Z. Y. 1968. *Turkey — The Challenge of Growth.* Leiden: E. J. Brill.

Hoekman, B. M. and S. Togan. eds. 2005. *Turkey-Economic Reform and Accession to the European Union.* Washington, D.C.: The World Bank and The Center for Economic Policy Copublication.

Hoşgör, E. 2011. "Islamic capital/Anatolian tigers: Past and present." *Middle Eastern Studies*, 47(2): 343–360.

Kalaycıoğlu, E. 2005. *Turkish Dynamics.* New York: Palgrave Macmillan.

Karpat, K. 1959. *Turkey's Politics — The Transition to a Multi Party System.* Princeton: Princeton University Press.

Karpat, K. H. 2001. *The Politicization of Islam-Reconstruction and Identity, State, Faith, and Community in Late Ottoman State.* Oxford: Oxford Univesity Press.

Keyder, C. (1981). *The Definition of a Peripheral Economy, Turkey: 1923–1929.* Cambridge: Cambridge University Press.

Keyman, E. F. and Z. Öniş. 2007. *Turkish Politics in a Changing World.* İstanbul: İstanbul Bilgi University Press.

Koçak, C. 2010. *Türkiye'de İki Partili Siyasal sistemin Kuruluş Yılları(1945–1950) Cilt I: İkinci Parti.* [In Turkish] İstanbul: İletişim Yayınları.

Koçak, C. 2012. *Türkiye'de İki Partili Siyasal Sistemin Kuruluş Yılları(1945–1950) Cilt II: İktidar ve Demokratlar.* [In Turkish] İstanbul: İletişim Yayınları.

Kruger, A. 1974. *Foreign Trade Regimes and Economic Development — Turkey.* New York: Columbia University Press for The National Bureau of Economic Research.

Kuru, A. T. 2006. "Reinterpretation of secularism in Turkey — The case of justice and development party." In *The Emergence of a Modern Turkey: Democracy and the AK Partiy,* ed. Yavuz, M. H., pp. 136–159. Utah: University of Utah Press.

Kuru, A. T. 2007. "Passive and assertive secularism — Historical conditions, ideological struggles and state policies towards religion." *World Politics,* 59(4): 569–94.

Kuru, A. T. 2009. *Secularism and State Policies Toward Religion: The United States, France, and Turkey.* Cambridge: Cambridge University Press.

Kuru, A. T. and A. Stepan. eds. 2012a. *Democracy, Islam and Secularism in Turkey.* New York: Columbia University Press.

Kuru, A. T. and A. Stepan. 2012b. "Laïcité as an ideal type and a continuum: Comparing Turkey, France and Senegal." In *Democracy, Islam and Secularism in Turkey,* eds. Kuru, A. T. and A. Stephan, pp. 95–121. New York: Columbia University Press.

Morlino, L. 2009. "Are there hybrid regimes? Or are they just an optical illusion?" *European Political Science Review,* 1(2): 273–296.

Muftuler-Bac, M. 2005. "Turkey's political reforms: The impact of the European Union." *Southeast European Politics and Societies,* 10(1): 17–31.

Okyar, O. 1965. "The concept of Étatism." *The Economic Journal,* 75(297): 98–111.

Owen, R. and Ş. Pamuk. 1998. *A History of Middle East Economies in the Twentieth Century.* London: I.B. Tauris.

Öniş, Z. 2012. "The triumph of conservative globalism: The political economy of the AKP era." *Turkish Studies,* 13(2): 135–152.

Öniş, Z. and E. E. Keyman. 2003. "Turkey at polls: A new path emerges." In *Islam and the Democracy in the Middle East,* eds. Diamond, L, M.F. Plattner and D. Brumberg, pp. 177–189. Baltimore and London: The Johns Hopkins University Press.

Öniş, Z. and F. Şenses. 2007. "Global dynamics, domestic coalitions and reactive state: Major policy shifts in post-war Turkish economic development." *METU Studies in Development,* 34: 251–286.

Özar, Ş. 2009. "Small and medium enterprises in the periphery: The case of Turkey." In *Turkey and the Global Economy-Neoliberal Restructuring and Integration in the Post-Crisis Era,* eds. Öniş, Z. and F. Şenses, pp. 204–222. Oxon: Routldege.

Özel, S. 2003. "Turkey at polls: After the tsunami." In *Islam and the Democracy in the Middle East,* eds. Diamond, L, M. F. Plattner and D. Brumberg, pp. 162–172. Baltimore and London: The Johns Hopkins University Press.

Özbudun, E. 2012. "Turkey—plural society and monolithic state." In *Democracy, Islam and Secularism in Turkey,* eds. Kuru, A. T. and A. Stepan, pp. 61–94. New York: Columbia University Press.

Özkurt, K. 2007. "Transition to multi-part regime in Turkey. An attempt at re-periodization." *Journal of Historical Studies*, 5: 13–32.

Pamuk, Ş. 2000. "Intervention during the Great Depression, another look at Turkish experience." In *The Mediterranean Response to Globalization Before 1950*, eds. Pamuk, Ş. and J. Williamson, pp. 321–329. London and New York: Routledge.

Pamuk, S. 2008. "Agriculture and economic development in Turkey, 1870–2000." In *Agriculture and Economic Development in Europe since 1870*, eds. Lains, P. and V. Pinilla, pp. 375–396. Oxon: Routledge.

Sayarı, S. 2011. "Clientelism and patronage in Turkish politics and society." In *The Post-Modern Abyss and The New Politics of Islam: Assabiyah Revisited-Essays in Honor of Şerif Mardin*, eds. Birtek, F. and B. Toprak, pp. 81–94. İstanbul: Istanbul Bilgi University Press.

Sunar, İ. 2004. *State, Society and Democracy in Turkey.* İstanbul: Bahçeşehir University Publication.

Taymaz, E., A. Filiztekin, M. Fisunoğlu, Y. Kılıçarslan and A. Lenger. 2008. *Kobilerde Dönüşüm-Küçük Firmaların Büyük Başarıları.* [In Turkish] Istanbul: Turkonfed.

Thornburg, M. E., G. Spry and G. Soule. 1949. *Turkey — An Economic Aprraisal.* New York: Twentieth Century Fund.

Togan, S. 1994. *Foreign Trade Regime and Turkish Liberalization During the 1980s.* Aldershot: Avebury Press.

Togan, S. 2010. *Economic Liberalization and Turkey.* Oxon: Routledge.

Tuğal, C. 2009. *Passive Revolution: Absorbing The Islamic Challenge to Capitalism.* Stanford: Stanford University Press.

Turam, B. 2007. *Between Islam and The State — The Politics of Engagement.* Stanford: Stanford University Press.

Waterbury, J. 1994. "Democracy without democrats? The potential for political liberalization in the Middle East." In *Democracy Without Democrats? The Renewal of Politics in the Muslim World*, ed. Salamé, G. London: I.B. Tauris.

Yalman, G. L. 2009. *Transition to Neolibralism — The Case of Turkey in the 1980s.* İstanbul: İstanbul Bilgi University Press.

Yavuz, M. H. 2003. *Islamic Political Identity in Turkey.* Oxford: Oxford University Press.

Yavuz, M. H. (ed.) 2006. *The Emergence of a Modern Turkey-Democracy and AK Party.* Salt Lake City, Utah: The University of Utah Press.

Yavuz, M. H. 2009. *Secularism and Muslim Democracy in Turkey.* Cambridge: Cambridge University Press.

Chapter 9

SOCIAL ORDER, RENTS, AND ECONOMIC DEVELOPMENT IN IRAN SINCE THE EARLY 20TH CENTURY

Hadi Salehi Esfahani and Esra Çeviker Gürakar

1. Introduction

This Chapter examines the evolution of social orders in Iran since the early 20th Century and relates the country's economic performance to that process. The study is enriched by comparisons with Turkey. The implications of the analysis offer insights for the Arab countries that are going through political transformation in the aftermath of the Arab Uprisings. The experiences of Iran and Turkey are particularly interesting and relevant for the Arab countries because both societies share historical ties and significant cultural and social features with the Arab world. In addition, both Iran and Turkey have gone through major regime changes with notable similarities as well as differences. The two countries also claim to be offering competing models of institutional and policy framework for the Arab countries undergoing transformation. As a result, a study of the dynamics of social order in Iran and its comparison with the process in Turkey could hold important lessons for the Arab world.

Our methodology is based on a version of the framework developed by North *et al.* (2009, henceforth NWW), enriched by the insights provided by various contributions of Acemoglu and his associates, particularly (Acemoglu 2008). A central theme of the framework is that human societies have historically started to establish order, control violence, and enforce contracts through personal self-enforcing dealings. Such deals work when they entail rents that would be lost if either side reneges. This is typically achieved through repeated interactions among individuals who are connected in some way (e.g., via kinship, neighborhood, etc.). To boost their rents and to help make their deals work better, those who are party to a deal (insiders) have an incentive to restrict the access of others to the relevant resources. The rents generated can be used to control the production process and to further restrict access to enhance rents. This gives rise to conflict between the interests of outsiders who want to gain access to the rents and insiders who want to protect and enhance their rents.

Conflict over the distribution of the rents also exists among insiders. The outcomes of these conflicts are ultimately shaped by the ability of different groups to exercise violence. The settlement could take the form of dominance by individuals and groups that are more effective in organizing and controlling the means of violence. Naturally, in these situations the dominant groups will be in a better position to control rents and resources. Such distribution of rents can also help the dominant groups to gain a stake in the system and contribute to the control of violence, allowing for rents to be generated. An alternative possibility is the emergence of a set of rules that allows the different groups to share the control over the means of violence and use it to maintain order for their collective benefit. Such rules and beliefs based on them must ensure that while positions of power may rotate among different individuals and group, no subset of them can monopolize power and exclude others. One key characteristic of such rules is that they must be impersonal and self-enforcing.

The emergence of a dominant group that can control violence naturally leads to uneven distribution of access to rents and resources, an outcome that NWW call the "natural state", or Limited Access Order (LAO). As we explain in Section 2, LAOs may take a variety of different forms. In situations where the level of economic and institutional development is low, some forms of LAO may be conducive to increased production for a while by ensuring property rights for those who have access to the political and economic resources (the elite). However, such growth episodes cannot be long lasting because LAOs severely curb incentives and access to resources for the majority of the population. The alternative social order that is compatible with sustained prosperity and growth is the Open Access Order (OAO), which functions based on self-enforcing, impersonal rules that treat all members of the society equally. Such rules work when they are widely accepted and cannot be changed without broad support. The emergence of impersonal rules is a social process that often requires the prevalence of balance of power among organized groups over decades and the development of an understanding about the rules that serve their collective interests. Historically, such processes have been slow to emerge, particularly because any group that finds an opportunity to gain an upper hand *vis-à-vis* others tries to reshape the rules to serves its own interests by constraining others.[1]

Our case study focuses on the ways in which the Iran's politics and economy have developed under different forms of LAO and the reasons why the country has encountered difficulties in moving towards an OAO. In particular, we highlight the

[1] (Khan, 2010a and 2010b) suggests a related, but different, framework for the analysis of social orders that focuses more on "political settlements" in which growth enhancing rents are created and redistributed. As a key feature, the framework attributes social outcomes and processes to the attitudes of elite groups towards cooperation. For example, if a country suffers from predatory rent seeking by a new elite group, time may be required for them to mature and take more long term views of rent generation and appropriations. Initially, rent extraction by the newcomers may be needed to avoid chaotic situation where no economic project is implemented properly. As Khan (2010b) puts it, a proper understanding of the workings of an LAO in a specific context is vital for re-designing institutions in a way that "improve the ability of competing elites to develop 'live and let live' strategies that also allow growth to be sustained if not accelerated." In this Chapter, we consider such changes as part of the moves from fragile to basic and mature LAOs.

roles of initial conditions (existing institutions, beliefs, and social structure), natural resources, and superpower interventions. Our examples from Turkey complement this analysis by highlighting the transition opportunities that emerge under LAO and the constraints that the process faces. The long-term economic performances of the two countries are depicted and compared to those of developed and developing countries in Figure 9.1.

Our arguments can be summarized as follows. At the start of the 20th Century, for reasons that may be traced back to superpower rivalry and to the strength of tribes as the main agents of violence, Iran had very weak state institutions and a fragile social and political order. In the 1920s, the country came under dictatorial rule of a strong military leader, Reza Khan. He had managed to organize a small, but effective army that gained control of the central government through a coup and began to defeat the other warlords around the country, improving the conditions for revenue collection and providing more resources for the central army to grow stronger. Before long, Reza Khan was in a position to take over as the Shah and to establish a less fragile LAO. The new regime developed a modern bureaucracy and security forces with a fiscal system and a network of elites around the Shah that could encourage production, channel rents, and control violence. However, despite major

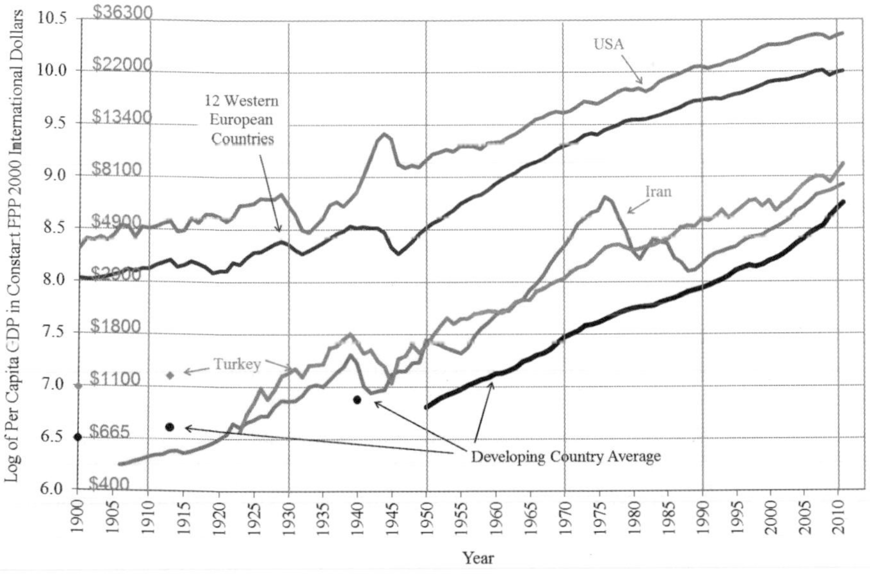

Fig. 9.1. Long-term economic development: Iran and Turkey vs. developing and developed countries. *Sources*: Authors' calculations based on the Maddison Project Database (see Bolt and van Zadan 2013, www.ggdc.net/maddison/maddison-project/data.htm), extrapolated using growth data from *World Development Indicators*, (available online at http://databank.worldbank.org/data/databases.aspx) and Khavarinejad (2003).

strides in stabilizing the political order and improving the economic conditions in the 1920s and 1930s, the system remained an LAO with a network of personal connections under the Shah, interwoven with the government and military organizations. As a result, when Reza Shah abdicated in 1941 following the invasion of the country by the allied forces, a period of chaos and instability ensued.

The post-Reza Shah political turbulence eventually came to an end and a more stable LAO reemerged in the mid-1950s, when one elite faction managed to stage a coup and re-establish dictatorial rule under Reza Shah's son, Mohammad-Reza Shah. Superpowers of the time participated both in adding to the intra-elite conflicts and to the reassertion of authoritarianism. Ultimately, the superior ability to organize the means of violence and, thereby, to control rent allocation was critical for the outcome. Though the Shah's firm grip over the system enabled him to stimulate economic growth and keep him in power for a quarter of a century after the coup, there was little institution building that could help the elite coordinate in less personal ways and take the social order towards a more mature system. Indeed, the regime's access to large oil rents and direct superpower backing led to extreme personalization of power and undermined institutional developments that might have helped the elite to coordinate in more impersonal ways. This feature put the system on shaky foundations that easily collapsed when some groups outside the ruling elite managed to coalesce around a high-ranking clergyman, Ayatollah Khomeini, and mobilized the mass of the population against the Shah in 1978–1979.

Although the revolutionary movement of 1978–1979 was led by the promise of freedom and equality, it ended up reproducing another LAO, the Islamic Republic. The revolution was followed by a violent struggle among a number of organized groups that contended for power. However, the victors were the coalition of clergy and lay men associated with Ayatollah Khomeini who had gained a better position in the process of revolution to recruit political support and to organize a new cadre of security forces. The Islamist ideology, the nature of the group formation, and the intensity of the post-revolution power struggle were important factors in drawing the boundaries of the new elite and shaping the institutions of the Islamic republic (Ghamari-Tabrizi 2008). The way in which the winning coalition had formed, had reached power, and its need to survive under threatening conditions gave primacy to personal relationships and limited the scope for impersonal institutions. The predominant position of Ayatollah Khomeini in the revolution became a model for establishing a pivotal office, the Supreme Leader, with ultimate say in all matters of the state. The office was designed to serve as a coordinator and gatekeeper for the elite. However, this institutional setup largely reinforced the personal nature of power in Iran. There have been a number of attempts in recent years to negotiate new deals that could reduce access restrictions and expand the role of impersonal rules. But, the gains in this respect have remained limited. The elite have mostly viewed such attempts as challenges to their power and have managed to suppress them, sometimes with violence. This process has strengthened the hands of the armed forces in the regime and in the allocation of rents. External interference in Iran and foreign threats of regime change have also added to this shift in the balance of power. These trends have contributed to high economic volatility and slow growth in recent years.

Turkey's experiences since the early 20th Century has similarities with the developments in Iran, but it also contains important contrasts that have helped the country become a more mature LAO and develop more impersonal institutions. Turkey emerged from a chaotic situation following the collapse of the Ottoman Empire at the end of World War I and, as in Iran, came under the control of a strong military leader, Ataturk. However, in contrast to the situation in Iran, Ataturk's regime inherited more advanced state institutions with more systematic control over violence. Also, Turkey's new leaders had been part of the modern Ottoman elites that had experimented with institution building and major state reforms. They had alliances with the regional elites and did not have to subdue them militarily. Moreover, they established a political party that complemented the government and military institutions for managing access to power. These features ensured that after the departure of the authoritarian ruler, there were sufficiently strong institutions to allow the elite factions to compete with each other without causing chaos. The military and the bureaucracy held veto powers and played key roles in steering the system through many episodes of economic and political instability. The elite came to increasingly rely on the court system for managing the intra-elite conflicts and, thereby, laid a foundation for the expansion of impersonal rules. Eventually state institutions and the private sector gained adequate strength to give the elected officials the upper hand *vis-à-vis* the military and bureaucratic elites. Two other factors seem to have helped this process as well: (1) third party enforcement from an OAO based organization; that is, the conditions for membership set by the European Union (EU), which required increased openness and reliance on formal institutions and (2) the rise of a large number of capitalists who started with small and medium size firms, but took advantage of Turkey's increased economic openness to export and accumulate capital. These groups formed a power base for the new political teams that have joined the ranks of the elite since the late 1990s. As a result, although personal connections still matter in Turkey, the country's LAO has matured and many impersonal rules have taken root in it. The consequence for the economy has been stable and robust growth over the past decade. Some risk of remaining an LAO exists in Turkey, as the elite groups currently dominant strive to control access to political and economic resources. But, the rise of new interests and impersonal rules along with the EU effect seems to have made the reversal of the progress unlikely.

In the rest of this Chapter, we first describe the theoretical framework of our study in more detail. We then examine Iran's transformation at various stages and compare it with that of Turkey. Finally, in the concluding section of the Chapter, we derive the implications of the study and offer lessons for the Arab countries that are being transformed in the aftermath of Arab Uprisings.

2. The Framework

According to the NWW thesis, prior to the formation of open political and economic systems (OAOs), human societies avoided chaos when relatively small and cohesive groups (the elite or oligarchy) managed to take charge of the main means of violence and restrict access to economic and political power. Once they controlled the tools of public policy and extracted rents from the rest of the society, the elite were able to support the organizations and social structures that helped maintain their power. The rents also motivated the members of the elite to value cooperation and to reduce risk of violence against each other and against the non-elite. This system (which NWW call the "natural state" or LAO) requires barriers against entry into the ranks of the elite as a means of preserving rents. This is specified through formal or informal rules, including culture and religion. However, control of violence is the ultimate guarantor of access restrictions.

Entry barriers play a central role in LAOs. Individuals in political office under LAO try to keep positions of power in order to increase their ability to run long-term projects and gain access to larger and longer lasting economic and political rents. Besides, incumbents may have the fear of being expropriated and prosecuted once out of power. Thus to preserve their positions, the ruling elite try preempt potential rivals by restricting access to power and resources. This requires some sort of coordination among the elite. The state is the organizational structure that brings about such coordination and governs the relationships within the elite and among them and the non-elite. An important implication of these aspects of the natural state is that private organizations will have difficulty surviving independently of the state under LAO.

Limits to entry, coordination among the elite, and the weakness of organizations outside the state may enable the elite to protect the returns to their investments against redistribution demands. This can strengthen the property rights of the elite and motivate them to invest, yielding economic growth compared to the bleak outcome of a competitive (and chaotic) system without such protection (Acemoglu 2008). However, the limitation of entry shrinks the pool of talented entrepreneurs among the elite and, thus, reduces productive investment and growth. Also, given the weak protection of property rights for those out of power under LAO, the potential turnover of the elite diminishes their incentives to invest. As a result, the system becomes increasingly inefficient.

Enforcement of rules and deals under an LAO is based on personal, self-enforcing relationships among the elites. This has important consequences for the forms and functions of LAOs. In particular, the variety of personalities and relationships that they can form causes LAO to take very diverse shapes, especially in structural details. In addition, the functions of the state under LAO have a personal nature and the delivery of government services always depends on whom the recipient is connected to. This feature enables the leaders of elite factions to build hierarchical following among the elite and non-elite for themselves, elicit their loyalty, and deliver discipline when they deem necessary. Vertical loyalties also tend to reduce trust across members of the hierarchies under each elite group leader, which in turn curtails the possibility of formation of horizontal associations outside the state, especially those that might challenge the LAO.

In contrast to LAOs, OAOs work based on impersonal rules and complex organizations. There are positions of power, especially offices that are in charge of controlling the means of violence. But, the individuals in those positions act as representatives held accountable by the public. They are bound by broadly-accepted, self-enforcing rules that are difficult to change and permit open access. The constraint on changes in the key rules under OAO is the costs of coordination and consensus building across large numbers of individuals and organizations. As a result, those who are elected to lead the state apparatus face constraints in getting other actors to help them change the rules in their favor, particularly because the other actors expect everyone else to hold them responsible if they deviate from the rules. The openness of access to political and economic leadership positions further means that those who are put in charge of political offices are easily replaceable by other contenders. So, they cannot expect to have much leverage over other members of the society to establish their own personal fiefdoms within the state. This in particular implies that the armed forces as state organizations cannot use their means of violence to gain direct or indirect control over the government. Rather, the military and security forces are placed under the consolidated control of civilians who represent the public

The diffuse and impersonal support for the rules under OAO can provide a third-party mechanism for the enforcement of new rules that are established through widely accepted procedures. This allows the organizational structure of the society to become increasingly complex and rich. In particular, it provides room for the emergence of all sorts of private associations and organizations outside the sphere of the state, ensuring competition for those in charge of policymaking and providing checks and balances for those acting within the state.

LAOs take different forms in terms of their ability to manage entry restriction and coordination among the elite. One way to classify them is in terms of the durability of institutions and the strength of private organizations present in the system. Using these criteria, NWW classify LAOs into three types: *fragile*, *basic*, and *mature*.

Fragile LAOs are rudimentary systems with many elite factions with their own direct access to violence. Balance of power among these factions could result in mutual deals and settlements that lead to the control of violence, possibly allowing production and rent generation to expand. Violence capacity would then serve as a principal determinant of the distribution of the rents. However, in the absence of institutional structures that allow for impersonal and long-term relationships, the deals among factions fall through once in a while and the power struggle may take violent forms. This inherent instability in the social order along with entry restriction severely limits the incentives to invest and produce under fragile LAOs. Even though output may expand in the short run, growth cannot be sustained. In the long run, fragile LAOs cannot perform well economically.

Basic LAOs emerge when one elite faction (often under the leadership of an individual) gains the upper hand and comes to regulate access to the political and economic resources. The dominant faction coordinates the other elite groups, balancing them against each other. It may even use its control over entry to create competition for other elite groups and to strengthen its own relative position. However, there are limits to the power of the leading elite because they need the other factions to help maintain the order and balance the potential challengers to the leadership. This implies that monopoly of violence may never be consolidated in an LAO. Suppressing all other factions soon brings about a breakup and factionalization of the dominant faction (or coalition) itself. As a result, although basic LAOs may go through periods of extreme concentration of power, their main mode of operation is the situation where factionalization among the elite persists with one faction or coalition enjoying dominance and serving as the coordinator and gatekeeper.

The dominance of one faction under basic LAO gives it some stability and provides an opportunity for state institutions to gain longevity. This can make the environment more hospitable for investment by the elite. The economic gains then reinforce the system. However, the nature of power remains highly personal and private organizations outside the sphere of the state are hardly tolerated.

Mature LAOs are social systems that go beyond basic LAOs and manage to develop more complex and impersonal institutions for regulating entry and intra-elite relationships. In particular, these take the form of stronger judicial and legislative bodies that regulate elite rivalries and elite-non-elite relations on less personal and arbitrary bases. In contrast to the basic LAOs, where the coordinators and gatekeepers tend to deal with conflicts personally and informally, the elite try to resolve their differences more formally in the legislature or in courts. Also, to select policymakers for political offices, they tend to hold elections that allow the non-elite to vote for competing elite factions. These features reduce the need for the dominance of one faction as a coordinator and guarantor of stability. The LAO becomes more mature as it comes to rely more on rules and formal mechanisms.

Mature LAOs allow for the formation of private organization within some range. Such opportunities enable the social and political entrepreneurs among the non-elite to build new coalitions and to penetrate the elite ranks or create pressure for lowering entry barriers. This process diminishes the rents that can be appropriated by the dominant coalition. If society's institutions are sufficiently developed and impersonal at that stage, the system might be able to transit into an open access order. However, it is also possible that the erosion of rents weakens the elite's incentive to maintain the institutions, preventing effective transition or even pushing the system into more basic or fragile LAOs.

The transition among various social orders does not follow any teleological process and may take many directions. The transition from a fragile to basic LAO is associated with the emergence of a dominant faction that can help maintain the stability of the system and allow some institutionalization of the state. The reverse transition may also take place. The demise of the dominant faction or its overzealous efforts to gain absolute power could push the system into a fragile state. The move from a basic to a mature LAO requires increased sophistication of state institutions and weakening of the dominant faction. The reverse move can come about if a faction that has the upper hand at some point tries to perpetuate its rule by undermining the system's institutions. For transition to an OAO, the society must have developed some institutional capabilities that can only exist in mature LAOs. NWW summarize such doorstep conditions as:

1. Rule of law for elites
2. Perpetually-lived organizations in the public and private spheres
3. Consolidated political control of the military by civilian leaders

Historically, institutionalization of rules, which plays a crucial role in reducing the arbitrary and personal nature of state power, has often been brought about as an unintended consequence of actions by elite groups or by accidental coordination among them. However, learning from other societies and accumulation of experience about rules that work or don't work can prepare the ground. External forces, such as threats from other states or promises of beneficial exchange with other countries, can also act as catalysts. For example, the potential for entering the European Union seems to have helped Turkey move closer to the doorstep of OAO. Of course, foreign forces may also adversely affect the maturing of an LAO by actively undermining institutions, intervening in elite rivalries, and the like. For example, US intervention in Iran in 1953 and the Iraqi invasion of Iran in 1980 seem to have adversely affected the development of institutions in Iran.

A question that has not yet been explored much in the social orders literature, but is particularly important for MENA countries, is the role of resource rents in the performance and development of LAOs. Self-enforcing personal deals that play a key role in basic LAOs depend on the rents that each agreement generates for the parties involved. When there are opportunities for generating rents through production, mutually beneficial agreements among the elite are more likely to entail provisions that facilitate investment and productivity. However, when there are significant resource rents to be distributed, the arrangements among the elite may entail less concern about rents derived from production. Furthermore, in pursuit of capturing more of the resource rents for themselves, the dominant elite may prefer weaker institutions and less constraint on their actions.

Another important issue that deserves greater attention is the notion of elite formation and circulation. While the social orders literature has emphasized the capacity to exercise violence, elite groups also need to have the ability to persuade people, to coordinate them, and to manage the production process, including capital accumulation (Mills 1956). Often, different members of an elite faction have different talents and complement each other. For example, elite leaders who are capable of influencing and mobilizing people often do not exercise violence themselves. Rather, they recruit or are joined by other individuals with the capacity for violence.

Also, entrepreneurs who can engage in production may gather around such an alliance to receive protection and greater rent appropriation opportunities in exchange for sharing the generated rent. However, since trust is central for the survival of such alliances, recruiting is limited and sometimes members of the same elite faction circulate among these roles. For example, in French 'pantouflage,' the same persons occupied leading positions in the military, the government, and the private sector over their careers (Kolabinska 1912; Bottomore 1993). The importance of trust also helps explain why kinship plays a major role in individuals' access to elite positions (Heying 1995). Ideological bonds could also help elite cohesion, though such bonds often do not last long. As Higley and Burton (2006) point out, "ideologically united elites" typically originate in revolutionary circumstances in which a movement articulates a specific ideology to overthrow the existing elites. Once the revolutionary fervor is over and some rival groups have been eliminated, stability returns when new alliances lead to the formation "consensually united elites". In this "elite settlement" process, "rival elite camps manage to bring their major disputes to a close and establish a basis for mutual trust" (Higley and Burton 2006).

An alternative formulation of elite dynamics is Vilfredo Pareto's concepts of "innovators" versus "consolidators". In his view, the circulation of elites has a wider meaning than the replacement of existing power elite by new ones. Rather, "consolidators replace innovators, and innovators replace consolidators" (Pareto 1991, p. 8). Pareto further argues that "when the new elite becomes victorious, it starts subjugating its erstwhile allies, shows a proclivity to monopolize all rewards and becomes more rigid and more exclusive" (Pareto 1991, p. 13). However, as we have argued above, they may also try to form new alliances or bring in new players to the game to balance the forces that may be pushing for change from within. The new entrants may be individuals or groups from the non-elite who manage to pass the entry barriers.

In applying this framework to the study of Iran, we first identify the nature of social order in each period. We then examine the entry restriction and rent appropriation mechanisms in that period. We also explore the ways in which the social order has shaped investment opportunities and economic performance. Next, we study the dynamics of the system and project its possible trajectories in the coming years. Finally, we derive the implications of our findings for Arab countries, especially those experiencing major transformation in the aftermath of Arab Uprisings.

3. Social Order and Economic Conditions in Iran in Early 20th Century

The elite strata in Iran traditionally consisted of the members of the royal court, top bureaucrats and military leaders, tribal chiefs and warlords, high clergy (*ulama*), and local notables (major landlords and merchants). The central government was weak and violence capacity was widely dispersed among the elite, especially tribal chiefs, in various localities. When the government needed to defend its territory against an external enemy or suppress a rebellious warlord, it called upon tribes and other warlords to send troops to join its limited forces. As a result, state power largely depended on how well it could balance the tribes and other organizations with violence capacity against each other and on the support it could muster from them. Rabi and Ter-Oganov's (2012) study of army in 18th and 19th Century Iran concludes:

> "The central authorities continued to use the provincial militias to keep order in the provinces and to balance the power of the tribes. They further ensured a balanced and loyal administration by dividing civil and military power between the *beglarbegi* (high provincial governor) and *sardār* (high military commander in the province). Finally, to check the irregular militias and cavalry, Qajar shahs, like their Safavid and Afshar predecessors, had in their service a standing and most loyal force — the Shah's bodyguard." (p. 354)

When power balances shifted, the tribes with their own dynastic ambitions did not hesitate to undertake armed opposition to the government, leading to the frequent and violent turnover of Iranian dynasties until the 20th Century: between the early 18th Century and the early 20th Century, power shifted from one dynasty to another four times.

The rise of religious leaders to the elite status rested upon a specific historical event: the ambition of the Safavids to strengthen their monarchy as a *Shiite* state against the neighboring *Sunni* Ottoman Empire. Accordingly, Safavid monarchs espoused Shiism as a state religion and provided economic resources and political support for Shiite religious bodies within the framework of the state. The expansion of Shiism further enhanced the ulama's independent sources of funding through religious taxes, contributions, and control of *waqf* property (religious endowments under Islamic law). The collapse of the Safavid state in 1736 and the interregnum of 58 years with tribal and dynastic conflicts provided the Iranian ulama with the opportunity to institutionalize their power more or less independently of state apparatus. This process gathered strength with the establishment of Qajar dynasty in 1794. Qajars "... were of nomadic descent, and for them the administration of a country was far more complex than that of a tribe.... The growth of the ulama was thus reinforced by their ability to perform educational, judicial, and legitimating functions of the Qajar state" (Moaddel 1986, pp. 522–523). When the 19th Century global developments made change inevitable in Iran, the ulama were politically and institutionally strong and could claim that they had the ability to lead the society morally and politically through the process of change. Meanwhile, in the Ottoman Empire the continuity of the strong state was considered as the sole guarantor of the preservation of social order and the spread of Islam. Thus, secular imperial politics and the most liberal and pragmatic branch of Sunni Islam, Hanafi School of Law, was adopted. Accordingly, the Ottoman ulama's duty was only serving as experts in "legitimizing" the decisions taken by the government (Gencer 2008). As a result, during the 19th Century reformist "Tanzimat" movement, the bureaucratic elite easily excluded the ulama from the decision making process arguing that the latter had lost their connections with the political reality in the modern world. The ulama lost their financial independence when the government took over religious endowments and turned the clergy into paid officials of the state (Ahmad 1993, p. 25).

Global developments and superpower rivalry also played a role in the functioning of Iran's fragile LAO in the 19th Century. Iran was a buffer between the territories controlled by Britain and Russia. So, each power had an interest in gaining greater ground in Iran and fending off the other. In doing so, they developed alliances among the central elite as well as the local warlords, with Britain focusing on the southern and Russia on the northern regions of the country. Neither saw a strong central government in their interest, but neither found it feasible to change the balance and replace the central government with its own allies. As a result, the weak Qajar dynasty became more durable it predecessors

The weak but durable central government in the 19th Century changed the nature of land relations in Iran and led to landlordism. The central government weakness allowed the elite members to treat the stretches of land under their control over as private property (Lambton 1969). When Amir Kabir, a modernizing chief minister, tried to reform the system in the 1840s, he was assassinated through palace intrigue. His reforms were defeated and large scale landlordism strengthened. The large landowners mainly composed of members of the royal family, top bureaucrats, tribal leaders, and local magnets, who had obtained land by conquest, inheritance, gift, or purchase. In addition, many ulama also came to won large tracks of land through inheritance, purchase, state grants and pensions, and sometimes through usurpation of the *waqf* properties under their supervision.

The rise of landlordism in Iran was in sharp contrast with the developments in Ottoman Turkey in the 19th Century and had significant consequences for the transformation of Iran's social order in the 20th Century. It is notable that until the mid-19th Century the institutional structures of land relations in the Ottoman Empire and Iran were rather similar in their essentials. However, their trajectories began to diverge in the second half of 19th Century as the Ottoman government began to removing tax collection intermediaries, establish private property rights, and distribute the state lands to small peasantry as a means of increasing government revenues (Karpat 1968). The relative strength of the state and its drive to raise revenues for the bureaucracy and the military were major factors in this process. Although the creation of private property rights allowed some to come to own large tracks of land that they did not cultivate themselves, the landlord class did not grow strong in many parts of the 19th Century Ottoman-Turkey because the central state bureaucracy managed to keep control of state lands and defeated the local notables through its reforms.

An important development in the structure of Iranian society in the 19th Century was the growth of the merchant class, which was made possible by the durability of the Qajar state and the rise of global trade in 19th Century. As merchants accumulated wealth, they acquired land and some of them managed to join the ranks of the elite. Also, their religious contributions increased and, as a result, they built closer ties with the clergy.

By the late 19th Century, landlordism and the rise of merchants and Shiite clergy had changed the balance of power in the Iranian society and the old social order was no longer viable. Indeed, in the early 20th Century, a coalition of merchants and clergy led a revolution, the Constitutional Revolution of 1905, that initiated the process of state modernization in Iran. However, the transition from fragile to basic LAO proved quite turbulent and prolonged. As the Qajars and some elite factions fought to maintain their relative power, a wide range of tribal leaders and local notables mobilized their armed men in support of the constitutionalists. Eventually the supporters of the old regime were violently defeated, but then conflict among the constitutionalists broke out and plunged the country into chaos during the 1910s. The ripple effects of World War I and the Bolshevik Revolution in Russia added to the turmoil.

Instability came to an end in the 1920s when Reza Khan, a Brigadier General in Iran's military, rose to power. Following a *coup d'état* in 1921, Reza Khan gained control of the military and the treasury and began to build a centralized army, which in turn made it possible to collect taxes more effectively, thus strengthening the central government. Within a few years, he had subdued the key warlord around the country and obliged a wide range of the elite to enter into alliance with him. In 1925, the alliance helped Reza Khan depose the Qajars and declare himself as the Shah. He became Reza Shah Pahlavi and the founder of a new dynasty.

4. Transformation of Social Order under Reza Shah

The rise of Reza Shah brought some changes to the patterns of land ownership and rent allocation, a process that was also influenced by the dominance of private ownership of land as a key channel of rent extraction. During the early years of Reza Shah's reign the government confiscated considerable areas of land from rebel warlords — mainly tribal chiefs — and other large landowners and local notables. Reza Shah himself sought, mostly through forced sales, to acquire as much land as possible in the form of crown property (Moghadam 1996). The large rents from these lands were needed not so much for covering court expenses that allowed the Shah to reward loyalty and service to him. Indeed, in spite of Reza Shah's modernization attempts, by the 1930s he had become the country's largest landlord. The government also extended its supervision over *waqf* endowments, reducing the top clergy's control over land and weakening the economic source of their independence.

While expropriating some landlords and undermining the economic source of many clergymen's power, Reza Shah built alliances with the rest. Some of the expropriated and state lands were also granted to military and bureaucratic leaders, thus nudging them to join the landlord class. This expanded the elite's interest in strengthening private property over land and led to a new legal basis for land ownership in the form of land-registration law of March 1932 (Ashraf and Banuazizi 1992).

The increasing power of the central army and the resources devoted to it gradually enabled its leading cadres to replace the defeated warlords as an elite group specialized in the use and control of violence. To keep the military under control and to ensure that the ambitions of the officers were checked, the armed forces were divided along different lines and monitored by intelligence units. However, prospects of benefiting from land rents played an instrumental role in maintaining the order. Indeed, as the political power and autonomy of the large landlords were weakened, some bureaucratic land military leaders advanced their positions in elite spheres through land acquisitions (Lambton 1953, pp. 182–189; 241–242; 259–262). Land grants from the government and the court also expanded these possibilities. In addition, the retiring top echelons of the military were often appointed by the shah to consequential positions, e.g., province governorship and bureaucratic high offices, foundation headship, corporate directorship, or seats in the Senate (the upper house of parliament). This *pantouflage* made the officers hopeful of receiving rents beyond active duty and ensured that they remain loyal to the Shah and refrain from interference with his policies or decisions of his appointees.

The role of the military in Iran was in sharp contrast with the situation in Turkey, where the Armed Forces saw themselves as the guardians of the country's secular republican system and began to intervene in politics as an institution after Ataturk and his close associates had left the scene (Ahmad 1993, pp. 121–147). In the absence of land rents and a coordinating leader, Turkish military leaders sought to enforce a set of rules in a collective fashion. To this end they tried to formalize and institutionalize their role in the country's politics and policymaking process. In Iran, the loyalty of the armed forces took a personal form: they were rewarded by the Shah for being loyal to him and for all matters of politics they deferred to him. They tried to follow the Shah's orders and not to have an opinion of their own. The allocation of land rents during Reza Shah's reign (and oil rents under his son's reign) was a critical element that made the arrangement work.

The LAO that emerged under Reza Shah was no longer a fragile one. The state started to gain more institutional capability and sophistication. New military and bureaucratic elites began to emerge with Reza Shah's efforts to develop a modern army and an efficient centralized bureaucracy. Similar to the aims of the *Harbiye* and *Mülkiye* — the civil and military bureaucratic schools in the 19th Century Ottoman Empire, in Iran many youngsters were sent to European military academies and universities for training in the 1920s and 1930s. Although an indigenous academy, *Dar ul-Funun*, had been established by the reformist chief minister in the 1840s, its activities never expanded enough to help train the sizable cadres needed for a modern state. With the return of Iranians educated in the West and the expansion of the domestic educational system, the civil bureaucracy expanded dramatically and its leadership rose in status. As mentioned above, some acquired land and gained greater access to rents. Others managed to join the elite sphere via membership in the parliament (*Majles*) (see Table 9.1), though this role became increasing low status among the elite as the power of the Shah grew. It should be noted that according to

Table 9.1, the share of ex-bureaucrats in the parliament was initially high, but those were most members of the old oligarchy who happened to hold jobs with the government. The rise of the bureaucrats' share in later years, on the other hand, indicates the entry of new members to the elite circles.[2]

As in other basic LAOs, all major economic organizations were linked to the dominant elite and provided them with the means to maintain or advance their positions. As for political organizations, all non-clandestine ones were dominated by the government, in which the shah was the pivotal player. The parliament (*Majles*) was weakened substantially and the judiciary, although reformed and expanded, came under full control of the government. Reza Shah applied patronage through the military, bureaucracy, and the royal court and seized upon the Iranian traditional web-type power relations and put himself in the center (Bill 1972). All the cabinets of this period "remained in office until they lost the confidence not of the *Majles*, but of the Shah" (Abrahamian 1982, p. 138). These aspects explain the weaknesses of institutional development and the relative failure of progress toward a mature LAO in Iran compared to Turkey, where institutions had started to take impersonal forms by the 1940s.

Reza Shah's rise to power broke an old impasse that had kept Iran's social order a fragile one for centuries. The defeat of multiple holders of violence capacity and the expansion of the central military organization allowed the bureaucracy to grow and endow the state with more durable institutions. This eventually laid the foundation for a basic LAO in mid 20th Century. The acquiescence of many elite groups was important in this transformation, especially the major landlords, merchants, bureaucrats, and professionals who found Reza Shah's dictatorship preferable to the past fragile equilibrium or chaos. The influence of institutional, organizational, and technological advances in the West were also non-trivial. A key loser in this process was the clergy, whose members were deprived of some of their resources and privileges (e.g., as reflected in the share of clergy in the parliament shown in Table 9.1). As in Turkey several decades earlier, the new dominant coalition in Iran did not find a useful role for the clergy in its ranks, especially in its effort to build a modern state based on the Western model of institutions.

Foreign influence in Iranian politics diminished after the rise of Reza Shah. The increased coordination among Iranian elite reduced opportunities for foreign powers to incite warlords against the central government or play different factions against each other. The superpower drive to interfere in Iran also diminished in the 1930s, when they became pre-occupied with the Great Depression. Once World War II loomed, Iran began to attract more attention again as the importance of its strategic location and oil resources got increasingly recognized. Like Turkey, Iran tried to take a neutral position in the War. But, that was not acceptable to the Allied forces that needed Iran as a military supply route to the Soviet Union. They invaded Iran in

[2] The active military officers were prohibited from joining the parliament. Those who joined after retiring have been listed in Table 9.1 based on other occupations that they had taken on.

Table 9.1. Occupational backgrounds of parliament members in Iran (1906–1979).

(Percent of Total)					
Occupation	1906–26	1926–41	1941–63	1963–7	1975–9
Cleric	24	11	4	0.3	0.3
Merchant	11	11.4	9.2	7.7	6.8
Landowner	28.5	40.4	40.4	23.2	9.8
Bureaucrat	32.1	26.9	32.6	45.8	40.8
Professional	12	17	19	13.8	21.3
Private Sector	3	2	2	3.7	3.2
Worker-Unionist	—	—	—	3	4.9

Source: Ashraf and Banuazizi (1992).

September 1941 and forced Reza Shah to abdicate in favor of his young son, Mohammad-Reza.

5. Economic and Political Change under Mohammad-Reza Shah

The fall of Reza Shah removed the coordinator of the Iranian elite and opened up the space for freer exchange. However, Iran did not have the necessary impersonal institutions to sustain a real democratic process. The outcome was a rather chaotic process that became increasingly violent, returning the country into a fragile LAO. An important added feature compared to the past was Iran's oil resources that were yielding increasing rents, though mostly captured by the British, who controlled the extraction and shipping of oil. These rents as well as geopolitical rivalries boosted the superpowers' incentives to intervene in Iran. The West chose to support the Shah and the elite groups around him (mostly the military leaders, some top bureaucrats, and many large landowners). The Soviet Union, on the other hand, opted to expand its influence through Iran's communist party (Tudeh Party), which secretly penetrated the military and developed a significant armed wing. This situation had helped line up a large and diverse set of elite groups in the form of the National Front against both Eastern and Western Bloc influences. Control over oil rents was at the top of the Front's agenda. The clergy, who had lost part of their influence among the elite, mostly rejected the three groupings and formed a forth faction. The multilateral elite game soon became complex and violent.

The standoff among elite factions was eventually resolved with a CIA-backed coup in 1953 that largely decimated the National Front and the Tudeh Party and substantially strengthened the Shah's faction of the elite. The dominant group had a rather similar character to the one that prevailed under Reza Shah, consisting of landlords, military leadership, and top bureaucrats. However, now oil rents were becoming quite sizeable compared to the land rents. This shift enabled the Shah to begin expanding his power in the new system. New technocrats were recruited to join the ranks of the elite, while the decline in the relative positions of the clergy and merchants resumed (see Table 9.1 for seat shares in *Majles*, reflecting these trends).

Another new element after 1953 was the response to the relatively wide appeal of the Tudeh and discovery of communist infiltrators and National Front sympathizers in all the ranks of the armed forces. To deal with this concern, the Shah established a secret police organization, SAVAK, that would be allowed to use violence with little accountability. The SAVAK also addressed another concern of the Shah: the opposition from large segments of the clergy and the merchant class that had lost their places in the dominant coalition, but had mass appeal and could generate significant resistance. They had also started to support and fund armed groups that engaged in assassinations of the ruling elite members.

As the gatekeeper for entry into the elite circles, the Shah used oil rents to recruit new elite members who would owe allegiance directly to him and would help strengthen his position *vis-à-vis* the more entrenched elite groups. He particularly preferred professionals who could run the bureaucracy and implement his preferred projects. This required expansion of infrastructure and education, especially for the middle classes, which together with the rising oil rents and other factors gave rise to high economic growth rates (Esfahani 2002).

The stabilization of the LAO in Iran under Mohammad-Reza Shah coincided with increasing interest on the part of the West, especially the US, to help Iran develop economically as a means of reducing the risk of a communist-instigated uprising, similar to those in China, Vietnam, and elsewhere. The landlords, who had some influence in the system, especially the parliament, were not very helpful in promoting this goal. Also, with oil rents and new elite members on his side, the Shah no longer needed the landlords or the rents from the Crown lands, which were costly to manage. As a result, in the early 1960s he decided to undermine the landowners' source of power through a major land reform, which redistributed most of their lands to their tenants. Before the land reform of 1963, members of the royal family, large landowning clans, and a few hundred other families owned about 62% of the agricultural land in Iran. Waqf endowments and the state domains accounted for another 18%. The remaining 20% belonged to about 750,000 small landowners and peasants (Ashraf and Banuazizi 1992). The Shah first distributed part of the Crown lands and then set a maximum limit on land holding by other holders. The land taken away from landlords would be compensated by giving them shares in the stocks of state-owned companies, priced by the government.

The land reform went well beyond passing land title to peasants. It enabled the regime to expand its control over the agriculture surplus through interventions in input and output markets and to move large scores number of agricultural workers to industry and service sectors. More importantly, it was combined with a series of other reforms, such as privatization of state owned enterprises, voting rights for women and use of military conscripts for education and healthcare development. These measures were meant to appeal to parts of the population and help weaken the landlords and the clergy as much as possible. However, ironically, the land reform may have unintentionally provided the clergy with more political power because it removed landlords as one of their main political rivals at the regional level. Since unlike the situation in Turkey, the Iranian army was not an independent player in the political game, powerful landlords used to serve important roles in the exercise political control at the local level. Thus, demolishment of their power created more space for the clergy. This is an important way in which the characteristics of the dominant collations of the LAOs in Turkey and Iran made a difference in the transition period.

The reform package met with strong opposition from segments of the clergy, merchants, and landlords. The demonstrations instigated by this opposition and led by a prominent clergyman, Ayatollah Khomeini, were violently suppressed in 1963 and the leaders were either put in jail or exiled. The Shah emerged victorious as a stronger dictator, but ended up relying on a narrower coalition. The elite factions driven to the sidelines and aspiring individuals outside the elite circles tried to organize and bring down the Shah's coalition, some forming or supporting armed groups. However, initially they met with little success as the government's security forces managed to keep the opposition at bay through violent repression. The Shah also tried to cultivate moderate and less political religious organizations as competitors for more radical religious groups and as a bulwark against the left.

By the mid-1960s, the Shah had recruited many professionals into the elite ranks and, using Iran's increasing oil revenues, he managed to encourage them to support investment and economic growth. His stronger role as a coordinator, his increased control over means of violence, and his prospects of living a few more decades created a stable environment in which production could expand. As a result, Iran experienced very high growth rates in the 1960s and early 1970s (Esfahani 2002).

Under the Shah, the state apparatus had firm control over generation and distribution of rents. The incentives of the elite were partly aligned through appointments to government positions and lucrative government contracts that rewarded service and loyalty. The Shah and his family also exerted influence through a series of foundations that they had established to manage their properties. The Shah's own foundation, the Pahlavi Foundation, was by far the largest and the most influential. These foundations generated and channeled rents in support of the Shah in various ways. For example, in Iran's imperfect markets, private companies needed help with ensuring access to inputs, credit, and marketing. Granting a chunk of a company's stock freely to the Pahlavi Foundation could generate vital support. The Foundation would appointment its well-connected representatives to the company's board of directors to deal with any problem the company encountered. These representatives were typically retired high-level military officers and bureaucrats who would receive part of the company's rents as reward. They would also monitor the company's finances to ensure that the Foundation receives its share of the profits. This system was similar to the one exercised under Reza Shah, but instead of granting control over land rents, it offered positions in modern companies.

The Shah's basic LAO began to unravel in the 1970s despite sharp increases in its oil rents. The elite groups that had been excluded from power and wanted to gain access to political and economic resources were already quite large. In addition, the

Shah did not want to give much ground to the new elite that he had recruited in the 1950s and 1960s. Many of them had helped improve the administrative system and were responsible for Iran's rapid growth after 1963. As a group, they had accomplished a great deal and had amassed significant professional credentials and experience in the 1960s and early 1970s. They had also developed a sense of *esprit de corps*, which was helping improve the quality of state institutions. However, the Shah was wary of sharing power with them and giving them substantial roles. So, he followed the same strategy that had worked for him earlier: recruit new elite members who would owe allegiance to him only. But, the strategy had significantly diminishing returns. The continuation of the strategy was adding to the ranks of disgruntled elites and even made the new recruits unsure of the long-term benefits of loyalty to the Shah. As a result, Iran's basic LAO become fragile again.

The turnover of the bureaucratic elite under the Shah undermined his regime's policymaking process because acting professionally and raising questions about the Shah's preferred policies would impair one's promotion in the system. For example, when the oil rents rose sharply in the first half of the 1970s, many top technocrats advised against rapid expansions of government expenditure and investment, which the Shah favored. Those professionals were quickly set aside in favor of new comers who would be willing to go along the policy. The result was high inflation rates in the mid-1970s that forced the government to cut back on spending slowing down the economy to check inflation. The slowdown and the cut back in rents fueled the growing discontent with the regime and, before long, a vast spectrum of opposition groups began to mobilize against the Shah.

The election of Jimmy Carter as US president in 1976 had important consequences for the Shah and his control over the social order. Carter had campaigned with a promise of support for human rights, which was a signal to everyone in Iran that the Shah may be under pressure to reduce political repression. Indeed, there were some relaxation of restrictions on speech and political gatherings and some constraints on the use of violence by the regime. This emboldened the opposition and revolutionary fervor gathered momentum. In this situation, religious opposition groups had clear advantages over their secular counterparts because religious rituals had provided opportunities for them to build and maintain effective networks, especially through mosques. In fact, after the removal of the landlords as political competitors, the suppression of secular opposition had opened up more space for the networks of the clergy, bazar merchants, and religious groups to grow strong. As a result, they were most successful in organizing the opposition to the Shah and soon helped establish Ayatollah Khomeini as the leader of the revolutionary movement that encompassed a wide range of groups.

As the revolutionary forces gathered momentum, the Shah's support crumbled. The elite recruited by the Shah could not act as a unified coalition to maintain the regime. They were connected to each other largely through their personal relations with the Shah, and he had kept them more as rivals than coalition partners. Many elite members were already disgruntled and some joined the opposition. Most of the rest also started to desert the Shah once his position became shaky. This was also true of the security forces. The Iranian military leaders all took orders from the Shah and, unlike their Turkish counterparts, were not in a position to act as a team independently of the Shah to preserve the system that they were supposed to serve. Some of them left the country and those who remained were imprisoned and executed soon after the Shah was overthrown in February 1979.

Turkey's experience between from the start of World War II till the end of 1970s had more contrast than similarity with those of Iran. Like Iran, Turkey had economically suffered during World War II. Also, expanding demands from the new propertied groups that had emerged under Ataturk and encouragements from the West convinced the ruling Turkish elite to allow for a certain degree of political liberalization. A new party, Democrat Party (DP), with support from the new elite factions came to office in 1950 and reduced the influence of the bureaucratic and military elites who had ruled Turkey since the inception of the republic. However, once in office, the DP applied populist policies, while trying to monopolize power. This was initially associated with increased economic growth, but the economy soon slowed down and tensions between the DP and the bureaucratic and military elites intensified. In 1954, the DP passed a law that entitled the government to dismiss any public employee, except army officers and judges. Eventually, after the economy entered a crisis in the late 1950s and the opposition to DP became more widespread, the DP was brought down by a military coup in 1960. In some ways the process looked like Iran's brief democratization and coup episodes after World War II. However, the military in Turkey had a very different character and its coup yielded a different outcome. In contrast to the case of Iran's 1953 coup that reestablished dictatorship, in 1960 the Turkish military acted as the guardian of the republic and refrained from directly intervening in the political process. Rather, through a set of complex institutional mechanisms defined in the new constitution (e.g., the Constitutional Court and the National Security Council), it let other elite groups to run the system collectively. For instance, the Constitutional Court of Turkey, which was established in 1962 as a response to a series of laws that had been passed by the DP majority government to weaken the military and bureaucratic elite, became the foremost veto playing institution in the judiciary. When the Court first became operative in 1962, it was introduced as a major innovation that would counterbalance the ills of majoritarian democracy and thus contribute to the consolidation of pluralistic democracy in the country. However, with the further empowerment of the Court *vis-à-vis* the republican institutions of the state in the 1982 Constitution, the guardian role of the Court was more forcefully codified. While the Court was initially given the authority to review the violation of civil rights, the idea of 'core rights' was abolished in the 1982 Constitution. In addition, the Court could vet the legality of political parties and enforce state secularism.

The new dominant coalition in Turkey in the 1960s did keep the access to power and resources generally restricted, but this was done through formalization and institutionalization of roles of various groups and organizations. This aspect allowed new independent organizations such as trade unions and business or religious association to grow and ultimately play important roles in the maturation of the Turkish LAO. Of course, the military carved out a special position for itself in the new system; e.g., through the National Security Council and Military Courts.

After the 1960 coup, the turnover in the top political offices was relatively frequent, but roughly the same elite groups rotated in power and the overall policy framework was rather stable. The military had a watch on policymakers and would intervene whenever its leaders felt that the system was moving, in their view, in the "wrong" direction. Turkish economy grew robustly between the early 1960s and mid-1970s, coinciding with the period of rapid growth in Iran, though not quite at the same rate (see Figure 9.1). In the mid-1970s, Iran's growth was fueled by injection of large oil rents, while in Turkey foreign debt was accumulating fast and driving the country towards a balance of payments crisis. Interestingly, both countries started to experience economic slowdown and rising political tensions in the second half of the 1970s. The process in Iran led to the formation of a broad coalition against the Shah's regime, ending with a revolution in 1979. In contrast, in Turkey different factions where battling each other and causing turmoil, which prompted the military to intervene and impose order with a coup in 1980. In the late 1970s, Turkey appeared to be moving backwards towards a fragile LAO. But, its long-lived military and bureaucratic organizations were strong enough to put the country back on its path.

6. Formation of the Islamic Republic under Ayatollah Khomeini

The first decade after the revolution of 1979 was a formative period for the new regime that took shape by Ayatollah Khomeini's coalition. The vision projected by the Ayatollah and his associates was one of an open access order in which everyone would be treated equally and could freely participate in the county's political and economic life through a democratic process. In addition, they wanted the new system to pay special attention to social justice, hence serving the masses and eliciting their support. But, they also wanted the new system that wanted to establish, the Islamic Republic, to be guided closely by their view of Islam and be ruled by people they could fully trust. Naturally, many groups that had participated in the revolution disagreed and serious conflicts and violence emerged, which ultimately ended with the establishment of another basic LAO.

The anti-Shah coalition was quite broad and represented wide segments of the population. However, since impersonal institutions in Iran were weak, it was clear from the start that the coalition would not continue after the overthrow of the Shah. Personal relations, especially ties with the leadership of the revolution, were critical for surviving in the dominant coalition. For others who lacked such ties and were essentially going along with the movement because they wanted to see the Shah toppled, the future was very uncertain. Indeed, well before the fall of the Shah, a number of opposition organizations had focused on arming themselves to strengthen their positions in the power struggle that was expected to emerge after the revolution. Some ethnic, linguistic, and religious minority groups at different corners of the country tried to seek autonomy or claim territory. A number of armed organizations also saw those territories as havens and joined them. Meanwhile, the factions close to Khomeini had developed their own armed organizations, some of which served as the foundation for the Iranian Revolutionary Guard Corps (IRGC) and its auxiliary militia, *Basij*.

Ayatollah Khomeini's role as the leader of the revolution made him a natural coordinator and gatekeeper for the new ruling elite. Initially, he seemed to be interested in keeping as much of the coalition together as possible. He appointed the leading liberal members of his coalition to form the first post-revolution government. However, he also appointed the people in his inner circle to a Revolutionary Council, which stood above the government and exercised real power. Such arrangements gave Khomeini and his close associates time to prepare better for establishing and running a new order. It was also an opportunity to assess various groups and individuals and to decide which ones were worth keeping in the ruling coalition and which ones had to be discarded. In this setting, some contenders to power who felt marginalized came into conflict with those closer to Khomeini and soon lines were drawn. Some of these groups were only political. But, many had armed wings and applied their violence capacities. Assassinations, bombings, and executions killed many political activists, politicians, and officials (Abrahamian 1982). The political and armed organizations supporting Khomeini managed to defeat their challengers in the early years of the revolution. Later on, they took on other groups that were not using violence, at least not at the time, some of which were even supportive the regime, but could not be trusted (e.g., the pro-Soviet Tudeh Party).

The use of violence by marginal groups did not always lead to their elimination. In fact, some such groups proved useful to the revolutionary elite and managed to rise in elite ranks. The best example of this is the Muslim Students of the Imam Khomeini Line, who took over the US embassy in November 1979. The revolutionary government at the time was opposed to this move and Khomeini also initially hesitant to endorse or reject them. But, he soon recognized the opportunity that the takeover had offered in dealing with internal and external threats and put his full weight behind them. Taking the embassy staff as hostages created a sense of crisis that made it easier for the new regime to take on the opposition groups and to establish a new order based on Khomeini's vision. It also marginalized many groups whose loyalty to that vision was in doubt. This included the liberals who were running the first post-revolution government and were forced to resign. The government passed on to people closer to Khomeini. The hostage crisis also caused serious cleavages among leftist groups accelerated their elimination, as they were pondering the anti-imperialist credentials of the Islamic Republic. During the prolonged negotiations to free the American hostages, the leaders of the Line of Imam Students ended up strengthening their bargaining positions and establishing themselves as an important elite group.[3]

[3]For more information, see http://en.wikipedia.org/wiki/Muslim_Student_Followers_of_the_Imam's_Line and http://en.wikipedia.org/wiki/Abbas_Abdi.

The power struggle after the revolution made it necessary for Khomeini and his associates to come up with an elite coalition with the ability to maintain itself and run the country. The key membership criterion was 'practical commitment' to Islam and the Islamic Republic, as determined by the regime leadership. Such commitment at the time included allegiance to and direct or indirect personal ties with Ayatollah Khomeini. These criteria initially entailed some cohesion and coordination among the elite. However, once the competitors and Ayatollah Khomeini were out of the picture, an effective organizational structure was needed to hold the coalition together and make it functional. The structure that emerged was the byproduct of the specific historical events at that time and the result of some trial and error, rather than pre-planning.

Since the interactions among the elite groups under the new regime were not institutionalized, Ayatollah Khomeini's role among them provided a model mechanism for handling coordination. The experiences of conflicts within and outside the coalition were key driving forces in the developments of the new order. To control intra-elite conflict, the coalition leaders opted for a powerful office for a "Supreme Leader" with an indefinite term for life. After Khomeini, the office was to be held by a clergyman selected by the Assembly of Experts (consisting entirely of the clergy). This was meant to insulate the office from political competition and allow the Supreme Leader to regulate the relations among factions in ways that would be considered fair. The Supreme Leader, as a sovereign Islamic jurist, would also be the guarantor of the compatibility of the system with Islamic Law (Schirazi 1997, p. 1).[4] This function was to be exercised through the Council of Guardians of the Constitution of the Islamic Republic (the Guardian Council), dominated by six senior members of the clergy appointed by the Leader. The Council was also charged with part of the gatekeeping responsibility of the Leader: All candidates for the presidency, the parliament, and the Assembly of Experts had to be vetted by the Guardian Council. The Leader was also given full control over the judiciary by enabling him to appoint the head of the branch from among Islamic jurists, subject to no checks. The judiciary was made organizationally independent.[5] Thus, while Khomeini had suggested before the revolution that he and other clerics would not hold positions in the government other than guiding the politicians to ensure that they follow the Islamic Law and the interests of the masses, the outcome turned out

[4]For centuries before the 1979 Revolution, the Shia clergy had formed an independent source of political power in Iran, funded by the proceeds of *waqf* properties and the contributions of the believers. The theory behind this power was that the true reign over the government belonged to the Hidden Imam, who was the only one capable of bringing about justice. Fallible humans running the government could not do justice and should only be true believers and prepare for the emergence of the Hidden Imam. This implied that the clergy did not have to take over the government and become sovereign. They could leave the government to secular politicians and focus on strengthening the faith. Ayatollah Khomeini's view was different. He argued that despite their fallibility, clergymen who were well trained in Islam's teachings could do better than laymen, whose government could become evil.

[5]The judiciary's total budget is determined through negotiations that it holds with the legislature, as is the case for a number of other independent bodies of the state.

to be very different (Ghamari-Tabrizi 2008, p. 49). Indeed, Khomeini later admitted that his initial suggestion to "the clergy to attend to their spiritual and guiding role after the revolution" had been a mistake and, after observing the tensions and conflicts, he changed his view and "asked the clergy to run the country" (Ghamari-Tabrizi 2008, p. 60). The clerics ended up playing a major role at the top echelons of all organs of the state. This can be seen for example in the composition of the members of *Majles* in the early and mid-1980s, about half of which were clerics and almost two-thirds had had some formal religious education (see Table 9.2). It should be noted that although the turnover in *Majles* was relatively high (Table 9.2), the positions rotated among the regime "insiders", who were a small group with relatively well-defined boundaries that are guarded by formal and informal barriers.[6] For example, most of the deputies who left Majles ended up in other top positions and their replacements were insiders.

To manage violence, the control of all armed forces was consolidated under the Leader. The regular army inherited from the Shah's regime was kept, but its role changed as the regime developed parallel revolutionary organizations. Its mission became more focused on protecting the boarders and training conscripts. Various security services under the Shah were integrated into one organization in charge of maintain order along the Basij and IRGC, when they were needed. The IRGC was launched at the onset of the revolution as an army with an ideological character and loyalty to the Leader to guard the system. It was also given the role to guide the Basij militia, which it also used as a recruiting ground. The Basij act as a volunteer auxiliary force with strong ideological ties to the regime. They carry out a range of functions including internal and external security, policing of various sorts, and

Table 9.2. Distribution of the members of the Islamic consultative assembly (*Majles*).

Session of the *Majles*	1	2	3	4	5	6	7	8
Year of Election	1980	1984	1988	1992	1996	2000	2004	2008
Actual number of MPs	327	277	278	268	265	297	285	285
First-time MPs	327	171	153	162	142	190	159	152
Percentage of total	*100%*	*62%*	*55%*	*60%*	*54%*	*64%*	*56%*	*53%*
Clerical Background								
Clerical	161	149	80	63	53	37	43	44
Percentage of total	*49%*	*54%*	*29%*	*25%*	*20%*	*12%*	*15%*	*15%*
With some formal religious educ.	49	26	32	23	32	16	26	11
Total with religious education	210	175	112	86	85	53	69	55
Percentage of total	*64%*	*63%*	*40%*	*32%*	*32%*	*18%*	*24%*	*19%*

Source: Arjomand (2009).

[6]Ehsani (2002) mentions a study of the elite of the Islamic Republic that shows that all the positions of power since the revolution have been controlled by about 2,700 individuals who have been rotating in those positions.

social and religious services. IRGC quickly gained a pivotal role in establishing order when numerous insurrections broke out across the country after the revolution and the ensuing chaos had to be controlled. About a year and a half later, when Iraq invaded parts of Iran, IRGC, and the Basij were called upon to defend the country along the regular army. However, soon they gained the upper hand *vis-à-vis* the army and played key roles in defending the regime internally and externally.

Under the new system, a great deal of economic resources came directly under the control of the Office of the Supreme Leader through a series of foundations (*bonyad*) that support the IRGC and Basij veterans and the families of martyrs or engage in charitable, ideological, and religious activities. Most notably the property confiscated from the elite of the Shah's regime, including foundation assets, were assigned to new foundations under the office of the Leader. In addition, some of the foundations received abandoned property and confiscated assets of the individuals convicted of certain illegal activities.[7] The Leader's office and many of the foundations were also given allocations from the government, though they are not accountable to the government or the parliament. As in Shah's time, the foundations became mechanisms to provide consequential positions for the retired IRGC leaders and other elite members. In addition, they offered employment opportunities for other retired members of the armed forces.

Articles 57 and 110 of the Constitution of the Islamic Republic of Iran (IRI) give the Supreme Leader the mandate to intervene in all matters of the state policy. Ayatollah Khomeini interpreted this as a rule enabling the Leader to issue "governmental ordinances" (*ahkaam-e hokumati*) that are above all law (Arjomand 2009, pp. 32–34). This power was institutionalized by Khomeini after a series of policies adopted by the government and supported by him were questioned by the Guardian Council jurists as incompatible with Islamic Law. Khomeini argued that exigency and expediency for the preservation of the state were more important than the law. Though some grand ayatollahs objected to this interpretation, the chorus of support for it from the rest of the elite eventually brought all factions into line. In 1988, the constitution was amended to elevate this rule to the Absolute Mandate of the Jurist, which according to Khomeini was "the most important of the divine commandments and has priority over all derivative divine commandments . . . . [It is] one of the primary commandments of Islam and has priority over all derivative commandments, even over prayer, fasting and pilgrimage to Mecca." (Quoted in Arjomand 2009, p. 34).

---

[7] After 1989, this latter set of assets was channeled to a new foundation, Headquarters for Executing the Order of the Imam, formed following an edict by Ayatollah Khomeini. A recent report by Reuters (see www.reuters.com/investigates/iran) estimated the asset of the Headquarters at about $95 billion and claimed that it has used the edict to acquire the property of some Iranians who have resided outside the country, even though they have not abandoned their property or been convicted for any crime. The executive director of the Headquarters had estimated its assets at $50 billion in early 2011 (see fa.wikipedia.org/wiki/ستاد_اجرایی_فرمان_امام)

Although the Leader could issue "governmental ordinances" to address contentious issues, Khomeini and other dominant clergy saw it more practical to set up an "Expediency Council" to reconcile conflicts among elite groups. The Council would be at the service of the Leader with his appointees running it, but would also include representatives from various state organizations. Yet another source of formal power for the Leader was his prerogative to appoint Friday prayer leaders, who lead group prayers and give political and religious sermons every Friday in cities across the country. In addition, he was to appoint representatives in various government organizations and provinces. Finally, the Leader was given command over the national media (official news agency, radio, television, and some newspapers).

The extensive powers formally vested with the office of the Supreme Leader were partly a reflection of Khomeini's charisma and his ability to mobilize the masses and to lead the elite. They were also driven in part by the exigencies of the existential threats that the regime faced at the time and the war with Iraq, both of which required discipline and coordination on the part of the elite. But, there was another more fundamental and overarching factor as well: concentration of power reflected the lack of institutional mechanisms to resolve the conflicts that regularly emerged among the heterogeneous elite factions brought to power by the Islamic Revolution. Even when some factions were sidelined to reduce tensions, the winning coalition would soon split up and engage in intra-elite rivalry (Moslem 2002). The Leader would then be called upon to settle the disputes one way or another. However, the arrangement seems to have had a reverse effect as well. The role of the Leader as the ultimate arbiter has tended to prevent the development of institutions and organizations that could bring about coordination in less personal ways. In other words, while factionalism may have given rise to a powerful office for leadership and coordination, power concentration has in turn contributed to continued factionalism and arrested institutionalization, which has been a notable feature of the politics of the Islamic Republic.

An important manifestation of the institutionalization problem was the failure to form and run large and effective political parties (Moslem 2002). One reason for the absence of effective political parties after the revolution may be ideological. Early after the revolution, some leading members of the elite argued that support for the Islamic Republic was based on mass mobilization by the charismatic Leader of the Revolution. In that context, party activity was viewed as divisive and counter to the Leader's efforts to unify the people. Since for the sake of unity the Leader had to ultimately agree with policies to be adopted, each group was supposed to try to convince the Leader of the positions that it advocated. The Leader would then make a decision based on all such input and communicate his positions to the masses and to the government. Indeed, Khomeini himself was skeptical of political parties, fearing that their activities would lead to dissension and division within the Muslim community (Arjomand 2009, p. 33). Other prominent figures in the system also echoed similar views, ranging from the claim that the "cleric is the father of the people" to the view that parties sow dissension and destroy the sacred unity of the community (Moslem 2002, p. 103).

The reasons why parties failed to take root in Iran after the revolution go beyond ideology. After Khomeini's death, the ideological argument was maintained by the elite camps associated with his successor, Ayatollah Ali Khamenei, but not by their rivals, who tried to establish many parties. It appears that the argument had remained functional for the former because they were connected with the main source of power in the country and did not find it helpful to have organized groups opposing them. Another reason seems to be Khomeini's role as the ultimate arbitrator among the elite, who lacked impersonal conflict resolution institutions at the start of the revolution. When elite groups faced a disagreement, they quickly referred the dispute to Khomeini, rather than coming up with impersonal procedures for consensus building. In fact, each side raced to check whether Khomeini was on its side or not, and if not, it tried to make its case before him. This was true of many disputes between parties as well as within each party. Hence, there was no point in keeping the party.

The prime example of this phenomenon is the fate of the Islamic Republican Party (IRP), which had been established to act as an encompassing state party sanctioned by Khomeini. The IRP's root went back to 1963 when in the process of the uprising against the Shah, a mix of clergy and lay followers of Ayatollah Khomeini formed a clandestine organization called the Coalition of Islamic Societies (known as Mo'talefa). The organization served as a network of Islamist political activists and provided moral and financial support for the families of those who were jailed or killed by the Shah's regime. It also had an armed wing that assassinated Prime Minister Hasan-Ali Mansur in 1966. In 1977, in preparation for the revolution, the clerical members of the network formed their own separate organization and called it the Society of Militant Clergy, SMC (Arjomand 2009, p. 21). Both branches played important roles in organizing demonstrations against the Shah, broadcasting Khomeini's declarations from exile, and bringing about regime change. After the revolution, the leaders of the SMC formed the main body of the Revolutionary Council, which set the main policy parameters for the provisional government appointed by Khomeini in 1979. At the same time, to prepare for political dominance in the years that followed, they established the IRP, led by the SMC clergy, but included a wide range of lay members as well. Soon after the hostage crisis, the provisional government was removed and the members of the IRP took many of the positions in the executive and the legislature. While IRP members all agreed on following Ayatollah Khomeini and supported a broad notion of the Islamic Republic, they had little agreement about the nature of the new state and the policies to be followed. They disagreed across many lines; e.g., how much the government should intervene in the economy or engage in redistribution. Naturally, to promote their policies and to channel rents and resources in their preferred directions, they also tried to take control of various state organizations and public foundations, while getting Khomeini's blessing. Increasingly intense disputes erupted over these matters and over why some have more access to Khomeini than others. Eventually in 1987, IRP leaders went to Khomeini and asked him to disband the party, which he did. Since similar tensions existed within SMC, it also split in the following year, again with

Khomeini's permission. This time the left wing of the group split away and formed a new organization called the Association of Militant Clergy, AMC. The centrists and the conservative/right-wing members remained organized as SMC.

The war with Iraq (1980–1988) took a very heavy toll on Iran in terms of human lives and economic hardship. But, it provided an important context for the regime to develop its revolutionary armed forces (IRGC and the Basij), suppress the opposition, and consolidate its grip on power. By mid-1982, Iran had gained the upper hand in the war and the West and many Arab countries had begun to support Iraq and prevent an Iranian victory (Bulloch and Morris 1989). However, despite the signs that tide could be turning, the government of Iran insisted in continuing the war. A declared goal was to punish the aggressor. But, internal situation was also part of the agenda. For example, in October 1982 Khomeini stated "This [war] was a blessing for us. In the continuity and maintenance of the revolution and growth of human potential this played an important role.... The war confronted our people with great difficulties but made our people more committed to the revolution and hardened their will and determination." (Zabih 1988, p. 158).[8] Iran eventually accepted a UN resolution for ceasefire in 1988 after it had been economically and militarily weakened and it was clear that it would not be allowed to emerge as the winner of the war.

The Iranian economy transformed significantly after the revolution. In 1979, all banks and large firms were taken over by the government or the new foundations. The government also imposed tight controls over trade and capital movements. These takeovers and controls, along with the departure of large number of business people and professionals from the country, lowered GDP per capita significantly. At the same time, the rents available to the country were quickly shrinking because oil exports as well as oil prices were falling precipitously. The controls enabled the new elite to channel the rents towards the war effort, internal security, and social base support. For example, the official exchange rate was kept at extremely overvalued rates and then allocated through a rationing system that subsidized the targeted organizations and individuals who enjoyed access to the leaders. Most products were also rationed via a coupon system, with special allocations to the families of martyrs, war veterans, and those serving IRGC and Basij. As the war continued, shortages intensified and the value of such allocations increased. But, the number of claimants was also rising fast and the available rents were shrinking. As a result, the amount offered to each family was diminishing and making it increasingly difficult to maintain the system. This factor, together with the realization that the war was unwinnable, convinced the leadership that continuing the war would jeopardize the survival of the regime.

Another major source of transformation of the economy was the new regime's effort to expand its base in the lower strata of the society and prevent the professionals who did not belong to the elite circles from getting access and exerting influence. The top positions in the bureaucracy and large economic enterprises went

[8]See also IMESS (2004) for the views of Iran's political and military leaders on the reasons for the continuation of the war.

to the elite members who were trusted, but did not necessarily have the skills required for those jobs. This realignment led to the migration of large numbers of professionals, depriving the country of their expertise and lowering productivity in many parts of the economy. On the other hand, the effort to reach out to the poor gave rise to new organizations that could help alleviate poverty, except during the second half of the 1980s when resources were extremely limited. An example of such an organization was Imam Khomeini Relief Foundation (IKRF), which is a bonyad formed by some Mo'talefeh members and run under the auspices of the Leader. Another example is the Reconstruction Crusade organization, formed to help develop rural areas. These organizations contributed a great deal to the reduction of poverty rates after the end of the Iran-Iraq war.

Over time, the new military and security forces, bonyads, and other revolutionary organizations became stronger organizations and their top ranks became proactive in gaining influence over policymaking offices. They built closer ties with the regime's leaders and promoted their own kinds and allies in the system. Initially, they worked mostly in cooperation with each other and occasionally in competition. Their main competition in the 1980s consisted of clerical groups that had been formed before the revolution and were in stronger positions in the early years of the revolution. However, as time passed, the leaders of the new organizations gained ground and competed with the clergy and others more effectively. This phenomenon can be seen in Table 9.2, which documents the rapid decline in the share of *Majles* seats occupied by the clergy after the mid-1980s. Table 9.3 further shows the concomitant rises in the shares of those with administrative, military and security backgrounds.

Table 9.3. Prior occupations and careers of the *Majles* deputies after Khomeini.

Session of the *Majles*	1	4	5	6	7	8
Year of Election	1980	1992	1996	2000	2004	2008
Educators and teachers	127	47	33	52	74	79
Percentage of total	*39%*	*18%*	*23%*	*18%*	*25%*	*28%*
Clerical professors and seminarians	101	29	15	9	14	12
Percentage of total	*31%*	*11%*	*6%*	*3%*	*5%*	*4%*
Medical and other professionals	35	14	16	25	18	18
Agriculturalists	13	1	0	0	0	0
Bazaar merchants	5	1	0	0	0	0
Workers	2	0	1	0	0	1
Private sector managers	1	4	3	4	3	3
Public and bonyad managers	1	3	6	9	6	8
Civil employees and local admins.	11	97	121	127	117	104
Percentage of total	3%	38%	45%	43%	40%	36%
Military and security staff	7	37	53	45	24	35
Percentage of total	*2%*	*14%*	*20%*	*15%*	*8%*	*12%*
Judiciary staff	11	15	11	16	15	16
Leadership personnel	2	7	8	7	8	6
Other (including the press)	11	1	2	3	13	3
Total	327	256	269	297	292	285

Source: Arjomand (2009).

The similarities and contrasts between Iran and Turkey in the 1980s are interesting. In both countries, new basic LAOs formed in the early 1980s. In Iran, a group of clergy organized new military and security forces and drew rather sharp access limits in the course internal and external struggles during the decade. The outcome was a relatively stable basic LAO. In Turkey, the military used the 1980 coup to assert its predominance and strengthen its formal role through a new constitution drawn in 1982. It enjoyed important veto powers and major access to resources, while restricting the participation of many politicians and organizations in politics until the late 1980s. However, the main institutions of the state had been maintained and there were expectations and pressures from both inside and outside the country for the system to return to its old path, albeit with some modifications. In particular, new rules were designed to give rise to large parties and to help reduce the fragmentation of the polity. However, once the restrictions on political participation diminished, the country began to experience political and economic instability again. As a result, the economy, which had grown at a decent pace during most of the 1980s following major export-oriented reforms in 1980, began to experience slowdown and high inflation. This was in contrast with Iran's economy that had experienced decline in most of the 1980s after becoming highly controlled in 1979–1980, but started to recover at the end of the decade.

7. Reconstruction, Reform, and Reaction

Ayatollah Khomeini passed away in 1989 and Ayatollah Ali Khamenei was selected to replace him as the Supreme Leader. Ali-Akbar Hashemi-Rafsanjani, the Speaker of *Majles* at the time, was elected as President under the amended constitution that had merged the position of the Prime Minister into that of the President and made it more a powerful office. Both Khamenei and Rafsanjani belonged to SMC, which after the split by AMC, consisted of the centrist and conservative clerics. Khamenei had served as the President in the previous eight years, sharing power with the left-leaning Prime Minister, Mirhossein Mousavi, who was supported by AMC. The transition was initially associated with increases in the relative powers of the centrist elite groups associated with Rafsanjani. The elite factions on the conservative side gathered around the office of the Supreme Leader and tried to exert influence on the system through offices and organizations under his control (Gheissari and Nasr 2005).

Some elite members with backgrounds in the military, bonyads, or administrative units such as the Reconstruction Crusade used their connections with the voters to get into the *Majles* (see the middle rows of Table 9.3). The left-leaning groups that had dominated the government during the war in the 1980s, especially those associated with the AMC, were mostly sidelined by the Rafsanjani administration. Quite a few of the individuals in this group joined cultural organizations, universities, and think tanks, where they carried out studies on culture, philosophy, political science, sociology, and economics.

The government of Rafsanjani announced a major reconstruction and reform program in 1989 to rebuild the economy and make it more market-oriented. This required rechanneling of rents towards investment, especially in the country's infrastructure that had fallen into serious disrepair during the war. The resources flowing to many organizations, most importantly to the armed forces and veterans, had to shrink, causing dismay among them. Rafsanjani's solution to the problem was to ask those organizations to seek revenues of their own. For IRGC, the Basij, and the foundations supporting the veterans, this meant engaging in economic activity and earning their share of the rents while contributing to the reconstruction. The IRGC already had many enterprise activities to bolster its budget during the war. However in 1990, it formed enterprises to carry out contracts for the government or produce goods in a large scale. One example of such a unit is *Ghorargah Sazandegi Khatam Alanbia*, which in time became "one of Iran's largest contractors in industrial and development projects, and today is considered the IRGC's major engineering arm" (Wehrey *et al.* 2008, p. 60).[9]

Rafsanjani's approach looked practical at the time, but it proved fateful for the economy because it set in motion a process by which the armed forces became involved not only in economic activity, but also in efforts to influence a variety of economic policies in highly distortionary ways (Wehrey *et al.* 2008; Borger and Tait 2010). As we have seen above, such organizations had promoted their representatives in the legislature and the executive by the second half of the 1980s. Hence, they were particularly effective in getting policies selectively turned in their favor. This included government contracts, regulations, insider information, and impositions on the private sector to share assets and profits. Rafsanjani's approach stabilized the political and social system for a while and postponed the urge to reach a more fundamental solution to the economic policy quagmire in Iran. However, it strengthened the role of personal connection and enabled those with better connections to power to strength their position and to limit the access of outsiders to resources. It ensured the continuation of the basic LAO that had been established after the revolution and made it less likely for impersonal rules to emerge and help the LAO to mature.

The reconstruction policy initially proved successful in helping the economy quickly rebound from its abyss in the second half of the 1980s. But, after a few years, the economy entered a balance of payments crisis that led to very high inflation and several years of economic stagnation. A key source of the problem was the way market liberalization was followed while the organizations that had access to power were expanding their roles in the economy. In particular, in the early 1990s the government of Iran decided to unify the exchange rates and open up the country's capital account. This removed part of the rents captured by the firms and organizations that had good connections and benefited from the pre-existing multiple exchange rate system. But, it presented them with a new profit opportunity. Given

[9]For a recent list of the economic interests of IRGC, see Iran Focus (2010a, 2010b). It should be kept in mind that the data presented in these articles are partly guesswork and in some cases depend on dubious sources. See also the Wikipedia page on IRGC, available online at http://en.wikipedia.org/wiki/Iranian_Revolutionary_Guard_Corps.

the openness of the capital account, they started to borrow heavily in international markets on a short term basis. They did not seem to be worried about bankruptcy because they expected the government to come to the rescue. In fact, since many firms were borrowing short term and there was a risk of balance of payments crisis, every firm that was in a position to borrow had strong incentives to stock up inventories of imported goods or foreign currency reserves, waiting to make large profits in case of a devaluation. The lenders were also counting on the government's incentive to help out the borrowers with its oil revenues. However, during 1993–1994 when a large amount of short-term foreign debt was coming due, oil prices declined and the government was confronted with a balance of payment crisis (Pesaran 2000). The Iranian rial quickly lost a great deal of its value and the borrowers claimed that they could not pay back their foreign currency debts at the new exchange rate. The government ended up providing them with foreign currency at the pre-crisis exchange rate, in effect assuming a big chuck of their debts for free. It also began to ration some of its foreign currency revenues at low rates to ensure that certain staples were imported at affordable prices. The result was a full-circle return to the multiple exchange rate system and its concomitant rent allocation to the organizations that enjoyed access to the policymakers. The deficit caused by these subsidies led to monetary expansion and validated the inflationary pressures from the devaluation cost push. Dealing with the debt crisis and stabilizing the prices curbed Iran's economic growth until the late 1990s.

The economic stagnation of the mid-1990s in the context of continuing cultural limitations and access restrictions imposed on the population under the Islamic Republic led to growing frustrations among broad segments of the Iranian society. Meanwhile, the left-leaning elite groups that had been sidelined by the Rafsanjani administration were strategizing a comeback and saw the growing discontent as an opportunity. They coalesced around a charismatic AMC cleric, Mohammad Khatami, who had served at high positions after the revolution. They advocated political reform to make it possible for the democratic potentials of the constitution to be utilized under the Islamic Republic. Khatami won the presidency in landslide election in 1997. The left-of-center reformist elite were soon on the ascendency. Once in control of the executive branch, they began to push against the conservative/right-wing elite and Rafsanjani's associates in various arenas. In particular, they opened up multiple news media channels to campaign against the conservatives and some centrists, especially Rafsanjani, and discredit them. The reformists also tried to curb the flow of government resources to their opponents. For example, part of the budget going to the IKRF was reallocated to new NGOs backed by the reformists to restructure welfare services (Esfahani 2005). These moves bred strong reactions among the conservatives and alienated the centrists, who had hoped to get along with the reformists. Some groups on the right mobilized pressure groups to use violence to intimidate and undermine the reformists. This included an assassination attempt on a leading reformist, who barely survived, and the murder of a number of intellectuals. These acts did not deter the reformists, who were attracting sympathy.

In 1999, the reformists organized elections for local councils for the first time after the revolution. They received 75% of the vote. The victory emboldened the reformists and their non-elite supporters. In particular, many student groups began demonstrating and demanding greater openness and change. However, the reaction from the conservative side grew stronger and student protests in the summer of 1999 were violently suppressed. Still, the reformists had a great deal of momentum and won almost 70% of the vote in Majles elections in February 2000.

With the executive and the legislature under their control, the reformists seemed to be dominating the political game in Iran and promising to bring about changes in the social order. But, there were at least two factors that worked against them. The first and foremost factor was the basic institutions of the Islamic Republic that gave disproportionate power to the organizations under the office of the Supreme Leader, where the conservative elite groups had gathered. In particular, according to the constitution, the conservatives could disqualify the reformists from running for national offices, and they did take advantage of this prerogative in later elections. The reformists wanted to reduce such powers and bring about many other changes. But, all those steps required the consent of the conservative elite. The reformists had no real strategy to deal with this hurdle because they had wanted to stick to the constitutional rules and the conservatives had no intention of yielding power voluntarily.

The second adverse factor was that the elected offices had little control over the state's means of coercion. The conservatives used those means to systematically arrest and try some reformists, but the latter would only publicize such practices in their media. The reformists avoided moves that would lead to significant mobilization or public protest by their supporters. They were concerned about violent confrontations and cautious about new entry into the elite circles that could bring new competitors for them. The result was a war of attrition between the reformists and their opponents, which turned into a frustrating experience for the public. Although Khatami remained personally popular and was reelected with another landslide in 2001, participation rate in the subsequent local and *Majles* elections went down sharply, which worked against the reformists. In 2004 *Majles* elections, the Guardian Council disqualified many reformist candidates, ensuring a conservative victory.

Curiously, despite the political confrontations in the first half of 2000s, the economy started to grow and gathered speed. There were two reasons behind this trend. First, Iran's oil revenues began to rise after 1999 when oil prices recovered from their lows during the East Asian crisis of 1997–1998. Second, having been blocked in their efforts to reform the political system, many reformist policymakers focused on economic policy. Many of them had also learned more about growth-oriented policies by then and helped the government rationalize and streamline many economic policies. In the early 2000s, the exchange rate was unified, many quota restrictions on trade were turned into tariffs, and trade barriers were generally lowered. The government improved it budget balance and established a foreign currency saving fund to help stabilize the foreign currency flows. However, growth proved highly unequalizing. Although the system had safety nets, they worked only for the very poor and left a large range of the population from lower and middle classes behind (Esfahani and Karimi 2013). By 2005, this factor along with the failure of the reformists' political agenda turned many voters towards a populist political entrepreneur, Mahmoud Ahmadinejad, who offered to bring the country's oil revenues to the dinner tables of common Iranians. Ahmadinejad had been a member of the IRGC and had served as a province governor in the 1990s and Mayor of Tehran during 2003–2005.

The political tensions during 1997–2005 and the reformists' efforts to redirect parts of the rents away from organizations associated with the conservative camp led to greater solidarity and mobilization on that side against the reformists. The centrists had also been undermined by both the right and the left after the early 1990s, although in the early 2000s they began to mend fences with the reformists. In 2005, this situation handed a victory to Ahmadinejad, who had the support of the security forces and conservative organizations. In return, Ahmadinejad's administration redirected the government's resources to serve the interests of the enterprises under the control of those organizations more than ever before (Wehrey *et al.* 2008; Borger and Tait 2010; Habibi 2013). One mechanism of this rent allocation was to increase the contracts allocated to IRGC-affiliated enterprises and to facilitate their participation in investment, production, and trade projects (Habibi 2013). The activities related to oil and gas sector were especially useful for this purpose. Another related mechanism was the use of state banks to offer preferential loans to those enterprises and to families associated with the IRGC and the Basij (Habibi 2013).

The other mechanisms used by Ahmadinejad to deliver rents to those connected with the security forces served broader purposes as well and helped fulfill his promises to the poor that they would receive a share of the oil rents. The prime example of this was the privatization program, which had started under the Rafsanjani administration, but had progressed slowly because of opposition from the conservative camp (Harris 2013). Ahmadinejad redesigned the program to ensure that its benefits go mainly to his constituencies that were shared by other conservatives as well. Under his plan, which tremendously accelerated privatization, 40% of the shares of some 2000 state-owned enterprises were to be sold on the stock market. In practice, "most shares of privatized firms were purchased either by semi-government enterprises or by investors who had close ties to security forces or government officials" (Habibi 2013). Another 40% of the shares were designated as "Justice Shares" to be distributed to the "lower" strata of the society, though the criteria for eligibility were not necessarily household income (Harris 2013). As Habibi (2013) puts it,

> The distribution of justice shares also served as an indirect mechanism by which to reward the low-income supporters of the regime, particularly the Basij militia, for their loyalty and support. The veterans of the Iran-Iraq war, the families of war martyrs, and households that had received income support from government welfare agencies — all were declared eligible to receive justice shares.

Another important policy that served multiple purposes was the restructuring of the budget process and the dissolution of the Budget and Management Organization (BMO). The BMO was a central professional bureaucracy that controlled the budget and recruitment processes of the government and tried to impose some economic cost-benefit analysis on public expenditures. In this sense, it acted as a constraint on political allocations of public funds. Ahmadinejad turned the central part of the BMO into an advisory bureau in the office of the President and placed its provincial offices under the control of province governors (Kian-Mehrzad 2013). This change removed an important constraint on discretionary recruiting and use of public fund at all levels, making high offices much more rewarding to the office holders. He "appointed a record number of current or former members of the IRGC and the Basij to key government positions and to upper-level management slots in public enterprises... [who in turn] used every opportunity to appoint former IRGC and Basij officials to lower-tier government posts and positions in state-owned enterprises" (Habibi 2013). With these changes in the administration, Ahmadinejad increased the budget allocations of the provinces where his governors could redistribute them with relatively free hands. Also, he himself traveled to provinces on a regular basis to be in direct contact with his constituencies in various corners of the country and hand money to those whom he or his staff deemed needy. Meanwhile, oil prices were going up sharply and were bringing the government larger windfall rents to be distributed.

A third major multiple-purpose policy adopted by Ahmadinejad was the so-called "Quick-Returns Projects." This program was meant to provide financing for small projects to create jobs expeditiously. The banks were obliged to offer a myriad of loans on preferential terms without much scrutiny, with implicit guarantees from the Central Bank and the government. This provided ample opportunities for rent allocation to the government's constituencies, both in security forces and the population at large. Naturally, the mechanisms used and the amounts distributed under this program were highly inefficient and inflationary (Amuzegar 2010). The default rate was quite high and few jobs were created (Habibi 2013). However, because of accelerating inflation, the program had to stop and the government and the central bank had to apply contractionary policies in 2008. By the first half of 2009, when Ahmadinejad was engaged in his reelection campaign, the economy was still suffering from high inflation and slowdown in the wake of "Quick-Returns Projects" program.

Although Ahmadinejad's distributive policies had gained him the support of a sizable part of the population, dissatisfaction was also on the rise in many other parts. This gave the reformist an opening to plan a return to office via the ballot box. Their main candidate was Mirhossein Mousavi, the Prime Minister in the 1980s, who had not been politically very active for two decades. The election in June 2009 became quite contentious, and when Ahmadinejad was announced as the winner, the reformist candidates claimed fraud and demanded that the result to be annulled and a new election to be held. The Supreme Leader directed the objecting candidates to file their complaints with the Guardian Council, which ruled that there had not been any cheating of significance. However, the reformists did not trust the Guardian Council's ruling. The Supreme Leader, the conservative camp, and the security forces stood fast behind the verdict, while the supporters of the reformist candidates took it to the streets of major cities to protest, thus launching the so-called "Green Movement". After a few days, the Supreme Leader ordered the protesters to stop and disband. But the sentiments were strong and the demonstrations continued. Soon the security forces entered the picture and violent confrontations erupted for several months until the Green Movement protests were suppressed. Many reformists were arrested, tried, and imprisoned.

In the wake of the Green Movement protests, the IRCG and other security forces gained further prominence among the elite. For example, their profile in the cabinet rose sharply. During Ahmadinejad's first term, "the number of cabinet ministers with IRGC or Basij backgrounds varied between six and ten. When he appointed the former IRGC commander, Gholamreza Rostami, oil minister in July 2011, the number of ministers with such a background in his 21-member cabinet rose to 12" (Habibi 2013).

In his second term, Ahmadinejad championed two major policies that are a major part of his legacy. One was a vast home construction project for low-income households (*Maskan-e Mehr*). The other was a massive energy subsidy reform that raised energy prices sharply and made a uniform cash subsidy to everyone in the country. The initial plan for the cash subsidy was to be set such that it would use only one half of the proceeds of the energy price increases. The other half was supposed to be utilized to expand the infrastructure and to enable the industry to adjust to the new relative prices. However, both policies turned into major liabilities. The housing project proved very costly and caused large deficits. The energy price reform turned out to have promised cash transfers much larger than the proceeds from price increases. The government tried to reduce the monumental deficit that it faced by cutting investment and other expenditures. But this proved to be contractionary.

At the same time, the government of Ahmadinejad was engaged in a confrontation with the West over Iran's nuclear energy program and remained defiant despite the threat of international sanctions. This confrontation seemed to have the support of the conservative elite and security forces since it gave primacy to security concerns and enhanced their relative positions, a purpose similar to the one that the war with Iraq had served in the first half of the 1980s. However, in 2012, as the difficulties due the domestic economic policies were becoming clear, tough sanctions went into effect as well and led to serious stagflation in Iran. When Iranians went to the polls to elect a new president in June 2013, they delivered a resounding verdict against Ahmadinejad's approach and in favor of a candidate who promised to resolve the nuclear dispute and pursue more responsible economic policies. The candidate also called for the armed forces to reduce their roles in the economy. The ballot box served as a dispute resolution mechanism, though the range of individuals who participated as candidates remains quite limited. Also as of December 2013, courts and many other potentials mechanisms are still under the control of the conservative side.

The contrast between the social orders in Iran and Turkey increased after the 1990s. In Iran, the circle of the elite remained closed and some groups were even expelled. Despite the slogans and efforts by many elite groups, especially those on the left, the nature of power remained highly personal. Intra-elite disputes ultimately entailed the use of violence and the settlements favored the organizers of the more effective means of violence. A substantial share of the rents produced in the economy or flowing from energy resources went to those who organized and supported violent groups in the form of subsidized good, services, credit, and foreign exchange. This was done through contracts with or transfers to the households and enterprises associated with the elite groups managing the means of violence. When dispute settlement mechanisms such as courts were used, they were aligned with the powerful groups rather than acting as impartial and impersonal referees.

In Turkey, the military that had the monopoly of legitimate use of violence continued to exercise power over the political and economic process, but it was acting as a collective and had to follow rules within itself and its relations with other groups. The army leaders could not act in an arbitrary manner and had to justify their actions. They did, for example, pressure Necmettin Erbakan, the Islamist Prime Minister 1996–1997, to step down and took him to court to ban him from politics. However, the incident taught the next generation of Islamist leaders about the ways in which they could navigate to power with less conflict with the military. They also found ways of making the rules less stringent. The European Union was particularly helpful in this regard because of its requirements for the countries that wanted to apply for accession. Meanwhile, the expansion of the economy and its global reorientation after 1980 was changing the social forces in the country. In particular, the lowering of trade barriers had enabled a host of new firms from Anatolia to grow and give rise to a powerful bourgeoisie that was more religious and socially conservative than the secular elite that had dominated Turkey since the beginning of the republic. This group provided a social base for new Islamist politicians who saw their opportunity to join the elite by advocating the rule of law and engagement with Europe and the rest of the world. As a result, they could get support from the EU to bear pressure on the military to open the political space for them. Their conservative social roots and outward economic outlook also found wide appeal among Turkish middle classes and gave them a large constituency, thus enabling them to work as a more unified political force than the traditional secular parties in Turkey. Since the latter were quite divided and could not form stable governments to stabilize the economy, the economic booms and busts of the 1990s help build stronger support for the Islamist parties that seemed able to form unified governments. Eventually after the banking crisis and deep recession of 2001, the Justice and Development Party (AKP) won the majority of seats in the 2002 parliamentary election and form the first single party government since mid-1980s.

Once in power, AKP leaders followed the logic of LAOs and tried to dominate the Turkish politics. They adopted the policy reforms that had been introduced after the 2001 crisis and ensured that the rate of inflation went down and the economy grew fast. This provided positive feedback and raised their chances of staying in power. However, to ensure success, they started to drive out their rival elite groups. Most significantly, AKP leaders challenged the military through the court system, which had become the preferred means of conflict settlement among the Turkish elite and was also acceptable to the EU. Of course, their longevity in office had provided them with ample opportunities to appoint new judges, which enabled AKP leaders to assert themselves quite effectively through the court system. The control that civilian leaders have gained over the military and the long-lived organizations and impersonal rules that have grown in Turkey seem to have brought it closer to the doorstep of an OAO. However, this is far from clear at this point because the domination of AKP over Turkish politics have also given it the chance to personalize part of the rent distribution and power relations. Over time, this process may move the system towards a more basic LAO. The following two examples highlight the recent setbacks in Turkey and draw parallels and contrasts with the situation in Iran.

In a process reminiscent of the dissolution of the BMO in Iran, the authority of the Turkish Court of Accounts, responsible for oversight of the use of public resources, has been curtailed over the past several years. The legal procedure for which the Court was to inspect the reliability and accuracy of financial reports of public administrations and scrutinize whether public resources were used efficiently was abandoned. Moreover, the principle of the independence of the audit was destroyed by the regulation that stipulated that the Court cannot form a report contrary to the views of public administrations' audit authorities (e.g., auditors in the state ministries and in social security institutions). The amendments were partly annulled by the Constitutional Court in December 2012 in what the media considered to be a 'revolution'. Yet, only three months later, AKP submitted another proposal amending the Court of Accounts Law. With the new amendments, audit reports will no longer be sent to Turkish Parliament for review but will only be discussed within the Court of Accounts. Moreover, the auditors will not have the authority to automatically launch an investigation if they detect a problem. Rather, if auditors determine that there was a mishandling of finances at a public institution, the Court of Accounts Council (comprised of the President and five other members elected by the government) will determine whether or not an investigation should be launched. Also, very recently Turkey's Court of Accounts decided to exclude the 'public loss' section from its audit reports for the year 2011, which would be sent to Parliament in 2013, allowing the losses by state institutions to go unrecorded.

Another example that seems to reflect the recent move away from impersonal relationships with the state in Turkey, with a parallel in Iran, is the developments in the housing sector under AKP domination. In 2004, the government passed a law that transferred all the duties and the authority of the Urban Land Office to another entity, Housing Development Administration (TOKI) and allowed the latter to form partnerships with the private sector to provide affordable housing. TOKI also received 64.5 million square meters of urban land, which have been its main asset in these partnerships and have provided opportunities for strengthening patron-client relations through TOKI. The distribution of contract values has been highly skewed: out of 817 partner firms in 2011 being granted contracts worth $18 billion, 30 firms received 42 percent of the total and another 45 firms received 20 percent of the total. The contracts have been associated with significant increase in the profitability of larger firms and are being questioned for their appropriateness. The size and activities of TOKI have some resemblance with the Masken-e Mehr project in Iran, with the difference that in Turkey the investment financing come from the private sector, which benefit from the land rents provided by TOKI, while in Iran the land and the financing are both provided by the government and the contractors are companies connected with security forces.

8. Conclusion

Iran started the 20th Century as a society with a very fragile limited access order. It lacked economic development, rule of law, and basic security of human life and property. A coup by an effective military leader changed that equilibrium into a basic LAO, where he became the shah and dominated as a dictator. This was associated with stability and economic growth, but offered few opportunities for broader access and impersonal rule development. The replacement of the dictator with his son as the new Shah in 1941 made it possible for the elite to interact in a less centralized fashion, with a potential for impersonal rules to develop. However, instead the elite factions intensified their conflicts and organized violent groups to dominate each other. Ultimately, one group led by the Shah managed to win the game with support from Western superpowers. The system returned to a basic and harsh LAO, though stability and availability of resources enabled it to do economically quite well for some time. Once the good performance created opportunities for some elite members to gain power, the Shah and his close associates undermined them to maintain their own dominance. However, in doing so, they also lost allies and succumbed to the revolutionary forces that could mobilize the public much more effectively.

After the revolution of 1979, many groups contested for power. While the characteristics of these groups and their power struggle gave rise to violence, the violence in turn shaped the system that was established after violence came under control. The faction associated closely with Ayatollah Khomeini was a much more effective mobilizer of the masses and took the lead in the power struggle. They managed to form new security forces that defeated other power contenders. At the same time, they came up with mechanisms to ensure that access remained limited to the new elite or 'insiders' as they have come to be known. Since personal connections and trust has been the main criterion for identifying the insiders, the mechanisms could not be rule based. The arbitrariness of the access restrictions has been an important impediment to the expansion of impersonal rules as determinants of social interactions. The mechanism has also been a key factor shaping the intra-elite struggles as it has been used by some factions to marginalize or exclude others. The tensions and conflicts caused by the struggle among elite groups to gain control of state organizations and access mechanisms has made the system unstable and caused economic growth to be relatively anemic. The sidelining of most of the country's professionals as outsiders who can not be trusted by insiders has also restricted the regime's access to expertise and has hurt economic performance.

In recent years, the poor policy design and weak implementation together with tightening foreign sanctions have substantially reduced the rents available in the Iranian economy. The GDP has declined and inflation has been rampant. The dominant coalition has put forward a moderate candidate, Hassan Rowhani, for presidency to ease tensions internally and externally and help the economy to recover. Large segments of the population have welcomed the move and have endorsed it by participating in the elections, where a majority voted for Rowhani. This has affirmed elections as a mechanism for settling intra-elite conflicts in the Islamic Republic. However, the episode has also affirmed the system's vetting process, which lacks impersonal rules. As a result, while elections serve as a non-violent mechanism for settling contests among the Iranian elite, the access restrictions and most essential features of the social order remain intact. In this sense, entry barriers are likely to remain high and become source of new disputes between the elite and non-elite and among the elite groups. Also, long-lived private organizations independent of the state are yet to develop. Thus, Iran's social order appears to have remained a basic LAO and slow to mature.

Turkey's social order managed to go further and develop long-live private organization such business association and labor and trade unions, especially after 1960. The institutional role of the military and the expanding connections with the European Union played important roles in allowing some impersonal rules to emerge and a more mature LAO to form. However, progress came at the cost of significant instability. Once new entry into the system allowed a stable dominant coalition to form, the economy also grew more robustly. This, however, is no guarantee for the transition to an OAO. Indeed, the case of Turkey shows the risk that the dominant elite groups may try to undermine the new institutions, reinvigorate access restrictions, and take the system back towards personal rule to preserve their own power.

The social orders framework applied in this paper has a number of implications of for the Arab countries experiencing change since 2011. A key point is that OAOs do not emerge from basic LAOs in a short time periods because impersonal rules that allow access to be open to the population at large have to emerge and become widely accepted and deeply ingrained in the collective understanding of the society. As a result, many transitions from an LAO are likely to end up with another LAO even though the discourse of those who lead the change may be one of openness. However, the nature of the transition and the character of the LAO that emerges matter for the possibilities for the system's institutions to mature. When the power structure in an existing LAO begins to crumble, many groups aspire to gain power and in the chaotic situation that arises, armed organizations present themselves as solutions to the society more broadly that desires order and to individual groups that want to maintain their power or dominate. Naturally, some conflict and violence among these groups may be inevitable. In some cases, violence could be minimized if some existing institutions have already reached some level of maturity under the pre-existing LAO. This appears to have been the case in Tunisia, where organizations such as labor unions had maintained some degree of independence from the state and could help make the transition more orderly (Kienle 2012). In other cases, the level of violence could remain high after the toppling of the old regime, as seems to be the case in Libya. Thus, the new system that is emerging there is likely to be a fragile or basic LAO for quite some time, while Tunisia could be on its path to establish more mature institutions. Oil rents in Libya, as in Iran, may add to the intensity of conflict over access and rent distribution, stifling productivity of the economy.

In the case of Egypt, the army and Muslim Brotherhood were two long-lived organizations with potentials to dominate the new order. The Brotherhood got a chance to rule, but proved relatively weak in controlling violence, establishing order, and reviving the economy that had declined after the downfall of the mass uprisings of early 2011. This led to widespread discontent and large anti-government demonstrations, partly supported by wealthy groups that had been influential under the Mubarak regime. The context of popular disgruntlement provided an opportunity for the army to push the Brotherhood aside and to start establishing its own new order. The outcome may take the path that Turkey took after 1960, with a gradual maturing of the new LAO, if the army carves out a rule-based position for itself as the guardian of the system and allows independent private organizations to grow. However, it is also possible that the continuing conflicts and security concerns take the system in a more basic LAO direction, where access remains restricted to some elite groups and individuals based on personal trust.

Current conditions and choices made by the political actors in the Arab world are quite critical and are likely to have very long-term consequences. An awareness about the form and nature of such effects is likely to matter for the decisions that the contenders for power make and for the subsequent social repercussions.

References

Abrahamian, E. 1982. *Iran between Two Revolutions*. New Jersey: Princeton University Press.

Abrahamian, E. 2008. *History of Modern Iran*. New York: Columbia University Press.

Acemoglu, D. 2008. "Oligarchic vs. democratic societies." *Journal of the European Economic Association*, 6(1): 1–44.

Amuzegar, J. 2010. "Iran's fourth plan: A partial assessment." *Middle East Policy*, 17(4): 114–130.

Arjomand, S. A. 2009. *After Khomeini: Iran Under His Successors*. United Kingdom: Oxford University Press.

Ashraf, A. and A. Banuazizi. 1992. "Classes in medieval Islamic Persia." In *Encyclopedia Iranica V*: 658–667.

Ahmad, F. 1993. *The Making of Modern Turkey*. London, UK: Routledge.

Bill, J. 1972. *The Politics of Iran: Groups Classes and Modernization*. Columbus: Charles E. Merrill.

Bolt, J. and J. L. van Zanden. 2013. "The first update of the Maddison Project; Re-estimating growth before 1820." Maddison Project Working Paper 4. Available online at http://www.ggdc.net/maddison/maddison-project/data.htm.
Borger, J. and R. Tait. 2010. "The financial power of the Revolutionary Guards." *The Guardian* (London), February 15. Available online at http://www.theguardian.com/world/2010/feb/15/financial-power-revolutionary-guard.
Bottomore, T. 1993. *Elites and Society.* New York: Routledge.
Brown, J. 1989. "The military and society: The Turkish case." *Middle Eastern Studies*, 25(3):387–404.
Buğra, A. and O. Savaşkan. 2010. "Yerel sanayi ve bugünün Türkiyesi'nde i dünyası [Local industry and business world in today's Turkey]." [In Turkish] *Toplum ve Bilim*, 118:92–123.
Bulloch, J. and H. Morris. 1989. *The Gulf War: Its Origins, History and Consequences.* London, UK: Methuen.
Cizre Sakallıoğlu, Ü. 1997. "The anatomy of the Turkish military's political autonomy." *Comparative Politics*, 29(2):151–166.
Dodd, C. H. 1965. "The social and educational background of Turkish officials." *Middle Eastern Studies*, 1(3):268–276.
Ehsani, K. 2002. "The strategies of democracy." *Aftab*, No. 16 (in Persian).
Esfahani, H.S. 2002. "Political Economy of Growth in Iran, 1963–2002." Working Paper, Growth Research Project, Global Development Network, Delhi, India.
Esfahani, H.S. 2005. "Alternative public service delivery mechanisms in Iran." *The Quarterly Review of Economics and Finance*, 45(2–3):479–525.
Esfahani, H.S. and S. M. Karimi. 2013. "The distributional consequences of economic growth and public spending programs in Iran." Manuscript. University of Illinois at Urbana-Champaign.
Findley, C. V. 1980. *Bureaucratic Reform in the Ottoman Empire: The Sublime Porte, 1789–1922.* New Jersey: Princeton University Press.
Gencer, B. 2008. *Islamda Modernlesme: 1839–1939.* [In Turkish] Istanbul: Lotus.
Ghamari-Tabrizi, B. 2008. *Islam and Dissent in Postrevolutionary Iran: Abdolkarim Soroush, Religious Politics and Democratic Reform*, London, UK: I.B. Tauris.
Gheissari, A. and V. Nasr. 2005. "The conservative consolidation in Iran," *Survival: Global Politics and Strategy*, 47(2):175–190.
Habibi, N. 2013. "The economic legacy of Mahmoud Ahmadinejad." Middle East Brief, Crown Center for Middle East Studies, Brandeis University.
Harris, K. 2013. "The rise of the subcontractor state: Politics of pseudo-privatization in the Islamic Republic of Iran." *International Journal of Middle East Studies*, 45(1):45–70.
Heying, C. 1995. "Civic elites, civic institutions, and the urban growth dynamic." Unpublished doctoral dissertation. United States: University of North Carolina, Chapel Hill.
Higley, J. and M. G. Burton. 2006. *Elite Foundations of Liberal Democracy.* Maryland: Rowman and Littlefield Publishing Group, Inc.
Institute for Middle East Strategic Studies (IMESS). 2004. "Viewpoints of the Iranian political and military elites towards the Iran-Iraq war." Available online at http://en.merc.ir/default.aspx?tabid= 98&ArticleId= 272.
Iran Focus. 2010a. "IRGC's dominance over Iran's politics and economy — Part 1." May 10. Available online at http://www.iranfocus.com/en/index.php?option=com_content&view=article&id=20355:irgcs-dominance-over-irans-politics-and-economy–part-1&catid=29:exclusive-reports&Itemid= 121.
Iran Focus. 2010b. "IRGC's dominance over Iran's politics and economy — Part 2." May 12. Available online at http://www.iranfocus.com/en/index.php?option=com_content&view=

article&id=20364:irgcs-dominance-over-irans-politics-and-economy-part-2&catid=29:exclusive-reports&Itemid=121.

Jenkins, G. 2007. "Continuity and change: Prospects for civil-military relations in Turkey." *International Affairs*, 83(2):339–355.

Karasipahi, S. 2009. "Comparing Islamic resurgence movements in Turkey and Iran." *Middle East Journal*, 63(1):87–107.

Karpat, K. H. 1968. "The land regime, social structure, and modernization in the Ottoman Empire." In *Beginnings of Modernization in the Middle East: The Nineteenth Century*, ed. Polk, W. R. and R. L. Chambers. Chicago: University of Chicago Press.

Khan, M. H. 2010a. "Political settlements and the governance of growth-enhancing institutions." Manuscript.

Khan, M. H. 2010b. "Bangladesh: Economic growth in a vulnerable LAO." Paper presented at the World Bank, June 4.

Khavarinejad, A. 2003. *The Estimation of Gross Domestic Product of Iran (1315–1337)*. Monetary and Banking Research Academy, Central Bank of the Islamic Republic of Iran.

Kian-Mehrzad, M. 2013. "Dissolution of Thoroughly Studies of Budget and Plan Organization," *Alef*. 2 Tir 1392. Available online at http://alef.ir/vdcjhyeviuqehoz.fsfu.html?190895. (Retrieved on November 1, 2013. In Persian).

Kienle, E. 2012. "Egypt without Mubarak, Tunisia after Bin Ali: Theory, history and the 'Arab Spring'." *Economy and Society*, 41(4): 532–557.

Kolabinska, Marie. 1912. *La Circulation Des Elites En France*. Paris, France: Imprimeries Reunies.

Lambton, A. K. S. 1953. *Landlord and Peasant in Persia: A Study of Land Tenure and Land Revenue Administration*. Oxford: Oxford University Press.

Lambton, A. K. S. 1969. *The Persian Land Reform: 1962–1966*. Oxford: Clarendon Press.

Mills, C. W. 1956. *The Power Elite*. Oxford: Oxford University Press.

Moaddel, M. 1986. "The Shi'i Ulama and the state in Iran." *Theory and Society*, 15(4):519–556.

Moghadam, F. E. 1996. *From Land Reform to Revolution: The Political Economy of Agricultural Development of Iran 1962–1979*. London, UK: I.B. Tauris.

Moslem, M. 2002. *Factional Politics in Post Khomeini Iran (Modern Intellectual and Political History of the Middle East)*. United States: Syracuse University Press.

North, D. C., J. J. Wallis, S. B. Webb, and B. R. Weingast. 2010. "Limited access orders: An introduction to the conceptual framework." Manuscript.

North, D. C., J. J. Wallis, and B. R. Weingast. 2009. *Violence and Social Orders: A Conceptual Framework for Interpreting Recorded Human History*. Cambridge: Cambridge University Press.

Paroto, V. 1991. *The Rise and Fall of the Elites: An Application of Theoretical Sociology*. New Jersey: Transaction Publishers.

Pesaran, M. H. 2000. "Economic trends and macroeconomic policies in post-revolutionary Iran." In *The Economy of Iran: The Dilemmas of an Islamic State*, ed. Alizadeh, P., pp. 63–99. New York, NY: I.B. Tauris.

Rabi, U. and N. Ter-Oganov. 2012. "The military of Qajar Iran: The features of an irregular army from the eighteenth to the early twentieth century." *Iranian Studies*, 45(3):333–354.

Rizvi, M. M. A. 2012. "Evaluating the political and economic role of the IRGC." *Strategic Analysis*, 36(4):584–596.

Rustow, D. A. 1964. "Turkey: The military." In *Political Modernization in Japan and Turkey*, eds. Ward, R. E. and D. A. Rustow, pp. 352–388. Princeton: Princeton University Press.

Saylan, G. 1986. *Capitalism, Bureaucracy and Political Ideology in Turkey*. Ankara: V Press.

Schirazi, A. 1997. *The Constitution of Iran: Politics and the State in the Islamic Republic.* London and New York: I.B. Tauris.

Shambayati, H. 2004. "A tale of two mayors: Courts and politics in Iran and Turkey." *International Journal of Middle East Studies*, 36(2):253–275.

Szyliowicz, J. S. 1971. "Elite recruitment in Turkey: The role of Mulkiye." *World Politics*, 23(3): 371–398.

Wehrey, F., J. D. Green, B. Nichiporuk, A. Nader, L. Hansell, R. Nafisi and S. R. Bohandy. 2008. *The Rise of the Pasdaran: Assessing the Domestic Roles of Iran's Islamic Revolutionary Guards Corps.* National Defense Research Institute. Santa Monica, CA: Rand Corporation.

Yavuz, H. 2003. *Islamic Political Identity in Turkey.* Oxford: Oxford University Press.

Yucekok, A. N. 1971. *Turkiye'de Dernek Gelisimleri (1946–1968).* [In Turkish] Ankara: Ankara Universitesi SBF Yayinlari.

Zabih, S. 1988. *The Iranian Military in Revolution and War.* London, UK: Routledge.

Zurcher, E. J. 1993. *Turkey: A Modern History.* London, UK: I.B. Tauris.

Chapter 10

WHAT HAPPENED IN THE EARLY YEARS OF DEMOCRACY: INDONESIA'S EXPERIENCE

Akhmad Rizal Shidiq and Philips Jusario Vermonte

1. Introduction

We discuss democratization and what might follow after a political crisis by showing some illustrative examples from Indonesia's experience. In 1998, the country was severely hit by the Asian Financial Crisis that turned into a massive economic and political crisis and eventually put an end to a 32-year-old strong authoritarian regime. In the aftermath of that crisis, particularly between 1999 and 2000, a series of reforms was undertaken to restore order. The country embarked on implementing economic and political reform, the latter being broadly defined as electoral democratization and decentralization.

On the economic front, reform was centered around stabilization and adjustment of microstructural problems. Despite the rhetoric, all post-crisis administrations more or less followed standard stabilization policies for monetary and fiscal conservatism, including tight money policy, minimum budget deficit and subsidies cuts, and privatization of government enterprises. Trade was generally liberalized, and many banking sectors underwent massive overhaul and recapitalization. In the political sphere, modern electoral democracy, including free press, was reintroduced. Legislative power has since been restored and political parties are no longer subject to political restrictions. Electoral democratization reached provincial and district levels along with significant decentralization both in terms of government public policy functions and inter-government fiscal arrangement.

More than a decade after such reform, Indonesia has by all means, managed to grow beyond many observers' expectations. With the exception of the long-time politically problematic East Timor secession, the country remains intact, the economy is robust, and the middle class is growing fast. Democracy has also been consolidated to some extent and decentralization has not resulted in disruptions of public service provision at the expense of locals.

Of numerous instructive features of the Indonesian reform experience, we first illustrate how reform paved the way for political Islam, which was repressed during the Suharto years, to emerge in mainstream politics. In particular, we look at the ups-and-downs of political parties as the backbone of democracy, with a particular reference to Islamic political parties, at the national level. Second, we discuss decentralization and proliferation of district splits to illustrate the power struggle at sub-national politics. We find that in Indonesian consolidated democracy — which includes both newly emerging political Islam and old Suharto-related politicians — more secular political elites have been constrained by electoral democratic institutional settings that require moderation for reaching now crucial popular voters. We also show from our discussion on district splits that local politics have become an interplay of among various political identities, from religion to ethnicity to right to economic rent, and the institutional setting provides mechanism and flexibility for limited power redistribution.

2. Prelude to Crisis

What caused the 1998 political crisis in Indonesia? For one, it was the Asian banking and financial crisis that brought the economy down to its knees. The currency crisis in Thailand led to a sudden reversal of capital flow from the region including Indonesia. The combination of bubble economy fueled with cheap capital inflow, moral hazard from implicit government guarantee, and post financial liberalization weak regulatory capacity, sent the country down from a promising new Asian Tiger to a paper tiger (Pangestu and Habir 2002).

This economic crisis however would have been less likely to explode as a massive political crisis if there had been no growing popular resentment against the structure of Suharto political machinery especially in late 1990s. Prior to 1998, the most remarkable feature of Suharto politics was the effective use of centralized military and Golkar's (the ruling party during the Suharto era) bureaucracy network circulation. Centered around Suharto himself, the network served as a means to accumulate and distribute economic surplus, but without severely predate the growth (Sidel 1998). Initially a Jakarta-based network circulation, the effective military and bureaucracy rotation policy designed from the center was eventually able to fully displace the local power holders.

While Suharto was in power, Indonesians lived under a pseudo electoral democracy. Most modern democratic apparatus and procedures (such as general elections, political parties, and lawmaking bodies) were in place but by any definition they cannot be assumed to have been run within modern democratic rules and convention. Political repression was rampant and the non-elected military's role in politics was dominant. The number of political parties were deliberately limited and very constrained. Bureaucracy was politically abused and the press was tightly controlled. Politics and political activities were orchestrated, often times by applying violence threats. Supported by the military and bureaucracy under Partai Golongan Karya

(Golkar, Party of the Functional Groups)[1], the regime managed to marginalize the country's two major political powers: left-leaning nationalists and political Islam.

However starting in the early 1990s, this circulation and wealth accumulation started to show some signs of defects. Suharto started to lose control over his junior army officers and a new distributional conflict arose from the entrance of Suharto's children into the circuit. In fact in the last years of Suharto's years, excessive involvement of his children and their close cronies into business became a critical issue and major concern of many Indonesians. By then, the aging Suharto's regime was also in question and frought with an uncertain future (Fisman 2001). In these years, modern political Islam reemerged within military-Golkar network, thanks to Habibie's — one of Suharto closest allies — role in creating Ikatan Cendekiawan Muslim Indonesia (ICMI, Indonesian Association of Muslim Intellectuals).

Moreover, regional discontent against a heavily centralized inter-regional fiscal arrangement gained political traction in the 1990s. Arguably an old issue since the country's independence, yet, the timing in wider grievance articulation is interesting as it occurred neither during oil boom period in the 1970s nor export oriented period of the 1980s. Booth (2011) argues that in the 1970s, centralized transfer arrangements for infrastructure development were effective in raising the availability public infrastructure for everyone. In the 1980s, despite experiencing a significant decline of oil revenue, the government remained politically committed and did not reduce fiscal transfers to regions. By that, it is probably not just a coincidence that the rise of economic grievances started to emerge at a time when Suharto started to lose control over the regions which by then, had a better informed and more responsive middle class who was perceptive to economic injustice.

The defect was exacerbated by the fact that during the 1997–1998 economic storm, the Suharto administration was not able to restore financial stability to the system, partly due to his unwillingness to fully adhere stringent stabilization policies. It was also partly undermined by massive domestic discontent major elements within his patronage started to break away, making the policy consolidation impossible. Without control to his political machinery, Suharto had no option but to quit. When he did it, the whole stable distributional network associated with bad governance came to end. In the immediate aftermath of crisis, political Islam and sub-national political leverage started to develop in the late 1990s, and it moved to the forefront of mainstream politics through newly installed electoral democracy and decentralization.

3. Two Important Reforms: Electoral Democracy and Decentralization

Suharto fell from power on May 12, 1998. This event provided a critical junction for reform and in the critical years between 1999 and 2004, Indonesia undertook a series of major economic and political reforms which led to democratization that shaped Indonesia to become what it is today.

[1]The list of abbreviations is given at the end of the Chapter.

The economic reform mainly aimed to produce growth recovery and stabilization of the economy, which is inevitable after the country had experienced a GDP decline of 13% in 1998 and major adverse shocks in both real and monetary sectors. Against this backdrop, economic reform consisted not only restoring fiscal and monetary conservatism, but also market liberalization and privatization to reduce micro inefficiency and structural problems. Center to this micro-adjustment process are banking sector restructuring, privatization, and trade liberalization.

Perhaps a telling story on how economic reform affected Suharto's power structure can be seen from IMF conditionalities for standby loan stated in a series of Letters of Intent (LOI). In the first LOI (October 31, 1997)[2], the Government of Indonesia (GOI) for the first time officially acknowledged inefficiency in state owned enterprises and planned for privatization. More surprisingly, given that Suharto was still in the office, the GOI would also eliminate import and marketing monopolies, the major sources of Suharto rent franchises income. The second LOI[3] (January 15, 1998) was even more explicit in attacking Suharto's franchise network by abolishing BULOG's (a state agency dealing with food logistics which was notoriously abused by Suharto's cronies) import monopolies, cement marketing monopoly, and, to many observers surprise, clove marketing board associated with his youngest son, Tommy. The third LOI[4] (April 10, 1998 — a month before Suharto's fall) took further steps by acknowledging off budget rents by the Investment and Reforestation Fund and discontinuation of state facilities privilege's of Tommy Suharto's National Car Project and then Vice President Habibie's Nusantara Aircraft Industry.

Yet, for the purpose of this Chapter, we do not elaborate this economic reform further since it is less-relevant to Egypt and other Arab countries as democratization is not taking place amid an economic crisis (as of 2014) the way Indonesia experienced in 1998. Instead, we discuss at length Indonesian democratization and its consolidation and decentralization.

3.1. *Electoral reform*

Suharto's downfall triggered a wave of political system and electoral democracy reform. Right after the downfall of Suharto, Indonesian highest assembly, the MPR (People's Consultative Assembly) amended the constitution. Essentially, the amendment implied, first, removal of MPR power in to be electing President as the latter directly elected by the people. Second it restores lawmaking power to the DPR (People's Representative Council) and all DPR members are now elected. Indirectly it also means that military political power, exercised from their

[2]Letter of Intent of the Government of Indonesia, International Monetary Fund, October 31, 1997. Available online at: http://www.imf.org/external/np/loi/103197.htm.
[3]Letter of Intent of the Government of Indonesia, International Monetary Fund, January 15, 1998. Available online at: http://www.imf.org/external/np/loi/011598.htm.
[4]Letter of Intent of the Government of Indonesia, International Monetary Fund, April 10, 1998. Available online at: http://www.imf.org/external/np/loi/041098.htm.

non-elected seat portion in DPR, had been significantly reduced and eventually stripped off.

This new law on elections and political parties was passed to regulate the 1999 election. The new law replaced the three-party system of the New Order era with a multi-party system. 90% of the eligible population participated in the election, which can be considered as one of the highest turnouts in the world. Nevertheless, Law no 3/1999 on the legislative election (see Table 10.1) stipulates that Indonesia adopts the PR close-list system, no different from the New Order government. It means that voters would vote for political parties, not for candidates. Changes in the electoral system continued until the 2009 election. The barriers for entry to electoral completion and for entry in the parliament were higher than the previous elections, with the 7% electoral threshold and 2.5% parliamentary threshold. Voter turnout, not unexpectedly, declined to 70%. Table 10.2 compares features between the 1999, 2004, and 2009 elections to highlight important continuities and changes of the electoral system.

Prior to the 2009 election, the Constitutional Court made a radical decision that replaced the semi-open election system with a fully open-list system in 2009 election. With this new system, voters have greater freedom to cast their votes for a candidate or a party, and parties have to allocate their seats to the candidates from their party who obtain the largest vote regardless of their rank order in the party lists. This is different from what was initially stipulated in the election law which specified that

Table 10.1. Major laws as legal basis for political reforms and decentralization.

Laws	Major Theme/Issues
Constitutional Amendment	Reorganizing political power structure of MPR (Highest People Assembly), DPR (Legislative), and President
Law 33/1999	Elections and Political Parties
Law 22/1999	Decentralization of government functions
Law 25/1999	Decentralization of inter-governmental fiscal transfer

Source: Authors.

Table 10.2. Changes in the Indonesian legislative election system.

Features	1999 Election	2004 Election	2009 Election
Electoral Threshold	None	3%	7%
Electoral Constituency	Province	Several districts	Several districts
District Magnitude	4–82	3–12	3–10
System	PR	PR	PR
List	Closed	Semi-open	Fully open
Seat allocation	Quota and largest remainder	Quota and largest remainder	Largest votes
Parties in Election	48	24	38

Source: Authors.

rank ordering in the party list could only be bypassed when a candidate won 30% of the quota value within his or her electoral district.

3.2. *Decentralization*

The political economy of decentralization cannot be separated from power struggle at the central level immediately developed after Suharto's resignation. As a successor of Suharto, B. J. Habibie did not enjoy a solid political support from traditional machinery: the bureaucracy under Golkar and the military. Habibie found out that to defend his political credibility and survival chance for next election in 1999, he could not rely on the now disarrayed and internally fragmented central committee of Golkar and, having no military background himself, on the military support. He then looked for a new basis of political support: the regions political elites (most notably non-Java Golkar politicians) who aspired to achieve a greater degree of decentralization.

Against this backdrop, the decentralization plan was developed and finally was passed as Law, and set at district level. It requires major transfer of resources from central government all the way to district government, and in many ways bypassing provincial government. Hofman and Kaiser (2002) estimated that there would be transfer of 2.5 million public servants and 16,000 public facilities to local government. Nevertheless, legitimate concerns that district government might not have the capacity to administer such massive transferred functions did prevent the Law for being passed. New intergovernmental fiscal relations substantially changes central government fiscal transfer form from mainly earmarked grants through *Subsidi Daerah Otonom* (Subsidies to Autonomous Region) for recurrent expenditure and civil servant's salary and *Inpres* for development (investment) spending, to balancing fund transfer system (*Dana Perimbangan*).

One major concern on this Law is the limited transfer of local taxing power since major taxes, such as property, income, and value-added tax, are still collected and administered by central government, leaving the regions with limited abilities to exercise (budgetary) public accountability feature of decentralization and rigidities in spending. Nevertheless, despite limited revenue and taxing power, a large bulk of government functions and expenditure is now in the hands of local government.

4. What Has Been Achieved: Continuation and Moderation of Reforms

At a glance, the Indonesian political crisis was an abrupt change of a 32-year-old strong authoritarian regime. Massive popular protests may give strong impressions that the crisis completely turned the old order upside down and completely wiped out Suharto's distributional coalitions and network. So much for those popular beliefs, we argue that this is neither the case nor an accurate depiction of reform and transition in Indonesia.

Our idea is simple: political crises and the fall of a dictator provide critical junctures for reforms. We argue that external shocks resulted in a deep economic crisis reduces the cost for collective action of citizens in articulating their long-time grievances and bring Suharto's regime down. Following the argument put forth by Acemoglu and Robinson (2007), Indonesia has managed to shift increasing *de facto* political power of non-elites (popular voters and political power basis formerly marginalized in Suharto's network, such as political Islam) to *de jure* political power through a series of political reforms in this critical juncture period. From the non-elites' perspective, those reforms set credible commitment for power redistribution. From the now-disarrayed perspective of Suharto-connected elites (from the Golkar network of military and bureaucracy and his economic cronies), giving up some of their political power was a less costly option than having further social unrest that was arising opposing power redistribution. In other words, Indonesia has been democratized.

Yet, the focus of this Chapter is on how to have sustainable and consolidated democracy. Acemoglu and Robinson (2007) suggest that democratization and reforms that survive critical juncture shall also limit the power shift to non-elites because otherwise the cost of reform becomes too high for the elites and they have strong incentives for generating collective action against reforms and, if sufficiently high, revert democratization. Therefore, this approach predicts that in a consolidated democracy, there would be a continuation and moderation of both elites' political power and roles. To test this prediction, we qualitatively examine two cases of Indonesian democratic reforms: first, the rise of political Islam in electoral democracy and second, decentralization and proliferation of district splits.

4.1. *Political reform and the rise of political Islam*

4.1.1. *Electoral political reform*

In the political sphere, Indonesia is now at best described as a consolidating democracy[5] and one clear evidence is the proliferation of new political parties. 48 political parties competed in the 1999 election, the first democratic election after the demise of Suharto's authoritarian regime. In the 2004 election, 24 political parties joined the contest and in 2009, 38 political parties, despite higher electoral threshold.

Furthermore in 2004, the country took one step further by adopting direct presidential and parliamentary election systems. Within a decade, Indonesians have successfully elected four presidents successively and the newly-formed political parties have slowly been institutionalized. Indonesian voters on their part, to borrow the term from Tworzecki (2003), are "learning to choose" rather quickly. This is quite remarkable, given the fact that during 32 years of the Suharto's New Order government, only three political parties were allowed to contest in the elections. The three political parties were Golkar, which was the ruling party for the whole period of the New Order regime from 1966 to 1998; Partai Persatuan Pembangunan (PPP, United

[5]We argue that both reforms of electoral democracy have been followed, albeit at slower pace, by positive development of democratic institutions such as active civil society and anti-corruption measures.

Development Party), which claimed to be an Islamic party; and Partai Demokrasi Indonesia (PDI, Indonesian Democratic Party), a nationalist-secular party.

In the 1999 election, Partai Demokrasi Indonesia Perjuangan (PDI-P, Indonesian Democratic Party of Struggle), which was basically the new name of old PDI, garnered the largest vote, while Golkar finished second in the tally. Interestingly, in the 2004 election, the incumbent party PDI-P lost to Golkar, the party that has perennially been associated with the discredited New Order regime. Golkar won the 2004 legislative election and therefore commanded the majority of seats in the parliament. Apparently, PDI-P failed to claim credits for the relatively stable financial as well as political situation they have brought about in the aftermath of dramatic turmoil in the period of 1997 to 1999. Islamic parties as a group altogether garnered 33.71% of the popular votes, highlighting the comeback of political Islam.

In the 2004 election, only 24 parties competed due to the 2% electoral threshold that was applied following the 1999 election. The results of the 1999 and 2004 elections are rather similar, although now Golkar won the election (see Table 10.3). From the perspective of the reward-punish model, this is surprising. The PDI-P led government implemented political liberalization and decentralization policies, particularly fiscal decentralization that transferred economic resources from the central government to the local governments. Yet, despite regional variations in the support for PDI-P and Golkar, PDI-P failed to claim this credit and was defeated by Golkar in this election.

While there is evidence of electoral volatility, the data presented also points to the fact that an observed pattern of stable partisan identities is discernible, especially for the Islamic parties and, to a lesser extent, Golkar. This situation, where volatility coexists with relatively stable partisan identity, is an anomaly to theoretical expectation of party identification in the literature of voting behavior. The theory of party identification, which refers to "long term, affective attachment to a specific political party" (Tworzecki 2003), expects a stable partisan loyalty. Therefore, stable partisan identity is expected to be associated with less electoral volatility.

Table 10.3. Partial election results 1999 and 2004.

	Vote (%) 1999	No. of Seats 1999	Vote (%) 2004	No. of Seats 2004
PDI-P	33.73	153	18.53	109
Golkar	22.43	120	21.58	127
PKB (Islam)	12.60	51	10.57	52
PPP (Islam)	10.70	58	8.15	58
PAN (Islam)	7.11	34	6.43	53
PBB (Islam)	1.94	13	2.62	11
PK (Islam)	1.36	7	7.34	45
PBR (Islam)	—	—	2.44	14
PD	—	—	7.45	56

Source: Authors' compilation.

Another radical feature of Indonesian political reform is the adoption of a direct presidential election system the 2004 election. While political parties are "lacking of meaningful platforms, experiencing the high frequency of party-switching and short-term coalition building" (Ufen 2006); political campaigns are now personalized, focusing not on the political parties but more on individual candidates. Individuals who are aspiring to become a presidential candidate set up their own parties which paves the way for the rise of 'presidential parties'. The prime examples are President Susilo Bambang Yudhoyono (SBY), who established the Partai Demokrat (PD, Democratic Party) to be his political vehicle in 2004.

Indeed, the direct presidential election system adopted in 2004 has necessitated the presidentialization of the Indonesian political parties. Party mechanisms are necessary, but they are not sufficient to attract votes. In some cases, candidates have to bypass their party mechanism especially when a party has two or more candidates running for office. The case in point is Jusuf Kalla of Golkar when he paired with SBY as the latter's vice-presidential candidate in 2004. As SBY's running mate, Kalla was campaigning against the Golkar party's presidential candidate Wiranto, who won the nomination through the party's convention. As a result, Kalla had to rely not on Golkar's party mechanism, but more on his own personal network.

The results of the 2004 elections seem to suggest that there is a degree of disconnection between vote choice in the parliamentary and presidential elections. In 2004, SBY won the presidential election despite the fact that his party, Partai Demokrat (PD), only secured a very small number of votes/seats in the parliamentary election. That year SBY embarked on a successful presidential campaign in which he handily defeated his main contender, Megawati Sukarnoputri, by the margin of 20% in the presidential run-off. In contrast, Golkar's electoral success in the 2004 parliamentary election did not translate into another success in the presidential election. Golkar's presidential candidate, Wiranto, was defeated as he came third in the first round of the two-round election. It indicates that voter preferences in 2004 were volatile and partisan identification was low. Voters were not 'ideologically' attached to political parties and split their preferences between the parliamentary and presidential elections.

From parliamentary and presidential elections results, we draw several findings. First, the significant presence and performance of PDI-P and Islamic parties as groups in elections indicated that political reform has indeed redistribute power to previously non-elites (nationalist and Islamic). Second, it can be seen that Golkar, the representative of old elites, has also been going strong in all elections after the crisis. This fact confirms our theoretical prediction that democracy is more likely to be consolidated if reforms produce significant but limited power redistribution. Golkar's strong performance in the immediate parliamentary election after the crisis in the 1999 also sent credible signal to elites that there is significant incentive to join in new political process and institutional settings. Third, direct presidential election results suggest that it provides citizens with more political outlets and institutions to express their political power, albeit the incoherence with parliamentary elections. For politicians, this also provides alternatives in reconciling internal disputes by allowing them to run beyond party's boundaries, thus another incentive to support reform.

4.1.2. *Islamic parties and the election*

During the early period of Indonesia's transition to democracy, probably the most important question is how the relationship between the state and Islam reemerged and is redefined. As briefly discussed earlier, with the establishment of ICMI, Suharto seemed to be more sympathetic to Islam. ICMI then became very influential in the country's political dynamic in the 1990s. ICMI was chaired by Suharto's most trusted aide Habibie, who then became the successor of Suharto in 1998. ICMI then become a focal point of Indonesian Muslims enlarged political activism that was previously very limited. When Suharto was forced to resign in 1998, the nervous military swung to the Islamic groups to hold onto power and backed Habibie. The military continued to reform and formally withdrew from politics. Meanwhile this also gave more moderate political Islam space to grow in the sphere of electoral politics.

We apply a simplified categorization of Islamic parties in Indonesia: the purist and the moderate. The purist Islamic parties are PPP, Partai Keadilan Sejahtera (PKS, Prosperous Justice Party), and Partai Bulan Bintang (PBB, Crescent Star Party), all were founded based on strict Islamic principles; and the moderates are Partai Amanat Nasional (PAN, National Mandate Party) and Partai Kebangkitan Bangsa (PKB, National Awakening Party), supported by members of the two largest Islamic mass organizations, Muhamadiyah and Nahdlatul Ulama. The latter are formally running on an inclusive platform. This different root of support, as a result of different interpretation of Islamic teaching, somehow explains the differences between the two and the root of Islamic party segmentation. Unless otherwise noted, our definition of 'Islamic parties' covers both camps.

Despite the strong performance of Islamic parties as a group the last three elections also witnessed the decline of vote share win by Islamic parties. Table 10.4 shows that the purist Islamic parties only managed to secure about 14% of the total votes in the 1999 election; while the moderates secured 20%. Thus, the total votes obtained by the Islamic parties as a group were about 34%. The figure consistently dropped over time, from 35% in 2004 election 26% in 2009 elections.

There are at least four explanation as to why the Islamic parties have experienced declining support from the electorate. First, pure instrumentalism among voters may be occurring. Being rational, voters see that the Islamic parties are too fragmented so none of the parties has a clear chance to win the election. As a result, voters throw their support to other parties.

Second, relevant to the first, Muslim voters may have chosen alternative channels outside the electoral arena to pursue their interests. Indeed, non-party Islamic organizations have mushroomed since the fall of Suharto in 1998. Most of these new Islamic groups share the same agenda, advocating the implementation of Islamic

Table 10.4. Vote shares of the largest Islamic parties in the DPR.

Party	1999 Votes (pct)	1999 Seats	2004 Votes (pct)	2004 Seats	2009 Votes (pct)	2009 Seats
PAN	7.12	34	6.44	53	6.01	43
PBB	1.94	13	2.62	11	1.8	0
PKB	12.61	51	10.57	52	4.94	27
PKS	1.36	7	7.34	45	7.8	57
PPP	10.7	58	8.15	58	5.3	39
Total	33.73	163	35.12	219	25.85	166

Source: Hamayotsu (2009).

laws in the country. In many cases, these non-party organizations are more articulate in advancing their agenda than the existing Islamic parties (Effendy 2003).

Third, political parties tend to always shift to the center, trying to project the image as parties that are not too secular or too Islamic as to find a middle ground (Tanuwidjaja 2010). The nationalist parties pursue strategies to accommodate the aspiration of the conservative electorate. Examples are abound, including the fact that Golkar and PDI-P are in favor of the implementation of *sharia* (Islamic by-laws) in various districts (Buehler 2008; Bush 2008). While more conservative voters still will not favor the secular-nationalist parties, such as PDI-P, Islamic voters with a secular view of religion and politics might be attracted to them. It is important to note, however, that the Islamic parties have pursued moderate agendas to attract less-religious Muslim voters too. Mietzner (2009) argues that the Islamic parties have shifted their electoral strategy to what he calls "new centrism" by portraying themselves as pluralistic and inclusive parties in order to seek support from the largely moderate and secular Indonesian society.

Fourth, unlike their counterparts in some Islamic countries, including the AKP in Turkey and Muslim Brotherhood in Egypt, major Islamic parties in Indonesia lack strong economic bases that deprive them the ability to provide social services to the society. The nationalist secular parties, such as Golkar and PDIP, have better access to resources that allow them to provide such social services that eventually help them in maintaining their support base (Rahman 2013).

As a result of competition, some of the Islamic parties have even distanced themselves from the Islamist agenda, particularly that of turning Indonesia into an Islamic state. Two purist Islamic parties, PPP and PKS, are no longer supportive of the inclusion of a controversial paragraph, which is called the Jakarta Charter, into the country's Constitution that will require all Indonesian Muslims to strictly abide by *sharia*. Moderation is also believed to be the key behind PKS' success in the 2004 election that saw its vote share increase significantly (Liddle and Mujani 2005, Mietzner 2009). Bubalo *et al.* (2008) note the shift of PKS strategy by launching political campaigns for more secular, clean and caring party, anti-corruption, wealth distribution, and social welfare was adopted prior to the 2004 election. PKS also did not pursue and explicitly specific religious agenda, such as *sharia* law and the establishment of an Indonesian Islamic state (Tanuwidjaja 2012).

Decentralization also exerts some effects on the strategies pursued by political parties. Studies by Buehler (2008) and Bush (2008) can illustrate how decentralization advantages the Islamic parties in Indonesia. Buehler observes that the adoption of *sharia* laws by local governments in Indonesia has been on the rise since 2001, which coincides with the implementation of the decentralization program. His case studies in the South Sulawesi province of Indonesia reveal that decentralization policy allows district government to adopt regional *sharia* by-laws, thus changing political strategy of political parties operating at local level.

Buehler (2008) and Bush (2008) assert that districts implementing such by-laws are not necessarily governed by regents from the Islamic parties. In fact, as they rightly note, most of the by-laws in many districts are initially proposed and implemented in districts headed by figures from Golkar and even PDI-P. Buehler (2008) argues that the *sharia* by-laws are used, especially by Golkar, to consolidate power. However, such by-laws certainly create an Islam-friendly atmosphere during election times that eventually works in favor of the Islamic parties in the subsequent election time.

In sum, the decline of vote share gained by Islamic parties in Indonesia illustrates the moderating effect brought about by electoral politics. The Islamic political parties moved to be come more moderate, while the secular-nationalist parties, in their attempt to reach moderate muslims, started to accommodate Islamic issues. The more conservative Islamic parties tend to articulate their political aspirations outside electoral politics.

4.2. *Decentralization and proliferation of district splits*

4.2.1. *Mixed result of decentralization*

As for decentralization, the then legitimate concern on the capacity of local governments to handle the transfer without disrupting public service delivery has never materialized. Despite an ambitious scope and tight timeline for implementation, decentralization of government functions and inter government transfers in fact went through as scheduled. In particular, we observe that there has been significant increase in ratio of central government transfer to total central government expenditure after decentralization is implemented (see Fig. 10.1), indicating serious commitment to decentralization. We do not have counter-factual evidence, but if history is used as a guide, it is not clear if a more gradual approach could have produced better results. Another piece of evidence that decentralization is a credible policy is that the looming threat for secession in the early year of decentralization has also significantly decreased (Tadjoeddin 2011).

In term of growth performance, in the first five years after decentralization had been launched (2000–2005), Indonesia experienced growth convergence across districts (McCulloch and Sjahrir 2008)[6]. However, the major concern of such massive

[6]What is rather unclear is the main determinants of growth still cannot explain the variation of the districts' growth.

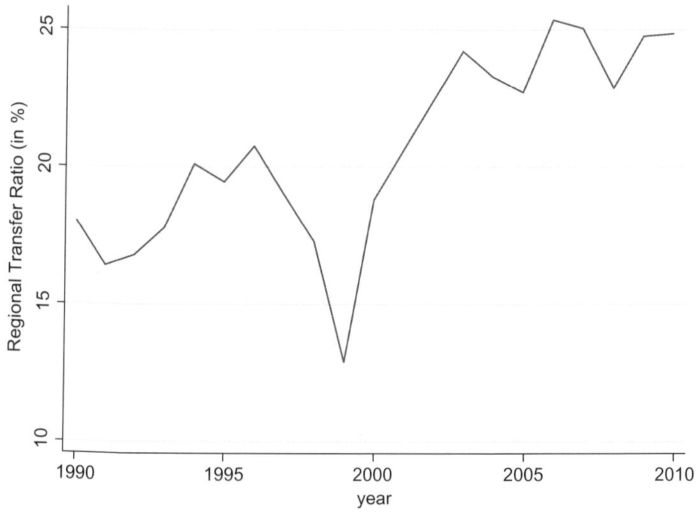

Fig. 10.1. Ratio of transfer to region to total central government expenditure.
Note: Calculated from CEIC database.

decentralization is on governance impact. Patunru and Wardhani (2008) noted that in the early years of its implementation, local governments excessively exercised their newly obtained lawmaking power and authorities in extracting revenue (Smeru 2001; LPEM-FEUI 2002), resulting in explosions of new local regulations, many of them distorted the economy. As of December 1, 2008, the Ministry of Finance found that out of 11,638 local laws examined, 2,431 are recommended to be amended for distorting the economy.

Upon further examination, many negatively concluded that the impact of decentralization on governance is problematic. It is not clear if decentralization *caused* higher corruption levels. One of the most glaring issue comes from the fact that there have been no reported indicators for corruption at district level that are comparable across periods before and after decentralization. Moreover, while decentralization is part of one massive political reform package, those reports fail to sufficiently control for other political reforms variables, such as electoral reform, that may also affect corruption levels as well as to address endogeneity and omitted variable bias problems.

Nevertheless, decentralization allows us to observe changes in rules of administering public policy across districts. Henderson and Kuncoro (2004) links corruption with one of the change of rules affecting bureaucracy incentive for taking bribes, intergovernmental transfer, and find that higher fiscal demand and/or lower fiscal transfer from central government increases demand for bribes. Moreover, between 2001 and 2004, Henderson and Kuncoro (2011) show that the Dewan Permusyawaratan Rakyat Daerah (DPRD, Regional House of Representatives) composition, as a direct result for political decentralization and elections, affects corruption level. They find that higher PDIP–Golkar's (two largest secular nationalist parties) share of votes in local assembly increases the bribe ratio, but voters were aware of it and vote for non PDIP–Golkar in districts with high corruption. Voters got the corruption reduction they wanted because non-PDIP-Golkar winning elites are now aware that reducing corruption reaps in rewards during local elections.

In terms of public spending, Skoufias *et al.* (2011) find that first, districts with directly elected head has higher government expenditure, except in health sectors, and higher local owned revenue. Following the political cycle, expenditure also increases when the timing for direct elections are imminent. Yet, they also find that *Pilkada* has no impact on quality and availability of public services and weak response on district's service needs. Shidiq (2010), estimating the impact of district government expenditure on public service performance and efficiency in the period of 2000–2005, finds that an increase of expenditure is associated with *lower* public service performance and efficiency. Arguably, the period of observation might be too short, but this finding raises question on where the money has actually been spent and whether government bureaucracy grabbed them for personal and non-public service uses.

These findings underline the mixed results of decentralization. Decentralization changed an incentive structure that affects elites' behavior on corruption and public service provision. Citizens can now assert higher constraints on bureaucracy behavior and elites have had to respond accordingly, suggesting limits of bad governance. Nevertheless, there is a strong indication that elites are still able to sustain their considerable control over rent extraction under new structures and accountability mechanism.

The other important reform related to decentralization that affect local political institutions is the direct election of local Head (*Pilkada, Pemilihan Kepala Daerah Langsung*) under Law 32/2004. We do not discuss *Pilkada* because this development more or less follows similar pattern at national level for shifting power balance between local assembly (legislative) and local head (executive) as by granting local head more 'presidential' power through direct election, instead of appointment by local assembly as in earlier period. Instead, in the next section, we discuss proliferation of provinces and districts splits to capture changes in power of local administration — which is not necessarily exercised through local election.

4.2.2. *Proliferation of districts splits*

After maintaining relatively steady number of administrative boundaries during Suharto's rule of 32 years, Indonesia saw a sudden increase of number of provinces and districts, especially after decentralization in 2000. The new provinces and districts came out by sub-dividing an original district into two or more jurisdictions through a law passed by the DPR and approved by President based on local initiative proposal.

There has been an escalating trend in the number of districts. According to Ministry of Home Affairs, from the day of issuance of Government Regulation 129/2000 to thc year 2009, Indonesia had an additional seven provinces and 198 districts, splitting from their respective original existing provinces and districts (see Table 10.5). In addition, as recent as 2011, there have been more than 150 proposals for

Table 10.5. Number of new provinces and cities and municipalities by year.

Year	No. of New Provinces	No. of New Cities	No. of New Municipalities	Total
1999	2	34	9	45
2000	3	0	0	3
2001	0	0	12	12
2002	1	33	4	38
2003	0	47	2	49
2004	1	0	0	1
2007	0	21	4	25
2008	0	27	3	30
2009	0	2	0	2

Source: Ministry of Home Affairs, Indonesia (2011).

new districts submitted to Ministry of Home Affairs and around 20 proposals to the Parliament. These statistics suggest that district splits are likely keep going in the near future.

Moreover Booth (2011) identifies that most of district splits are located outside Java, indicating that demand for splitting is aligned with the fact that previously marginalized local non-Java political elites have gained more political power along with decentralization and democratization. The largest district splitting rate occurred in Riau and Papua provinces, that happened to be also provinces with longtime economic and political grievances toward Jakarta.

Why does a district 'split'? Theoretically, the size of a district or administrative jurisdiction is an equilibrium between the benefit of economics of scale for public services production and the cost of organizing an effective administration in larger area. The latter includes not only logistical and geographical issues, but also managing conflicts that have arisen from higher heterogeneity in larger districts. With pervasive problems of governance, it also includes rent-seeking competition (i.e., on natural resources). The popular discourse in the wake of decentralization implementation suggests that decentralization would reduce the cost of organizing polity both at central and local government level, particularly to reduce grievances and secessionist tendency among regions in outer Java.[7] Yet, combined with local electoral democratization, we argue that decentralization increased the cost of organizing polity at provincial and districts level due to more fragmented political power.

Some critical events after the 1998 crisis also induced proliferation of new districts. The first one is East Timor referendum, that led to the country's separation in 1999. The referendum and its subsequent result suggest the limited ability of central government to keep the nation intact. Second, the Megawati administration's decision in 2003 to split Papua into three provinces and several districts sent signals to the regions that provincial and district splits are politically feasible and possible. This also illustrates that anti-secessionist policy and Megawati's main motive for

[7]Tadjoeddin (2011), for example, finds that decentralization, in particular new inter-regional fiscal transfer, has met its objective for appeasing secessionist tendencies at the provincial level.

subdividing Papua has produced an unintended consequence of increasing number of district splits requests.

Nevertheless, the crucial question is what makes a district in Indonesia more likely to split. Fitrani *et al.* (2005), using the data of 300 districts in Indonesia for period of 1998–2000 (before decentralization) and 2001–2003 (after decentralization), find that in before-decentralization period, a district is more likely to split if it has larger area and population size, higher share of natural resource in its budget, lower share of wage in budget, and lower share of votes for Golkar. In the post-decentralization period, a district split is more likely to occur in areas area with larger population and area size, ethnically more fragmented at sub-district (*Kecamatan*) level, higher share of civil service wage in local budget, less share of development expenditure in local budget, and higher share of secondary education and poverty rate.

The different determinants for the probability for a district to split before and after decentralization period suggests that decentralization affects the dynamic of district proliferation. Before decentralization, district split seems to be more related to local government attempts in claiming natural resources revenue located in the region from the central government. After decentralization, a district split serves as a political resort local elites in tapping and enlarging access to government revenue and rent transfer from central to local government under new decentralized arrangement. In other words, instead of promoting a more decentralized fiscal arrangement, a district split stresses out local government dependency on central government revenue transfer. This unintended consequence of decentralization and fiscal transfer was very unlikely anticipated by its initiator (Nordholt and van Klinken 2007).

For our analysis, we focus on the cost of organizing local government bureaucrats. In interpreting their estimates, Fitrani *et al.* (2005) assume variable wage share to total expenditure as a cost of running bureaucracy. Thus, higher wage share in the budget represents higher costs for civil services. On the other hand, share of development expenditure (investment expenditure, as oppose to recurring expenditure) in local government budget is a proxy for the availability of non-salary income source for bureaucrats. Development expenditure is traditionally the object for local bureaucrats' off-budget income coming from kickbacks, illegal commission, or other forms of corruption, thus a lower share of development expenditure implies that this kind of bureaucrats' income source is more limited. Combined with a high wage share, it shows the increase of cost of organizing bureaucracy in a district. Faced with this problem, instead of rationalizing the number of civil servants, elites at district level allow administrative splits to share the burden of increasing costs with central government through inter-regional transfer from central government. In particular, on top of allocation based on district's economic and demographic characteristics, a new district can expect the fixed portion of the General Allocation Fund (DAU) assignment formula for each district.

It is important to emphasize that at district level the main local elites are local bureaucrats (*pegawai negeri*). These elites are supported by heavy central government revenue transfers to local government administration as well as rent distribution out of political functions assigned to the local government. The nature and longevity of Suharto's regime dictated that only those who are connected to bureaucracy or military can have access to resources and power, thus basically eliminating non-bureaucratic elites in the region.

Along with their counterpart of military territorial organization, they have been crucial elements during the 32 years of Suharto's power network. The network also effectively internalize the power of local aristocracy into the structure. In Suharto's regime, the center picked the district head and military commando in regular rotational basis, partly to prevent them forming own local political and resource basis. Yet, regardless of such control mechanism, the ranks below top position the ranks were largely occupied by locally cultivated bureaucracy, either by the indigenous people (*putra daerah*) or long-time migrant residents. In the post-Suharto era, it is inevitable that these local elites-cum-bureaucrats were in better position to run for offices and continued to shape the direction of local politics (Hadiz 2010).

Nevertheless, these elites are now located in more democratic environment. With the absence of a strong centralized power network, they are also more fragmented and subject to local political competition. To win the office and capitalize their political power, they need to compete and credibly differentiate themselves to each other. To do so, competing elites need to take up some identities to get some political power leverage by aligning themselves with popular voters or citizens. Two most observed identities being taken up are religious affiliation and ethnicity, which previously had been effectively suppressed under Suharto's regime for security and conformity reasons, and it has also been evident in the process of district splits.

Three studies on district splits in Poso, Mentawai, and West Sumba look at the detail of the importance of such political identity. A major recurring theme of these studies is that splits take places in districts where elites wanting for split can effectively coordinate themselves around religious and ethnic boundaries. Aragon (2007) shows that in the case of Poso district split, previous ethno-religious conflict enhanced the political power of ethno-religious identities in local politics and encouraged for districts splits along this line. Poso district eventually split into new districts of Morowali and Tojo Una-una. In this formation, new elites associated with Islam and ethnic Bungku conceived Morowali, while those who are closely identified as Islam and Tojo ethnic have Tojo Una-una. Meanwhile the Protestant and Pomona ethnic is now majority in the original Poso district.

In Mentawai, Eindhoven (2007) points out that the proposal for the new district of Mentawai Archipelago was motivated by grievances over cultural and religious dominance of the district of origin, mainland Padang Pariaman. Mentawai is majority non-muslim and does not share Padang Pariaman's Minangkabau culture. Mentawai was granted a district before decentralization mostly due to intensive lobby by elites, namely Mentawaian university students/alumni in Padang and *adat* (local custom) leaders promoted through NGO campaign, that identify themselves around this ethno-religious lines. Nevertheless, subsequent developments suggest that this split is also motivated by lucrative rent redistribution in the country's logging industry.

The case of a failed split in West Sumba district is also instructive (Vel 2007). The initial proposal was to split West Sumba into Central Sumba, West Sumba, and Southwest Sumba. But unlike most of successful district split proposals, West Sumba has homogeneous ethno-religous identity, making arguments for elite regrouping more difficult. As a result, despite strong support from Sumbanese elites in Jakarta power ring, as for 2007, the proposal failed to materialize. The fact that West Sumba has limited sources of rents such as natural resources also did not help in putting forward the proposal.

It is probably too early to fairly assess the overall impact of district splits on public service and local economies. However some preliminary findings suggest that in term of public service, district splits have not shown positive impact yet. In its evaluation study on the impact of district split between 2001 and 2007 on limited number of districts observed, the Indonesia National Planning Agency (Bappenas 2008) found that economic performance and public service at new districts had been below optimal, their economic growth is more fluctuated, and there is little evidence for poverty reduction catch-up. The Ministry of Home Affairs (MOHA 2011) also shared similar sentiments in their evaluation to 205 new districts. Yet, due to methodological issues in these reports, we argue that whether districts splits brought positive or negative economic and public service impact remains subject to further rigorous research. In term of ethno-religious conflict, the finding is clearer: districts splits, by homogenizing the district population, effectively reduce conflict (Toha 2012; Booth 2011; Diprose 2009).

For our purpose and framework, proliferation of district splits illustrates the process of moderation of local elites power in original districts. Moderation of these elites' political power depends on their ability to bear the cost of organizing themselves, and the ability to provide income from local government budget and other off-budget rent sources. Burgess *et al.* (2011) neatly show that district split and direct election lead to more deforestation and illegal logging. It also depends on the ability of opposing elites wanting the split in generating political power from different political legitimacy bases. In our district split case, political power takes the form of ethnic and religious identities.

5. Conclusion

Our observations on electoral reform suggest that Indonesia has managed to implement extensive reform and has held regular elections for legislative and executive at both national and local levels. Those elections witnessed the rise of formerly repressed political Islam as well as the persistent presence of old ruling party of Golkar. The last three elections results also indicated a certain level of stable partisanship for these two major political bases. In addition, it is evident there has been a significant shift of political power from political elites to citizen that has been credibly institutionalized in series of democratic political reforms. On decentralization, while the country also managed to live beyond initial negative expectations, we find mixed results of this reform. Decentralization has clearly changed political structures and, by that, incentives and behavior of local elites (the bureaucrats in the local administration), are now more constrained by citizens' political power. Yet, 14 years down the road, such changes in political elites' behavior have not yet delivered significantly better governance and public service provision.

Nevertheless, contemporary Indonesia can best be described as a consolidating democracy. Based on instructive features in our discussion on Indonesian electoral result, the rise of political Islam, district splits and good governance practice, we find that Indonesia's consolidation of democracy is characterized by continuation and moderation of old elites political power. Moderation implies that, under democracy, power has been shifted away from the old elites, including new elites of political Islam to citizens as popular voters. However, as the continuation story suggests, this power shifting is also limited as elites have managed to maintain considerable political and economic power even within reformed political institutions. Since limited political power redistribution provides Suharto-related elites, mainly Golkar, bureaucracy, and the militaries, with incentives to support reform and democratization, we argue that this continuation element is extremely crucial in any consolidating democracy.

List of Abbreviations

DPR: Dewan Perwakilan Rakyat (People's Representative Council)
DPRD: Dewan Permusyawaratan Rakyat Daerah (Regional House of Representatives)
Golkar: Partai Golongan Karya (Party of the Functional Groups)
ICMI: Ikatan Cendekiawan Muslim Indonesia (Indonesian Association of Muslim Intellectuals)
MPR: Majelis Permusyawaratan Rakyat (People's Consultative Assembly)
PAN: Partai Amanat Nasional (National Mandate Party)
PBB: Partai Bulan Bintang (Crescent Star Party)
PD: Partai Demokrat (Democratic Party)
PDI: Partai Demokrasi Indonesia (Indonesian Democratic Party)
PDI-P: Partai Demokrasi Indonesia Perjuangan (Indonesian Democratic Party–Struggle)
PKB: Partai Kebangkitan Bangsa (National Awakening Party)
PKS: Partai Keadilan Sejahtera (Prosperous Justice Party)
PPP: Partai Persatuan Pembangunan (United Development Party)

Acknowledgments

We thank Djayadi Hanan, Risa J. Toha, and the participants of the Economic Research Forum's Workshop on "The Political Economy of the Arab Awakening", held in Cairo on 24 March 2012, for helpful comments and discussions. We also thank Ishac Diwan and two anonymous referees for extensive and extremely useful comments. This Chapter was first written when Shidiq was a Research Fellow at Ash Center, Harvard Kennedy School.

References

Acemoglu, D. and J. A. Robinson. 2007. *Economic Origins of Dictatorship and Democracy.* New York, USA: Cambridge University Press.

Aragon, L. 2007. "Elite competition in Central Sulawesi." In *Renegotiating Boundaries: Local Politics in Post-Suharto Era,* ed. by Nordholt, H. S. and G. van Klinken, pp. 39–66. Leiden, The Netherlands: KITLV Press.

Bappenas. 2008. "Studi Evaluasi Dampak Pemekaran Daerah." Discussion paper, Badan Perencanaan Pembangunan Nasional (Bappenas) and United Nations Development Programme (UNDP).

Booth, A. 2011. "Splitting, splitting and splitting again: A brief history of the development of regional government in Indonesia since independence." *Bijdragen tot de Taal-, Landen Volkenkunde,* 167(1): 31–59.

Bubalo, A., G. Fealy and W. Mason. 2008. "Zealous democrats: Islamism and democracy in Egypt, Indonesia, and Turkey." Institute Paper 25, Lowy Institute for International Policy.

Buehler, M. 2008. "Sharia by-laws in Indonesian districts: An indication for changing patterns of power accumulation and political corruption." *Southeast Asia Research,* 16(2): 165–195.

Burgess, R., M. Hansen, B. A. Olken, P. Potapov and S. Sieber. 2011. "The political economy of deforestation in the tropics." Working Paper 17417, National Bureau of Economic Research.

Bush, R. 2008. "Regional Sharia regulations in Indonesia: Anomaly or symptom?" In *Expressing Islam: Religious Life and Politics in Indonesia,* ed. by Fealy G. and S. White, pp. 174–191. Singapore: ISEAS.

Diprose, R. 2009. "Decentralization, horizontal inequalities and conflict management in Indonesia." *Ethnopolitics,* 8(1): 107–134.

Effendy, B. 2003. *Islam and the State in Indonesia.* Singapore: ISEAS.

Eindhoven, M. 2007. "New colonizers? Identity, representation and government in the post-New Order Mentawai archipelago." In *Renegotiating Boundaries: Local Politics in Post-Suharto Era,* ed. by Nordholt, H. S. and G. van Klinken, pp. 67–90. Leiden, The Netherlands: KITLV Press.

Fisman, R. 2001. "Estimating the value of political connections." *The American Economic Review,* 91(4): 1095–1102.

Fitrani, F., B. Hofman and K. Kaiser. 2005. "Unity in diversity? The creation of new local governments in a decentralising Indonesia." *Bulletin of Indonesian Economic Studies,* 41(1): 57–79.

Hadiz, V. R. 2010. *Localising Power in Post-Authoritarian Indonesia: A Southeast Asia Perspective.* California, USA: Stanford University Press Stanford.

Hamayotsu, K. 2009. "Beyond faith and aliran: Mobilizing Islamic youth in a democratic Indonesia." Paper presented at the American Political Science Association Conference, September 3–6.

Henderson, J. V. and A. Kuncoro. 2004. "Corruption in Indonesia." NBER Working Papers 10674, National Bureau of Economic Research.

——— 2011. "Corruption and local democratization in Indonesia: The role of Islamic parties." *Journal of Development Economics,* 94(2): 164–180.

Hofman, B. and K. Kaiser. 2002. "The making of the big bang and its aftermath: A political economy perspective." Paper Presented at the Conference: Can Decentralization Help Rebuild Indonesis? A Conference Sponsored by the International Studies Program, Andrew Young School of Policy Studies, Georgia State University, May 1–3, Atlanta, Georgia.

Liddle, W. R. and S. Mujani. 2005. "The rise of Susilo Bambang Yudhoyono." *Asian Survey*, 45(1): 119–126.

LPEM-FEUI 2002. "Construction of regional index of doing business." Research Report, Institute for Economic and Social Research, Faculty of Economics, University of Indonesia, Jakarta.

McCulloch, N. and B. S. Sjahrir. 2008. "Endowments, location or luck? Evaluating the determinants of sub-national growth in decentralized Indonesia." Policy Research Working Paper Series 4769. Washington, DC: The World Bank.

Mietzner, M. (2009). *Military Politics, Islam, and the State in Indonesia: From Turbulent Transition to Democratic Consolidation.* Singapore: ISEAS.

Ministry of Home Affairs (MOHA). 2011. "Evaluasi 205 Daerah Otonom Hasil Pemekaran." Discussion paper, Ministry of Home Affairs, Indonesia.

Nordholt, H. S. and G. van Klinken. 2007. *Renegotiating Boundaries: Local Politics in Post-Suharto Era.* Leiden, The Netherlands: KITLV Press.

Pangestu, M. and M. Habir. 2002. "The boom, bust and restructuring of Indonesian banks." IMF Working Papers 02/66. Washington, DC: International Monetary Fund.

Patunru, A. A. and S. B. Wardhani. 2008. "Political economy of local investment climates: A review of the Indonesian literature." PAPI Background Paper: Political Economy of the Local Investment Climate in Indonesia Project.

Rahman, A. A. 2013. "Islamic parties at an impasse, need reform to avoid the worst." *The Jakarta Post*, February 25.

Shidiq, A. R. 2010. "What makes a bad municipal government in Indonesia." Mimeo, Department of Economics, University of Indonesia, Jakarta.

Sidel, J. T. 1998. "Macet total: Logics of circulation and accumulation in the demise of Indonesia's New Order." *Indonesia*, 66: 158–195.

Skoufias, E., A. Narayan, B. Dasgupta and K. Kaiser. 2011. "Electoral accountability, fiscal decentralization and service delivery in Indonesia." Policy Research Working Paper Series 5614. Washington, DC: The World Bank.

SMERU 2001. "Otonomi Daerah dan Iklim Usaha: Temuan dari SMERU." [In Indonesian] Research Report, SMERU Research Institute, Jakarta.

Tadjoeddin, M. Z. 2011. "The economic origins of Indonesia's secessionist conflicts." *Civil Wars*, 13(3): 312–332.

Tanuwidjaja, S. 2010. "Political Islam and Islamic parties in Indonesia. Critically assessing the evidence of Islams political decline." *Contemporary Southeast Asia*, 32(1): 29–49.

——— 2012. "PKS in post-Reformasi Indonesia: Catching the catch-all and moderation wave." *South East Asia Research*, 20(4): 533–549.

Toha, R. J. 2012. "Ethnic riots in democratic transition: A lesson from Indonesia." Ph.D. thesis, UCLA.

Tworzecki, H. 2003. *Learning to Choose: Electoral Politics in East-Central Europe.* California, USA: Stanford University Press.

Ufen, A. 2006. "Political parties in post-Suharto Indonesia: Between 'Politik Aliran' and 'Philippinization'." Working Paper 37. Hamburg: German Institute of Global and Area Studies.

Vel, J. 2007. "Campaigning for a new district in West Sumba." In *Renegotiating Boundaries: Local Politics in Post-Suharto Era*, ed. by Nordholt, H. S. and G. van Klinken, pp. 91–120. Leiden, The Netherlands: KITLV Press.

Index